INTERNATIONAL LAW

International Law

ANDERS HENRIKSEN

OXFORD
UNIVERSITY PRESS

Great Clarendon Street, Oxford, OX2 6DP,
United Kingdom

Oxford University Press is a department of the University of Oxford.
It furthers the University's objective of excellence in research, scholarship,
and education by publishing worldwide. Oxford is a registered trade mark of
Oxford University Press in the UK and in certain other countries

Published in the United States of America by Oxford University Press
198 Madison Avenue, New York, NY 10016, United States of America

British Library Cataloguing in Publication Data
Data available

Library of Congress Control Number: 2016963286

ISBN 978-0-19-875301-8

Printed in Great Britain by
Ashford Colour Press Ltd

Preface

This book seeks to introduce law students and legal practitioners to the basic purposes and principles of public international law. It is first and foremost intended for undergraduate law students who study public international law for the first time. The overarching aim is to enhance the understanding of international law by presenting and exploring that part of the lawyer's legal toolbox that contains the answers that are needed to resolve questions involving two or more sovereign states. As an experienced teacher of public international law at the Faculty of Law, University of Copenhagen, I found a gap in the existing market with regard to a concise and accessible presentation of public international law that would be useful to law students and legal practitioners from non-common law jurisdictions. Hence, the ambition of this book has been to compile a textbook of appeal to students and universities across Europe.

In practice, of course, there are many approaches to the presentation of the field of public international law. This book offers a fairly pragmatic approach to international law and it deliberately refrains from offering a highly theoretical account of the law. In fact, one of its core ambitions is to highlight the occasional tension between, on the one hand, stability and order and, on the other, certain notions of 'justice'. Where possible, the book has sought to illustrate the points made through brief presentations of cases.

The book combines presentations and discussion of both general topics of public international law (such as its history, structures, sources, subjects, jurisdiction, immunity and state responsibility) as well as many of its specialized sub-disciplines (including the law of the sea, human rights law, environmental law, economic law, dispute settlement, the regulation of the international use of force, the law of armed conflict and international criminal law). For pedagogical purposes, all chapters contain a brief introductory list of the central issues covered in the chapter, a concluding summary, some suggestions for further reading and a range of questions for discussions.

Public international law is a field prone to constant rapid developments and, while every effort has been made to ensure the book is as up to date as possible at the time of publication, the law has been stated as at 1 November 2016.

I wish to thank those who have assisted in this project in different ways. First, I wish to thank former Oxford University Press sales representative Johannes Björkman who was the first to suggest I wrote a textbook myself. I must also thank Lucy Read who was my initial editor at OUP. Special thanks are due to Tom Randall at OUP for his very professional and dedicated job at commissioning the incredibly useful reviews to the draft chapters as well as ensuring that I kept (most of) the deadlines along the way. I would also like to thank the following reviewers who undertook the laborious job of reading and commenting on the draft chapters as they were being completed:

Mikael Baaz, University of Gothenburg, Sweden
Freya Baetens, Leiden University, Netherlands

Christian Franklin, University of Bergen, Norway
Magne Frostad, University of Tromsø, Norway
Larissa van den Herik, Leiden University, Netherlands
Ralph Janik, University of Vienna, Austria
Märta Johansson, Örebro University, Sweden
Pétur Dam Leifsson, University of Iceland, Iceland
Francesco Montanaro, Bocconi University, Italy
Daniela Obradovic, University of Amsterdam, Netherlands
Otto Spijkers, Utrecht University, Netherlands
Ingrid Westendorp, Maastricht University, Netherlands
William Worster, The Hague University of Applied Sciences, Netherlands.

Thank you also to those reviewers who wished to remain anonymous.

I don't know who you are but thank you for your patience and useful suggestions. I have tried to ensure that the many recommendations made have found their way into the final product.

I would also like to thank those at our law faculty here at the University of Copenhagen who made valuable comments on individual chapters along the way, so thank you, Yoshi Tanaka, Peter Pagh, Jens Elo Rytter, Amnon Lev and Astrid Kjeldgaard-Pedersen.

Finally, I would like to thank Caisa who provided me with not only love but also with the the assistance, flexibility and space to prepare and complete this book.

Anders Henriksen
University of Copenhagen, Denmark
November 2016

Guide to the Book

International Law is written with the student in mind. Its user-friendly style will ensure you gain a sound understanding of the subject area and a range of supporting features throughout will help you to consider the latest debates and reflect upon the issues at hand.

    This guide shows you how to use those features so that you can get the most out of your studies.

CENTRAL ISSUES

overview of   3. It also provides an over
onal law and   ondary sources of internatic
as article 38   a description of unilateral st

Central issues

Central issues boxes highlight the key issues and introduce you to the key principles within the topics covered and the critical areas of debate to consider as you read each chapter.

Summary

is concerned with the authority of a stat
als or property. The rules can be divide
to prescribe, jurisdiction to enforce and

Summaries

Chapter summaries provide an overview of the topics covered in each chapter, allowing you to review the essential concepts and points discussed.

Recommended reading

jrisdiction in international law, see Cedric
(Oxford University Press, 2008). See a
nternational Law and How We Use It (O

Recommended reading

At the end of each chapter is a list of recommended further reading, carefully selected to help supplement your knowledge and develop your understanding of key topics.

Questions for discussion

he cultural relativist critique of human
at the human rights debate before the H

Questions for discussion

Questions at the end of each chapter allow you to test your understanding of the topics covered. You will find guidance on how to answer these questions on the accompanying Online Resource Centre.

Outline Contents

Detailed Contents

Table of Cases

European Union

International Criminal Court (ICC)

Table of Treaties and International Instruments

EUROPEAN LEGISLATION

Table of Statutes

1

Foundations and structure of international law

CENTRAL ISSUES

1. This chapter introduces the reader to the subject of public international law and provides an overview of its most important elements.

2. It contains a brief historical overview of the development of modern international law from the late Middle Ages until the present.

3. It also introduces the various structures within international law, consisting of the international law of coexistence and the international law of cooperation.

4. The chapter discusses the issue of enforcement in international law and touches on the tension between notions of justice and stability/order that is a consequence of the existing state-centric configuration of international law.

1.1 Introduction

Public international law deals with legal issues of concern to more than one state. It is traditionally defined as the system of law that regulates the interrelationship of sovereign states and their rights and duties with regard to one another. But to that must be added a host of other actors, most notably international organizations and individuals that may also possess rights and/or obligations under international law. Public international law must be distinguished from 'private international law' that consists of national laws that deal with conflicts of law and establish rules for the treatment of cases that involve a foreign element.[1]

Like all law, international law reflects the society to which it applies. Therefore as international society becomes ever more specialized and intertwined, so does international law. In 2006, the American Society of International Law (ASIL) identified 100

---

[1] In this book, the term 'international law' refers to public international law.

ways international law shapes and affects our lives and the world in which we live.[2] The issues highlighted by ASIL included, of course, many of the more fundamental topics of concern to international society that we shall explore in this book, such as the prevention and regulation of conflict, the principles for governing the seas and oceans, the protection of core human rights, the prevention of international crime and terrorism and diplomatic and consular protection. But the issues also covered a lot of the more mundane aspects of our lives. In fact, although we primarily associate international law with the highly pertinent and 'big' issues of global concern, such as when a people—whether Basque, Kurdish or Kosovo Albanian—have the right to statehood, how to fight international terrorism, if Russia can annex Crimea, how climate change can be limited, what international trade agreements should look like or—more recently—what to make of China's dubious claims to major swathes of the South China Sea, international regulation is actually everywhere around us. It is present in the cars we drive, the phone calls we make, the food we eat, the wine we drink, the clothes we wear, the movies we watch, the medicine we use and so on and so forth. Indeed, the preparation, production and shipping of the very book you hold in your hands were subject to a host of international legal instruments.[3]

One of the consequences of the seemingly ever expanding reach of international law has been the gradual development of a myriad sub-disciplines, such as international human rights law, the international law of the sea, international environmental law, international economic law, the laws of armed conflict etc. As we shall see throughout this book, the different sub-disciplines often have their own distinct institutions and occasionally also adjudicatory bodies.[4] Another characteristic of contemporary international law is that legal issues formerly dealt with exclusively within one of the sub-disciplines are increasingly scrutinized in several of them. For instance, while up until a few decades ago it was sufficient for experts on the international regulation of armed conflicts to be familiar with the law and developments within the laws of war—a branch of international law particularly created for the purposes of regulating armed conflict—this no longer suffices. The expansive reach of human rights law and the establishment of a range of international criminal tribunals mean that genuine expertise on how armed conflicts are regulated internationally also requires extensive knowledge of human rights law and international criminal law.

Despite its increasing practical relevance, though, as we shall see throughout this book, international law remains a system of law that is very different from the national legal systems most lawyers are familiar with. Most notably, unlike in a domestic legal system, there is neither a legislative nor an executive branch in the international legal

---

[2] American Society of International Law, 'International Law: 100 Ways It Shapes Our Lives' (2006) www.asil.org/sites/default/files/100%20Ways%20Booklet_2011.pdf (accessed 20 July 2016).

[3] In the event that you consider copying and distributing the book, you may also find it useful to know that international law contains instruments that seek to protect intellectual property and copyright.

[4] On so-called 'fragmentation' of international law, see, inter alia, Jan Klabbers, Anne Peters and Geir Ulfstein, *The Constitutionalization of International Law* (Oxford University Press, 2009). See also ILC, 'Fragmentation of International Law: Difficulties Arising from the Diversification and Expansion of International Law' (13 April 2006), UN Doc. A/CN.4/L.682, para. 492.

system. Similarly, although a number of international courts have been created over the years, there is no mandatory and well-established procedure for the settlement of legal disputes. In general, international law remains a decentralized legal system in which it is primarily up to the legal subjects themselves to create, interpret and enforce the law.

This introductory chapter begins in Section 1.2 with a brief historical overview of international law before Section 1.3 presents the international legal system consisting of different structures of legal rules and principles. Subsequently, Section 1.4 discusses the basis of international legal obligation and Section 1.5 offers a brief overview of the relationship between international law and national law. Section 1.6 deals with the issue of enforcement. The chapter concludes in Section 1.7 with some remarks about the alleged inadequacies of international law and the tension between notions of justice and order that is so prevalent within the international legal system.

1.2 A brief history of international law

Cultures and communities have traded and interacted with each other for millennia and there are numerous historical records of the creation of more or less formal practices and mutual expectations that may be considered to be early traces of what we today call international law. [5] Whatever their preferences, cultures and traditions, political communities have felt a need for international rules and principles and the certainty and predictability they bring to their international relations.[6] But since international law as we know it today was invented in Europe, it is also where our brief overview of its history should begin. Europe in the *late Middle Ages* (15th and 16th centuries) was characterized by both multiple levels of different allegiances and rights and obligations as well as the universal political and religious forces of, respectively, the Holy Roman Empire and the Catholic Church. By providing the spiritual authority of the Western world, the Pope in particular was able to exert considerable influence over the various princes, emperors and kings who governed their territories. But also the networks of knights and merchants were of a transnational nature and the populations at the time often felt a closer sense of allegiance to such communities than to their fellow 'nationals'. It was also a time when ideas about the normative structure of the world were dominated by more or less developed theories of natural law originally developed in the classical eras. Natural law contained an all-embracing set of ideas about natural and social life in the universe and, though primarily focused on the individual and his or her relations to the world, it also applied to states by virtue of the fact that rulers were also individuals and therefore subject to it. Next to natural law (*jus naturale*) was *jus gentium* that was considered a law of people/nations and

---

[5] The historical overview is built on, among others, the works of Wilhelm G. Grewe, *The Epochs of International Law* (rev edn, De Gruyter, 2010); Stephen C. Neff, *Justice Among Nations: A History of International Law* (Harvard University Press, 2014); and Bardo Fassbender and Anne Peters (eds), *The Oxford Handbook of the History of International Law* (Oxford University Press, 2012).

[6] See also Alexander Orakhelashvili, 'The Idea of European International Law' (2006) 17 *European Journal of International Law* 315.

hence inferior to natural law, at times simply perceived as being derived from the more overarching principles of the latter. Despite the absence of an elaborate international legal structure, legal obligations and contracts were created in day-to-day relations of the communities at the time leading to numerous agreements on the treatment of merchants, maritime traders and diplomatic envoys and the conduct of war and the exchange and ransoming of prisoners of war.

The period was also the dawn of colonialism, and the early confrontations between Spanish explorers and native Indian populations and kingdoms in the New World posed a particular challenge to the philosophers and legal scholars of the time. In a series of famous lectures from 1532—*De Indis et De Iure Belli Relectiones*—the Spanish Dominican professor Francisco de Vitoria (1483–1546) concluded that the native populations of the New World were part of the society of the human race and that the acts of the Spanish conquistadores were thus governed by natural law. Vitoria also rejected the claim that the Spanish could justify their conquests of the new areas based on notions of 'discovery' (it is, after all, hard to discover something that the locals have already 'found') or by grant of the Pope. To Vitoria, like all other wars, the waging of war against the natives of the New World had to be 'just' and the acts of the Spanish could only be justified on the basis of alleged local resistance to the activities of the Christian missionaries and opposition to the free passage and trading policies of the Spaniards.[7]

It is, however, not until the *17th and 18th centuries* that we begin to see the contours of a modern international legal system. For one thing, a much clearer distinction was introduced between *jus naturale* and *jus gentium* and it is from the latter that international law as we know it subsequently developed as a discipline. A leading figure in this period was the Spanish Jesuit Francisco Suárez (1548–1617), who in 1612 published his important work *A Treatise on Laws and God the Lawgiver*. Suárez was succeeded by the, arguably, most famous international lawyer of all time, the Dutchman Hugo Grotius (1583–1645) whose major contributions to the development of international law include *The Freedom of the Seas* and *On the Law of War and Peace* published in, respectively, 1609 and 1625. Among other things, Grotius was instrumental in applying natural law to the conduct of international relations and developing the law of nations to make it a practical tool for regulating a variety of areas of international relations. Another influential figure was Emmerich de Vattel (1714–1767) whose *Law of Nations* from 1758 contains useful legal guidance for practitioners of international law.

The international legal system that we recognize today is generally tied to the emergence and consolidation of nation states in Europe.[8] The 'birth' of the international state system is usually traced back to the 1648 Peace of Westphalia that brought an end to the Thirty Years War that had ravaged continental Europe. In the peace treaties of Westphalia, consisting of the Peace of Munster and the Treaties of Munster and Osnabruck, the major European powers sought to establish a semblance of order and structure in an otherwise anarchical and disorderly European world. The idea was to

---

[7] See also Matthew Craven, 'Colonialism and Domination' in Fassbender and Peters (n 5) 863–869.

[8] See also Antonio Cassese, 'States: Rise and Decline of the Primary Subjects of the International Community' in Fassbender and Peters (n 5) 49–70.

reduce the powers of transnational forces, like empire and religion, and instead compartmentalize territory and individuals into sovereign states. In turn, over time, this helped to establish the state as the primary source of authority paving the way for an increasing sense of allegiance among citizens to their respective states of nationality. By attempting to create an international order derived from agreed rules and limits and basing it on a multiplicity of 'states' of equal legal importance, Westphalia was a decisive turning point. What had initially been conceived of as a concept of order for war-torn continental Europe, spread to the rest of the world and to this day remains a key building block of international law. Before the Peace of Westphalia, the French lawyer Jean Bodin (1530–1596) had already conceptualized the all-important notion of state sovereignty that—as we shall see in Section 1.4—is vital to understanding the purposes and functions of international law. Bodin was influenced by the chaos and turmoil of the raging wars of religion in France and he felt the need for a system that contained a clear and unquestionable source of authority. In his *Six Livres de la République*, published in 1576, he developed the theory of a sovereign who possessed 'absolute and indivisible' power and was answerable only to God. The sovereign would be above the law and could both create and break the law at his own discretion. In a sense, the sovereign stood above society and was bound by no one. Bodin's hugely influential thoughts were later supplemented by the equally important conceptions of sovereignty developed by Thomas Hobbes (1588–1679) and John Locke (1632–1704).

The *19th century* was dominated by a full-on assault on the idea that acts of states could be judged according to whether or not they conformed to transcendent ideals of fairness or divine will. In international law, this was the era of 'positivism', the primary tenant of which was that the only true source of law was state will. Consequently, positivism attached primary importance to state consent, whether expressed explicitly in the form of a treaty or implicitly by customary practices adhered to by states due to a belief that the practice was legally binding. According to the 'consensual theory', unless a state has consented to be bound by a rule, no international legal obligation exists and the state remains entitled to act as it pleases. Unlike natural law, then, positive law does not envisage a universal legal system but rather one that is fragmented and in which states are bound by different legal obligations. As we shall see in the next chapter, positivism and the consensual theory remain fundamental influences on the theory of international legal sources. The British legal scholar John Austin (1790–1859) is arguably the most radical exponent of legal positivism. He developed the so-called 'command theory' and defined law as the command of a sovereign, backed up by sanctions. To Austin, the absence of a sovereign in the international system meant that international law could not be perceived as a genuine legal system, merely as laws of positive morality.

Positivism owed much of its appeal as a theory of international law to the emergence of formal institutions of international law, including the 1865 International Telegraph Union and the 1874 Universal Postal Union. It was also during this period that the first multilateral treaties regulating armed conflict were concluded. In 1856, for example, the *Declaration of Paris* set legal limits to the capture of private property at sea and the 1868 Declaration of St Petersburg banned the use of explosive bullets and stipulated that the only permissible aim of war is to defeat the armed forces of the enemy. Of even greater importance were the two Hague Conferences in 1899 and 1907 that led to the adoption of a number of important conventions on, respectively, the conduct of war and the establishment of a permanent Court of Arbitration. The latter half of the century also saw a peak in colonialism in Asia and in particular Africa. Although most of the states in South America gained independence from their European colonizers in the first half of the 19th century, at the 1884–1885 Berlin Conference the major European powers gathered to discuss the criteria for the partition of Africa ('the Scramble for Africa')[9] and, at the outbreak of the First World War in 1914, 90 per cent of Africa was under European control.[10]

Not surprisingly, it was the destruction and carnage of the First World War that were to dominate the events in the *interwar period*. The primary development was the creation in 1919 of an organization tasked with maintaining world peace. The organization—the League of Nations—was a creation of US President Woodrow Wilson (1856–1924). While the League did not prohibit war, it did try to limit its outbreak by requiring states to submit potential destabilizing disputes to one of a number of settlement mechanisms and to desist from resorting to war until a certain period had elapsed following the decision by that mechanism.[11] Efforts to outlaw war were not attempted until 1928 when the *Treaty of Paris* (also known as the Kellogg–Briand Pact) obliged parties to refrain from going to war as a means of settling their international controversies and as an instrument of national policy.[12] A major achievement of the interwar period was the successful establishment of the Permanent Court of International Justice (PCIJ) based in The Hague in the Netherlands. Although the Court did not have compulsory jurisdiction, it did build a substantial body of case law and was the forerunner to the present day International Court of Justice (ICJ).[13]

The period *immediately after the Second War World* was a time of major achievements in international law. For one thing, one of the ways in which the world (or, more correctly, the victorious states in that war) reacted to the atrocities of the Nazis was to prosecute top German officials for international crimes before a war crimes tribunal in Nuremberg, thereby setting an important precedent in international criminal law.[14] More importantly, the League of Nations was replaced by the United Nations (UN) which was entrusted with the maintenance of international peace and

[9] Craven (n 7) 879–887.

[10] For studies of colonialism and international law, see the major works by Anthony Anghie, *Imperialism, Sovereignty and the Making of International Law* (Cambridge University Press, 2004); Martti Koskenniemi, *The Gentle Civilizer of Nations: The Rise and Fall of International Law 1870–1960* (Cambridge University Press, 2011).

[11] Covenant of the League of Nations (adopted 28 June 1919, entered into force 10 January 1920), art. 12.

[12] Treaty Between the United States and Other Powers Providing for the Renunciation of War as an Instrument of National Policy (adopted 27 August 1928, entered into force 24 July 1929) 94 LNTS 57 (Kellogg–Briand Pact).

[13] See also Ole Spiermann, *International Legal Argument in the Permanent Court of International Justice* (Cambridge University Press, 2005).

[14] Major Japanese war criminals prosecuted before an international military tribunal in Tokyo. See Chapter 15.

security. The UN is built on solid 'Westphalian' principles and is based on respect for the principle of equal rights and self-determination of peoples and on the sovereign equality of all its members.[15] The founding treaty of the UN—the Charter of the United Nations—introduced a ban on the use of force and gave a collective organ—the Security Council—the competence to maintain international peace and security and, to that end, if necessary, to authorize forceful measures. From then on, the maintenance of peace and the conduct of war were to be a collective effort. In practice, however, from the outset the activities of the UN were marred by the outbreak of the Cold War and the struggle between the Great Powers of the East and West. Consequently, the Security Council remained by and large inactive throughout the Cold War. It was not until after the collapse of communism and the successful UN-sanctioned ousting of Iraq from Kuwait in 1991, that the collective security system in the UN began to live, to some extent, up to its promises.[16]

The UN Charter also established a General Assembly where all members are represented. Although the Assembly only has a consultative role, it offers an organizational structure where all states—including those of marginal importance—can voice their opinions and raise their concerns. The Assembly has also been instrumental in the promotion of a wide range of goals of global interest. One of the best examples is the important role it played in the decolonialization process. When the UN was created, almost one-third of the world's population lived in territories which were in some way dependent on a colonial power. In 1960, the Assembly adopted a landmark declaration on the granting of independence to colonies that affirmed the right of all people to self-determination and proclaimed that colonialism should be brought to a speedy and unconditional end.[17] Today, 80 former colonies have gained their independence.[18] The Assembly has also helped to advance the development of international law. In 1946, it established the International Law Commission (ILC) whose primary purpose is to promote the 'progressive development of international law and its codification'.[19] The ILC has been instrumental in the adoption of important treaties, such as in the law of the sea, diplomatic and consular relations, human rights and on treaty law itself. With the creation of the UN, the current International Court of Justice (ICJ) also replaced the PCIJ and gradually assumed an increasingly important role.

The UN also serves as an umbrella structure for a number of important international organizations. A 1944 conference at Bretton Woods in the United States, created the most important international organizations for the regulation of trade and monetary policy: the International Monetary Fund (IMF), the International Bank for

---

[15] See, respectively, Charter of the United Nations (adopted 26 June 1945, entered into force 24 October 1945), arts 1(2) and 2(1).

[16] The regulation of the use of force is the subject of Chapter 13.

[17] Declaration on the Granting of Independence to Colonial Countries and Peoples, GA Res. 1514 (II) (14 December 1960), UN Doc. A/RES/1514(XV).

[18] For an overview, see 'The United Nations and Decolonization' www.un.org/en/decolonization/nonselfgov.shtml (accessed 26 July 2016).

[19] Statute of the International Law Commission, GA Res. 174 (II) (21 November 1947), UN Doc. A/RES/174(II), art. 1. For an overview, see Alan Boyle and Christine Chinkin, *The Making of International Law* (Oxford University Press, 2007) 171–183.

Reconstruction and Development (the 'World Bank') and the General Agreement on Tariffs and Trade (GATT). While the GATT was created to liberalize world trade by reducing tariffs and other barriers to trade, the IMF was established to ensure exchange stability and to make resources available to states with balance of payment difficulties. To supplement the IMF, the World Bank provides loans to developing countries. In 1995, the World Trade Organization (WTO) replaced the old GATT system.[20]

The creation of the UN and its various 'sister organizations' illustrates that states often further their goals of common interest by creating international organizations. Membership of these organizations varies according to purpose and region. An important regional organization is the North Atlantic Treaty Organization (NATO) whose members agree to offer each other mutual defence in the event of an attack by an external actor. NATO was created in 1949 to counter the threat from the Soviet Union but it remains of vital importance. Institutional cooperation has been particularly strong in Europe, where the European Union (EU) stands out as an impressive example of what ambitious states can accomplish. Like the UN, the impetus for the creation of what later became the EU was the motivation to avoid large-scale conflict. In 1951, six European states established the European Coal and Steel Community and a common market for coal and steel.[21] In 1957, the same states adopted the Treaty of Rome that created the European Economic Community (EEC) consisting of an economic common market and a customs union.[22] By 1993, the EEC had developed into a single market. The 1992 Maastricht Treaty created the European Union[23] and the 1999 Treaty of Amsterdam brought the members of the Union even closer together. On 1 May 2004, the EU was expanded with ten new member states thus bringing the total membership to 25.[24] Today it stands at 28.[25] The EU consists of a number of important institutions, including the European Council, the Council of the European Union, the European Parliament, the European Commission and the Court of Justice of the European Union (CJEU). Some of these may adopt legally binding instruments or render binding decisions.

Mention should also be made of the 1949 Council of Europe created to strengthen intergovernmental and inter-parliamentary cooperation.[26] In 1950, the Council adopted the European Convention on Human Rights (ECHR) which remains the

---

[20] International economic law is covered in Chapter 11.

[21] The states were Belgium, France, Germany, Italy, Luxembourg and the Netherlands.

[22] In 1973, Denmark, Ireland and the UK joined the EEC. Greece joined in 1981 and Portugal and Spain in 1986.

[23] In referendum on 2 June 1992, a narrow majority of Danish voters rejected the Maastricht Treaty. In a subsequent referendum on 18 May 1993, a majority of Danish voters accepted Danish ratification of the Maastricht Treaty on the basis of an agreement entered into in Edinburgh according to which Denmark was granted four exceptions to the Treaty (EU citizenship, participation in the economic and monetary union, defence and justice and home affairs).

[24] The new states were Cyprus, the Czech Republic, Estonia, Hungary, Latvia, Lithuania, Malta, Poland, Slovakia and Slovenia. Austria, Finland and Sweden had joined in 1995.

[25] In 2007, Bulgaria and Romania were admitted to the EU. Croatia joined in 2013.

[26] See Statute of the Council of Europe (adopted 5 May 1949, entered into force 3 August 1949), ETS No. 1. See also the overview in Chapter 12.

central instrument for the protection of human rights in Europe. The Convention established the European Court of Human Rights (ECtHR) in Strasbourg, France, that hears complaints from individual citizens and may render binding decisions.

The extensive institutional cooperation in Europe means that there have been increasingly fewer political issues that national policymakers can freely decide. In recent years, the perceived loss of national sovereignty and allegations of unjustified judicial activism by the CJEU in Luxembourg and the ECtHR in Strasbourg have caused somewhat of a popular backlash around Europe. A growing number of European politicians criticize the European institutions for making unwarranted encroachments on national sovereignty, in particular in sensitive areas such as social security, asylum and migration and national security. In a historical referendum on 23 June 2016, in what may well be a sign of more profound popular dissatisfaction with the speed and breadth of European integration, a majority of British voters decided that the UK should leave the EU.[27]

Important regional organizations have also been created outside Europe. In the Americas, for example, the 1948 Organization of American States (OAS) was established to create a peaceful order and to promote solidarity and collaboration and to defend the sovereignty, territorial integrity and independence of its members.[28] It has 35 member states and consists of, among other things, a General Assembly and an Inter-American Commission on Human Rights (IACHR). In Africa, the 2001 African Union (AU) grew out of the 1963 Organisation of African Unity and works to ensure a prosperous and secure African continent.[29] It has 54 member states[30] and its most important organs include an Assembly, an Executive Council, a Pan-African Parliament and a Court of Justice.

1.3 The structures of international law

The international legal system consists of different structures of rules reflecting the historical evolution of the law and the political configuration of the world.[31] The structures are built on the configuration of the sovereign state as the primary actor in the international system.[32] In fact, the reason why the 1648 Peace of Westphalia is generally perceived as being a pivotal moment in the development of international law is because it founded the principle that sovereign states are the primary actors in the

---

[27] At the time of writing, the legal consequences of 'Brexit' remain unknown.

[28] The predecessor of the OAS was the 1890 International Union of American Republics.

[29] See Constitutive Act of the African Union (adopted 11 July 2000, entered into force 26 May 2001), OAU Doc. CAB/LEG/23.15.

[30] Morocco is the only state on the African continent that is not a member of the AU.

[31] See also the approach of the so-called English School in the international relations theory, inter alia, the seminal works of Hedley Bull, *The Anarchical Society: A Study of Order in World Politics* (Palgrave Macmillan, 1977). See also Wolfgang Friedmann, *The Changing Structure of International Law* (Stevens & Son, 1964). For an excellent and more recent account of the structures of international law, see Spiermann (n 13) ch. 2.

[32] Bull (n 31) 65.

international system and that they enjoy equal legal status as well as protection from outside intervention. From then on, the international society has first and foremost been a society of *individual sovereign states*.

The conception of the state as a (national) sovereign helps to explain the role and primary purpose of international law.[33] International law is best conceived of from the standpoint of national law and as a response to a lawyer's need for legal rules and principles to complement those found in his or her national legal system. National law is perfectly adequate to regulate the vast majority of legal disputes that merely involve the relationship between citizens of a sovereign state or between the citizens and the state. But mutual respect for sovereignty dictates that national law is ill-suited to a situation where the interests of more than one sovereign state collide. Whenever a lawyer encounters an issue of importance to more than one state, he or she must look to international law to find the legal answer needed. In essence, then, international law serves as a supplement to national law—as a residual legal system—the scope of which cannot be determined independently of national law. It is only when an issue is of interest to more than one national sovereign that international law enters the picture. The *scope* of international law is thereby determined by the inadequacy of national law. The *content* of international law, and thus the concrete answers to the questions that cannot be answered in national law, on the other hand, must be found in international law.[34]

The two ways in which an issue becomes of interest to more than one state define the two substantive structures of international law. The first is where two or more states are likely to have a colliding interest in the substance of the issue. Here, the mere fact that international society is composed of a multitude of sovereign states with different interests is sufficient to make the issue international. The second way an issue becomes of interest to more than one state is when the involved states have agreed in a treaty to turn the issue (that would otherwise have been dealt with by national law) into one of an international character. In practice, therefore, a matter may become an issue for international law either due to its *content* or due to its *form*. While the former is governed by the international law of coexistence, the latter is dealt with under the international law of cooperation.[35]

The *international law of coexistence*—also referred to as 'general international law'—contains the answers required to separate the powers of the sovereign states and thereby uphold peaceful coexistence. Thus, it is here the lawyer finds the classic topics of international law. These topics include issues related to the delimitation of—and title to—territory, the criteria for statehood and the recognition of new states and governments, jurisdiction and immunity, the use of force, the conduct of armed hostilities and neutrality in times of armed conflict. Also included are the fundamental principles of treaty law and the secondary legal principles on state responsibility.[36] As a legal structure, the international law of coexistence is primarily *horizontal* in the

---

[33] The following approach is taken from Spiermann (n 13) ch. 2.
[34] Spiermann (n 13) 46–48. See also 85.   [35] Ibid, 49–50, 69–70.
[36] For views on the scope of the international law of coexistence, see also Bull (n 31) 66–67 and Spiermann (n 13) 83–87.

sense that it is mainly concerned with the manner in which sovereign states interact with—and between—each other. It is less preoccupied with how sovereign authority is constituted or exercised in relation to the citizens within the state. Such issues are matters for international law because states have made them the object of a treaty, in which case they form part of the international law of cooperation (see below). It is also important to note that the international law of coexistence is similarly not concerned with binding states closer together in some sort of unified international 'community'. It merely seeks to ensure that states can pursue their different and separate interests (whatever they may be) in a way that respects the sovereignty of other states. As a fundamental structure of international law, the international law of coexistence is relatively stable and not subject to much change. But there is an inherent vagueness to the *content* of the law and easily recognizable rules are rare.[37] In fact, there has always been an element of 'law-creation' in the process of resolving issues in which the interests of two or more states collide.

The second substantive structure of international law—the *international law of cooperation*—contains the legal answers to issues that are not inherently of interest to two or more states but which have nevertheless been turned into matters of international concern through the adoption of a treaty. The reason why the issue is of an international character (and thus ill-suited to be dealt with by national law) is because treaties are international agreements that are governed by international law. As an international legal structure, the international law of cooperation is much 'younger' than the international law of coexistence. As the previous historical overview has illustrated, in the period immediately after the end of the Second World War states began to create organizations that were given competence to deal with issues that had until that time been considered to be of an entirely national interest.[38] The result was the emergence of a new structure of international law involved in the promotion of a variety of 'societal' goals. International law thereby began to be concerned with the manner in which sovereignty authority was exercised within individual states. Topics covered by the international law of cooperation include international human rights law, the majority of international environmental law and international economic law. EU law is a particularly good example of a legal regime solidly situated in the international law of cooperation.

It is important to understand that states are only inherently bound by the international law of coexistence and that they must agree to all other international legal obligations. The international law of cooperation is therefore 'optional' in the sense that states decide for themselves if they want to turn a matter previously dealt with by national law into a matter of international law. It is the consensual character of the international law of cooperation that explains why a state like the UK is free to leave the EU if it wants to do so[39] or why a state can withdraw from the ECHR if it no longer

---

[37] Spiermann (n 13) 88–92.
[38] Friedmann (n 31) 61–71. See also Wolfgang Friedmann, 'The Changing Dimensions of International Law' (1962) 62 *Columbia Law Review* 1147.
[39] See also art. 50 of the Treaty on European Union (TEU).

wants to be bound.[40] It also helps to explain the pace—or rather the lack thereof—with which international society deals with wider societal goals, such as the reduction of poverty or curbing climate change. To tackle such issues requires agreement by states and that is often hard to come by.

1.4 The basis of international obligation

The question of why states are bound to observe international law has dominated international legal theory for centuries.[41] As the historical overview has illustrated, the theoretical debate has traditionally been dominated by proponents of natural law and positivism. While the former derives the binding force of international law from the claim that dictates of nature require certain behaviour of states, the latter bases international obligation in the 'consensual theory'. One of the issues international legal theory has struggled with has been how to reconcile state sovereignty with international obligations.[42] Surely, if a state is sovereign and the legal subject of no one, it cannot be bound by international law. To uphold the binding character of international law seems to imply the negation of sovereignty and it would therefore appear that *either* the state is sovereign, and hence not bound by international law, *or* it is bound by international law, and thus not sovereign.

But as we saw in the previous section, there need not be an irreconcilable tension between sovereignty and international legal obligations. Indeed, if one looks outside the law for the answer to the question of why international law is binding, things become less complicated.[43] The existence of a plurality of sovereign states justifies the binding character of international law. It is not, in other words, a matter of choosing between upholding either state sovereignty or international legal obligations but, rather, of perceiving international legal obligations as a logical consequence of sovereignty.[44] Just as domestic societies must impose limits on the way individuals exercise their liberties, if liberty for all is to be respected, it is only by limiting the manner in which sovereign states may exercise their sovereignty that international society can ensure respect for the sovereignty of all states. The peaceful coexistence of sovereign states requires the existence of a number of basic rules that dictate how states may behave and may not behave in their mutual relations. Even sovereign states are bound by the rules of the society of which they form part.

---

[40] Withdrawal from the ECHR is regulated in art. 58. A state will, however, remain bound by the content of a provision of a treaty that reflects customary international law. See also Chapter 2.

[41] See also Oscar Schachter, 'Towards a Theory of International Obligation' (1967–1968) 8 *Virginia Journal of International Law* 300.

[42] A classic discussion is H. L. A. Hart, *The Concept of Law* (Clarendon Press, 1961) 220–226. For a critical account, see Martti Koskenniemi, *From Apology to Utopia: The Structure of International Legal Argument* (Cambridge University Press, 1989); David Kennedy, 'Theses about International Law Discourse' (1980) 23 *German Yearbook of International Law* 353.

[43] See also Spiermann (n 13) 44.   [44] Ibid, 45–47.

In practice, of course, all states accept that they are members of a *society of states* and that they all benefit from the rules required for maintaining peaceful coexistence within the society they form.[45] They also participate in the working of the rules of the system. This, of course, does not mean that states may not disagree about the content of the law or that individual states may not decide to occasionally violate the law. Although Louis Henkin was right when he famously noted that 'almost all nations observe almost all principles of international law and almost all of their obligations almost all the time',[46] breaches of international law are not hard to find. The important point to note is that states never question whether they are bound by international law. When a state is accused of torturing its citizens, it does not respond by arguing that it is not generally bound by the prohibition against torture. Instead, it argues that the allegations of torture are incorrect or that it was somehow justified in violating the prohibition. When Russia intervened in Ukraine and annexed Crimea in 2014, it did not claim that it was not bound by international law, including the prohibition on the use of force, but instead that its acts fell outside those prescribed by international law. By justifying its actions with international legal arguments, Russia in reality affirmed the existence of the international legal system.

1.5 The relationship between international law and national law

A few points must be noted about the relationship between international law and national law. First of all, as we shall see throughout this book, *international law asserts its own supremacy over national law*. A state cannot justify a breach of its international legal obligations by arguing that compliance would be at variance with its national law.[47] International law is not, however, generally preoccupied with *how* a state lives up to its international obligations and leaves it to each state to determine how it will implement its international commitments.[48] What is of interest are actual breaches of international legal obligations in the form of concrete results that follow from acts or omissions. There are exceptions, however, and member states of the EU may be under obligations to implement EU regulations and directives in their domestic legal systems in a certain manner.[49] A number of conventions in international criminal law also require state parties to take effective domestic measures to ensure that certain prescribed acts constitute

---

[45] For a debate on the notion of a 'society of states' in the international system, see Bull (n 31) 13–19, 25–26, 38–44.

[46] Louis Henkin, *How Nations Behave* (Columbia University Press, 1979) 47.

[47] See also Vienna Convention on the Law of Treaties (adopted 23 May 1969, entered into force 27 January 1980), 1155 UNTS 331, art. 27.

[48] See also ILC, 'Draft Articles on the Responsibility of States for Internationally Wrongful Acts' (A/56/10, 2001) art 12; *LaGrand (Germany v United States of America)*, Judgment [2001] ICJ Rep 466, para. 125.

[49] For a classic case, see Case 6/64 *Costa v ENEL* [1964] ECR 585.

offences under national law and allow states to establish jurisdiction over those offences.[50]

A second point relates to the manner in which *international law is applied in national legal systems by the legislature and national courts*. National implementation and concrete application of international law is a constitutional issue that varies from state to state. Most presentations begin the analysis with the two different approaches that have dominated legal theory: monism and dualism. *Monism* holds that international law and national law essentially form a single legal order or a set of mutually intertwined legal orders that are presumed to be coherent. The monist approach therefore also holds that international law can be applied directly in the national legal system of states and that the international norm prevails in the case of conflict. The best known exponent of monism was Hans Kelsen (1881–1973) who argued that international law and national law form a single legal system because they both derive their validity from the same ultimate source, the *Grundnorm*.[51] *Dualism*, on the other hand, holds that international law and national law are two separate legal systems that operate independently. While international law primarily regulates the relationship between states, national law governs the relationship between citizens or the citizens and the state. Following a dualistic approach, neither of the two legal systems creates rules for the other, and if international law is applied domestically it is because it is 'translated' into the national legal system, in most cases through the adoption of national legislation. However, neither monism nor dualism is able to explain the myriad ways in which international law is applied by national legislatures and courts. In part, this is due to the post-1945 growth in treaties in areas that were traditionally dealt with solely under national law. The theoretical debate has therefore gradually moved away from the dichotomy between monism/dualism and instead turned to pluralism.[52]

In practice, each legal system determines how the norms of other legal systems are taken into account. As already noted, the extent to which international law is integrated into a national legal system depends on the constitutional approach of the state in question. In general, however, national courts are more willing to apply norms derived from customary international law than treaty-based norms. Since it is in customary international law that one finds the answers required to separate the powers of sovereign states (the international law of coexistence), this is not surprising. National courts are well aware that disputes inherently involving the interests of more than one state must be answered by international—and not national—law. Both civil law and common law jurisdictions therefore apply customary international law directly

---

[50] See, inter alia, Convention Against Torture and Other Cruel, Inhuman or Degrading Treatment or Punishment (adopted 10 December 1984, entered into force 26 June 1987), 1465 UNTS 85, arts 4–5. See also Convention on the Prevention and Punishment of the Crime of Genocide (adopted 9 December 1949, entered into force 12 January 1951), 78 UNTS 227, art. 5.

[51] Hans Kelsen, *General Theory of Law and State* (Harvard University Press, 1945) 564.

[52] James Crawford, *Brownlie's Principles of Public International Law* (8th edn, Oxford University Press, 2012) 50. See also Giorgia Gaja, 'Dualism—A Review' in Janne Nijman and André Nollkaemper (eds), *New Perspectives on the Divide Between National and International Law* (Cambridge University Press, 2007) 52–53.

in their legal systems and often stipulate that it takes precedence over domestic legislation.[53] But since a treaty may govern an issue that is not inherently of an international nature, it will not necessarily be applied in a national legal system. In return for tight parliamentary control over the ratification of treaties, some civil law states in Europe accept treaties on an equal footing with national legislation.[54] Other civil law states, however, including the Nordic states, adopt a more 'dualistic' approach and require treaties to be formally incorporated into national law before they are given direct effect.[55] Incorporation of treaties generally takes one of two forms. The treaty is either incorporated into national law by a short statute with the treaty as an annex or through a more thorough reformulation and interpretation in new—or an amendment to existing—legislation. Incorporation is also a requirement in the common law system in England.[56] In the United States, there is no requirement of incorporation and the decisive issue is the extent to which the national court deems the treaty to be 'self-executing'.[57] In practice, however, national courts will always try to avoid a breach of an international obligation and, to that end, seek to interpret national legislation in accordance with the content of an international obligation. Courts will usually work on the assumption that the legislature did not intend to violate international law.

1.6 The issue of enforcement of international law

As noted in the introduction, one of the ways in which the international legal system differs from a national legal setting is in its lack of an international police force and a mandatory judicial system that can enforce the law. Despite its shortcomings, though, enforcement is not totally absent from international law. In fact, when it comes to *adjudication* of disputes significant progress has been made since the Second World War. As we shall see throughout the book, a number of judicial dispute settlement bodies with competence to settle disputes and/or determine complaints of violations of international law do exist, the most notable example being the ICJ. Other examples include the Permanent Court of Arbitration (PCA), International Tribunal for the Law

---

[53] For an overview of selected jurisdictions, see Crawford (n 52) 88–93. See also Eileen Denza, 'The Relationship between International and National Law' in Malcolm D. Evans (ed.), *International Law* (4th edn, Oxford University Press, 2014) 418–425. See e.g. art. 25 of the Basic Law for the Federal Republic of Germany and art. 10(1) of the Italian 1948 Constitution. For France, see Crawford (n 52) 88–89. For an overview of relevant practice from Sweden, see Michael Bogdan, 'Application of Public International Law by Swedish Courts' (1994) 63 *Nordic Journal of International Law* 3, 4–6. For Denmark, see the analysis in Ole Spiermann, *Moderne Folkeret* (3rd edn, Jurist—og Økonomforbundets Forlag, 2006) 156–161. For Norway, see Morten Ruud and Geir Ulfstein, *Innføring i Folkerett* (4th edn, Universitetsforlaget, 2011). For the UK and the US, see respectively, Crawford (n 52) 67–71, 80–82.

[54] See the overview of selected jurisdictions in Crawford (n 52) 93–102.

[55] For Italy, see Crawford (n 52) 98. Incorporation is generally required in the Nordic states, see for Sweden: Bogdan (n 53) 611 and also NJA 2004.225 H. For Denmark, see UfR 2006.770 H and UfR 1986.898 H and the overview in Ole Spiermann (n 53) 151–154. For Norway, see NR 1997.580 H and NR 2000.1811 H.

[56] See the overview in Crawford (n 52) 63–65.

[57] For the—complicated—US practice, see Crawford (n 52) 77–80. See also the American Law Institute, *Restatement (Third) of the Foreign Relations Law of the United States* (1987) ch. 2.

of the Sea (ITLOS) and the dispute mechanisms in international economic law. In addition, the UN has created a number of monitoring bodies with varying competences in the realm of human rights law. In Europe, adjudication is particularly strong and both the CJEU and the ECtHR are competent to issue binding decisions on matters that may potentially constitute violations of the relevant treaties.

The picture is less promising when it comes to 'policing' and *actual enforcement* of breaches of international law. In some cases, as we shall examine in more detail in Chapters 12 and 13, an aggrieved state may try to seek redress before the UN Security Council but enforcement by the Security Council is rare. To that end, it is also worth noting that the Security Council was not set up to enforce international law but to uphold international peace and security and the Council is therefore more influenced by political and strategic considerations than by law. If the Council *does* decide to take action, however, it has a wide range of options available to it culminating in the authorization of the use of force. In some cases, the Council will seek to maintain peace and security (and by implication also help to enforce violations of international law) by imposing a variety of forms of sanctions. Mention should also be made of the practice of establishing peacekeeping operations in the form of deployment of UN personnel to an area of dispute in an attempt to uphold international peace and security and in many cases to prevent further violations of international law. As we shall see in Chapter 15, the Council may also established criminal tribunals tasked with prosecuting serious international crimes.

In practice, of course, collective action that may help to enforce international law may also take place outside the framework of the UN, including in regional organizations. The EU, for example, has an elaborate system for enforcing breaches of EU law. In response to Russia's annexation of Crimea, a number of states and organizations, including the EU, decided to impose sanctions against Russia and Russian interests.

In most cases, however, an aggrieved state is left with no choice but to adopt its own measures in response to another state's violation of international law. Such measures of self-help may take a number of forms that take account of the reciprocal nature of many parts of international law. For one thing, as Chapter 7 will demonstrate, international law generally allows a state to respond to a breach of international law by employing proportionate and non-forceful 'countermeasures' and breach its international legal obligations towards a delinquent state. In addition—as Chapter 3 demonstrates—if the violation of international law relates to a breach of a treaty obligation, the aggrieved state will often be allowed to respond by suspending its own performance of the treaty. A state may, furthermore, respond to a breach of international law by adopting measures of 'retorsion' that are unfriendly—but lawful—acts, such as halting foreign aid, suspending trade, severing non-legally binding agreements, cancelling state visits or downgrading or even breaking off diplomatic contact.

The limited means of actually enforcing violations of international law makes it all the more important that states usually have a strong incentive for complying with their international obligations. As mentioned earlier, most states generally honour their legal obligations towards each other. States comply with international law for a number of reasons.[58] There is a strong element of reciprocity in the international legal system: for one thing, states are well aware of the long-term benefits to everyone of a well-functioning international legal system where promises are kept and agreements are honoured. In addition, like most individuals, states generally care about their reputation and will go to great lengths to be seen as a respectable and law-abiding member of international society. In fact, one of the implications of increasing global interconnection is the rising cost of acquiring a reputation for being unreliable and untrustworthy.[59] To reap the benefits of an international organization, participating states are generally expected to abide by the established norms, practices and institutions.

1.7 The alleged inadequacy of international law in the 21st century

One of the recurring criticisms of international law is that the existing state-centric configuration of the world is outdated and at times counterproductive to creating a more fair and just world. For example, respect for state sovereignty sometimes stands in the way of benevolent efforts to alleviate the suffering of a distressed civilian population. Likewise, the consensual character of treaty-making makes much needed progress on issue of global concern—such as the eradication of poverty, fair trade agreements or combating climate change—hard to achieve.[60] While there is no denying the occasional tension between the state-centric system and 'justice' (whatever that is[61]), it is important to remember that the construction of a legal system around sovereign states was never motivated by a desire to create a more just and equitable world. It was instead led by a desire to find an organizing principle for upholding international order and stability. It was, in other words, less about justice than it was about order. In fact, while it sounds harsh, it is a misconception to assume that the primary purpose of international law is to create a more just world. As we shall see throughout this book, when balancing notions of 'justice' and stability and order, international law often prioritizes the latter. As we saw earlier in the chapter, international law is primarily preoccupied with finding the answers that are required to

---

[58] There is a growing literature on state compliance with international law, see, among others, the classic work by Thomas M. Franck, *The Power of Legitimacy Among Nations* (Oxford University Press, 1990). See also Andrew Guzman, *How International Law Works: A Rational Choice Theory* (Oxford University Press, 2008) 33–71. A critical view is found in Jack L. Goldsmith and Eric Posner, *The Limits of International Law* (Oxford University Press, 2006).

[59] On reputation, see Rachel Brewster, 'Unpacking the State's Reputation' (2009) 50 *Harvard International Law Journal* 231; Abram Chayes and Antonia H. Chayes, *The New Sovereignty: Compliance with International Regulatory Agreements* (Harvard University Press, 1995) 273.

[60] A well-known critique of the classic approach to state sovereignty and an endorsement of a world of global networks, is Anne-Marie Slaughter, *A New World Order* (Princeton University Press, 2004).

[61] On the meaning of 'justice' in world politics, see Bull (n 31) 74–94.

separate the powers of the sovereign states and to ensure the maintenance of order and stability.

In practice, of course, order may also be a value in itself. Those who argue for less respect for state sovereignty should remind themselves that it is often hard to realize broader societal goals in a society without order and stability. Indeed, when considered through a lens of stability, the many unwarranted inroads into state sovereignty in recent years—whether in the form of Russian interferences in Ukraine or Western-led 'humanitarian interventions' without UN backing—constitute one of the most serious threats to international society. Critics of the state-centric configuration of the world also tend to underappreciate the fact that the current system, however 'unjust' it may appear to be, ensures a level of global representation by far surpassing that offered by possible alternatives—including, of course, that offered by the various 'anti-globalization' movements who proclaim to speak on behalf of an ill-defined 'global community'.

On a final note, it is worth noting that the 'Westphalian' configuration of international society is not the only conceivable way of structuring international society. Indeed, as the brief historical overview illustrated, when seen from a wider historical perspective the emergence of sovereign states is a fairly recent phenomenon. It was not inevitable that states were to assume the primary role in the international system and it cannot be ruled out that future generations may want to rethink the current configuration of the world and decide that the world should instead be structured around, say, ethnic or religious lines or by a 'world government'. At present, however, the state system remains alive and well, and states seem destined to remain the principal international legal actors for the foreseeable future. While states frequently disagree about whether or not the existing system should be more responsive to a variety of more or less pertinent 'global issues', there are currently no serious attempts to replace the state-centric system with something else. Despite its weaknesses, there is an overall recognition that the existing system is the best option on offer.

Summary

Public international law is the legal system that deals with issues of concern to more than one state. It consists of different structures that reflect historical legal evolution and the principles and political configuration of the world. The most fundamental principle is the one that constitutes the nation state as the most important legal actor in the international system. The international law of coexistence—or general international law—contains the answers required to separate the powers of sovereign states. The international law of cooperation provides the legal answers to issues that have been turned into matters of international concern pursuant to the adoption of a treaty. The existence of a plurality of sovereign states provides the theoretical justifications for the binding character of international law. A state cannot justify a breach of its international legal obligations with the claim that it would breach its national laws if it were to comply. The application of international law in national law is governed by the constitutional principles of each state and thus varies substantially. In practice, however, most states will apply customary international law domestically. Treaty-based obligations, on the other hand, often require incorporation. Enforcement of international law remains a challenge but it is not totally absent. In addition, non-legal incentives often move states towards compliance with their international obligations. There is an undeniable tension between the existing state-centric system and wider notions of 'justice'. The current configuration of the world was, however, never motivated by a specific desire to create a more just and equitable world or to facilitate the realization of wider 'community' goals. Instead, it was derived from a desire to find an organizing principle that could uphold international order and stability in world affairs.

Recommended reading

For classic works on the history of international law, see Arthur Nussbaum, *A Concise History of the Law of Nations* (Macmillan, 1947); Wilhelm G. Grewe, *The Epochs of International Law* (De Gruyter, 2010).

More recent contributions include Stephen C. Neff, *Justice Among Nations: A History of International Law* (Harvard University Press, 2014); Alexander Orakhelashvili, 'The Idea of European International Law' (2006) 17 *European Journal of International Law* 315; Bardo Fassbender and Anne Peters (eds), *The Oxford Handbook of the History of International Law* (Oxford University Press, 2012).

For the structures and purposes of international law, see the seminal work by Hedley Bull, *The Anarchical Society: A Study of Order in World Politics* (Palgrave Macmillan, 1977); Wolfgang Friedmann, *The Changing Structure of International Law* (Stevens & Son, 1964). An excellent and more recent account is available in Ole Spiermann, *International Legal Argument in the Permanent Court of International Justice* (Cambridge University Press 2005) ch. 2.

For a classic discussion of the basis of legal obligation, see H. L. A. Hart, *The Concept of Law* (Clarendon Press, 1961) 220–226.

There is a rich literature on state compliance with international law, see, inter alia, the classic work by Thomas M. Franck, *The Power of Legitimacy Among Nations* (Oxford University Press, 1990). Other works include Andrew Guzman, *How International Law Works: A Rational Choice Theory* (Oxford University Press, 2008) 33–71; Christian Reus-Smit, 'Politics and the International Legal Obligation' (2003) 9 *European Journal of International Relations* 591. For a critical view, see Jack L. Goldsmith and Eric Posner, *The Limits of International Law* (Oxford University Press, 2006).

Questions for discussion

1. Why was the Peace of Westphalia perceived as a crucial turning point in the history and development of public international law?

2. What is the difference between natural law and legal positivism? Do you see any reflections of the two theories in contemporary debates on public international law?

3. How would you describe the relationship between international law and national law in the legal system of your state?

4. Why does the conception of a national sovereign help to explain the role and primary purposes of international law?

5. What is the difference between the international law of coexistence and the international law of cooperation? Why is the law of coexistence a more stable structure?

6. Where do you see a (potential) tension between order and justice in international law?

7. Can you think of any way that international society can be structured other than around states? And what consequences might an alternative configuration have?

2

Sources of international law

CENTRAL ISSUES

1. This chapter provides an overview of the legal sources in international law and takes its point of departure in article 38 of the Statute of the International Court of Justice.

2. It discusses the primary sources of international law: the treaty, customary international law and general principles.

3. It also provides an overview of the secondary sources of international law as well as a description of unilateral statements.

4. The chapter lists those legal sources deemed to be of a higher normative value than other sources and discusses the issue of so-called soft law and the legal value of, among other things, resolutions and declarations from the United Nations General Assembly.

2.1 Introduction

Sources of law determine the rules of legal society and, like national legal societies, the international legal society has its own set of rules. Thus, when we look for the content of international law, we consult the sources of international law. In essence, the sources of international law contain the legal answers to the questions that cannot be answered in national law. In domestic law, the identification of relevant legal sources is rarely a problem and there is traditionally a very definite method of ascertaining the law in any given subject matter. In most constituencies, the domestic lawyer will simply consult parliamentary legislation as well as potentially relevant court cases in order to identify the relevant information about the law. This method also reflects the hierarchical nature of the domestic legal order. In international law, however, the situation is very different. As we shall see throughout this book, the lack of a universal legislature and a system of courts with compulsory jurisdiction often make the task of uncovering the law more difficult. Furthermore, since international law is a decentralized legal system, legal obligations may derive from more than one particular source.

Legal sources enable legal subjects to distinguish between norms of a legal character and those of a 'merely' political, moral or ethical nature. The International Court of Justice (ICJ) has stressed the difference between law and politics on a number of occasions. In the *South West Africa* cases, the Court stated:

> Throughout this case it has been suggested, directly or indirectly, that humanitarian considerations are sufficient in themselves to generate legal rights and obligations, and that the Court can and should proceed accordingly. The Court does not think so. It is a court of law, and can take account of moral principles only in so far as these are given a sufficient expression in legal form. Law exists, it is said, to serve a social need; but precisely for that reason it can do so only through and within the limits of its own discipline. Otherwise, it is not a legal service that would be rendered.[1]

In practice, sources of international law are the argumentative tools available to the international lawyer.

The concept of a legal source is tied to the theories about the basis and structure of international law we discussed in Chapter 1. So while proponents of natural law find sources of international law in what they consider to be elementary dictates of justice, positivists will look for evidence of state will. The modern theory of sources as reflected in article 38 of the ICJ Statute is based on the (positivist) consensual theory. Thus, whether expressed *explicitly* in a treaty or more *tacitly* in an international custom accepted as law or in a general principle already recognized by states, all international legal obligations are considered to be derived from the consent of the state. This book adopts a more pragmatic approach to legal theory. Not all answers in international law can be found in freely undertaken obligations. It is, nevertheless, a fallacy to assume that states cannot be bound by an obligation to which they have not consented. Whether they have consented or not, all states are bound by those behavioural rules that are required for the maintenance of peaceful coexistence in the society of which they form part.

We begin our discussion in Section 2.2 with article 38 of the ICJ Statute. Section 2.3 discusses treaties, Section 2.4 covers customary international law and Section 2.5 turns to general principles of international law. Attention then shifts to the two additional sources listed in article 38. Section 2.6 discusses judicial decisions and Section 2.7 examines academic contributions. Section 2.8 discusses the role played by unilateral statements. We then turn to the issue of a hierarchy of sources in Section 2.9 and conclude in Section 2.10 with a discussion of non-binding instruments and so-called 'soft law'.

---

[1] *South West Africa, Second Phase (Ethiopia and Liberia v South Africa)*, Judgment [1966] ICJ Rep 6, paras 49–50. See also *Barcelona Traction, Light and Power Co., Ltd (Belgium v Spain)*, Judgment [1970] ICJ Rep 3, para. 89.

2.2 Article 38 of the Statute of the International Court of Justice

The classical attempt at listing the sources of international law is found in article 38 of the ICJ Statute:

1. The Court, whose function is to decide in accordance with international law such disputes as are submitted to it, shall apply:
   a. international conventions, whether general or particular, establishing rules expressly recognized by the contesting states;
   b. international custom, as evidence of a general practice accepted as law;
   c. the general principles of law recognized by civilized nations;
   d. subject to the provisions of Article 59, judicial decisions and the teachings of the most highly qualified publicists of the various nations, as subsidiary means for the determination of rules of law.
2. This provision shall not prejudice the power of the Court to decide a case *ex aequo et bono*, if the parties agree thereto.

Since the ICJ essentially continues the work of the 1922 Permanent Court of International Justice (PCIJ), article 38 is almost identical to the corresponding article in the statute of its predecessor. The preparatory works for the ICJ therefore also date back to the drafting process of the PCIJ in 1920. Of particular relevance is the work carried out by an Advisory Committee of Jurists that was created to formulate a first draft for the original court. [2] Although article 38 is purely directed to the Court, it is considered of *general* relevance. It has been the subject of much academic debate about whether the list of sources in the article is exhaustive.[3] In practice, the ICJ has relied on sources not mentioned in the article 38—most notably unilateral statements.

Article 38 distinguishes between primary and secondary sources of law. While the former is constituted by conventions (treaties), customary law and general principles, the latter refer to judicial decisions and scholarly contributions. Another approach holds that the first three sources are law *creating* because they create (new) rights and obligations whereas the latter two are law *identifying* since they merely apply or clarify the content of existing law.

2.3 Conventions (treaties) as a legal source

The adoption of a convention—also called a 'treaty'—is the most direct and formal way for states to create rights and obligations under international law. Indeed, as we

---

[2] For a historical background, see Ole Spiermann, 'Historical Introduction' in Zimmermann and others (eds), *The Statute of the International Court: A Commentary* (2nd edn, Oxford University Press, 2012) 47–71. On the PCIJ, see also the same author in *International Legal Argument in the Permanent Court of International Justice: The Rise of the International Judiciary* (Cambridge University Press, 2005).

[3] See Hugh Thirlway, *The Sources of International Law* (Oxford University Press, 2014) 19–30.

shall see throughout this book, the most important legal sources within a given area of international law are often treaty-based. In fact, the treaty is the only instrument available to two or more states that want to enter into some sort of formal legal relationship. The legal basis of treaty-based obligations is state consent and a treaty can therefore only create legal obligations for the consenting states. So while it is a mistake to assume that all international legal obligations derive from state consent, in treaty law consent *is* decisive. The effect of a treaty is expressed in the principle *pacta sunt servanda* according to which states are bound to honour their treaty-based obligations.

As we shall examine in more detail in Chapter 3, treaties come in many forms and the title of the instrument is immaterial. A treaty concluded by two states—a *bilateral* treaty—often governs a particular issue of mutual interest, such as the construction of joint infrastructure, and resembles a contract. Treaties between larger groups of states—*multilateral* treaties—often have general application and possess 'law-making' features. When a treaty establishes an international organization it is referred to as a 'constituent treaty'.[4] Some constituent treaties create international organizations with the competence to adopt legally binding instruments. The Charter of the United Nations, for example, gives the Security Council the competence to adopt resolutions binding on all members of the UN.[5] Within the EU, the European Parliament and the Council of the European Union can adopt binding 'EU legislation'. The instruments in question derive their binding character from the constituent treaty and are therefore 'treaty-based'. A state that becomes party to the constituent treaty consents to be bound by any subsequent legal instruments adopted pursuant thereto.[6]

2.4 Custom as a source of international law

2.4.1 Introduction

Often in societies, the way things have always been done becomes the way that things *must* be done. Indeed, to some extent all law begins with custom.[7] Undoubtedly, the absence of an international 'law-maker' has made custom a particularly important source of international law and many well-known legal principles are derived from common usage and interstate practice. Furthermore, while the exact content of customary law may not be as detailed as treaty law, it is based on the everyday interaction of states and therefore has the ability to adapt to changing circumstances. As a legal source, however, custom is controversial and volumes have been written on the theoretical difficulties associated with the acceptance of custom as a source of international law.[8]

---

[4] On international organizations as subjects of international law, see Chapter 4.
[5] See more in Chapter 13.   [6] See also Thirlway (n 3) 33–34.
[7] David J. Bederman, *Custom as a Source of Law* (Cambridge University Press, 2010).
[8] See, e.g., Jorg Kammerhofer, *Uncertainty in International Law: A Kelsian Perspective* (Routledge, 2011) 59–86.

International customary law arises when a particular way of behaving is: (1) followed as a general practice among states; and (2) accepted by those states as legally binding.[9] Thus, there is both an *objective* element (state practice) and a *subjective* element (the belief that the practice is legally binding).[10] One of the challenges is to identify the point in time when behaviour—the custom—ceases to be optional and becomes legally required.

Customary rule binds *all* states (unless a state persistently objects, on which see Section 2.4.2) including a state that has not taken part in the formation of the practice. Customary legal norms need not be universal in scope, though. In *Right of Passage over Indian Territory*, the ICJ stated that 'long continued practice between two States accepted by them as regulating their relations' can form the basis of mutual rights and obligations between those states.[11] Customary international law may also develop *regionally* between a particular group of states.[12] Thus, in the *Asylum Case*, Colombia claimed that a Latin American custom existed which granted safe conduct from its embassy in Lima, Peru, for a political opponent of the Peruvian government. Although the ICJ denied the existence in customary law of that particular entitlement, it implicitly acknowledged that the practice could potentially constitute a local custom binding (only) on the regional states.[13] In Europe, democratic governance may qualify as an example of regional customary international law.[14]

2.4.2 The objective element–state practice

Before a specific pattern of state behaviour becomes legally binding, it must be 'the way things are done'. In most cases, this requires *consistent repetition of a particular behaviour*; meaning that for a considerable period of time states have behaved in a certain (identical) manner when confronted with the same facts. This, of course, raises the question of what counts as acts of a state. In theory, all state acts may be taken into consideration: both physical acts—such as the conduct of military operations, the seizure of foreign vessels etc.—and verbal acts—like diplomatic statements, press releases, official manuals and statements in international organizations.[15] But verbal acts must be public, and internal documents and memoranda do not qualify as state

---

[9] *Jurisdictional Immunities of the State (Germany v Italy: Greece intervening)*, Judgment [2012] ICJ Rep 99, para. 55; *North Sea Continental Shelf Cases*, Merits [1969] ICJ Rep 3, para. 77.

[10] For the historical background to the merger of an empirical and will-based approach to customary international law, see Stephen C. Neff, *Justice Among Nations: A History of International Law* (Harvard University Press, 2014) 226–259, in particular 252–253.

[11] *Case concerning Right of Passage over Indian Territory (Portugal v India)*, Merits [1960] ICJ Rep 6, 39.

[12] See also Michael Wood, 'Third Report on identification of customary international law' (ILC, 2015), UN Doc. A/CN.4/682, paras 80–84.

[13] *Colombian–Peruvian Asylum Case*, Judgment [1950] ICJ Rep 266, 277–278.

[14] Steven Wheatley, 'Democracy in International Law: A European Perspective' (2002) 51 *International and Comparative Law Quarterly* 225, 234.

[15] See also Michael Wood, 'Second Report on identification of customary international law' (ILC, 2014), UN Doc. A/CN.4/672, paras 37–42.

practice.[16] Resolutions and declarations by international organizations constitute the sum of individual acts by the participating states and may therefore also be relevant.

Conceptually, state practice can be divided into three elements: consistency, duration and generality of practice. The element of *consistency* requires that practice is reasonably uniform.[17] In *Right of Passage over Indian Territory*, the Court found that a *'constant and uniform practice'* on the part of the rulers of India of allowing free passage to Portuguese individuals, civil officials and goods constituted practice for the purposes of creating customary international law.[18] In *Nicaragua*, however, the Court stated that it is not to be expected that states have acted 'with complete consistency'. As long as the conduct is *generally* consistent with the rule, and inconsistent conduct is by and large treated as a breach of the rule rather than an indicator of the recognition of a new rule, the conduct may suffice.[19] Thus, minor departures from a collective uniformity may be acceptable. In *Jurisdictional Immunities of the State*, the Court used the term 'settled practice'.[20]

As for *duration*, practice evolves slowly and gradually over time, often through years of repeated behaviour. But as the ICJ stated in the *North Sea Continental Shelf Cases*, 'the passage of only a short period of time is not necessarily, in itself, a bar to the formation of a new rule of customary law'.[21] Consistency and representation are therefore of greater importance that mere duration. Indeed, in situations of rapid change state practice may be formed in a very short time potentially paving the way for the creation of so-called 'instant custom'.[22] The international reaction to the terrorist attacks on the United States on 9/11 may be an example of instant custom. The overwhelming response to the attacks indicated that states were suddenly willing to accept that armed attacks under article 51 of the UN Charter could be perpetrated by a non-state actor.[23]

The third and potentially most difficult element of the identification of practice relates to the *generality* of the practice and the question of how widespread participation in the practice must be. While unanimity is not required, practice should include the majority of states.[24] In the *North Sea Continental Shelf Cases*, the ICJ stated that the practice by states 'whose interests are specially affected' was of particular relevance.[25] The task is therefore not simply to determine how many states participate in a given

---

[16] Ibid, para. 47. See also ILC, 'Guiding Principles applicable to unilateral declarations of States capable of creating legal obligations' (2006), UN Doc. A/61/10, principle 5 (ILC Guiding Principles).

[17] Wood, 'Second Report' (n 15) paras 55–57.

[18] Ibid, para. 40. The same was not the case, however, with regard to the passage of armed forces, armed police and arms and ammunition which had always required the permission of the local authorities, ibid, para. 43. See also *The Case of the SS Lotus (France v Turkey)*, Judgment, 1927, PCIJ, Series A, No. 10, 26–30.

[19] *Military and Paramilitary Activities in and against Nicaragua (Nicaragua v United States)*, Merits [1986] ICJ Rep 14, para. 186. But see *Asylum Case* (n 13) 277 and *Fisheries Case (UK v Norway)*, Judgment [1951] ICJ Rep 116, 131.

[20] *Jurisdictional Immunities* (n 9) para. 55.   [21] *North Sea Continental Shelf Cases* (n 9) para 74.

[22] Bin Cheng, 'United Nations Resolutions on Outer Space: "Instant" International Customary Law?' (1965) 5 *Indian Journal of International Law* 23. See also Michael Scharf, *Customary International Law in Times of Fundamental Change* (Cambridge University Press, 2013).

[23] See also Chapter 13.   [24] See also Wood, 'Second Report' (n 15) paras 52–55.

[25] *North Sea Continental Shelf Cases* (n 9) para. 74.

practice, but *which* states. States which are particularly active in a given area are more likely to be devoted to developing applicable practices than other states.

A state may avoid being bound by an emerging customary rule by *persistently objecting* to the practice.[26] The law therefore protects a state from the imposition by a majority of other states of new obligations upon it while simultaneously allowing that same majority to progressively develop the law without having to wait for acceptance of it by every state involved. In the *Fisheries Case*, the ICJ noted that the emergence of a potential ten-mile rule for the closing line of bays would 'be inapplicable as against Norway inasmuch as she has always opposed any attempt to apply it to the Norwegian coast'.[27] In a similar vein, in the *Asylum Case* the ICJ noted that an alleged Latin American practice of diplomatic asylum could not be binding on Peru because it had explicitly repudiated the practice in question.[28] The persistent objector rule only applies, however, in relation to new and *emerging* customary rules. Once a rule has come into existence, it can no longer be objected to. New states are also bound by existing customary law. Lastly, the persistent objector rule does not apply to peremptory norms/*jus cogens* (discussed in Section 2.9).

2.4.3 **The subjective requirement—*opinio juris***

State practice, however general and representative, only creates a legally binding custom when it is accepted as law—the so-called requirement of *opinio juris sive necessitatis*. The purpose of the subjective requirement is to differentiate between acts motivated by a desire to honour—or create—a legal obligation and those that are not.[29] The subjective element is controversial and there is no denying that some of the theoretical difficulties lie in the requirement that a state must participate in a practice believing it to be legally required. How does one ascertain what states believe to be the law? States rarely explain why they act or refrain from acting as they do. Also, since practice has to start somewhere, it seems far-fetched to insist that a state that begins to depart from an existing custom acts in the belief that the new behaviour is legally mandated.

According to the International Law Commission (ILC), the existence of sufficient general and representative state practice (the objective element) is *usually* sufficient to create a binding custom and evidence of *opinio juris* is usually only looked for if there is reason to believe that a particular behaviour stems from non-legal motivations.[30] If no general and representative practice exists, however, a state initiating a new practice cannot realistically be said to have a belief in its legality. There is, in other words, a

---

[26] See also Wood, 'Third Report' (n 12) paras 85–95; Jonathan I. Charney, 'The Persistent Objector Rule and the Development of Customary International Law' (1985) 56 *British Yearbook of International Law* 1.

[27] *Fisheries Case* (n 19) 131.   [28] *Asylum Case* (n 13) 277–278.

[29] See also *Nicaragua* (n 19) paras 207–208; Wood, 'Second Report' (n 15) para. 61.

[30] International Law Association, 'Final Report of the Committee, Statement of Principles Applicable to the Formation of General Customary International Law' (London Conference 2000) part III, para. 16. For a similar approach, see Maurice Mendelson, 'The Subjective Element in Customary International Law' (1996) 66 *British Yearbook of International Law* 177, 204–207. For the argument that there is a 'sliding scale' in the sense that the level of *opinio juris* is relative to the amount of existing state practice, see Frederic L. Kirgis Jr, 'Custom on a Sliding Scale' (1987) 81 *American Journal of International Law* 146.

distinction between behaviour at a time when a particular rule begins to be formed (where it cannot be a requirement that the states believe their behaviour is permitted or required by law) and behaviour at a time when it has already been established (where such a belief is presumed to exist).[31]

The subjective requirement is particularly important where circumstances indicates that a given practice stems from non-legal motivations.[32] Thus, if the conduct is ambiguous, proving *opinio juris* is a requirement. In the *Lotus* case, the PCIJ did not find that an alleged practice, whereby criminal prosecutions for acts committed by ships on the high seas only occurred before the courts of the state whose flag was flown, was based on a conscious decision on the part of states that they were under a duty to abstain from prosecutions not falling within that practice.[33] And in the *Asylum Case*, the ICJ found that the practice in question had been so 'much influenced by considerations of political expediency' that it was not possible to discern a usage that was 'accepted as law'.[34] Indeed, according to the Court, rather than any feeling of legal obligation, the practice in question was motivated by 'extra-legal factors', such as good-neighbour relations.[35]

The subjective element is particular important when a state acts contrary to an existing customary rule. While breaches of an existing custom may lead to the formation of new custom, much will depend on the justification offered. In *Nicaragua*, the Court noted that if a state defends its breach of a rule of customary international law 'by appealing to exceptions or justifications contained within the rule itself', its attitude will actually confirm and not weaken the rule.[36] Indeed, even repeated breaches of customary norms will not do away with the binding nature of the latter as long as *opinio juris* of their normative status continues to exist.[37]

We saw earlier that a customary rule is binding on all states, including those that have not have not taken part in the formation of the practice, unless a state persistently objects. But while it is not generally necessary to prove that a state has given its consent to a rule of customary international law, proof that it *has* consented will usually suffice.[38] To that end, it is important to remember that customary law can also arise between a limited set of states.

2.4.4 The relationship between custom and treaty law

When a treaty codifies customary international law, the parties to the treaty will be bound by the treaty as well as customary international law while non-parties are only bound by the latter. But in practice, of course, all states are under the same substantial obligation. The ICJ confirmed the potential existence of such 'parallel obligations' in

---

[31] International Law Association (n 30) part III, para. 16.
[32] *North Sea Continental Shelf Cases* (n 9) para. 77.   [33] *Lotus* (n 18) 28.
[34] *Asylum Case* (n 13) 277.   [35] Ibid, 286; *Jurisdictional Immunities* (n 9) 55.
[36] *Nicaragua* (n 19) para 186.
[37] See also Rosalyn Higgins, *Problems & Process: International Law and How We Use it* (Oxford University Press, 1994) 20–22.
[38] Mendelson (n 30) 192–193. See also International Law Association (n 30) part III, para. 18.

Nicaragua, where it stated that the use of interstate force is regulated in both the UN Charter as well as in customary international law and that the two norms retained a separate existence.[39] Treaty-based obligation may also be identical to obligations in customary international law if the treaty has a 'crystallizing' effect whereby its content develops into customary law. In *The Wall*, for example, the ICJ indicated that the provisions of the 1907 Hague Regulations had *over time* developed into customary law.[40] When a treaty contains elements of both codification of existing customary law and progressive developments, non-parties are only bound by the former. If, however, state practice develops along the lines of the progressive parts of the treaty, the latter may also become binding on the states that are not parties to the treaty.

When the content of a treaty-based and a custom-based obligation is identical, the two sources will complement and reinforce each other. If the content of the two obligations are not exactly identical, a potential conflict can often be avoided through interpretation.[41] When conflicting content cannot be reconciled, the question arises which of the two sources prevails.[42] As we shall see later, if one of the two norms has a peremptory/*jus cogens* character, it prevails. It is more uncertain how a conflict is resolved in other situations. Since the adoption of a treaty is a deliberate act of law-creation, the treaty normally prevails over custom between the parties to the treaty. The situation is less clear when the customary norm has developed *subsequent* to the inconsistent treaty-based rule. In many instances, the conflict will be governed by the principle of *lex posterior* whereby that which is later in time prevails. A more pragmatic approach is to let the subsequent customary norm modify the content of the treaty-based rule. If there is a conflict between a norm of a general and a more detailed character, the *lex specialis* principle stipulates that the latter prevails.

2.5 General principles as a source of law

The third source in article 38 is that of 'general principles of law recognized by civilized nations'. Although the ICJ rarely refers to general principles, it is clear that such principles are never far from the minds of the judges. Indeed, it is often in 'general principles' that the lawyer finds the legal answers that cannot be found in domestic law. General principles of law were inserted into article 38 because the drafters of the PCIJ Statute were concerned that treaties and custom were insufficient to provide all the legal answers needed. General principles of international law would prevent the Court being unable to decide a dispute due to a shortage of applicable law—so-called

---

[39] *Nicaragua* (n 19) para. 179.

[40] *Legal Consequences of the Construction of a Wall in the Occupied Palestinian Territory*, Advisory Opinion [2004] ICJ Rep 136, para. 89.

[41] See also ILC, 'Conclusions of the Study Group on the Fragmentation of International Law: Difficulties Arising from the Diversification and Expansion of International Law', UN Doc. A/61/10, 2006, paras 2 and 4.

[42] Ibid.

non liquet.[43] General principles were thus also primarily intended as 'gap fillers' that only needed to be consulted when a dispute could not be resolved on the basis of a treaty or customary international law. The phrase 'recognized by civilized nations' is meant to illustrate that the general principles are limited to those common to developed national legal systems as a means to prevent arbitrariness on the part of the judges.[44] Today, the reference to 'civilized nations' is devoid of meaning.

The most relevant 'general principle of international law' is *equity.*[45] In the *Diversion of Water from the Meuse* case, Judge Hudson of the PCIJ stated that 'principles of equity have long been considered to constitute a part of international law'[46] and that the Court 'has some freedom to consider principles of equity as part of the international law which it must apply'.[47] The ICJ has also made many references to equity, most notably in cases concerning maritime delimitations. In the *North Sea Continental Shelf Cases*, for example, the Court relied on equitable principles when it delimited the continental shelf between West Germany, the Netherlands and Denmark.[48] It has also referred to equity in relation to the delimitation of boundaries on land.[49] The Court considers reliance on equity to be a logical and integral part of the application of law that only influences the application of substantive rules and is unrelated to more overarching considerations of 'justice'.[50] In *Maritime Delimitation in the Black Sea*, it reiterated that the role of equity in delimitation cases is 'to achieve a delimitation that is equitable' not 'an equal apportionment of maritime areas'.[51]

International law also contains a general principle of *good faith* that stipulates that states must act honestly in the fulfilment of their international obligations.[52] The ICJ referred to the principle in the *Nuclear Tests Cases*.[53] Another general principle of international law is the principle that international agreements are binding—also known as *pacta sunt servanda*. In *Nicaragua*, the Court also referred to the rules in

---

[43] For the historical background, see Bin Cheng, *General Principles of Law as Applied by International Courts and Tribunals* (Cambridge University Press, 1953) 1–26.

[44] See also PCIJ, Advisory Committee of Jurists, 'Procés-Verbaux of the Proceedings of the Advisory Committee, June 16th–July 24th with annexes' (Van Langenhuysen Brothers, 1920) 310, 318. See also Cheng, *General Principles* (n 43) 19–25.

[45] Thirlway (n 3) 110. Some scholars believe that equity should be considered as a distinct legal source not covered by art. 38, see the discussion in Thirlway (n 3) 104–110 and in Cheng, *General Principles* (n 43) 19–20. Article 38 (2) of the ICJ Statute specifies that the Court may decide a case on the basis of what it considers fair and right—*ex aequo et bono*—if the parties to a case agree. This has yet to occur.

[46] *Diversion of Water from the Meuse*, Individual Opinion by Mr Hudson, 1937, PCIJ, Series A/B, No. 70, 76.

[47] Ibid, 77.   [48] *North Sea Continental Shelf Cases* (n 9) paras 85–88.

[49] *Frontier Dispute (Burkina Faso v Republic of Mali)*, Judgment [1986] ICJ Rep 554, para. 150.

[50] *North Sea Continental Shelf Cases* (n 9) para. 88. See also *Continental Shelf (Libyan Arab Jamahiriya v Malta)*, Judgment [1985] ICJ Rep 1, para. 45; *Fisheries Jurisdiction (UK v Iceland)*, Merits [1974] ICJ Rep 3, para. 78; *Land and Maritime Boundary (Cameroon v Nigeria: Equatorial Guinea intervening)*, Judgment [2002] ICJ Rep 303, para. 294; *Continental Shelf (Tunisia v Libyan Arab Jamahiriya)*, Judgment [1982] ICJ Rep 18, para. 71.

[51] *Maritime Delimitation in the Black Sea (Romania v Ukraine)*, Judgment [2009] ICJ Rep 61, para. 111.

[52] Cheng, *General Principles* (n 43) 103–160.

[53] For almost identical cases, see *Nuclear Tests Case (New Zealand v France)*, Judgment [1974] ICJ Rep 457, para. 49 and *Nuclear Tests Case (Australia v France)* [1974] ICJ Rep 253, para. 46.

Common article 3 to the four 1949 Geneva Conventions as constituting 'a minimum yardstick' that reflect 'elementary considerations of humanity'.[54] It also referred to 'elementary considerations of humanity' in its advisory opinion on the *Legality of the Threat or Use of Nuclear Weapons*.[55] In *Corfu Channel*, the ICJ made reference to a number of principles that could be candidates for general principles of international law. In addition to 'elementary considerations of humanity', the Court found that Albania had violated 'the principle of the freedom of maritime communication' as well as 'every State's obligation not to allow knowingly its territory to be used for acts contrary to the rights of other States'.[56] In international environmental law, the latter principle is known as the 'no harm' principle.[57] International rules on procedure and evidence are often based on legal principles derived from national law. In the *Genocide Convention* case, the ICJ referred to a general principle of *res judicata* according to which a decision is final and binding on the parties.[58] The principle ensures that litigation comes to an end at a certain point. In *Corfu Channel*, the Court also relied on circumstantial evidence and noted that such 'evidence is admitted in all systems of law'.[59]

2.6 Judicial decisions

Judicial decisions are a subsidiary source of law. This is also reflected in the reference in article 38(1)(d) to article 59 of the Statute according to which the ICJ's decisions are only binding on the parties to the case. Judicial decisions may, however, carry substantial interpretative weight. As the principal judicial organ of the UN, the decisions and advisory opinions of the ICJ are particularly carefully examined. In practice, of course, there may be a thin line between those instances where the Court merely *identifies* rather than *develops* the law. In the *Genocide Reservations* case, for example, the Court adopted a new approach to treaty reservations.[60] The Court's approach to the measurement of the territorial sea in the *Anglo-Norwegian Fisheries* case has also had a major impact on the development of international law.[61] The ICJ is not bound by its earlier decisions but it strives to maintain judicial consistency and usually makes reference to its case law. At times, the Court's earlier decisions even constitute the natural point of departure for the analysis, as was the case in *Cameroon v Nigeria*. Here, the Court simply referred to its earlier case law and noted that the 'real question is whether, in

---

[54] *Nicaragua* (n 19) para. 218.
[55] *Legality of the Threat or Use of Nuclear Weapons*, Advisory Opinion [1996] ICJ Rep 226, para. 79. See also *The Wall* (n 40) para. 157.
[56] *Corfu Channel (UK v Albania)*, Merits [1949] ICJ Rep 4, 22. See also *Nuclear Weapons* (n 55) para. 29.
[57] *Trail Smelter (United States v Canada)* (1905) III RIAA 1965.
[58] *Application of the Convention on the Prevention and Punishment of the Crime of Genocide (Bosnia and Herzegovina v Serbia and Montenegro)*, Judgment [2007] ICJ Rep 43, paras 115–116.
[59] *Corfu Channel* (n 56) 18.
[60] *Reservations to the Convention on Genocide*, Advisory Opinion [1951] ICJ Rep 15.
[61] *Fisheries Case* (n 19) 116.

this case, there is cause not to follow the reasoning and conclusions of earlier cases'.[62] The judgments ('awards') from courts of arbitration also contain important contributions. Prominent examples include the *Alabama Claims* arbitration,[63] the *Island of Palmas* case[64] and the *Trail Smelter* case.[65] A recent award that could well have an important impact on international law is the award by a court of arbitration in July 2016 in the *South China Sea Arbitration*.[66] Certain decisions from the international criminal courts also carry substantial interpretive value; the most notable examples include the major judgments from the 1946 International Military Tribunal (IMT) at Nuremberg[67] and the International Criminal Tribunal for the former Yugoslavia (ICTY).[68] The Iran–US Claims Tribunal, set up after the 1979 revolution in Iran, has rendered many noteworthy decisions, in particular on issues relating to investment protection and the legal effects of expropriation of foreign property.[69] Other relevant international courts include the European Court of Human Rights (ECtHR) and the Court of Justice of the European Union (CJEU). Finally, depending on the circumstances, decisions by national courts, in particular those of courts of last instance, such as supreme courts and constitutional courts, may also be of relevance. Municipal decisions may additionally constitute state practice for the purposes of customary international law.[70]

2.7 Scholarly contributions and the ILC

Of the sources listed in article 38(1), 'the teachings of the most highly qualified publicists of the various nations' is the least important. While writers and thinkers like Suaréz, Grotius and Vattel have historically influenced the development of international law, academics today play a much less significant role. Although some courts refer to academic analysis,[71] the ICJ rarely makes any references to academics.[72]

---

[62] *Land and Maritime Boundary between Cameroon and Nigeria*, Preliminary Objections [1998] ICJ Rep 275, para. 28. See also *Application of the Convention on the Prevention and Punishment of the Crime of Genocide (Croatia v Serbia)*, Preliminary Objections [2008] ICJ Rep 412, para. 53.

[63] *Alabama claims of the United States of America against Great Britain* (1872) XXIX RIAA 125.

[64] *Island of Palmas (Netherlands v United States)* (1928) II RIAA 829.

[65] *Trail Smelter* (n 57) 1965.

[66] *The Republic of the Philippines and the People's Republic of China*, Award, PCA Case No. 2013-19, 12 July 2016.

[67] See, inter alia, *Judgment of the Nuremberg International Military Tribunal 1946* (1947) 41 *American Journal of International Law* 172.

[68] Arguably the most important of the decisions is the Appeals Chamber decision in *Tadić*, see *Tadić*, Decision on the Defence Motion for Interlocutory Appeal on Jurisdiction, ICTY-94-1 (2 October 1995).

[69] For a thorough account, see George H. Aldrich, *The Jurisprudence of the Iran–United States Claims Tribunal* (Oxford University Press, 1996).

[70] See, in particular, *Jurisdictional Immunities* (n 9) para. 64.

[71] Michael Wood, 'Teachings of the Most Highly Qualified Publicists (Art. 38(1) ICJ Statute)' in Rüdiger Wolfrum (ed.), *Max Planck Encyclopedia of Public International Law* (Oxford University Press, 2010) para. 14.

[72] For an exception, see *Nottebohm (Second Phase) (Liechtenstein v Guatemala)*, Judgment [1955] ICJ Rep 4, 22; *Lotus* (n 18) 26.

Academic positions and interpretations may, of course, influence practitioners or those who develop international law.[73]

The contributions of the ILC play a special role in international law. The ILC was established in 1947 with the primary purpose of promoting the 'progressive development of international law and its codification'.[74] The composition of the Commission is intended to be representative of all the principal legal systems of the world and the members sit in their individual capacities. Among other things, the Commission selects topics and makes proposals for draft conventions and codifications. Usually, once a topic has been chosen for consideration, a working group will be formed and a Special Rapporteur will be appointed who will produce a series of reports that may contain concrete proposals. In turn, these may lead to the adoption of important conventions. When that is the case, the Commission's draft articles and commentaries thereon serve as valuable interpretive tools.[75]

2.8 Unilateral statements

Case law from both the PCIJ and the ICJ show that unilateral statements by state representatives can create obligations under international law. Importantly, there would not seem to be any requirements of form and both oral and written statements may suffice.[76] Like treaties, binding unilateral declarations can be issued by heads of state, heads of government and ministers for foreign affairs.[77] In *Eastern Greenland*, the PCIJ interpreted a declaration issued by a Norwegian foreign minister—the so-called 'Ihlen Declaration'—as a statement that was legally binding on Norway.[78] In the course of a bilateral Danish–Norwegian dialogue on the status of Eastern Greenland, the Foreign Minister of Norway (Mr Ihlen) referred to Danish claims to the whole of Greenland and stated that his country 'would not make any difficulties in the settlement of this question'.[79] When Norway later contested Danish sovereignty over the area, the Court found the earlier statement 'unconditional and definitive' and therefore binding on Norway.[80] In the *Nuclear Tests Cases*, the ICJ concluded that a series

---

[73] See also Jean d'Aspremont, *Formalism and the Sources of International Law: A Theory on the Ascertainment of Legal Rules* (Oxford University Press, 2011) 209–211.

[74] Statute of the International Law Commission, GA Res. 174 (II) (21 November 1947), UN Doc. A/RES/174(II), art. 1.

[75] For practical examples of the ILC's contribution to codification and progressive development of the law, see Alan Boyle and Christine Chinkin, *The Making of International Law* (Oxford University Press, 2007) 183–200.

[76] *Nuclear Tests Case (New Zealand v France)* (n 53) para. 48; *Nuclear Tests Case (Australia v France)* (n 53) para. 45. See also *Temple of Preah Vihear (Cambodia v Thailand)*, Preliminary Objections [1961] ICJ Rep 17, 31. For a critique of the Court's reasoning in the *Nuclear Tests Cases*, see Alfred P. Rubin, 'The International Legal Effects of Unilateral Declarations' (1977) 71 *American Journal of International Law* 1.

[77] ILC Guiding Principles (n 16) principle 4. See also Chapter 3.

[78] *Legal Status of Eastern Greenland (Denmark v Norway)*, Judgment, 1933, PCIJ, Series A/B, No. 53. See also James W. Garner, 'The International Binding Force of Unilateral Oral Declarations' (1933) 27 *American Journal of International Law* 493.

[79] *Eastern Greenland* (n 78) para. 58.   [80] Ibid, paras 195, 201.

of clearly unilateral public statements by, among others, the French president were legally binding on France.[81] The cases concerned French atmospheric nuclear tests in the South Pacific that caused radioactive fall-out in, among other places, New Zealand and Australia. The Court found that official French statements testified to an intention to be legally bound to cease atmospheric tests.[82] According to the Court, 'nothing in the nature of a *quid pro quo*, nor any subsequent acceptance of the declaration, nor even any reply or reaction from other States, is required' for a unilateral statement to be legally binding.[83]

It will often be difficult to determine if a state intends to bind itself *legally* when it makes a particular statement. Weight must be given first and foremost to the text of the declaration, together with the context and the circumstances in which it was formulated.[84] A unilateral declaration should, however, only be considered binding if it is stated in clear and specific terms.[85] In the *Nuclear Tests Cases*, the ICJ stressed that a 'restrictive interpretation' is called for when states make 'statements by which their freedom of action is to be limited'.[86]

2.9 Hierarchy of sources

One of the characteristics of a national legal system is a hierarchy of legal norms. It is a vertical system in the sense that constitutional norms have a higher legal status than legislation and administrative regulation. The international legal system, on the other hand, is by and large a horizontal legal order without a hierarchy.[87] Apart from the distinction between primary and secondary sources of law in article 38 of the ICJ Statute, all legal sources are deemed to have the same normative status. Conflicts between sources are therefore not generally resolved by granting one of the sources a higher normative value than the other but by determining which of the conflicting norms should prevail in the particular case. For example, as we saw earlier, cases of conflict between treaties and customary international law are usually—but not always—resolved by giving priority to a treaty-based rule because the adoption of a treaty can be seen as a more deliberate act of law creation than the creation of customary law.

---

[81] *Nuclear Tests Case (New Zealand v France)* and *Nuclear Tests Case (Australia v France)* (n 53).

[82] *Nuclear Tests Case (New Zealand v France)* (n 53) paras 51–53 and *Nuclear Tests Case (Australia v France)* (n 53) paras 49–51.

[83] *Nuclear Tests Case (New Zealand v France)* (n 53) para. 46 and *Nuclear Tests Case (Australia v France)* (n 53) para. 43. See *Nuclear Tests Case (Australia v France)*, Dissenting Opinion of Judge de Castro (n 53) 374–375.

[84] See also ILC Guiding Principles (n 16) principle 7. See also *Frontier Dispute* (n 49) paras 39–40.

[85] ILC Guiding Principles (n 16) principle 7.

[86] *Nuclear Tests Case (Australia v France)* (n 53) para. 47. See also ILC Guiding Principles (n 16) principle 7. See also the debate in Thomas Franck, 'Word Made Law: The Decision of the ICJ in the *Nuclear Test Cases*' (1975) 69 *American Journal of International Law* 612, 617.

[87] A classic work on the issue of hierarchy in international law is Prosper Weil, 'Towards Relative Normativity in International Law?' (1983) 77 *American Journal of International Law* 413.

In practice, however, all legal systems have norms that are considered to be of greater importance than others, and international law is no exception. In fact, there are at least three exceptions to the general presumption of normative equality.[88] First, as we shall see in Chapter 3, article 53 of the Vienna Convention on the Law of Treaties (VCLT) stipulates that a treaty is void if it 'conflicts with a peremptory norm of general international law'.[89] Peremptory norms—also referred to as *jus cogens*—are norms 'accepted and recognized by the international community of States as a whole as a norm from which no derogation is permitted and which can be modified only by a subsequent norm of general international law having the same character'. Although the concept of *jus cogens* is not free from theoretical difficulties,[90] international courts have increasingly accepted its existence. In a 2006 preliminary judgment in the *Armed Activities* case, the ICJ referred to the prohibition of genocide as a peremptory norm of general international law.[91] And in *Obligation to Extradite or Prosecute*, it similarly stated that the prohibition against torture is not only part of customary international law but also 'has become a peremptory norm (*jus cogens*)'.[92] It is not clear what norms possess a *jus cogens* character and the ILC has explicitly decided against trying to make a list.[93] On the basis of the case law mentioned above, genocide and the ban on torture appear to be obvious candidates. Other likely norms include the ban on slavery, the prohibition of aggression, the ban on crimes against humanity, the prohibition of piracy and the prohibition of apartheid and other forms of gross racial discrimination.[94]

The second exemption to the normative equality of international legal norms is obligations *erga omnes*. *Erga omnes* obligations are normatively superior in the sense that they are not merely owed to another state but to the 'international community as a whole'. The ICJ made reference to the concept of *erga omnes* in the *Barcelona Traction* case where it did not find that Belgium had legal standing on behalf of shareholders in Belgium in a Canadian company in a case against Spain. To the Court,

> an essential distinction should be drawn between the obligations of a State towards the international community as a whole, and those arising vis-à-vis another State in the

---

[88] See also ILC, 'Fragmentation of International Law' (n 41) paras 324–409.

[89] See also VCLT art. 64. An early contribution is Alfred von Verdross, 'Forbidden Treaties in International Law: Comments on Professor Garner's Report on "The Law of Treaties"' (1937) 31 *American Journal of International Law* 571. A unilateral declaration that conflicts with a peremptory norm of general international law is similarly void, see the ILC Guiding Principles (n 16) para. 8, and VCLT art. 53.

[90] For a debate see, inter alia, Alexander Orakhelashvili, *Peremptory Norms in International Law* (Oxford University Press, 2006). See also Thirlway (n 3) 154–163. A critical position is found in Weil (n 87). A defence of the concept can be found in Antonio Cassese, 'For an Enhanced Role of Jus Cogens' in Antonio Cassese (ed.), *Realizing Utopia: The Future of International Law* (Oxford University Press, 2012) 158–171.

[91] *Armed Activities on the Territory of the Congo (New Application: 2002) (Democratic Republic of the Congo v Rwanda)*, Jurisdiction and Admissibility [2006] ICJ Rep 6, para. 64.

[92] *Questions relating to the Obligation to Prosecute or Extradite (Belgium v Senegal)*, Judgment [2012] ICJ Rep 422, para. 99. See also *Prosecutor v Anto Furundžija*, Judgment, ICTY-95-17/1 (20 December 1998) para. 153.

[93] ILC, Draft Articles on the Law of Treaties, with commentaries, *Yearbook of the International Law Commission*, 1966, vol. II, pp. 187, 248, para. 3.

[94] For a tentative list, see ILC, 'Fragmentation of International Law' (n 41) para. 374.

field of diplomatic protection. By their very nature the former are the concern of all States. In view of the importance of the rights involved, all States can be held to have a legal interest in their protection; they are obligations *erga omnes*.[95]

Thus, *erga omnes* norms possess a particular procedural feature in the sense that breaches of the norms, unlike breaches of other legal obligations, can be invoked by any state and not just by those which are the immediate beneficiaries of the obligation.[96] In practice, *erga omnes* obligations will include the norms of a peremptory/*jus cogens* character.[97] The ICJ has also referred to the right to self-determination as a principle with an *erga omnes* character.[98] It remains open whether the *erga omnes* category encompasses rights that are not of a *jus cogens* character but the concept of *erga omnes* obligations is increasingly referred to in international environmental law.[99]

The third and final category of privileged norms is that of obligations under the UN Charter. Article 103 of the Charter stipulates that obligations under the Charter prevail if they conflict with obligations under any other international agreement. Since article 25 of the Charter obliges members states to accept and carry out resolutions of the Security Council that have been adopted under Chapter VII of the Charter, the practical effect of article 103 is that states must comply with the Council's resolutions even if it means that they thereby violate other international legal commitments.[100] The primacy of Security Council resolutions is not absolute, however, and the Council does not seem able to oblige states to disregard norms of a *jus cogens*/peremptory character.[101] This was also the conclusion reached by the Court of First Instance of the EU in the seminal *Kadi* case concerning the EU's incorporation of obligations under the sanctions regime in Security Council Resolution 1267.[102] In a controversial 2008 judgment in the same case, the CJEU held that *all* measures adopted by the Union—including those implementing resolutions adopted by the Security Council—must be compatible with fundamental rights.[103]

---

[95] *Barcelona Traction, Light and Power Co, Ltd*, Judgment [1970] ICJ Rep 3, para. 33.

[96] See also ILC, 'Fragmentation of International Law' (n 41) paras 380–409.

[97] *Barcelona Traction* (n 95) para. 34.

[98] *Case Concerning East Timor (Portugal v Australia)*, Judgment [1995] ICJ Rep 90, para. 29. See also *Legal Consequences for States of the Continued Presence of South Africa in Namibia (South West Africa) notwithstanding Security Council Resolution 276*, Advisory Opinion [1970] ICJ Rep 16, 31; *The Wall* (n 40) para. 88.

[99] See Chapter 10.   [100] For the competences of the Security Council, see also Chapter 13.

[101] See also ILC, 'Fragmentation of International Law' (n 41) para. 346.

[102] Case T-315/01 *Kadi v Council and Commission* [2005] ECR II-3659, paras 224–226.

[103] Cases C-402 and 415/05 P *Kadi and Al Barakaat International Foundation v Council and Commission* [2008] ECR I-6351, paras 281ff. See also Juliane Kokott and Christoph Sobotta, 'The *Kadi* Case—Constitutional Core Values and International Law—Finding the Balance?' (2012) 23 *European Journal of International Law* 1015–1024. See also ECtHR, *Nada v Switzerland*, App. no. 10593/08, 12 September 2012, paras 171, 176 and 212. However, in neither of the cases did the Courts question the prima facie normative priority of the resolutions in question. See also Astrid Kjeldgaard-Pedersen, 'Nationale domstoles behandling af international normkonflikter' (2013) *Ugeskrift for Retsvæsen* 75.

2.10 Non-binding commitments and the concept of 'soft law' instruments

When states utilize the legal sources we have examined so far they create an expectation of behaviour that is legally binding. It is not uncommon, however, for states to create norms of behaviour of a non-legally binding nature. While legally binding norms are generally referred to as 'hard law', those of a non-binding nature may be termed 'soft law'.[104] Importantly, then, whether a rule is 'hard' or 'soft' relates to its normative character and not to the precision of the norm.[105] As we shall see in Chapter 10, soft law is particularly prevalent in international environmental law where some of most cited instruments, including the 1972 Stockholm Declaration and the 1992 Rio Declaration, are of a non-binding character. The creation of soft law and non-binding 'norms of behaviour' is also visible in the young and highly politicized field of international cyber security. Compared to hard law, the creation of a soft law instrument is generally a faster and more flexible way to establish an expectation of behaviour and, while a violation of the soft law norm will not be met with legal sanctions, the political price associated with violating the norm may be high.[106] The determination of whether an instrument is legally binding or a mere political pledge—and thus 'soft law'—revolves around the intention of the parties. Did the parties intend the instrument to be binding?

The soft law category includes a wide range of instruments, such as resolutions of international organizations, interpretative declarations, reports adopted by international agencies or in international conferences. A particularly important type of soft law commitment is that of *resolutions and declarations adopted by the United Nations General Assembly*. In contrast to the UN Security Council, the General Assembly only holds recommendatory powers and is not competent to adopt legally binding resolutions and declarations. In practice, however, the instruments may have an impact on the formation of customary international law as both a reflection of state practice as well as *opinio juris*.[107] Examples of important General Assembly resolutions include the 1960 Declaration on the Granting of Independence to Colonial Countries and Peoples,[108] the 1963 Legal Principles Governing the Activities of States in the Exploration and Use of Outer Space[109] and the 1970 Declaration on Friendly

---

[104] See Daniel Thurer, 'Soft Law' in Rüdiger Wolfrum (ed.), *Max Planck Encyclopedia of Public International Law* (Oxford University Press, 2009).

[105] For such an approach, see Weil (n 87) 414.

[106] The view that different legal norms carry a variety of differing impacts and legal effects, see Richard R. Baxter, 'International Law in "Her Infinite Variety"' (1980) 29 *International and Comparative Law Quarterly* 549, 563, is hard to reconcile with the inherent binary nature of international law, see also Jan Klabbers, *The Concept of Treaty in International Law* (Kluwer, 1996) 13; Jan Klabbers, 'The Redundancy of Soft Law' (1996) 65 *Nordic Journal of International Law* 167.

[107] See also *Nuclear Weapons* (n 55) 70 and the extensive reliance on General Assembly instruments in *Nicaragua* (n 19).

[108] GA Res. 1514 (XV) (14 December 1960), UN Doc. A/RES/1514(XV).

[109] GA Res. 1962 (XVIII) (13 December 1963), UN Doc. A/RES/1962(XVIII).

Relations.[110] In practice, then, the declarations and resolutions from the General Assembly illustrate that while soft law instruments are not legally binding on their own terms, they may in certain circumstances assist in the 'crystallization' of customary law and *on that basis* assist in the creation of (hard) international law. In particular, this will be the case if the instrument in question is adopted with broad or even universal support.[111]

Summary

The international legal society has its own legal sources and the discussion therefore takes its natural point of departure in article 38 of the ICJ Statute. According to that article, sources of international law can be divided into those of a primary and those of a secondary nature. While treaties, customary international law and general principles constitute the primary and undoubtedly most important legal sources, judicial decisions and scholarly contributions are listed as merely secondary sources of law. Article 38 is not exhaustive, however, and international legal answers may be found elsewhere too, most notably in unilateral statements by states. While the sources of international law are generally considered to possess the same normative value, exceptions do exist. Examples include norms of a peremptory character (*jus cogens*), *erga omnes* obligations and those legal obligations that derive from the UN Charter. 'Soft law' refers to commitments undertaken by states that are not legally binding. Depending on the circumstances, soft law commitments may pave the way for the creation of customary international law and thus hard law norms.

Recommended reading

For more on legal sources in general, see Hugh Thirlway, *The Sources of International Law* (Oxford University Press, 2014); Jean d'Aspremont, *Formalism and the Sources of International Law: A Theory on the Ascertainment of Legal Rules* (Oxford University Press, 2011).

On article 38 of the ICJ Statute, see Alain Pellet, 'Article 38' in Andreas Zimmermann and others (eds), *The Statute of the International Court of Justice: A Commentary* (2nd edn, Oxford University Press, 2012) and Ole Spiermann, 'Historical Introduction' in the same work.

On the PCIJ, see Ole Spiermann, *International Legal Argument in the Permanent Court of International Justice: The Rise of the International Judiciary* (Cambridge University Press, 2005).

For customary international law, see David J. Bederman, *Custom as a Source of Law* (Cambridge University Press, 2010) and the three reports by Michael Wood for the ILC on identification of customary international law, in particular 'Third Report on identification of customary international law' (ILC, 2015), UN Doc. A/CN.4/682. See also Maurice Mendelson,

---

[110] GA Res. 2625 (XXV) (24 October 1970), UN Doc. A/RES/2625XXV.
[111] Wood, 'Third Report' (n 12) paras 45–55.

'The Subjective Element in Customary International Law' (1996) 66 *British Yearbook of International Law* 177.

For *jus cogens* and peremptory norms, see Alfred von Verdross, 'Forbidden Treaties in International Law: Comments on Professor Garner's Report on "The Law of Treaties"' (1937) 31 *American Journal of International Law* 571; Alexander Orakhelashvili, *Peremptory Norms in International Law* (Oxford University Press 2006).

On hierarchies in international law as such, see Prosper Weil, 'Towards Relative Normativity in International Law?' (1983) 77 *American Journal of International Law* 413.

For soft law, see Alan Boyle, 'Soft Law in International Law-Making' in Malcolm D. Evans (ed.), *International Law* (4th edn, Oxford University Press, 2014); Jan Klabbers, 'The Redundancy of Soft Law' (1996) 65 *Nordic Journal of International Law* 167.

Questions for discussion

1. Why is the theory of sources tied to more basic theories about international law and the basis of legal obligation?

2. What are the theoretical difficulties associated with the requirement of *opinio juris* as part of the formation of customary international law?

3. Where should one look for the practice of states for the purposes of the formation of customary international law?

4. What is the difference between primary and secondary sources of international law? What are the primary and secondary legal sources in the national legal system in your country?

5. In some cases, a conflict of norms may exist between the different sources of international law. Can you provide some examples of how international law tries to resolve such conflicts?

6. Is a 'soft law' instrument legally binding?

7. What is the legal significance of a soft law instrument?

3

The law of treaties

CENTRAL ISSUES

1. This chapter examines the principles and rules of the international law of treaties as reflected in the 1969 Vienna Convention on the Law of Treaties.

2. It discusses the treaty as a legal concept and provides an overview of the regulation of who can conclude treaties, how consent to be bound by a treaty is expressed, the rules on entry into force, treaty reservations, the interpretation of treaties, amendments and modifications, the invalidity of treaties and the termination of and withdrawal from treaties.

3. For the most part, the international law of treaties resembles domestic rules for the creation and operation of contracts.

4. The most contentious issues in the law of treaties relate to the subject of reservations and treaty interpretation.

3.1 Introduction

Like other communities, the community of states needs rules and guiding principles that govern the agreements entered into by its legal subjects. No society can function properly if its subjects are in constant disagreement on the application and interpretation of their agreements, and it is therefore in the interests of all actors in international society that a legal regime exists for governing international agreements. Not surprisingly, then, the law of treaties is one of the oldest areas of public international law and it is part and parcel of the international law of coexistence, without which stability and predictability would be difficult to maintain.

The primary rules and principles in the area of the law of treaties are found in the 1969 Vienna Convention on the Law of Treaties (VCLT) that was adopted by the UN Conference on the Law of Treaties in May 1969 and entered into force in January 1980. The draft articles of the Convention were prepared by a number of successive Special Rapporteurs of the International Law Commission (ILC). Since the Convention seeks to codify existing customary practices, it generally reflects customary international law. In fact, there has yet to be a case where the International Court of Justice (ICJ) has found that the content of a particular convention provision does *not* reflect customary law.[1]

The VCLT is meant to be applied to *all* types of written treaties and it therefore governs treaties as diverse as a bilateral agreement to construct infrastructure as well as a multilateral document such as the UN Charter. In practice, however, as this chapter will illustrate, the concrete application of the Convention may differ depending on the type of treaties. This is in particular the case in relation to the VCLT's principles of interpretation. Like domestic rules that govern the creation and operation of contracts, the law of treaties is not concerned with the material content of the instrument itself. That is a matter for the parties to the particular treaty.

The overview begins in Section 3.2 with a presentation of the treaty as a concept under international law. After that, Section 3.3 examines who possesses the authority to conclude treaties. Section 3.4 deals with treaties between states and international organizations and Section 3.5 discusses the different means whereby consent to be bound by a treaty can be given. The issue of entry into force and obligations in the so-called interim period is covered in Section 3.6 and Section 3.7 deals with the question of validity/invalidity. The complicated issue of reservations is discussed in Section 3.8 and treaty interpretation in Section 3.9. The chapter concludes in Sections 3.10 and 3.11 with, respectively, an overview of amendments and modifications, and termination and withdrawal from treaties.

3.2 The treaty as a concept under international law

A treaty is an *international agreement governed by international law concluded by two or more international subjects with treaty-making capacity*. The adoption of a treaty reflects a will among two or more international subjects to apply international law as a means of regulating their interests. The vast majority of treaties are concluded by two or more states and interstate treaties regulate an increasing array of international relations. As we saw in Chapter 2, the distinction between *bilateral* treaties (concluded by two states) and *multilateral* treaties (between larger groups of states) can prove useful. The VCLT applies to all types of written treaties concluded between states.[2] *International organizations* may also be parties to a treaty governed by international law but the treaty will not be governed by the VCLT. Instead, it will be regulated by the 1986 Vienna Convention on the Law of Treaties between International Organizations or between States and International Organizations. It is important to note that not all legally binding agreements entered into by states will be treaties governed by international law. In some circumstances, a state may enter

---

[1] Anthony Aust, *Modern Treaty Law and Practice* (3rd edn, Cambridge University Press, 2013) 11.

[2] Vienna Convention on the Law of Treaties (adopted 23 May 1969, entered into force 27 January 1980), 1155 UNTS 331, art. 2(1)(a).

into an agreement under national law in which case it will be governed by domestic as opposed to international law.

The legal basis of a treaty obligation is state consent. No one can force a sovereign state to enter into a legally binding agreement and a treaty only creates legal obligations for the parties. This is reflected in article 34 of the VCLT. So while state A and state B are free to enter into a treaty that governs their mutual relations, they cannot conclude a treaty that creates rights or obligations for state C unless the latter consents. When a state has consented to be bound by a treaty and has become a party to it, the state must comply with its terms. This is reflected in the principle of *pacta sunt servanda* that constitutes an essential part of general international law. The principle is reflected in article 26 of the VCLT whereby a treaty in force 'is binding upon the parties to it and must be performed by them in good faith'. Article 27 specifies that a state party may not invoke its national laws as justification for a failure to perform a treaty-based obligation.[3] Hence, a state is obliged to comply with its treaty-based obligation even if doing so requires breaching its national laws.

Importantly, despite the fact that the VCLT only applies to written treaties concluded by states, *oral* agreements are also 'treaties' for the purposes of international law. Article 3 of the VCLT explicitly stipulates that the fact that the Convention only applies to written treaties does not affect the legal force of other agreements. In the 1992 *Great Belt* case, a telephone conversation between the prime ministers of Finland and Denmark brought an end to a dispute between the two states concerning Denmark's decision to construct a bridge across 'Storebælt' (Great Belt).[4]

The title of the written instrument is immaterial for the purposes of determining if it is a 'treaty' governed by international law. Hence, depending on the intention of the parties, everything from 'minutes', 'protocols', 'exchanges of notes', 'memoranda of understanding' to 'covenants', 'charters' and 'conventions' may qualify as treaties.[5] As long as the instrument in question testifies to an *intention* to create rights and obligations it is a treaty for the purposes of international law.

If the parties to an agreement do not intend to create a *legal* obligation, the agreement does not constitute a treaty for the purposes of international law.[6] In fact, as we saw in the previous chapter, states make frequent use of a variety of instruments that are not intended to be legally binding.[7] It is only when a political pledge is accompanied

---

[3] But see the exception in art. 46.

[4] See *Passage Through the Great Belt (Finland v Denmark)*, Application Institution Proceedings, General List No. 86 [1991] ICJ Rep 1 and the subsequent Order [1992] ICJ Rep 348. For more on the case, see Martti Koskenniemi, 'Case Concerning Passage through the Great Belt' (1996) 27 *Ocean Development & International Law* 255.

[5] *Aegean Sea Continental Shelf (Greece v Turkey)*, Judgment [1978] ICJ Rep 3, para. 96; *Maritime Delimitation and Territorial Questions between Qatar and Bahrain (Qatar v Bahrain)*, Jurisdiction und Admissibility, Judgment [1994] ICJ Rep 112, para. 23.

[6] Charles Lipson, 'Why are Some International Agreements Informal?' (1991) 45 *International Organization* 494. See also Kal Raustiala, 'Form and Substance in International Agreements' (2005) 99 *American Journal of International Law* 581.

[7] Anthony Aust, 'The Theory and Practice of Informal International Instruments' (1986) 35 *International and Comparative Law Quarterly* 787. But see the scepticism voiced by Jan Klabbers, *The Concept of Treaty*

by a desire to create rights and obligations under international law that one can meaningful talk about a 'treaty' under international law. In practice, of course, it may be difficult to determine if an agreement is intended to be legally binding or merely a political pledge. States have an unfortunate tendency to be reluctant to state explicitly whether a commitment is supposed to legally binding.[8] What is decisive is the intention of the parties.[9] In some cases, the instrument in question will contain one or two provisions that assist in the determination of what the parties intended. In practice, both the terminology and the form of the instrument may provide guidance. A lack of precision in the wording and the use of very general and vague terms may indicate a lack of intention to create a legally binding commitment. Terms such as 'will' and 'ought' usually signal that the parties do not intend to make a binding commitment, whereas words like 'shall', 'rights', 'oblige' or 'must' indicate the opposite. Guidance may also be sought from the circumstances surrounding the conclusion of the instrument as well as the manner in which it is dealt with subsequent to its conclusion. If the instrument is submitted to the national parliament in accordance with domestic procedure for the conclusion of treaties, it indicates the existence of an intention to create a legally binding commitment. For example, the decision by the executive branch in the United States not to submit the December 2015 Paris Agreement on climate change for approval before the US Senate as required for treaties by the US Constitution, indicates that the US government does not believe that the agreement constitutes a legally binding agreement under international law. Article 102 of the UN Charter specifies that treaties and international agreements entered into by a member of the UN shall be registered with the UN Secretariat. While registration under article 102 is not decisive, it may indicate if the parties believe that they have entered into a legally binding instrument.[10]

Case law from the ICJ shows that it does not take much for a concrete disputed agreement to be considered a binding treaty under international law. In the *Aegean Sea Continental Shelf* case, for example, the Court did not rule out that a press communiqué without signatures or initials could be considered a legally binding treaty.[11] And in *Case Concerning Maritime Delimitation and Territorial Questions between Qatar and Bahrain*, the Court concluded that minutes from a meeting not only gave an account of discussions and summarized points of agreement and disagreement but also enumerated the 'commitments to which the Parties have consented'. It therefore created rights and obligations in international law for the parties.[12]

---

in *International Law* (Kluwer, 1996) and the critique of the British practice of concluding apparently non-binding memoranda of understanding in John H. McNeill, 'International Agreements: Recent US–UK Practice Concerning the Memorandum of Understanding' (1994) 68 *American Journal of International Law* 821. For a reply, see Aust, *Modern Treaty Law and Practice* (n 1) 46–49.

[8] Oscar Schachter, 'The Twilight Existence of Nonbinding International Agreements' (1997) 71 *American Journal of International Law* 296, 297.

[9] *Aegean Sea Continental Shelf* (n 5) para. 96. See also Aust, *Modern Treaty Law and Practice* (n 1) 29–35.

[10] *Maritime Delimitation and Territorial Questions between Qatar and Bahrain* (n 5) para. 29.

[11] *Aegean Sea Continental Shelf* (n 5) para. 96.

[12] *Maritime Delimitation and Territorial Questions between Qatar and Bahrain* (n 5) paras 25, 30.

3.3 The authority to conclude a treaty

All states possess the legal capacity to conclude treaties[13] but not all representatives of a state are considered competent to conclude a treaty on behalf of a state. The issue of 'representation' is dealt with in article 7 of the VCLT that refers to the concept of 'full powers'. In practical terms, a 'full power' is a document that authorizes a state representative to negotiate and conclude a treaty on behalf of the state. Hence, a representative who produces a document with an authority to negotiate and conclude a treaty on behalf of the state will be so authorized. But not all state representatives need to produce 'full powers'. According to article 7(2)(a), by virtue of their functions heads of state, heads of government and ministers for foreign affairs may perform *all acts* that relate to the conclusion of a treaty on behalf of a state without presenting full powers. Their positions mean that other states can rely on their ability to act on behalf of the state. Thus, in *Eastern Greenland* the Permanent Court of International Justice (PCIJ) concluded that the unilateral statement by the Norwegian Minister of Foreign Affairs was binding on Norway even though the minister was allegedly not competent under Norwegian law to bind Norway in the matter in question.[14] A more limited authority to represent a home state rests on heads of diplomatic missions[15] and representatives accredited by a state to an international conference or an international organization.[16] Depending on the circumstances, these individuals may participate in *the adoption of a text* of a treaty without full powers.

According to article 46(1) of the VCLT, a state may not invoke the fact that its consent to be bound by a treaty has been expressed in violation of its *national laws* as invalidating its consent unless the violation of national law was manifest and concerned a national rule of fundamental importance. Under article 46(2), the *violation of internal law* must be 'manifest' in the sense that it is objectively evident to any state conducting itself in the matter in accordance with normal practice and good faith. The threshold is high, and in *Land and Maritime Boundary between Cameroon and Nigeria*, the ICJ concluded that states are not obliged 'to keep themselves informed of legislative and constitutional developments in other States which are or may become important for the international relations of these States'.[17] If a person with no authority to conclude a treaty has nevertheless done so, the state may decide to avail itself of the opportunity to disavow the act of the person in question by subsequently endorsing the act and thereby establishing its consent to be bound.[18] The state will be held to have done so by implication if it

---

[13] VCLT art. 6.

[14] *Legal Status of Eastern Greenland (Denmark v Norway)*, Judgment, 1933, PCIJ, Series A/B, No. 53. See also *Maritime Delimitation and Territorial Questions between Qatar and Bahrain* (n 5) paras 26–27.

[15] VCLT art. 7(2)(b).   [16] VCLT art. 7(2)(c).

[17] *Land and Maritime Boundary between Cameroon and Nigeria (Cameroon v Nigeria; Equatorial Guinea intervening)*, Judgment [2002] ICJ Rep 303, para. 266.

[18] VCLT art. 8.

invokes the provisions of the treaty or otherwise acts in such a way as to appear to treat the act in question as effective.[19]

3.4 Treaties between states and international organizations

Both the ICJ's advisory opinions in the *Certain Expenses* case[20] and the *Legality of the Use by a State of Nuclear Weapons in Armed Conflict*[21] illustrate that, depending on the circumstances, international organizations may have some treaty-making powers. For example, since their (treaty-based) establishment, both the UN and the EU have entered into a substantial number of treaties that cover a wide variety of issues. The *Vienna Convention on the Law of Treaties between International Organizations or between States and International Organizations* was adopted in 1986 to regulate the treaty relations of international organizations. At the time of writing, however, it has not yet entered into force. The approach of the ILC when working on the draft articles was to use the 1969 VCLT as the basis for the new convention on international organizations and simply proceed from article to article in order to determine when modifications were called for. Thus, with a few exceptions, the 1986 Convention is identical to the 1969 Convention. The UN is a party to the 1986 Convention.

3.5 Consent to be bound

In order for a state to become legally bound by a treaty, it must consent to it. According to article 11 of the VCLT, consent may be expressed by a signature, an exchange of the instruments that constitute a treaty, ratification, acceptance, approval or accession 'or by any other means if so agreed'.[22] Hence, the VCLT is fairly flexible and leaves it to the parties to the treaty to determine the means by which the required consent may be expressed. Today, there is a widespread practice of simply expressing consent by signature—also known as a *definitive* signature.[23] Article 15 of the VCLT also permits consent by *accession*, where a state consents to be bound by a treaty, which it has already signed, in the following circumstances:

(a) if the treaty provides for it;

(b) if it is otherwise established that the negotiating parties were agreed that it should be possible; or

---

[19] ILC, Draft Articles on the Law of Treaties, with commentaries, *Yearbook of the International Law Commission*, 1966, vol. II, pp. 187, 194.

[20] *Certain Expenses of the United Nations (Article 17, paragraph 2, of the Charter)*, Advisory Opinion [1962] ICJ Rep 151, 168.

[21] *Legality of the Use of Nuclear Weapons in Times of Armed Conflict*, Advisory Opinion [1996] ICJ Rep 66, para. 19.

[22] See also VCLT arts 12–16.

[23] George Korontzis, 'Making the Treaty' in Duncan B. Hollis (ed.), *The Oxford Guide to Treaties* (Oxford University Press, 2012) 196.

(c) if all the parties have subsequently agreed that a state may express its consent by such means.

In practice, accession is primarily relevant in relation to multilateral treaties that gradually expand their list of participating states.

An important distinction is that between signature and *ratification*. In some circumstances, consent to be bound by a treaty requires not only a signature by the potential state party in question, but also a subsequent confirmation by the state that it intends to be bound by the treaty.[24] The purpose of ratification is to allow the signing state a period of time before it gives its binding consent, often by seeking the approval of its national parliament or, more rarely, at the hands of the general public through a referendum.[25] Hence, when subsequent ratification is required, the (initial) signature is not (yet) confirmation that the state intends to be bound by the treaty. Well-known examples of treaties that were subject to subsequent ratification were the 1992 Treaty on the European Union (Maastricht Treaty) and the 2007 EU Treaty of Lisbon. Indeed, the VCLT itself is subject to ratification.[26] According to article 14 of the VCLT, ratification is required if:

(a) it is specified in the treaty itself;

(b) it is otherwise established that the negotiating parties agreed that it was needed;

(c) the representative who signed the treaty did so subject to ratification; or

(d) it appeared from the full powers of the representative or it was expressed during the negotiation that that was the intention of the state.

If it is not specified or otherwise manifest that ratification is needed, there is a presumption that ratification is *not* required.[27]

3.6 Entry into force—obligations in the interim period

When a state has given its consent to be bound by a treaty, it has shown its intention to undertake the legal obligations it contains. In practice, however, it is not legally bound by the treaty until the treaty enters into force. According to article 24 of the VCLT, a treaty enters into force 'in such manner and upon such date as it may provide or as the negotiating states may agree'. In the case of simple *bilateral* agreements, the treaty may enter into force when both parties sign the agreement. But it is not unusual for a substantial amount of time to pass before a *multilateral* treaty enters into force. The VCLT itself did not enter into force until more than ten years after it was adopted.[28] If the treaty does not specify when it enters into force,

---

[24] VCLT art. 14.   [25] For an exact definition, see VCLT art. 2(1)(b).   [26] VCLT art. 82.
[27] Aust, *Modern Treaty Law and Practice* (n 1) 96.
[28] Art. 84 states that the Convention enters into force on the 30th day following the date of deposit of the 35th instrument of ratification or accession.

it will generally enter into force as soon as consent has been established for *all* the negotiating states.

A treaty that has not yet entered into force cannot create any legal obligations for the contracting states. But good faith requires that a state is not entirely free to act as it pleases in the period between when it gave its consent to be bound by the treaty and when the treaty enters into force—known as 'the interim period'. Article 18(b) of the VCLT specifies that during that period consenting states must refrain from acts which would 'defeat the object and purpose' of the treaty. Whether an act 'defeats the object and purpose' of a treaty must be determined on a case-by-case basis. The provision is easier to apply to treaties of a contractual nature than to more general law-making treaties.[29] As a point of departure, however, it will probably only be in those cases where a state's behaviour in relation to a treaty appears to be 'unwarranted and condemnable' and potentially motivated by bad intentions that it will be found to violate its interim obligations.[30]

3.7 Validity

All legal systems have rules that concern the validity—and invalidity—of its legal instruments, and the international law of treaties is no exception. Since the legal basis of a treaty obligation is the consent of the state party, it is not surprising that most of the grounds for invalidity relate to defects in the consent given by a state. Thus, with the exception of treaties in violation of *jus cogens*, the underlying rationale of a claim of invalidity will be that the consent to be bound was somehow defective, meaning that consent would not have been forthcoming had it not been for the circumstance in question.[31] The rules on invalidity are found in articles 46–53 and 64 of the VCLT, and they illustrate that it is very difficult to successfully raise a claim of invalidity. In fact, predictability, stability and mutual trust dictate that once agreed and entered into, even seemingly 'unequal' or 'unreasonable' treaties must be considered valid and legally binding.[32]

The first ground of invalidity has been noted previously in the chapter. Thus, according to article 46 of the VCLT a state can invoke the fact that its consent to be bound by a treaty was expressed in violation of its internal law. It requires, however, that the violation was 'manifest and concerned a rule of its internal law of fundamental importance'.[33] In practice this will means that 'it would be objectively evident to any State conducting itself in the matter in accordance with normal practice and in good faith'.[34] Article 46 must be distinguished from article 27 whereby a

---

[29] See also Jan Klabbers, 'How to Defeat a Treaty's Object and Purpose Pending Entry into Force: Toward Manifest Intent' (2001) 34 *Vanderbilt Journal of Transnational Law* 283.

[30] Ibid, 330.

[31] See also Jan Klabbers, 'The Validity and Invalidity of Treaties' in Hollis (n 23) 557.

[32] On 'unequal' treaties, see Matthew Craven, 'What Happened to Unequal Treaties? The Continuities of Informal Empire' (2005) 74 *Nordic Journal of International Law* 335.

[33] VCLT art. 46(1).   [34] VCLT art. 46(2).

state may not invoke its internal law as a justification for not fulfilling a treaty-based obligation.

Article 48 addresses *error* in the formation of treaties and stipulates that error can only be invoked if it 'relates to a fact or situation which was assumed to … exist at the time when the treaty was concluded' and if it 'formed an essential basis' of the consent expressed. In addition, under article 48(2), error cannot be invoked by a state if the latter contributed by its own conduct to the error or the circumstances were such that the state should have noticed 'a possible error'. Importantly, political miscalculations are different from errors and the VCLT works on the assumption that representatives of a state are able to make reasonable judgements in their actions.[35]

Article 49 specifies that a state can invoke *fraud* as invalidating consent if it has been misled or 'induced to conclude a treaty'. In a somewhat similar vein, article 50 specifies that *corruption of a representative of a state* may be a ground for invoking invalidity. Article 51 concerns coercion and stipulates that an expression of consent shall be without legal effect if it has been procured 'through acts or threats' directed against a state representative. A more relevant provision is article 52, according to which a 'treaty is void if its conclusion has been *procured by the threat or use of force in violation of … the Charter of the United Nations*'. The rule raises a number of questions, including in relation to the validity of peace treaties concluded on the basis of the use of force that may have doubtful legality under the UN Charter. Since some measure of coercion and pressure is endemic in international relations and negotiations, it is of some importance that the article only concerns military force.[36]

The most relevant of the provisions on potential invalidity is article 53 that relates to the issue of peremptory character/*jus cogens*. As we saw in Chapter 2, article 53 specifies that a treaty is void if it 'conflicts with a peremptory norm of general international law'.[37] Such norms are those that have been 'accepted and recognized by the international community of States as a whole as a norm from which no derogation is permitted and which can be modified only by a subsequent norm of general international law having the same character'. Article 53 differs from the other articles on invalidity in that it is the only one that focuses on the *content* of the treaty in question and thereby tries to limit the contractual freedom of the states. In practice, however, as mentioned in Chapter 2, there is little agreement on which norms are of a *jus cogens* character. Although it would be fairly obvious that the prohibition on genocide and the bans on torture, slavery and outright aggression may be covered by article 53, there is less certainty about the status of other core human rights. Article 53 should be read in conjunction with article 64 according to which an existing treaty becomes void and terminates if it conflicts with an emerging (new) peremptory norm. In contrast to article 53, the latter article concerns cases where a treaty was valid when concluded but

---

[35] Klabbers, 'The Validity and Invalidity of Treaties' (n 31) 565–566.   [36] Ibid, 569–570.

[37] A unilateral declaration that conflicts with a peremptory norm of general international law is similarly void, see ILC, 'Guiding Principles applicable to unilateral declarations of States capable of creating legal obligations' (2006), UN Doc. A/61/10 (ILC Guiding Principles) and VCLT art. 53.

subsequently becomes void due to the establishment of a new rule of *jus cogens*. An example would be a treaty previously intended to regulate the slave trade.

3.8 Reservations

International law may allow a state to take account of national political, social or cultural attitudes by becoming a party to a multilateral treaty without accepting all of its provisions and obligations.[38] Unilateral statements whereby a state may exclude or modify the legal effect of one or more provisions of a treaty in its application to the state are termed 'reservations',[39] and the rules and principles governing the character and legal consequences of reservations are among the most detailed and complicated in the field of the law of treaties.[40]

At the outset it is important to distinguish between 'reservations' and 'interpretative declarations'. Unlike a reservation, an *interpretative declaration* (which is not mentioned in the VCLT) does *not* seek to modify the treaty obligation but merely to *specify* or *clarify* the meaning or scope the declaring state attaches to the obligation in question. Hence, the purpose of such a declaration is to communicate to other parties what the declaring state understands the existing obligation to be. Often, the intention of an interpretative declaration is to ensure an interpretation of a treaty provision that is consistent with the domestic law of the state in question. Where applicable, the declaration may constitute an element that must be taken into account in interpreting the treaty in accordance with the general rules of treaty interpretation (see Section 3.9).[41] It is equally important not to confuse reservations with *derogations*. As we shall explore further in Chapter 9, some human rights treaties contain provisions that authorize a state to 'derogate'—and thereby not to apply certain provisions—in times of emergency or similar periods of national emergency. Article 15 of the European Convention on Human Rights (ECHR), for example, allows a contracting party to derogate from certain of its obligations in 'time of war or other public emergency threatening the life of the nation'.[42]

The concrete rules on treaty reservations owe much to the 1951 *Genocide Reservations* case where the ICJ issued an advisory opinion on the making of reservations to the 1948 Genocide Convention. [43] Up until then, reservations were not valid unless accepted by *all* the contracting parties. Although the ICJ reiterated that a state cannot be bound by a treaty without its consent and that no reservation can therefore be effective against a state without its agreement, it adopted a new and more flexible

---

[38] For an overview, see Aust, *Modern Treaty Law and Practice* (n 1) 114–144.

[39] For a definition, see VCLT art. 2(1)(d).

[40] For an overview, see Edward T. Swaine, 'Treaty Reservations' in Hollis (n 23) 277–301. In practice, of course, given their 'contractual' nature, reservations cannot be made to bilateral treaties.

[41] See also ILC, 'Guide to Practice on Reservations to Treaties' (2011), UN Doc. A/66/10, para. 4.7.1.

[42] See also International Covenant on Civil and Political Rights (adopted 16 December 1966, entered into force 23 March 1976), 999 UNTS 171, art. 4.

[43] *Reservations to the Convention on Genocide*, Advisory Opinion [1951] ICJ Rep 15.

approach to reservations that subsequently found its way into the VCLT.[44] According to the Court, reservations are generally acceptable if they are compatible with 'the object and purpose' of the treaty in question.[45] State practice is rich with examples of state reservations and reservations of minor significance are particularly prevalent in relation to human rights conventions, such as the UN Covenant on Civil and Political Rights. Denmark, for example, has made a number of fairly limited reservations to both the Covenant's protection of the right of appeal in criminal cases and to the right for juvenile offenders to be segregated from adults and accorded treatment appropriate to their age and legal status. Sweden and Norway have also made a reservation to the obligation to segregate juvenile offenders from adults, and Sweden has a further reservation to the obligation to prohibit propaganda for war.[46] Among the more well-known examples of treaty reservations are the Danish 'opt-outs' to the 1992 Maastricht Treaty on the establishment of the EU. In a May 1992 referendum, a narrow majority of Danish voters rejected the Maastricht Treaty. Since the Treaty had to be ratified by all member states, a solution to the 'Danish problem' was found at the Edinburgh Summit in December 1992 where the member states agreed to allow Denmark to 'opt out' of certain aspects of the Treaty.[47] In a subsequent referendum in May 1993, a majority of Danish voters accepted Danish ratification of the Treaty with the four 'opt-outs'. In essence, the opt-outs were treaty reservations that meant that Denmark would not be bound by certain provisions of the Treaty.[48]

Reservations to treaties are not always permitted. According to article 19 of the VCLT, reservations are excluded in three circumstances. First, reservations cannot be made if the treaty expressly stipulates that reservations are not permitted. Article 120 of the Rome Statute of the International Criminal Court, for example, specifies that no reservations may be made to the Statute. Secondly, some treaties provide that only certain reservations to the treaty can be made. The third and most important exception holds that a reservation cannot be made if it violates the object and purpose of a treaty. In such cases, the reservation will be null and void and without legal effect regardless of whether or not other states have objected to it.[49] According to the ILC, the object and purpose of a treaty is compromised if the reservation 'affects an essential element of the treaty that is necessary to its general tenour, in such a way that the reservation impairs the raison d'être of the treaty'.[50] An obvious example would be a reservation to a treaty according to which internal law may be invoked as a justification for a failure to perform a treaty-based obligation. It is often extremely difficult to identify

[44] Ibid, 21–22.   [45] Ibid, 24.

[46] For an overview of reservations to the Covenant, see https://treaties.un.org/pages/ViewDetails.aspx?src=TREATY&mtdsg_no=IV-4&chapter=4&clang=_en.

[47] European Council, 'Denmark and the Treaty on European Union', Edinburgh, 11 and 12 December 1992, 92/C 348/01.

[48] The reservations related to the third stage of Economic and Monetary Union and the introduction of the common currency (the euro), common defence policies, cooperation in the fields of justice and home affairs and provisions relating to EU citizenship.

[49] See also ILC, 'Guide to Practice on Reservations to Treaties' (n 41) paras 4.5.1–4.5.2.

[50] Ibid, para. 3.1.5.

the object and purpose of a treaty,[51] in particular as these have a tendency to become more elaborate and complex. However, both the title and a preamble may offer some guidance.[52] The issue is particularly relevant with regard to reservations to human rights conventions. As we saw earlier, many states have made minor reservations to human rights conventions, but it may be hard to draw the line between permissible and impermissible reservations to human rights conventions. A concrete example is the reservation by the United States to the obligation in the Covenant not to impose the death penalty for crimes committed by persons under 18 years of age.[53]

Articles 20 and 21 of the VCLT deal with the important—and controversial—issues regarding acceptance/objection to reservations and the legal effects of reservations. As a main rule, and as a natural consequence of the consensual nature of the law of treaties, a reservation will not become effective in relation to another contracting state unless that state has accepted it—either explicitly or implicitly. In short, if a state proposes a reservation the other states may accept or object to the reservation. If a state has not objected within 12 months, it is deemed to have accepted it.[54] Article 20 initially stipulates that acceptance is not required if the reservation is *expressly* authorized by the treaty.[55] If, however, it appears from the limited number of participating states and the object and purpose of the treaty that it is meant to apply in its entirety to all parties, reservation requires the consent of *all* those parties.[56] Unless otherwise provided, a reservation to a treaty that is a constituent instrument of an international organization requires the acceptance of the competent organ of that organization.[57] If nothing is provided in the treaty, reservations are governed by the following principles.

(a) If a state accepts a reservation by another state they will be parties to the same treaty.[58]

(b) If a state objects to another state's reservation the treaty will not enter into force between the two states <u>if</u> the objecting state expresses a definite intention for that to be the case.[59]

(c) A state's reservation is effective when at least one other contracting state has accepted it.[60]

With regard to the *legal effects* of reservations and objections, article 21 of the VCLT stipulates that a reservation modifies the provisions of the treaty for the reserving and the other state.[61] It does not, however, modify the provisions for the other parties *inter se*.[62] As a result of the Danish reservations to the Maastricht Treaty, then, while Denmark is not bound by the reserved parts of the treaty, the other non-reserving

[51] See also Jan Klabbers, 'Some Problems Regarding the Object and Purpose of Treaties' (1997) 8 *Finnish Yearbook of International Law* 138. For reservations to human rights treaties, see William A. Schabas, 'Reservations to Human Rights Treaties: Time of Innovation and Reform' (1994) 32 *Canadian Yearbook of International Law* 39.
[52] Klabbers, 'Some Problems Regarding the Object and Purpose of Treaties' (n 51) 156–158.
[53] See reservations by the United States in link in n 46.   [54] VCLT art. 20(5).
[55] VCLT art. 20(1).   [56] VCLT art. 20(2).   [57] VCLT art. 20(3).
[58] VCLT art. 20(4)(a).   [59] VCLT art. 20(4)(b).   [60] VCLT art. 20(4)(c).
[61] VCLT art. 21(1).   [62] VCLT art. 21(2).

states are bound vis-à-vis each other. If an objecting state has not expressly opposed the entry into force of the treaty between itself and the reserving state, the provisions to which the reservation relates do not apply between the two states.[63]

In practical terms, then, a state can react to another state's reservation in three ways: (1) it can accept the reservation in which event the treaty will enter into force between the two states with the reservation in force; (2) it can object to the reservation and express an intention that the treaty as a whole should not enter into force between the states—if that is the case, the treaty will not govern the two states' relations; or (3) it can object to the treaty but refrain from expressing an intention that the treaty as a whole should not enter into force between the two states. Then the treaty will enter into force between the two states with the reservation in force. In practice, therefore, the legal effect of options (1) and (3) is the same, and the choices for an objecting state are therefore not very favourable. Unless it wants the treaty *as a whole* not to govern the relations between itself and the reserving state, it will make no material difference if it accepts or objects to a reservation.

If a reservation violates a treaty's object and purpose, the reserving state cannot rely on it in its treaty relations with other parties. In practice, then, there would only appear to be two possible outcomes.[64] The first is that the invalidity of the reservation nullifies the instrument *as a whole* whereby the (reserving) state is no longer considered a party to the agreement at all. While this approach preserves the integrity of the treaty regime in question, it is a drastic step that the involved states themselves may not desire. The second option is to essentially ignore the reservation and conclude that the (reserving) state remains bound by the treaty, including the provision(s) to which the reservation related. However, this so-called 'severance' option goes against the consensual principle according to which a state is only bound by the treaty obligations to which it consents. While the latter approach has been supported by, among others, the European Court of Human Rights (ECtHR),[65] the Human Rights Committee[66] and the Nordic states,[67] the ILC has suggested a more modified and somewhat reasonable solution.[68] In a 2011 *Guide to Practice*, it introduces a *presumption* of severability according to which the reserving state will be considered a contracting state without 'the benefit of the reservation' unless it 'has expressed a contrary intention or such an intention is otherwise established'.[69] Thus,

---

[63] VCLT art. 21(3).

[64] See also Ryan Goodman, 'Human Rights Treaties, Invalid Reservations, and State Consent' (2002) 96 *American Journal of International Law* 531.

[65] *Belios v Switzerland*, App. no. 10328/83, 29 April 1998, para. 60. See also *Loizidou v Turkey*, App. no. 15318/89, Preliminary Objections, 23 March 1995.

[66] Human Rights Committee, 'General Comment No. 24: General comment on issues relating to reservations made upon ratification or accession to the Covenant or the Optional Protocols thereto, or in relation to declarations under article 41 of the Covenant' (4 November 1994), UN Doc. CCPR/C/21/Rev.1/Add.6, para. 18.

[67] See the overview in Jan Klabbers, 'Accepting the Unacceptable? A Nordic Approach to Reservations to Multilateral Treaties' (2000) 69 *Nordic Journal of International Law* 179.

[68] See the critique in Hugh Thirlway, *The Sources of International Law* (Oxford University Press, 2014) 38–44; Aust, *Modern Treaty Law and Practice* (n 1) 131; Klabbers, 'Accepting the Unacceptable?' (n 67) 190.

[69] ILC, 'Guide to Practice on Reservations to Treaties' (n 41) para. 4.5.3. See also Goodman (n 64) 555–559.

unless the state makes it manifest that it will *only* be a party to the treaty if it can benefit from the invalid reservation, it will be presumed to be a full party without benefitting from the reservation.

According to article 19 of the VCLT, a reservation must be made by a state 'when signing, ratifying, accepting, approving or acceding to a treaty', and there is no mention of a right to make a reservation after the treaty in question has been ratified. A reservation subsequent to ratification cannot therefore be effective unless it is accepted by the other contracting parties.[70]

A state that is not satisfied with an existing treaty obligation may in theory withdraw from the treaty and try to 're-accede' with a reservation that excludes the unwanted obligation in question.[71] While it may be hard to see why such a denunciation and subsequent re-accession with a reservation should not be an option, there is debate about its compatibility with international law.[72] A practical and sensible solution may be to allow the issue to be dealt with on a case-by-case basis depending on the attitude of the other contracting parties. It is important to recall, however, that a state that wishes to become 'un-bound' by a treaty obligation may still be bound by the content of the obligation if it has become binding as a matter of customary international law.

3.9 Interpretation

Most disputes in international law relate to the proper interpretation of a treaty, and treaty interpretation is therefore one of the most important skills of any international lawyer. The primary principles governing treaty interpretation are contained in articles 31 and 32 of the VCLT that reflect customary international law.[73] As always, it is the intention of the parties that is the key.

Article 31(1) articulates the general rule that a 'treaty shall be interpreted in good faith in accordance with the ordinary meaning to be given to the terms of the treaty in their context and in the light of its object and purpose'. The reference to 'good faith' derives from the *pacta sunt servanda* obligation in article 26. Article 31(1) illustrates that the interpretation of a treaty must consider three elements: the *text*, its *context* and the *object and purpose* of the treaty as desired by the parties. Thus, *all* elements

---

[70] See also Aust, *Modern Treaty Law and Practice* (n 1) 141–142.

[71] This, of course, requires that the obligation in question is not of such a nature that a reservation will violate the treaty's object and purpose.

[72] Aust, *Modern Treaty Law and Practice* (n 1) 141–141. See also Glenn McGrory, 'Reservations of Virtue? Lessons from Trinidad and Tobago's Reservation to the First Optional Protocol' (2001) 23 *Human Rights Quarterly* 769, 812; Laurence R. Helfer, 'Not Fully Committed? Reservations, Risk, and Treaty Design' (2006) 32 *Yale Journal of International Law* 367, 373.

[73] *Territorial Dispute (Libyan Arab Jamahiriya v Chad)*, Judgment [1994] ICJ Rep 6, para. 41; *Oil Platforms (Islamic Republic of Iran v United States)*, Preliminary Objections [1996] ICJ Rep 803, para. 23; *Kasikili/Sedudu Island (Botswana v Namibia)* [1999] ICJ Rep 1045, para. 18; *LaGrand (Germany v United States)* [2001] ICJ Rep 466, paras 99–101. See also ECtHR, *Golder v UK*, App. no. 4451/70, 21 February 1975, para. 29. See also Ulf Lindefalk, *On the Interpretation of Treaties* (Springer, 2010) 7.

must be considered and none are intended to be of greater weight than the others.[74] While it is usually fair to assume that the ordinary meaning of a word or term is what was intended by the parties to the treaty,[75] the text is only the natural starting point for the interpretation. Thus, if the wording of a treaty is clear but its application would lead to an unreasonable result, the other elements must be applied. In practice, it is usually only possible to grasp the 'ordinary meaning' of a text by considering its context and the overall object and purpose of the treaty. In order to determine, for example, what is meant by the terms 'force' or 'armed attack' in articles 2(4) and article 51 of the UN Charter, the interpreter must take account of both the structure of the Charter as well as the Charter's purposes as set out in the preamble and the opening articles. According to article 31(4), a 'special meaning' must be given to a term in a treaty provision if 'it is established that the parties so intended'.

According to article 31(2), the 'context' includes not only the treaty's preamble but also annexes as well as agreements and instruments made by the parties *in connection with the conclusion of the treaty*. Article 31(3)(a) and (b) permits consideration of agreements and practice established *subsequent* to the adoption of the treaty.[76] Since the manner in which a treaty is actually applied by the parties is a relatively solid indication of what they believe the treaty to mean, subsequent practice is a particularly relevant source of treaty interpretation. Indeed, if subsequent practice is sufficiently clear and either expressly or tacitly accepted by all parties, it can take precedence over an otherwise fairly clear wording of the text in a treaty. For example, while article 27(3) of the UN Charter stipulates that decisions by the Security Council on non-procedural matters must be made by an 'affirmative' vote of nine of its members including the 'concurring votes' of the five permanent members, practice subsequent to the adoption of the Charter has confirmed that the term 'concurring' should simply be interpreted as 'not objecting'. Thus, in its 1970 advisory opinion on *Namibia*, the ICJ concluded that, although the intention of the drafters of the Charter was different, 'the proceedings of the Security Council extending over a long period of time supply abundant evidence' that it will only be by casting a negative vote and relying on the power of the veto—and not merely abstaining—that a permanent member can block a decision.[77]

The *Namibia* case illustrates the difficulties that may be associated with determining if subsequent practice in the application of a treaty should be conceived of as an interpretation or an outright amendment of a provision.[78] In *Hassan v UK*, the ECtHR concluded that subsequent practice of the parties 'could be taken as establishing their agreement not only as regards interpretation but even to modify the text' of the ECHR.[79] The Court found that the detention of individuals on the basis of the

---

[74] See also ILC, Draft Articles on the Law of Treaties, with commentaries, *Yearbook of the International Law Commission*, 1966, vol. II, pp. 187, 219, para. 8; Richard Gardiner, *Treaty Interpretation* (Oxford University Press, 2008) ch. 5.

[75] See also *LaGrand* (n 73) para. 77.   [76] VCLT art. 31(3)(a) and (b).

[77] *Legal Consequences for States of the Continued Presence of South Africa in Namibia (South West Africa) notwithstanding Security Council Resolution 276 (1970)*, Advisory Opinion [1971] ICJ Rep 16, para. 22.

[78] See also Gardiner (n 74) 243–245. See also ECtHR, *Soering v UK*, App. no. 14038/88, 7 July 1989, paras 103–104 and *Öcalan v Turkey*, App. no. 46221/99, 12 March 2003, paras 162–165.

[79] *Hassan v UK*, App. no. 29750/09, 16 September 2014, para. 101.

Third and Fourth 1949 Geneva Conventions in the course of an international armed conflict would appear to be prima facie inconsistent with the right to liberty under article 5 of the Convention unless the detaining state has made a valid derogation from its obligations under that article. It also concluded, however, that subsequent state practice showed that the lack of a formal derogation should not prevent the Court from taking account of the Geneva Conventions when interpreting and applying article 5.[80]

Article 31(3)(c) of the VCLT specifies that, together with the context, treaty interpretation shall take account of 'any relevant rules of international law applicable in the relations between the parties'. Hence, the treaty must be considered in the wider context of international law where international obligations are interpreted in relation to their normative context.[81] In *Hassan v UK* mentioned above, the ECtHR relied on this provision when it concluded that the interpretation of a party's human rights obligations should take account of the existence of international humanitarian law. It found that the grounds for permitting deprivation of liberty set out in article 5 of the ECHR should be 'accommodated ... with the taking of prisoners of war and the detention of civilians who pose a risk to security under the Third and Fourth Geneva Conventions'.[82]

Article 32 of the VCLT concerns the status of the preparatory works to a treaty (*travaux préparatoires*), such as preliminary drafts of the treaty, records from conferences and explanatory statements. Such material is explicitly listed as a 'supplementary means of interpretation' and is only to be consulted 'in order to confirm the meaning resulting from the application of article 31, or to determine the meaning when the interpretation according to article 31' either leaves the meaning ambiguous or obscure, or will lead to a 'result which is manifestly absurd or unreasonable'.[83] In practice, however, although the interpretative value of preparatory work varies significantly and must be approached with care, the preparatory work will usually be consulted if it has anything meaningful to add about the intention of the parties to a treaty.

If a treaty is drafted in more than one language, it may give rise to a host of interpretative issues.[84] Article 33 of the VCLT states that if a 'treaty has been authenticated in two or more languages' 'the text is equally authoritative in each language' unless otherwise specified or agreed. The problem is sometimes overcome by a stipulation in the treaty that one of the languages will prevail in the case of inconsistency.

The interpretive principles in articles 31–33 of the VCLT are intended to govern the interpretation of all types of treaties. It would, however, be wrong to assume that

---

[80] Ibid, paras 101–103.

[81] On this, see ILC, 'Fragmentation of International Law: Difficulties Arising from the Diversification and Expansion of International Law', Report of the Study Group of the International Law Commission (13 April 2006), UN Doc. A/CN.4/L.682, 206–244. See also Gardiner (n 74) ch. 7.

[82] *Hassan v UK* (n 79) paras 102–104. See also WTO, *United States—Import Prohibition of Certain Shrimp and Shrimp Products* (12 October 1998) WT/DS58/AB/R, paras 126–134 and—somewhat controversially— *Oil Platforms (Iran v United States)*, Merits [2003] ICJ Rep 161, para. 41.

[83] *LaGrand* (n 73) para. 104.   [84] See e.g. *LaGrand* (n 73) 99–109.

approaches to interpretation are always the same. How much weight the interpreter assigns to, respectively, the text, context and object and purpose of a treaty often depends on the character of the treaty. Thus, while treaties of a contractual/reciprocal character may dictate an interpretative approach that centres around state consent and the intention of the parties involved, treaties of a more 'law-making' character may call for a teleological approach that places more emphasis on the treaty's stated object and purpose. In addition, a *constitutive treaty*, that establishes an international institution and specify the functions and competences of that institution,[85] is generally considered to be of a 'special nature' that calls less for interpretation in accordance with the intention of the parties that created the institution than an interpretation that stresses 'effectiveness' ('functionality').[86] Thus, in its 1949 advisory opinion in the 1949 *Reparations Case*, the ICJ concluded that the UN possesses those competences that are required for it to effectively discharge the functions entrusted to it by the member states.[87] In practice, it falls to the international organization itself to interpret the extent of its own powers.[88] In *Legality of the Use of Nuclear Weapons in Times of Armed Conflict*, the Court found that the World Health Organization (WHO) did not have the competence to request an advisory opinion on whether the use of nuclear weapons was lawful.[89] The constituent treaties of the EU are routinely interpreted by the Court of Justice of the European Union in a manner in which their purpose and 'effectiveness' are stressed. In the seminal 1963 case of *Van Gend en Loos*, the (then) European Court of Justice stated that the Treaty establishing the European Economic Community was 'more than an agreement which merely creates mutual obligations between the contracting states ... [it] constitutes a new legal order of international law' and should be interpreted accordingly.[90] *Human rights conventions* are also generally interpreted less according to the original intention of the parties and more in order to ensure the effective, real and concrete protection of the individuals who find themselves under the jurisdiction of the states in question. [91] The ECtHR, for example, has repeatedly stressed that the convention is a 'living instrument' that must be interpreted in the 'light of present-day conditions' and not 'solely in accordance with the intentions of their authors at the adoption of the treaty'.[92] A similar approach is visible in the practice of other human rights bodies.[93]

---

[85] See VCLT art. 5.

[86] See also Catherine Brolmann, 'Specialized Rules of Treaty Interpretation: International Organizations' in Hollis (n 23) 512–513.

[87] *Reparations for injuries suffered in the service of the United Nations*, Advisory Opinion [1949] ICJ Rep 174, 179–180. See also *Certain Expenses* (n 20) 157.

[88] *Certain Expenses* (n 20) 168.

[89] *Nuclear Weapons* (n 21) para. 19. See also *LaGrand* (n 73) para. 102.

[90] Cases 26–62 *Van Gend en Loos* [1963] ECR I-1, 12.

[91] See also Basak Cali, 'Specialized Rules of Treaty Interpretation: Human Rights' in Hollis (n 23).

[92] See, among others, *Tyrer v UK*, App. no. 5856/72, 25 April 1978, para. 31; *Loizidou v Turkey*, App. no. 15318/89, 23 March 1995, para. 71.

[93] See Human Rights Committee, 'General Comment No. 6, The Right to Life' (30 April 1982), UN Doc. HRI/Gen/1/Rev.7, paras 4–5; *19 Tradesmen v Colombia*, 5 July 2004, Inter-AmCtHR, Series C, No. 109 (2004), para. 173.

3.10 Amendments and modifications

As time passes and conditions and/or political sentiments change, parties to a treaty may feel the need to alter some of the provisions. As we have just seen, subsequent practice in the application of a treaty can have the practical effect of modifying the content of the treaty if it has been consented to by the parties. Under article 39 of the VCLT, a treaty may also be formally *amended* by the specific agreement of the parties—often termed 'protocols'. For example, over the years the ECHR has been supplemented by a large number of protocols.[94] Unless otherwise provided for in the treaty, the regular consent-centred formalities on the conclusion and coming into effect of treaties will apply to such amendments. In practice, many treaties, and most multilateral treaties, will contain provisions on amendments. Article 108 of the UN Charter, for example, states that the Charter can be amended and come into force for all members when the amendments have been adopted (and ratified) by two-thirds of the members of the General Assembly, including the five permanent members. Thus, an amendment may even bind states which have voted against it. In the absence of any specific provisions, a proposed amendment has to be notified to all contracting states.[95] Regardless of any modifications, article 41 of the VCLT states that two or more parties to a multilateral treaty may conclude an agreement *modifying* the treaty between them. It does require, however, that such a possibility is either provided for in the treaty or the modification in question is not prohibited by the treaty and does not affect the other parties' rights or obligations or relate to a provision from which derogation is incompatible with the effective execution of the object and purpose of the treaty as a whole.

When it is particularly obvious to parties that their treaty-based commitments need to take account of subsequent developments, they may decide to adopt a so-called framework convention. Unlike other treaties, a framework convention does not seek to exhaustively regulate a given topic but instead seeks to establish an organizational structure that will be competent to develop the substantive regulation. Framework conventions are particularly relied upon in international environmental law where a well-known example is the 1992 UN Framework Convention on Climate Change (UNFCCC).[96] While the Convention itself only contains few substantive provisions, it establishes a Conference of the Parties (COP) that is tasked with adopting the substantive measures required to reach the objectives of the Convention. Some framework conventions adopt a 'list technique' whereby obligations are linked to one or more periodically updated lists contained in protocols or annexes to the treaty.

---

[94] For an overview, see Council of Europe, 'Search on Treaties' at http://conventions.coe.int/Treaty/Commun/ListeTraites.asp?MA=3&CM=7&CL=ENG (accessed 28 July 2016).

[95] VCLT art. 39(2).   [96] See more in Chapter 11.

3.11 Termination and withdrawal

A treaty may come to an end and terminate if its purpose has been fulfilled or if it is clear that it is limited in time and that time has passed. Articles 54 and 57 of the VCLT state that a treaty also terminates in accordance with a provision in the treaty or by the consent of all the parties thereto. In other situations, article 56 specifies that a state may only denounce or withdraw from a treaty where the parties intended to permit such a possibility or where the right may be implied by the nature of the treaty. In such cases, a party must give no less than 12 months' notice of its intention to denounce or withdraw from the treaty.

A state may also be entitled to terminate a bilateral treaty if the other state materially breaches its obligations under the treaty. Under article 60(3) of the VCLT, a *'material breach'* consists of a repudiation of the treaty not permitted by the VCLT or the violation of a provision that is essential to accomplishing the object and purpose of the treaty. In cases of a material breach of a multilateral treaty, article 60(2) specifies that the other parties may, inter alia, unanimously decide to suspend the operation of the treaty in whole or in part or to terminate it either in relations between themselves and the defaulting state or as between all the parties.

In a limited range of situations, international law also permits a state to terminate or suspend its treaty-based obligations for a number of exceptional circumstances. First of all, under article 61 of the VCLT, a state may terminate or withdraw from a treaty if, due to the 'permanent disappearance or destruction of an object indispensable for the execution of the treaty', it becomes impossible for a state to perform the treaty-based obligation. Only a permanent impossibility will be relevant. Secondly, according to article 62, the same may apply in cases of *a fundamental change of circumstances* (*rebus sic stantibus*). The exception is narrow, however, and it may only be invoked if the change was unforeseen at the time the treaty was concluded and the existence of the now changed circumstances 'constituted an essential basis of the consent of the parties to be bound by the treaty' and the 'effect of the change is radically to transform the extent of the obligations still to be performed'. In addition, a state may not invoke its own conduct.[97] In *Gabčíkovo-Nagymaros Project*, the ICJ did not find that changes in environmental knowledge and awareness radically affected the obligations of the parties.[98]

The ICJ has noted that the provisions for the termination and suspension of the operation of treaties in articles 60–62 of the VCLT reflect customary international law.[99] The consequences of the termination or suspension of a treaty are listed in articles 70–72.

---

[97] Aust, *Modern Treaty Law and Practice* (n 1) 263.
[98] *Gabčíkovo-Nagymaros Project (Hungary v Slovakia)*, Judgment [1997] ICJ Rep 7, para. 104.
[99] Ibid, para. 46.

Summary

Like other societies, the society of states has rules and principles that govern the agreements entered into by its legal subjects, and the law of treaties is one of the oldest and most important areas of public international law. The primary rules in the area of the law of treaties are found in the 1969 VCLT that, for the most part at least, reflects customary international law. The 1969 Convention regulates the conclusion and entry into force of treaties, the application and interpretation of treaties and the validity, termination and withdrawal of treaties, and is intended to be applied to *all* types of treaties whether bilateral or multilateral. For the most part, the rules resemble domestic rules for the creation and operation of contracts and, as with national contract law, the law of treaties is not concerned with the material content of the instrument itself. While the majority of the rules and principles are uncontroversial, issues relating to treaty reservations and the interpretation of treaties remain contentious and therefore fairly complex.

Recommended reading

For a thorough contribution, see Duncan B. Hollis (ed.), *The Oxford Guide to Treaties* (Oxford University Press, 2012).

A classic work on the law of treaties is Lord McNair, *The Law of Treaties* (Oxford University Press, 1986). See also Richard R. Baxter, 'International Law in "Her Infinite Variety"' (1980) 29 *International and Comparative Law Quarterly* 549; Oscar Schachter, 'The Twilight Existence of Nonbinding International Agreements' (1977) 71 *American Journal of International Law* 296; Jan Klabbers, *The Concept of Treaty in International Law* (Kluwer, 1996). More recent works include Anthony Aust, *Modern Treaty Law and Practice* (3rd edn, Cambridge University Press, 2013) and the same author in 'The Theory and Practice of Informal International Instruments' (1986) 35 *International and Comparative Law Quarterly* 787. See also Hugh Thirlway, *The Sources of International Law* (Oxford University Press, 2014) ch. 2.

For other contributions to the literature on reservations, see William A. Schabas, 'Reservations to Human Rights Treaties: Time of Innovation and Reform' (1994) 32 *Canadian Yearbook of International Law* 39; Ryan Goodman, 'Human Rights Treaties, Invalid Reservations, and State Consent' (2002) 96 *American Journal of International Law* 531.

For a thorough work on treaty interpretation, see Richard Gardiner, *Treaty Interpretation* (Oxford University Press, 2008) and Ulf Lindefalk, *On the Interpretation of Treaties* (Springer, 2010).

Questions for discussion

1. In what ways does the interpretation of constituent treaties and human rights treaties differ from a more traditional approach to interpretation?

2. What is the meaning of *pacta sunt servanda* and how does the principle manifest itself in the law of treaties?

3. How should one determine if an agreement is a treaty governed by international law or is merely a political pledge?

4. It is often the case that a treaty does not enter into force after a certain amount of time has passed. While a consenting state cannot be bound by a treaty that has yet to enter into force it is not entirely free to act as it pleases. Why is that? From where is such an 'obligation' derived?

5. Can you provide some examples of when it is important to identify the object and purpose of a treaty?

4

The actors in the international legal system

CENTRAL ISSUES

1. This chapter introduces the reader to the various actors in the international legal system that possess rights, powers and obligations in international law.

2. It contains a thorough presentation of statehood and the criteria for the creation of new states, and briefly discusses the (limited) legal significance of recognition.

3. The chapter also discusses the modes by which a state can acquire title to new territory. In addition, it provides an overview of the issues of state succession and state extinction.

4. The chapter presents an overview of the legal personality of territorial entities other than states, international organizations, individuals and additional actors in the international legal system.

4.1 Introduction

We saw in Chapter 1 that international society is first and foremost a society of individual sovereign states. But while states remain centre stage, they are by no means the only relevant actors in international law. In fact, one of the consequences of the post-1945 expansion of international law into areas that had traditionally been of limited international interest has been the increasing legal importance of a variety of non-state actors, most notably international organizations and individuals. The answer to the question of who international law actually applies to is often found in the concept of 'legal subjectivity' or 'legal personality'.[1] The subjects of international law are those to whom the international legal system gives the capacity to hold rights, powers and obligations. Importantly, though, legal subjectivity/personality is relative and not all participants in the international legal system hold the same rights and obligations. As the International Court of Justice (ICJ) famously stated in the *Reparations* case, legal

---

[1] For a debate, see Roland Portmann, *Legal Personality in International Law* (Cambridge University Press, 2010).

subjects 'are not necessarily identical in their nature or in the extent of their rights, and their nature depends upon the needs of the community'.[2] The principal features of international legal personality include the capacity to bring claims in respect of breaches of international law, the capacity to conclude treaties and the enjoyment of privileges and immunities from the exercise of national jurisdiction. While states have all these capacities, other actors will only possess those rights and obligations they have been given by states.[3] In that sense, non-state actors derive their legal personality from states. In its 2010 advisory opinion on the *Unilateral Declaration of Independence in Respect of Kosovo*, the ICJ noted that it is not uncommon for the Security Council to make demands on actors other than states and international organizations and that it would require a case-by-case evaluation to determine 'for whom the Security Council intended to create legal obligations'.[4]

The purpose of this chapter is to present the different actors in the international legal system and to highlight their most important features. The presentation opens in Section 4.2 with an analysis of the state as a legal actor. Section 4.3 provides a brief overview of the legal personality of international organizations and Section 4.4 discusses the legal personality of individuals. Section 4.5 lists a number of other actors in the international legal system and Section 4.6 discusses non-governmental organizations.

4.2 The state

4.2.1 Introduction

One of the major developments of the 20th century was the emergence of a large number of new states. From around 50 states at the beginning of the century to about 75 immediately after the Second World War, the number of states skyrocketed with the decolonialization process in the 1960s and 70s. By July 2016, the number of states registered as members of the UN stood at 193.[5] The most recent additions to the club of states were South Sudan (2011) and Montenegro (2006). States are by far the most important actor among international legal actors and they are the only actor that can create international law. The purpose of this section is to analyse and discuss the state as a legal actor in international law. We begin the overview with a discussion of the significance associated with recognition (Section 4.2.2). We then examine the criteria for statehood in the Montevideo Convention on the Right and Duties of States (Section

---

[2] *Reparations for Injuries Suffered in the Service of the United Nations*, Advisory Opinion [1949] ICJ Rep 174, 178.

[3] See also James Crawford, *The Creation of States in International Law* (2nd edn, Oxford University Press, 2006) 28–29 and the same author in *International Law as an Open System: Selected Essays* (Cameron May, 2002) 19–22. See also the discussion in Astrid Kjeldgaard-Pedersen, *The International Legal Personality of Individuals* (forthcoming) 32.

[4] *Accordance with International Law of the Unilateral Declaration of Independence in Respect of Kosovo*, Advisory Opinion [2010] ICJ Rep 403, paras 116–117.

[5] See http://www.un.org/en/member-states/ (accessed 12 August 2016). The list does not include Taiwan, the Vatican or Kosovo.

4.2.3) and the issue of illegality in the creation of a state (Section 4.2.4). Attention then turns to the contentious issue of self-determination (Section 4.2.5) after which we discuss the acquisition of new territory (Section 4.2.6), state succession (Section 4.2.7) and finally the issue of state extinction (Section 4.2.8).

4.2.2 **The issue of recognition**

The special status afforded to states makes it all the more important to identify the rules and principles that govern the creation of states. It is therefore somewhat unfortunate that the issue is fraught with contention. The primary reason for the existing uncertainties about when an entity qualifies as a 'state' is due to diverging opinions about what role is played by other states in the recognition of an emerging state.

At the outset, it is important to note the distinction—often blurred—between the recognition of *a state* and that of *a government*. While the state is the legal entity under international law, the government is the representative of the state that is entitled to act on the state's behalf. The actual effects of lack of recognition of a state are of greater legal importance than those relating to lack of recognition of a government. A decision not to recognize a government that claims to represent a territorial entity is not the same as denying that the entity in question qualifies for statehood. For example, the widespread lack of recognition of the Taleban regime as the government of Afghanistan in the 1990s did not mean that there was a lack of recognition that Afghanistan constituted a state for the purposes of international law.[6]

Traditionally, the doctrinal debate about the effects of recognition of states has been dominated by two competing approaches. According to a *declaratory* view, the creation of states is first and foremost a matter of law and the fulfilment of legal criteria. Thus, as soon as an entity can be said to satisfy a number of predetermined requirements, it will enjoy the rights and duties of a state in international law. Under this approach, the relevant criterion for acquiring statehood is essentially one of *effectiveness*.[7] In contrast to the declaratory approach, the *constitutive* view holds that recognition by other states is a precondition for statehood. So, unless an entity that appears to bear all the hallmarks of a 'state' is recognized as such by other states, it is not a state for the purposes of international law.[8] The emergence of the constitutive view was tied to the rise of positivism and the pre-eminence of state consent in the 19th century. It subsequently served as a useful tool for the

---

[6] For more on recognition of governments, see Stefan Talmon, *Recognition of Government in International Law: With Particular Reference to Governments in Exile* (Oxford University Press, 2001).

[7] Crawford (n 3) 4–6.

[8] A pragmatic version of the constitutive view was proposed by Sir Hersch Lauterpacht who noted that *someone* has to ascertain if/when an emerging community fulfils the requirements for statehood and, in the absence of an impartial international organ, that task must be fulfilled by states. To him, the valid objection was not against the constitutive view as such but instead that states treat recognition as a matter of policy and not of legal duty, see Sir Hersch Lauterpacht, *Recognition in International Law* (Cambridge University Press, 1947) 55.

established (primarily Western) states to deny 'non-civilized' nations inclusion in the society of nations.[9]

In its practical application, the constitutive approach to recognition is highly problematic. For one thing, there is the issue of the relativism inherent in the constitutive position. If a state only exists in relation to another state that has recognized its existence, it would seem that absolute existence is not possible. That seems hard to accept. Surely, an entity must be a state or not a state. Another difficulty relates to the question of quantity. If recognition is indeed required before an entity becomes a 'state', how many states must recognize it? And is the recognition of some states more important than that of other states?

Contemporary international law is based on the declaratory approach. Thus, according to article 3 of the 1933 Montevideo Convention on the Rights and Duties of States, the 'political existence of the State is independent of recognition by other States'.[10] Practice also widely supports a declaratory view. In a 1920 advisory opinion on the legal aspects of the Aaland Islands, an International Committee of Jurists stated that the recognition by a number of states of a new state of Finland did not in itself 'suffice to show that Finland, from this time onwards, became a sovereign state'.[11] Instead, the Committee relied on the 'conditions required for the formation of a sovereign State'.[12] In similar vein, a 1991 legal opinion by an Arbitration Commission on the situation regarding the disintegration of Yugoslavia noted that 'the existence or disappearance of the state is a question of fact' and 'that the effects of recognition by other states are purely declaratory'.[13] It also bears noting that non-recognized states are routinely the object of legal claims by non-recognizing states. An example is Israel that is repeatedly accused of violating international law by the same Arab states that refuse to recognize Israel's existence as a state.

Two points must be noted, however. First of all, in a very limited number of cases that we shall return to later in this section, statehood seems to have been denied to entities that would otherwise seem to fulfil the formal criteria on the basis of the principle that legal rights cannot arise from wrongful conduct (*ex injuria jus non oritur*). The second point worth making is that general rejection of the constitutive theory does not mean that acts of recognition are entirely irrelevant. Acts of recognition have evidentiary value in the sense that they reflect the fact that other states accept that an entity fulfils the conditions for statehood. Since membership of the UN is only open to states,[14] UN membership provides very strong

---

[9] Crawford (n 3) 13–16.

[10] Montevideo Convention on the Rights and Duties of States (adopted 26 December 1933, entered into force 26 December 1934), 165 LNTS 19, art. 3.

[11] See International Committee of Jurists, 'Report of the International Committee of Jurists entrusted by the Council of the League of Nations with the task of giving an advisory opinion upon the legal aspects of the Aaland Islands Question', League of Nations Official Journal, Special Supplement No. 3, October 1920, 8.

[12] Ibid.

[13] See the Arbitration Commission of the Peace Conference on Yugoslavia, Opinion No. 1 (20 November 1991). See also Opinion Nos 8 and 10 (both 4 July 1992).

[14] Charter of the United Nations (adopted 26 May 1945, entered into force 24 October 1945), art. 4(1).

evidence of statehood and effectively resolves the matter of contention about an entity's status as a state.[15] But UN membership is not a requirement. Switzerland did not join the UN until 2002 and no one claimed that it was not a state before that time. An example of an entity that appears to fulfil the formal requirements for statehood is Taiwan. However, due to its delicate relationship with mainland China, it maintains a policy of deliberate ambiguity about its status and has never formally proclaimed its independence.[16] Palestine is a special case. In November 2012, the UN General Assembly granted Palestine status as a 'non-member observer State'. On that basis, it may now be referred to as a state—at least for the purposes of the UN.[17] On 2 January 2015, Palestine acceded to the Rome Statute of the International Criminal Court.

Recognition is also important because it is often a precondition for the establishment of bilateral relations, including the initiation of diplomatic representations and treaty relations. So, while a lack of recognition will not invalidate statehood, it may have important practical consequences for the non-recognized state. In that regard, it is worth noting that states are not obliged to have diplomatic relations with each other. Nothing precludes a state from conditioning its recognition of an emerging state and the initiation of bilateral relations on conditions that may be stricter that those found in the Montevideo Convention (see Section 4.2.3). The recognition policies of the United States and the European Community (EC), as it then was, in relation to the new states that emerged as a consequence of the disintegration of the former Soviet Union and the former Yugoslavia after the end of the Cold war illustrate this point.[18] In addition to the traditional criteria for statehood, the United States and the EC conditioned their recognition on the new states' adherence to democracy and the rule of law, including the commitments in the Conference on Security and Co-operation in Europe's 1975 Helsinki Act and the 1990 Charter of Paris for a New Europe.[19] The United State and the EC thereby used the political act of recognition as an incentive for the emerging states to commit to policies that served the interests of the potentially recognizing actors. The message that was sent was that if the emerging states wanted to reap the many benefits of bilateral relations with the United States and the EC, such as foreign aid packages and trade agreements, they would have to commit to democratic principles.

---

[15] On recognition and the practice of the UN, see John Dugard, *Recognition and the United Nations* (Grotius, 1987).

[16] See the overview in Crawford (n 3) 198–221.

[17] GA Res. 67/19 (4 December 2012), UN Doc. A/RES/67/19, para. 2. See also Report by the Secretary-General, 'Status of Palestine in the United Nations' (2013), UN Doc. A/67/738; UN Office of Legal Affairs, 'Issues related to General Assembly resolution 67/19 on the status of Palestine in the United Nations' (21 December 2012).

[18] Sean D. Murphy, 'Democratic Legitimacy and the Recognition of States and Governments' (1999) 48 *International and Comparative Law Quarterly* 545.

[19] See 'Testimony by Ralph Johnson, Deputy Assistant Secretary of State for European and Canadian Affairs, 17 Oct 1991' (1991) 2(3) *Foreign Policy Bulletin* 42; the European Community, 'Declaration on the Guidelines on the Recognition of New States in Eastern Europe and in the Soviet Union' (16 December 1991).

4.2.3 **The Montevideo criteria and the requirements
of effectiveness**

The 1933 Montevideo Convention on the Right and Duties of States contains the most
authoritative and accepted criteria for statehood. According to the Convention's
article 1, a 'state' must possess the following:

(a) a permanent population;

(b) a defined territory;

(c) a government; and

(d) a capacity to enter into relations with other states.

The list of criteria is clearly based on notions of effectiveness.

The first condition is the existence of a *permanent population* and it simply requires
that *someone* has made the territory their home. It is not a requirement that the population in question has a certain size. In fact, the population of tiny island states, such as
Tuvalu and Nauru, are limited to, respectively, around 10,000 and 11,000 inhabitants.
In Europe, 'microstates' include Liechtenstein and San Marino. The requirement that
the population is 'permanent' makes it unclear whether a population that is entirely
composed of nomadic tribes suffices. In *Western Sahara*, the ICJ simply concluded
that nomadic people 'possessed rights, including some rights relating to the lands
through which they migrated'.[20]

The second requirement is a *defined territory*. Like the requirement of a permanent population does not exclude entities with small populations from statehood,
nothing precludes an entity with a tiny landmass from fulfilling the requirement of
a territory. As we have just seen, microstates such as Tuvalu and San Marino are also
'states' for the purposes of international law. In addition, the entity's boundaries
need not be precisely demarcated and settled.[21] As long as the authorities control a
consistent area of undisputed territory, an entity is likely to fulfil the requirement
of defined territory. The lack of a definite territorial delineation of parts of Israel,
for example, did not prevent its acceptance as a state by a majority of states. In a
similar vein, the political uncertainties about the exact location of a potential territorial border between Israel and Palestine are not decisive to the issue of Palestinian
statehood.

The third condition concerns the existence of a *government*. Before a territorial entity with a population can be considered a state, it must have someone who can exercise
control over the territory and ensure its compliance with international obligations.
There must be some sort of entity in charge of running affairs and able to answer to the
outside world. In its 1920 advisory opinion on the Aaland Islands, the International
Committee of Jurists found that Finland would not fulfil the conditions for statehood
until 'a stable political organisation had been created and until the public authorities

---

[20] *Western Sahara*, Advisory Opinion [1975] ICJ Rep 12, para. 152.
[21] See also *Monastery of Saint-Naoum*, Advisory Opinion, 1924, PCIJ, Series B, No. 9 and *North Sea
Continental Shelf (Germany v Denmark and Netherlands)*, Judgment [1969] ICJ Rep 3, para. 46.

had become strong enough to assert themselves throughout the territories of the State without the assistance of foreign troops'.[22]

International law is indifferent to the form of the government in question. It is not, therefore, a requirement under the Montevideo Convention that a government is democratically elected or otherwise governs according to the wishes of the population of the territory in question. What is decisive is that the government in question is effective. In practice, though, what 'effective' means can vary. It seems that there is a need to distinguish between, on the one hand, those situations where the entity attempts to secede from within an existing state structure, in which case the secession will often be contested, and, on the other, instances where the claim to statehood flows from a grant of independence to the territory by a former sovereign. While the criterion of effectiveness is applied strictly in the former situation, the standard appears to be less stringent in the second.[23] The government in question does not necessarily need to be in a position where it can exercise its authority throughout the entire territory.

The requirement of an effective government ceases to be relevant once a state *has been* established. Somalia is a good illustration. Although Somalia has essentially been without an effective governance for decades, no one disputes that it remains a state for the purposes of international law. Similar considerations apply to Syria in relation to the ongoing civil war.

The last of the four Montevideo criteria is the requirement that a state must have the *capacity to enter into relations with other states*. What is of importance here is *legal* rather than political or economic independence. In short, to be a state an entity must have the ability to act without legal interference from other states.[24] Importantly, commitments and obligations undertaken or imposed under international law are not an impediment to statehood. In 1931 in the *Austro-German Customs Union* case before the Permanent Court of International Justice (PCIJ), Judge Anzilotti summed it up when he stated that the conception of independence has:

> nothing to do with a State's subordination to international law or with the numerous and constantly increasing States of *de facto* dependence which characterize the relation of one country to other countries ... As long as ... restrictions do not place the State under the legal authority of another State, the former remains an independent State however extensive and burdensome those obligations may be.[25]

In many cases, it is the lack of legal independence that prevents an otherwise 'state-like' entity from fulfilling the conditions for statehood. Scotland, for example, has a permanent population, a defined territory and extensive home rule through a parliament in Edinburgh. But it is still formally part of the UK with the UK Parliament in London retaining important powers.[26] In a referendum in September 2014, a

---

[22] See *Aaland Islands* (n 11) 9.   [23] Crawford (n 3) 56–60.

[24] See also *Island of Palmas (Netherlands v United States)* (1928) II RIAA 829, 838 and the discussion in Crawford (n 3) 62–89.

[25] *Customs Regime Between Germany and Austria*, Individual Opinion by M. Anzilotti, 1931, PCIJ, Series A/B, No. 41, 58.

[26] See Scotland Act 1998 and Scotland Act 2012.

majority of the population of Scotland decided *not* to seek formal independence from the UK.[27] A somewhat similar situation is that relating to the status of Greenland. Despite the existence of a permanent population in Greenland, a clearly defined territory and widespread self-rule, Greenland remains part of the Kingdom of Denmark with important competences, including substantial treaty-making authority, vested in Copenhagen.[28]

Temporary interference with an established state's independence and ability to enter into relations with other states—for example, belligerent occupation such as Iraq's unlawful occupation of Kuwait in 1990–1991—does not alter statehood.[29]

4.2.4 **The issue of illegality in the creation of a state**

There have been a few isolated instances where an otherwise effective territorial entity has been created in a manner that is deemed to be so illegitimate that it is met with essentially unanimous rejection by the international society. In those rare cases, one would be hard pressed to argue that the entity in question should nevertheless still be considered as a state for the purposes of international law. Although state practice is not entirely consistent, the decisive factor seems to be that the potentially emerging state was created in flagrant violation of basic norms of international law, potentially of a *jus cogens* nature.[30] Practice would thereby seem to confirm the *ex injuria jus non oritur* principle according to which no legal rights can arise from wrongful conduct.

First of all, the case of Rhodesia strongly indicates that an otherwise effective territorial entity may effectively be prevented from becoming a state for the purposes of international law if its creation *violates the local population's right of self-determination*.[31] On 11 November 1965, a white minority government issued a declaration of independence in the British colony of (South) Rhodesia. Even though it appeared to fulfil the formal criteria for statehood, Rhodesia was met with overall rejection of its claim to statehood, including from both the UN General Assembly and the UN Security Council. In a series of resolutions, the Security Council called upon all states to refrain from recognizing the 'illegal racist minority regime' and explicitly referred to the new government as an 'illegal authority'.[32]

Secondly, the establishment of the Turkish Republic of Northern Cyprus (TRNC) indicates that a territorial entity *created through the unlawful use of force* may also be effectively barred from statehood under international law. The TRNC was established in 1974 by Turkish forces in the northern part of Cyprus following the ousting of the president of Cyprus. To date, the TRNC is only recognized by Turkey. But state practice is not consistent, and the case of Bangladesh illustrates that the use of unlawful

---

[27] BBC News, 'Scottish referendum: Scotland votes "No" to independence' (19 September 2014) http://www.bbc.com/news/uk-scotland-29270441 (accessed 28 July 2016).

[28] See Act of Greenland Self-Government (Act no. 473 of 12 June 2009).

[29] Crawford (n 3) 73–74.   [30] Ibid, 99–107.

[31] Ibid, 128–131. For more on the right to self-determination, see Section 4.2.5.

[32] See, respectively, SC Res. 216 (12 November 1965), UN Doc. S/RES/216 and SC Res. 217 (20 November 1965), UN Doc. S/RES/217.

force may not always be an insurmountable obstacle to achieving statehood. In 1971, after massive internal tension and disturbances, India invaded what was then part of Pakistan (East Pakistan) and thereby paved the way for the subsequent creation of an independent Bangladeshi state. The different treatment of the TRNC and Bangladesh may be explained by a number of factors. Leaving aside pure politics, it is possible that the geographic separation of East Pakistan/Bangladesh and Pakistan may have had an impact. It also bears noting that the population in the seceding territory in Pakistan had been subjected to massive human rights violations at the hands of the Pakistanis. But, whatever the motivations, it remains a fact that the exact relationship between the use of force and the right to self-determination is unclear. While a territorial entity created through the use of illegal force in violation of the right to self-determination of the population on the territory is unlikely to be accepted as a state, the result may be different if the unlawful force is used in order to further the realization of the self-determination of a population.[33]

4.2.5 **The right to self-determination**

One of the most debated issues in international law relates to the relationship between statehood and the right to self-determination. The right to self-determination stipulates that all peoples have a right to freely determine their political status and pursue their economic, social and cultural development.[34] Although the existence of a potential right to self-determination was touched upon prior to 1945,[35] it did not emerge as a fundamental principle of international law until the decolonization process after the end of the Second World War.[36] Today, the right is found in a number of important legal documents. It is, for instance, listed in article 1 of the UN Charter.[37] The General Assembly has also referred to the right in a number of important resolutions, including the 1970 Declaration on Principles of International Law concerning Friendly Relations and Co-operation among States in accordance with the UN Charter.[38] It is also mentioned in the first part of article 1 in the 1966 UN Covenant on Human Rights.[39] In the *East Timor* case, the ICJ stated that the right to self-determination is an essential principle of international law that has an *erga omnes* character.[40]

---

[33] See also the discussion in Crawford (n 3) 134–146.

[34] See generally Antonio Cassese, *Self-Determination of Peoples* (Cambridge University Press, 1995).

[35] See *Aaland Islands* (n 11) 5–6.

[36] See also Matthew Craven, 'Statehood, Self-Determination, and Recognition' in Malcolm D. Evans (ed), *International Law* (4th edn, Oxford University Press, 2014) 226–227.

[37] See also UN Charter art. 73.

[38] GA Res. 2625 (XXV) Declaration concerning Friendly Relations (24 October 1970), UN Doc. A/25/2625.

[39] See art. 1 in both the International Covenant on Civil and Political Rights (adopted 16 December 1966, entered into force 23 March 1976), 999 UNTS 171 (ICCPR) and the International Covenant on Economic, Social and Cultural Rights (adopted 16 December 1966, entered into force 3 January 1976), 993 UNTS 3 (ICESCR).

[40] *Case Concerning East Timor (Portugal v Australia)* [1995] ICJ Rep 90, para. 29. See also *Legal Consequences for States of the Continued Presence of South Africa in Namibia (South West Africa) Notwithstanding Security Council Resolution 276 (1970)*, Advisory Opinion [1971] ICJ Rep 16, 31; *Legal*

The right to self-determination has also been referred to as a core legal norm by national courts.[41]

The practical application of the right to self-determination has been fraught and contentious. In the decolonialization process, a large number of former colonies relied on the right and successfully acquired independent status. The grant of independence to these states followed the logic of a 1960 General Assembly Declaration on the Granting of Independence to Colonial Countries and Peoples.[42] But while it quickly became clear that self-determination could be translated into a right to statehood for people *under colonial rule*, it has been less obvious whether the right also supports claims of secession for other people. The question resurfaced after the end of the Cold War following the collapse of the Soviet Union and the chaotic disintegration of the Socialist Federal Republic of Yugoslavia.[43] More recently, the issue arose with regard to Kosovo after it declared its independence in 2008. After years of fruitless negotiations about the future political status of the territory, in February 2008 a newly formed Assembly of Kosovo declared Kosovo's independence from Serbia and the establishment of a sovereign state. In a 2010 advisory opinion on *Accordance with International Law of the Unilateral Declaration of Independence in Respect of Kosovo*, the ICJ did not offer its views on whether international law confers a positive entitlement to Kosovo to secede. The Court simply noted that international law did not preclude Kosovo from issuing a declaration of independence.[44]

The current status of the law was summarized in 1998 by the Canadian Supreme Court in an opinion regarding, among other things, whether international law gives the province of Quebec a right to secede. In *Reference re Secession of Quebec*, the Court made a distinction between 'internal' self-determination/autonomy and 'external' self-determination/right to statehood. It noted that the right to self-determination of a people is normally fulfilled by internal self-determination (autonomy) according to which a people pursue their political, economic, social and cultural development *within* the framework of an existing state. A right to external self-determination/statehood, on the other hand, only arises in the most extreme of cases.[45] Colonial people and others who may otherwise find themselves subject to alien subjugation, domination or exploitation have a right to external self-determination that may entitle them to create their own independent state.[46] That right, however, need not materialize

---

Consequences of the Construction of a Wall in Palestinian Territory, Advisory Opinion [2004] ICJ Rep 136, para. 88.

[41] See, inter alia, *Reference re Secession of Quebec* [1998] 2 SCR 217, para. 114.

[42] See, inter alia, GA Res. 1514 (XV) Declaration on the Granting of Independence to Colonial Countries and Peoples (14 December 1960), UN Doc. A/RES/1514(XV).

[43] See, inter alia, Alain Pellet, 'The Opinions of the Badinter Arbitration Committee: A Second Breath for the Self-Determination of Peoples' (1992) 3 *European Journal of International Law* 178.

[44] *Accordance with International Law of the Unilateral Declaration of Independence in Respect of Kosovo*, Advisory Opinion [2010] ICJ Rep 403.

[45] *Reference re Secession of Quebec* (n 41) para. 126. On the distinction between internal and external self-determination, see also Committee on the Elimination of Racial Discrimination, 'General Recommendation 21: The right to self-determination' (8 March 1996), UN Doc. A/51/18, para. 4.

[46] *Reference re Secession of Quebec* (n 41) paras 132–133.

in an actual claim for statehood. A people with a right to independence may decide that their interests as a people are best served by remaining within an existing
state. An example is Greenland. In 1953, on the basis of an amendment to the Danish
Constitution, the colony of Greenland became an integral part of the Kingdom of
Denmark. The amendment was approved by the National Council of Greenland,
and in a 1954 Resolution, the General Assembly noted that 'the people of Greenland
have freely exercised their right to self-determination'.[47] The Danish government has
consistently recognized that 'the people of Greenland is a people pursuant to international law with the right of self-determination'[48] and have also proclaimed that it
will not seek to prevent Greenlandic independence. Up until now, at least, the people
of Greenland have preferred to remain part of the Kingdom of Denmark albeit with
extensive self-rule.[49]

It is extremely doubtful whether a people who are neither colonized nor subject
to alien subjugation, domination or exploitation can claim a right to external self-
determination/statehood.[50] Such peoples must exercise their right to self-determination within an existing state. Exceptions to this principle must require a situation
of extreme oppression and the almost total denial of meaningful internal self-determination for a people.[51] To that end, it should be noted that there is a clear trade-off
between the rights of the people who want their own state and the maintenance of
international peace and stability. While it is easy to sympathize with a host of 'peoples' around the world who feel that they deserve to have their own independent state,
predictability and global stability speak clearly in favour of keeping the territorial integrity of the 'mother-state' intact and require people to pursue their right to self-
determination within their existing state.[52] As we saw in Chapter 1, when balancing
'justice' and order, international law often prioritizes the latter. The need for order and
respect for existing territorial borders is reflected in the so-called 'safeguard clause'
that was first introduced in the 1970 Declaration on Friendly Relations.[53] The clause
stipulates that there can be no question of remedial secession in a state where the government represents the whole of the people or peoples within its territory on a basis of
equality and without discrimination.[54]

4.2.6 The acquisition of new territory

An issue that is somewhat related to statehood and the conditions for the creation
of states is that of an existing state's acquisition of additional territory. A state can
acquire title to new territory in a number of ways. First, a state can purchase territory from another state through *cession*. There are many historical examples of such

---

[47] See also GA Res. 849 (IX) (22 November 1954), UN Doc. A/RES/849(IX).
[48] Preamble to Act of Greenland Self-Government (n 28).
[49] For the latest grant of devolution, see n 28.
[50] *Reference re Secession of Quebec* (n 41) para. 138.   [51] See also Crawford (n 3) 119.
[52] See also *Aaland Islands* (n 11) 5.
[53] Declaration concerning Friendly Relations (n 38) para. 5(7).
[54] See also *Reference re Secession of Quebec* (n 41) para. 130.

'land purchases'. Among the more well known are the purchase by the United States of Alaska from Russia in 1867 and its 1917 acquisition of the Danish West Indies from Denmark. After the end of the Cold War, the United States also indicated that it would be interested in purchasing Greenland from Denmark.[55] Cession of territory was also the primary method by which European states acquired territory in Africa and Asia during the period of colonialization.[56] Cession of territory is governed by a few basic principles. The state that acquires the territory cannot obtain more rights to the territory than those possessed by the ceding state. Additionally, the acquiring state must respect the potential rights of third states.[57] Acquisition of territory by cession may be the result of an agreement to solve a border dispute between two or more states. The mutual transfer of territory—'land swap'—is, for example, likely to be an important element in a future final peace agreement between Israel and Palestine.[58]

The second way that a state can acquire title to new territory is through *accretion* where new land is gradually created naturally. On rare occasions, new islands are formed by volcanic eruption. In 1963, for example, volcanic eruptions off the coast of Iceland created the—new—island of Surtsey. The formation of new territory must be the result of natural forces, however, and man-made features are not covered. Artificial accretion will only be accepted as new territory if it does not infringe the rights of other states or if those states have given their consent. For a number of years, China has been constructing a string of artificial 'islands' on maritime features, such as reefs and low-tide elevations in the South China Sea. These entities cannot form the basis of Chinese claims to title in the areas in question. This was also the conclusion reached by a court of arbitration in a July 2016 award in the *South China Sea Arbitration*.[59] The court considered that the 'status of a feature be ascertained on the basis of its earlier, natural condition, prior to the onset of significant human modification'.[60] Very sudden or violent changes, for example as a result of storms or natural disasters, are referred to as *avulsion*. The distinction between accretion and avulsion is relevant in relation to alterations of rivers that form the territorial boundary between two states. It is only when a change to the course of the river is caused by accretion that it will move the boundary line between the two states.[61] *Erosion* is the opposite of accretion and refers to the gradual disappearance of territory caused by natural forces.

The next two means of acquiring title to additional territory bear certain similarities. The principles of *occupation* stipulate that a state can obtain title to territory that has never been the subject of any state—also known as *terra nullius* or simply

---

[55] Dansk Udenrigspolitisk Institut, 'Danmark under Den Kolde Krig' (1997).

[56] See Crawford (n 3) 266.   [57] *Island of Palmas* (n 24) 842.

[58] According to confidential documents leaked by Al Jazeera in 2011, the Israeli government and the leadership of the Palestinian Authority have been negotiating the mutual exchange of territory as an element in the peace process, see 'Summary of Olmert's "Package" Offer to Abu Mazen' (31 August 2008) http://transparency.aljazeera.net/files/4736.PDF (accessed 28 July 2016).

[59] *The Republic of the Philippines and the People's Republic of China (Award)*, PCA Case No. 2013-19, 12 July 2016.

[60] Ibid, para. 306. See also para. 511.

[61] *The Chamizal Case (Mexico v United States)* (1911) XI RIAA 309.

'no-man's land'.[62] As a legal concept, *terra nullius* is different from that of '*res communis*' that refer to an area that is not subject to the legal title of any state. The best example of the latter is the high seas.[63] Title is acquired when the state demonstrates that it exercises effective control over the territory and that it has the intention of obtaining title. While occupation is of limited relevance today, it was the basis for a range of historical claims to territory 'discovered' by European explorers, including Australia and the South Island of New Zealand.[64] Another historical example of a claim to title over *terra nullius* is the case of Svalbard (formerly known as Spitzbergen), an archipelago to the north of continental Europe in the Arctic Ocean.[65] While occupation is the means whereby a state acquires title to territory that does not belong to anyone, it is through *prescription* that it may gain title to territory previously under the sovereignty of another state. In contrast to occupation, the acquisition of territory by prescription is derived from the existence of a form of implied consent on the part of the state whose rights are being displaced by the acquiring state. The element of consent means that the acts of the acquiring state must be peaceful and that sustained protests and objections by the 'old' state will prevent prescription.[66]

In practice, it may be difficult to ascertain if a state's attempt to acquire territory should rightfully be considered as a case of occupation or one of prescription. Most territorial disputes involve contesting claims by states that have performed a series of more or less 'sovereign' acts. In most cases, title over the disputed territory will not be awarded because one of the states has been able to prove beyond any doubt that it holds title over the territory but, rather, because it has a claim that is superior to that of a competing state. Regardless of whether a claim to title is based in occupation or prescription, it must rest on the *effective possession* of the territory. The leading case on the issue of acquisition of territory remains Judge Huber's 1928 arbitral award in the *Island of Palmas* case.[67] The dispute originated in Spain's 1898 cession of the Philippines to the United States. The Netherlands and the United States were in disagreement about whether the cession included the Island of Palmas that is an isolated island located around halfway between the outermost island in the Philippines and the closest island in a group of islands that belonged at that time to the Netherlands. Judge Huber ruled in favour of the Netherlands and articulated the principle that 'the continuous and peaceful display of territorial sovereignty is as good as title'.[68] While the initial discovery of an as yet unknown territory could establish 'inchoate' title, the initial act of discovery must be followed up by effective occupation of the territory within a reasonable time.[69]

The requirement that a state must 'display territorial sovereignty' means that it must have behaved as a state in the disputed territory. The degree of sovereignty will vary according to the territory in question and even limited exercises of sovereignty

[62] *Western Sahara* (n 20) para. 79.   [63] See also Chapter 8.   [64] Crawford (n 3) 265–266.
[65] Geir Ulfstein, *The Svalbard Treaty: From Terra Nullius to Norwegian Sovereignty* (Aschehoug, 1995).
[66] *Land and Maritime Boundary between Cameroon and Nigeria (Cameroon v Nigeria: Equatorial Guinea intervening)*, Judgment [2002] 1CJ Rep 303, paras 67, 70.
[67] *Island of Palmas* (n 24).   [68] Ibid, 839.   [69] Ibid, 845–846. See also Crawford (n 3) 271.

may suffice in isolated and sparsely populated territory, such as remote islands or in areas of inhospitable terrain.[70] In the *Eastern Greenland* case, the Danish display of sovereignty mainly consisted of minimal acts of administration and the granting of concession rights in the area. Since what is decisive is the display of sovereignty, acts performed by private citizens or private companies without the assistance of state authorities does not count. It is also worth mentioning that the public acts must reflect an intention on the part of the state to acquire title.

A few more points are worth noting in relation to establishing title to contested territory. For one thing, geographical contiguity is not in itself decisive. It may well be the case that a contested island is not awarded to the state whose mainland is in closest proximity.[71] In addition, cases involving disputed territory often require the determination of a so-called 'critical date'. This is the moment at which the potential rights of the parties manifested themselves to such an extent that subsequent acts could not alter the legal positions of the parties. In the *Pulau Ligitan* case, the ICJ stated that it could not:

> take into consideration acts having taken place after the date on which the dispute between the Parties crystallized unless such acts are a normal continuation of prior acts and are not undertaken for the purpose of improving the legal position of the Party which relies on them.[72]

In the *Island of Palmas* case, the critical date was the date of Spain's cession of the Philippines to the United States. The identification of the critical date is important because the doctrine of 'intertemporal law' stipulates that the law to be applied in a concrete case is that which existed at the critical date. Thus, when Judge Huber decided who had title to the Island of Palmas in 1923, he relied on the law as it existed at the critical date in 1898.[73]

A final point must be made in relation to the acquisition of territory by prescription. An apparent display of sovereignty will not prevail and secure title to territory if another state can prove the existence of a pre-existing legal right to the territory, such as a treaty-based title. Thus, as the ICJ has stated in a number of cases, while a display of sovereignty may confirm legal title, it cannot by itself alter it. In the *Frontier Dispute* case, the Court stated that if the disputed territory 'is effectively administered by a State other than the one possessing the legal title, preference should be given to the holder of the title'.[74]

For most of history, *conquest* of territory through the use of force was a recognized means of acquiring title. This, however, is no longer the case. A state's military

---

[70] See also *Island of Palmas* (n 24) 840; *Legal Status of Eastern Greenland*, 1933, PCIJ, Series A/B, No. 53, pp. 50–51/32–33.

[71] *Island of Palmas* (n 24) 854-5. See also *Territorial and Maritime Dispute between Nicaragua and Honduras in the Caribbean Sea (Nicaragua v Honduras)*, Judgment [2007] ICJ Rep 659, para. 161.

[72] *Sovereignty over Pulau Ligitan and Pulau Sipadan (Indonesia v Malaysia)*, Judgment [2002] ICJ Rep 625, para. 135.

[73] *Island of Palmas* (n 24) 845–846.

[74] *Frontier Dispute (Burkina Faso v Mali)*, Judgment [1986] ICJ Rep 554, para. 63. See also *Land and Maritime Boundary* (n 66) paras 67–70.

occupation of the territory of another state will generally activate the international rules on belligerent occupation and the rights and obligations they entail, but the presence of the foreign state is considered to be of a temporary nature that does not result in a transfer of sovereignty.[75] The sovereign that is displaced by the occupation merely loses *de facto* possession of the territory but not *de jure* possession.[76] As Oppenheim famously stated, there 'is not an atom of sovereignty in the authority of the occupant'.[77] The prohibition against forceful territorial acquisitions is reflected in the 1970 General Assembly Resolution on Friendly Relation.[78] Thus, the Iraqi attempt to annex Kuwait following its invasion of that state in 1990 was unanimously rejected as having no legal validity.[79] In a similar vein, in the absence of an agreement to the contrary, Israel cannot obtain sovereignty over those parts of Palestine that it occupies.[80] With the exception of East Jerusalem and the Golan Heights, the latter of which has been annexed by Israel, this is also acknowledged by the Israeli Supreme Court.[81] On 18 March 2014, Russia annexed the Crimean Peninsula in Ukraine after a Russian intervention and a local referendum in which an overwhelming majority voted to leave Ukraine.[82] The General Assembly responded by reaffirming that state territory shall not be the object of acquisition by force and that attempts to disrupt the territorial integrity of a state are incompatible with the purposes and principles of the Charter.[83] It also underscored that the local referendum had no validity and 'cannot form the basis for any alteration of the status' of the area.[84]

4.2.7 **State succession**

It is vital for the maintenance of international stability and predictability that international society is able to manage the disappearance of old states or the emergence of new states in a stable and predictable manner. As a concept under international law, 'state succession' concerns 'the replacement of one state by another in the responsibility for the international relations of territory'.[85] Issues of state succession can arise

---

[75] See also SC Res. 252 (21 May 1968), UN Doc. S/RES/252.

[76] See also Yoram Dinstein, *The International Law of Belligerent Occupation* (Cambridge University Press, 2009) 49–50.

[77] Lassa Oppenheim, 'The Legal Relations between an Occupying Power and its Inhabitants' (1971) 33 *Law Quarterly Review* 363, 364. See also *Construction of a Wall* (n 40).

[78] Declaration concerning Friendly Relations (n 38).

[79] See, inter alia, SC Res. 662 (9 August 1990), UN Doc. S/RES/662.

[80] SC Res. 252 (21 May 1968), UN Doc. S/RES/252. See also SC Res. 478 (20 August 1980), UN Doc. S/RES/478; *Construction of a Wall* (n 40) para. 78.

[81] CA 1432/03, *Yinon Production and Marketing of Food Products Ltd v Qaraan et al.* [2004] 59(1) PD 345, 355–356.

[82] Steven Lee Myers and Ellen Barry, 'Putin Reclaims Crimea for Russia and Bitterly Denounces the West', *New York Times* (18 March 2014) http://www.nytimes.com/2014/03/19/world/europe/ukraine.html?_r=0 (accessed 28 July 2016).

[83] See the Preamble to GA Res. 68/262 (27 March 2014), UN Doc. A/68/L.39 and Add.1.

[84] Ibid, para. 5.

[85] Vienna Convention on Succession of States in Respect to Treaties (adopted 23 August 1978, entered into force 6 November 1996), 1946 UNTS 3, art. 2(1)(b).

in many circumstances and the legal regime governing successions is among the most complicated and disputed in international law. International law contains two conventions on state succession, the 1978 Vienna Convention on Succession of States in Respect of Treaties and the 1983 Vienna Convention on Succession of States in Respect of State Property, Archives and Debts. Although the latter is not yet in force, many of its provisions reflect customary international law.

Changes of statehood always raise a host of important legal questions, including issues relating to the status of existing treaties, membership of international organizations and nationality. The practical manner in which succession is dealt with varies from case to case and in many instances the 'old' and the 'new' states will settle the most important issues in a bilateral treaty. But whenever a new territorial entity emerges it is necessary to initially determine if the entity should be considered as a continuation of a pre-existing state or as a completely new and separate entity. When the Soviet Union disintegrated, the Russian Federation was generally considered to constitute the continuation of that state, albeit, of course, with a smaller territory. Russia was therefore allowed to continue the membership of the Soviet Union in relevant international organizations, including the UN. The outcome was different when the Socialist Federal Republic of Yugoslavia fell apart. In that case, the disintegration of the Yugoslavian state was considered to be so profound that it had ceased to exist as a 'state' for the purposes of international law.[86] As a result, Serbia and Montenegro was not allowed to simply continue the now dissolved Yugoslavian 'mother-state'.[87] Among other things, Serbia was denied the right to continue Yugoslavia's membership of the UN.[88] Issues of state succession also arise when two states merge and form a single state. In the case of the 1990 German unification, the German Democratic Republic was technically assimilated into the Federal Republic of Germany.[89]

The rules on succession to treaties are complex and largely depend on the subject matter at hand. But as a point of departure it will often make sense to accept that the emerging state is not bound by the treaties and agreements that were concluded by its predecessor. There are, however, a number of exceptions to this so-called 'clean slate' approach. The principle of *uti possidetis juris* stresses that geographical boundaries created by treaties remain in force regardless of whether or not the boundaries coincide with ethnic, tribal, religious or political affiliations.[90] Predictability and stability would be greatly jeopardized if territorial boundaries were subject to negotiation whenever a state changed its legal status. In the *Frontier Dispute* case, the ICJ applied the *uti possidetis* principle to an old colonial border and noted its 'exceptional importance for the African continent'.[91] This principle has also been applied in non-colonial

---

[86] See the Arbitration Commission of the Peace Conference on Yugoslavia, Opinion No. 8.

[87] Ibid, Opinion No. 10.

[88] See, inter alia, SC Res. 757 (30 May 1992), UN Doc. S/RES/757 and SC Res. 777 (19 September 1992), UN Doc. S/RES/777.

[89] Treaty on the Final Settlement with Respect to Germany (12 September 1990).

[90] Vienna Convention on Succession of States in Respect to Treaties (n 85) art. 11.

[91] *Frontier Dispute* (n 74) 20.

settings and to internal boundaries. In the *Territorial Dispute* case, the ICJ rightly noted that a boundary agreed upon in a treaty, 'achieves a permanence which the treaty itself does not necessarily enjoy. The treaty can cease to be in force without in any way affecting the continuance of the boundary.'[92]

If a state disintegrates and ceases to exist, as was the case with the former Yugoslavia, the clean-slate approach means that the population of the succeeding territory cases to be protected by human rights conventions until the emerging state decides to become a party. The UN Human Rights Committee has therefore adopted the view in a General Comment that protection under the UN Covenant on Civil and Political Rights, continues 'notwithstanding change in government of the State party, including dismemberment in more than one State or State succession'.[93] The Comment is not legally binding, though. In the *Genocide* case, two of the ICJ judges concluded that the Genocide Convention 'does not come to an end with the dismemberment of the original State, as it transcends the concept of State sovereignty'.[94]

4.2.8 Extinction

Once a state has been established, it is almost impossible for it to lose its statehood involuntarily. As we have already seen, the absence of an effective government, as is presently the case in both Somalia and Syria, will not cause a state to cease being a state, and a state will similarly not be extinguished through the unlawful use of force and subsequent efforts of annexation by another state, as was the case with Iraq's invasion of Kuwait in 1990.[95] As the disintegration of Yugoslavia illustrates, however, a state may cease to exist if it disintegrates and subsequent splits into a range of new states. A state may, of course, alter its legal status of its own free will and dissolve itself. Two or more states may decide to merge into a single state as occurred in 1990 with the unification of the German Democratic Republic (GDR, East Germany) and the Federal Republic of Germany (FRG, West Germany). Another example was the merger in the same year of North Yemen and South Yemen into a unified Republic of Yemen. A state may also cease to exist on a voluntary basis if it decides to split into two or more independent states. This took place in 1993 when the Czech Republic and Slovakia were created from the former state of Czechoslovakia.

---

[92] *Territorial Dispute (Libyan Arab Jamahiriya v Chad)*, Judgment [1994] 1CJ Rep 6, para. 73.

[93] Human Rights Committee, 'CCPR General Comment No. 26: Continuity of Obligations' (8 December 1997), UN Doc. CCPR/C/21/Rev.1/Add.8/Rev.1, para. 4.

[94] *Application of the Convention on the Prevention and Punishment of the Crime of Genocide*, Preliminary Objections, Separate Opinion of Judge Weeramantry [1996] ICJ Rep 595, 646. See also Separate Opinion of Judge Shahabuddeen, 636.

[95] On the rare cases of so-called *debellation*, see Michael N. Schmitt, 'Debellation' in Rüdiger Wolfrum (ed.), *Max Planck Encyclopedia of Public International law* (Oxford University Press, 2009).

4.3 International organizations

The international organization is an actor that plays an increasing role in international law. International organizations come in many forms and an all-encompassing definition of is not easy to find. The most authoritative definition is found in the International Law Commission's (ILC's) 2011 Draft Articles on the Responsibility of International Organizations. Here, an international organization is defined as:

> an organization established by a treaty or other instrument governed by international law and possessing its own international legal personality. International organizations may include as members, in addition to States, other entities.[96]

International organizations are created by treaty and they must not therefore be confused with so-called Non-Governmental Organizations (NGOs) that are private entities without legal personality in international law.[97] Organizations such as the UN, the North Atlantic Treaty Organization (NATO) and the institutions of the EU are international organizations whereas entities like Amnesty International, Human Rights Watch and the World Wildlife Federation (WWF) are NGOs.

The first international organizations were created in the 19th century when organizations such as the International Telegraphic Union and the Universal Postal Union were established in order to further technical cooperation and facilitate international communications. As the historical overview in Chapter 1 illustrated, however, it was not until after the turn of century that states began to set up organizations to deal with more contentious political matters, including issues relating to peace and security. The first such organization was the League of Nations that was created after the end of the First World War to maintain world peace. After the end of the Second World War, the League was replaced with the UN that quickly established itself as an umbrella organization for a myriad of international organizations. That period also saw the birth of a variety of regional organizations of great importance, including NATO, the European Coal and Steel Community that would eventually develop into the EU and the Council of Europe.[98]

The UN remains by the far most important international organization with a global reach. Its membership is practically universal and, as we shall see throughout this book, it covers a wide range of activities of vital importance to the effective functioning of international society. In addition, as noted in Chapter 2, it is generally presumed that obligations undertaken under the UN Charter must prevail over potentially competing international obligations.[99] Since most of the important

---

[96] ILC, Draft Articles on the Responsibility of International Organizations (2011), UN Doc. A/66/10, art. 2(a).

[97] See also Section 4.5 and the special case of the ICRC.

[98] See also Chapter 1. For a treatment of the Council of Europe, see Chapter 9.

[99] UN Charter art. 103.

features of the UN are dealt with elsewhere in this book, only a few of its characteristics will be noted here.

The UN is composed of six principal organs. The *General Assembly* has the competence to discuss and make recommendations on all matters that fall within the scope of the organization's constituent treaty—the UN Charter.[100] All 193 members of the UN have a seat in the Assembly. The *Security Council* is endowed with primary responsibility for maintaining international peace and security and is composed of 15 members, including five permanent members who retain a veto power. As discussed in more detail in Chapter 13, the Council possesses wide-ranging powers. The *Secretariat*, headed by the Secretary-General who is usually selected for a term of five years, services the different UN organs. António Guterres took over as Secretary-General at the beginning of 2017, following Ban Ki-moon who had been in the role since 2007. The *Economic and Social Council* (ECOSOC) holds the primary responsibility for economic and social matters within the UN and is composed of 54 members. Over the years, it has established a wide range of subsidiary organs. The *International Court of Justice* is the principal judicial organ of the UN. Its competences are dealt with in Chapter 12. The final principal organ of the UN is the now suspended *Trustee Council* which was set up to administer the Trustee system.

International organizations have the rights and obligations accorded to them by states.[101] This generally includes a power to conclude necessary agreements governed by international law[102] and immunity from the exercise of jurisdiction by national courts.[103] In the *Reparations* case, the ICJ clarified that the UN is a legal subject under international law capable of possessing international rights and duties and with a capacity to protect its rights by bringing international claims for injury to its personnel.[104] As noted in Chapter 3, the Court also stated that the extent of an organization's rights and obligations depend on 'its purposes and functions as specified or implied in its constituent documents and developed in practice'.[105] We shall see in Chapter 7 that international organizations may also be held responsible for breaching their legal obligations.[106]

---

[100] Ibid, art. 10. On the legal status of the resolutions by the General Assembly, see Chapter 2.

[101] *Legality of the Use of Nuclear Weapons in Times of Armed Conflict*, Advisory Opinion [1996] ICJ Rep 226, para. 25.

[102] See Vienna Convention on the Law of Treaties between States and International Organizations or between International Organizations (1986).

[103] *Difference Relating to Immunity from Legal Process of a Special Rapporteur of the Commission on Human Rights*, Advisory Opinion [1999] ICJ Rep 1999, 62.

[104] *Reparations for Injuries Suffered in the Service of the United Nations*, Advisory Opinion [1949] ICJ Rep 174, 179.

[105] Ibid, 180, 182. See also *Jurisdiction of the European Commission of the Danube between Galatz and Braila*, Advisory Opinion, 1927, PCIJ, Series B, No. 14, 64.

[106] See also ILC, Draft Articles on the Responsibility of International Organizations (n 96) art. 3.

4.4 Individuals

Like international organizations, individuals possess those rights and obligations that states bestow on them.[107] In the *LaGrand* case, the ICJ concluded that the United States had violated its obligations not only to Germany but also to two German nationals when it brought criminal proceedings against the German nationals without informing them of their rights under the Vienna Convention on Consular Relations. The Court noted that the clarity of the relevant provisions of the Vienna Convention, viewed in their context, 'admits of no doubt'. They created individual rights which 'may be invoked in this Court by the national State of the detained person'.[108] It is primarily in human rights law that international law bestows *rights* on individuals. As we shall discuss in more detail in Chapter 9, up until the middle of the 20th century the manner in which states dealt with their own citizens was generally of no concern to international law. Things began to change after the end of the Second World War when states adopted conventions bestowing rights on individuals under international law. As we shall see in Chapters 11 and 14, the increasing protection of the rights of individuals is also noticeable in international economic law, including in relation to the protection of foreign investments, and in the laws of armed conflict.

States have also imposed *obligations* under international law on individuals. In 1946, the International Military Tribunal (IMT) at Nuremberg famously rejected the argument that international law cannot serve as the basis for the criminal prosecution of individuals.

> Crimes against International Law are committed by men, not by abstract entities, and only by punishing individuals who commit such crimes can the provisions of International Law be enforced.[109]

As we will see in more detail in Chapter 15, individual responsibility under international law primarily manifests itself in relation to crimes deemed particularly serious by international society. The earliest example is the crime of piracy. More recently, the hijacking of aircraft, crimes against peace, crimes against humanity and war crimes have been added to the list of crimes under which individuals hold international responsibility.

4.5 Other actors in international law

4.5.1 Territorial entities other than states

States are not the only territorial entities that may possess rights and obligations under international law. In fact, there are numerous historical examples of *territorial entities*

---

[107] See the thorough overview in Kjeldgaard-Pedersen (n 3). For early jurisprudence, see *Jurisdiction of the Courts of Danzig*, Advisory Opinion, 1928, PCIJ, Series B, No. 15, 17–18.

[108] *LaGrand (Germany v United States)*, Judgment [2001] ICJ Rep 466, para. 77.

[109] *Judgment of the Nuremberg International Military Tribunal 1946* (1947) 41 *American Journal of International Law* 172, 221.

other than states with international legal personality. In most cases, the creation and management of the entities has been governed by treaty, as was the case in relation to the governing of Berlin from the end of the Second World War to the unification of Germany in 1990. Another example of international administration of territory was the post-First World War mandate system created by League of Nations for the administration of a number of territories that had belonged to the defeated states in the war.[110] The mandate system was replaced by a trustee system after the dissolution of the League of Nations and the creation of the UN.[111] When South Africa refused to place the territory of South-West Africa (today, Namibia) under UN trusteeship, the ICJ concluded that the presence of South Africa in the territory was illegal.[112] More recent examples of international administration of territories include the different UN regimes established with regard to the preparation of East Timor for independence after decades of Indonesian occupation[113] and the administration of Kosovo after the civil war in the former Yugoslavia.[114]

As noted previously, *Taiwan* does not claim to be a state. The territory does, however, possess separate legal personality with regard to at least certain issues, including in area of the law of the sea. It also has relations with several international organizations.[115] *Hong Kong* is another territorial entity with a degree of legal personality under international law. Since China took over the territory in 1997 from the UK, its status has been one of a 'Special Administrative Region' in China with the competence to enter into international agreements and participate in some international organizations.[116] Reference should also be made to the *Holy See* that serves to support the Holy See as a religious institution. Italy has recognized the Holy See as the holder of exclusive sovereignty and jurisdiction over the Vatican City in Rome, Italy.[117] As a legal person, the Holy See is a *sui generis* entity. It is, for example, a party to many treaties and also has diplomatic relations with a substantial number of states.

4.5.2 **Groups of individuals**

As collective entities, groups of individuals may also have legal personality. As we saw earlier in the chapter, the right to self-determination is based on the notion that *peoples* possess certain rights under international law. *Indigenous groups* are another example. In 2007, the General Assembly adopted a Declaration on the Rights of Indigenous Peoples.[118] Among other things, the Declaration stipulates that indigenous people have a right to the full enjoyment as a collective or as individuals of

---

[110] Covenant of the League of Nations (adopted 28 June 1919, entered into force 10 January 1920) art. 22.

[111] See Chapters XII and XIII of the UN Charter.

[112] *Namibia* (n 40). See also SC Res. 264 (20 March 1969), UN Doc. S/RES/264.

[113] See SC Res. 1272 (25 October 1999), UN Doc. S/RES/1272.

[114] SC Res. 1244 (10 June 1999), UN Doc. S/RES/1244.   [115] Crawford (n 3) 198–221.

[116] Sun Zhichao, 'International Legal Personality of the Hong Kong Special Administrative Region' (2008) 7 *Chinese Journal of International Law* 339.

[117] Lateran Treaty (adopted 11 February 1929) art. 3.

[118] GA Res. 61/295 Declaration on the Rights of Indigenous Peoples (13 September 2007), UN Doc. A/RES/295.

all human rights and fundamental freedoms and have the right to be free from any kind of discrimination.[119] *Insurgent groups* and *national liberation movements* are also endowed with rights and obligations in international law, most notably within the laws of armed conflict.[120] For example, the 1977 Additional Protocol I to the 1949 Geneva Conventions specifies that national liberation movements may under certain circumstances have rights and obligations under the Protocol. Such groups may also be granted a right to conclude treaties.

4.5.3 **Private corporations**

Whether *private corporations* have rights and—in particular—obligations under international law has been the focus of increasing attention, including in the field of human rights. In practice, rights may under certain circumstances be bestowed on private corporations under international human rights law and particularly in international economic law. As for obligations, there is a booming literature in the area of so-called 'Corporate Social Responsibility' (CSR) and in 2011 the UN Human Rights Council adopted a number of Guiding Principles on Business and Human Rights that stress the obligations of states to respect, protect and fulfil human rights and fundamental freedoms.[121] The Guiding Principles are not legally binding, however, and at present the obligations that corporations undertake in that area remain voluntary. International law does not, for example, recognize 'international corporate crimes'. Nevertheless, in some circumstances a contractual relationship between a state and a corporation will be governed by international law. For example, concession agreements for the extraction of oil are often 'internationalized'.[122]

4.6 **Non-Governmental Organizations**

Non-governmental organizations, including such organizations as Amnesty International, Human Rights Watch and environmental organizations, have a growing influence on the processes that lead to the creation of international law. In many cases, they enhance enforcement of international law by proving vital information to monitoring bodies. They also contribute to better transparency in international decision-making. Their increasing role is reflected in the 1991 European Convention on the Recognition of the Legal Personality of International NGOs and in the 1998 UN Declaration on the Rights of Human Rights Defenders. Currently, however, NGOs do not possess rights or obligations under international law and as such they do not possess legal personality. There are exceptions, however, and one of these relates to the

---

[119] Ibid, arts 1–2.

[120] See Liesbeth Zegveld, *Accountability of Armed Opposition Groups in International Law* (Cambridge University Press, 2008).

[121] See UNHRC Res. 17/4 (16 June 2011), UN Doc. A/HRC/17/L.17/Rev.1.

[122] See, inter alia, *Texaco Overseas Petroleum Co. v The Government of the Libyan Arab Republic* (1979) *Yearbook of Commercial Arbitration* 53, 177ff.

status of the *International Committee of the Red Cross* (ICRC). Although the ICRC is a private organization, its mandate (the provision of protection and assistance to victims in times of armed conflict) is grounded in international conventions.

Summary

The answer to the question of who international law actually applies to is traditionally found in the concepts of 'legal subjectivity' or 'legal personality'. Since being a subject or having 'personality' in a legal system means having the capacity to hold rights, powers and obligations that can be enforced in that system, the subjects of international law are those to whom the international legal system gives exercisable rights, powers and obligations. Importantly, though, not all participants in the international legal system hold the same rights and obligations and legal personality is a relative concept. International society is first and foremost a society of individual states and states remain the most central actor possessing those capacities in international law. States are not the only actors in international law, however, and other actors with rights and obligations under international law have been created. Such actors will possess the powers they are given by states. Apart from states, the primary actors are international organizations and individuals.

Recommended reading

On the issue of legal personality, see Roland Portmann, *Legal Personality in International Law* (Cambridge University Press, 2010); Rosalyn Higgins, *Problems & Process* (Oxford University Press, 1994) ch. 3; Jean d'Aspremont (ed.), *Participants in the International Legal System* (Routledge, 2011).

On statehood, see the seminar work by James Crawford, *The Creation of States in International Law* (2nd edn, Oxford University Press, 2006). See also Matthew Craven, 'Statehood, Self-Determination, and Recognition' in Malcolm D. Evans (ed.), *International Law* (4th edn, Oxford University Press, 2014).

A classic work on the role of recognition is Sir Hersch Lauterpacht, *Recognition in International Law* (Cambridge University Press, 1947). See also Stefan Talmon, *Recognition of Government in International Law: With Particular Reference to Governments in Exile* (Oxford University Press, 2001); John Dugard, *Recognition and the United Nations* (Grotius, 1987).

For a presentation and discussion of the right to self-determination, see Antonio Cassese, *Self-Determination of Peoples* (Cambridge University Press, 1995).

On international organizations under international law, see C. F. Amerasinghe, *Principles of the International Law of International Organizations* (2nd edn, Cambridge University Press, 2005); Jan Klabbers, *An Introduction to International Institutional Law* (Cambridge University Press, 2009); Dapo Akande, 'International Organizations' in Malcolm D. Evans (ed.), *International Law* (4th edn, Oxford University Press, 2014).

A solid discussion of the individual as a legal person is contained in Astrid Kjeldgaard-Pedersen, 'The International Legal Personality of Individuals' (forthcoming). See also

Robert McCorquodale, 'The Individual and the International Legal System' in Malcolm D. Evans (ed.), *International Law* (4th edn, Oxford University Press, 2014).

Questions for discussion

1. Why is legal personality a relative concept?

2. What is the problem with the two approaches to the role of recognition (the declaratory and the constitutive)?

3. What is the difference between an internal and an external right to self-determination? Why is the distinction important?

4. Does Kosovo have a right to secede from Serbia?

5. What did Judge Huber mean when he stated that 'the continuous and peaceful display of territorial sovereignty is as good as title'?

6. Is Palestine a state for the purposes of international law?

7. From where do international organizations derive their legal personality? How do you determine the extent of an international organization's rights and obligations under international law?

8. When it comes to the issue of statehood, can you provide some examples of where there might be a tension between, on the one hand, notions of justice and, on the other, international stability?

5

Jurisdiction

CENTRAL ISSUES

1. This chapter discusses the international legal concept of jurisdiction as well as the content of the relevant legal principles.

2. It presents the difference between, respectively, the jurisdiction to prescribe and the jurisdiction to enforce and the main elements thereof.

3. The chapter analyses the different principles of prescriptive jurisdiction (the principle

of territoriality, nationality, universality, protection and so-called passive personality) and discusses the issue of concurring jurisdictions as well as jurisdiction on ships and aircraft.

4. The chapter also discusses the prohibition on enforcing jurisdiction on the territory of another state as well as the legal consequences of violating that prohibition.

5.1 Introduction

International law primarily seeks to maintain international order by compartmentalizing territory and individuals into sovereign states. One of the defining aspects of sovereignty, then, is the exclusive right of each state to govern its internal affairs. As the Permanent Court of Arbitration famously stated in the *Island of Palmas* case: 'Sovereignty in the relations between States signifies independence. Independence in regard to a portion of the globe is the right to exercise therein, to the exclusion of any other State, the functions of a State.'[1] In the *Lotus* case, the Permanent Court of International Justice (PCIJ) also stressed how the 'first and foremost restriction imposed by international law upon a State is that—failing the existence of a permissive rule to the contrary—it may not exercise its power in any form in the territory of another State'.[2] The principle against physically exercising sovereignty in another state is countered by another principle that flows from state sovereignty. In the *Lotus* case, the PCIJ stated that the prohibition against physically

---

[1] *Island of Palmas (Netherlands v United States)* (1928) II RIAA 829, 838.
[2] *The Case of the SS Lotus (France v Turkey)*, Judgment, 1927, PCIJ, Series A, No. 10, 18–19.

exercising jurisdiction in other states did not mean that a state was also prohibited from exercising jurisdiction in its own territory, 'in respect of any case which relates to acts which have taken place abroad, and in which it cannot rely on some permissive rule of international law'.[3]

In international law, the dual aspects of sovereignty mentioned above are reflected in the principles of the lawful exercise of jurisdiction. The term jurisdiction relates to the authority of a state to exert its influence and power—in practice make, apply and enforce its rules—and create an impact or consequence on individuals or property.[4] In practice, the principles of jurisdiction translate into important distinctions between various means of jurisdiction, the primary ones being jurisdiction to *enforce* and jurisdiction to *prescribe*. In general, as the *Island of Palmas* and the *Lotus* cases illustrate, a state is entitled to *regulate* conduct that occurs abroad but it may not *enforce* its laws outside its territory. International law also operates with a jurisdiction to *adjudicate* that concerns the right of domestic courts to receive, treat and determine cases referred to them. The three forms of jurisdiction can be illustrated with a case of robbery. The *criminalization* of the robbery is an act of prescriptive jurisdiction while the physical *apprehension* of a suspected robber is a case of enforcing jurisdiction. Jurisdiction to adjudicate relates to the *subsequent* criminal prosecution of the individual. In this chapter, adjudicative jurisdiction is only dealt with in the discussion in Section 5.3 of prosecuting individuals who have been brought before a court in violation of the prohibition against enforcing jurisdiction in other states. The concept of 'extraterritorial' jurisdiction relates to those rare cases where a state may be authorized to enforce its jurisdiction on the territory of another state.

The principles of jurisdiction seek to balance the rights of a sovereign state to exert its influence over matters of its concern with the interests of other sovereign states not to be subjected to undue encroachment on their right to conduct their own affairs. The attempt by state A to exercise jurisdiction over individuals or events on the territory of state B will be perceived as an infringement of the sovereignty of state B because it interferes with how the latter exercises its own jurisdiction. By seeking to ensure that states do not assert jurisdiction over affairs that are properly the domain of other states, the principles of jurisdiction seek to prevent undue friction between states and are therefore part and parcel of the international law of coexistence.

The source of jurisdiction is state sovereignty and the role of international law is merely to limit the exercise of jurisdictional powers. As we shall see in Chapter 6, state immunity sometimes requires a state to refrain from exercising jurisdiction. In practice, respect for sovereignty often leads to conflicting interpretations of the limits of jurisdiction. Respect for the sovereignty of a state that wants to influence a matter speaks in favour of adopting an expansive view of jurisdiction, while respect for the sovereignty of a state that is subjected to the first state's exercise of jurisdiction dictates otherwise. Most states assert less jurisdiction than international law allows

---

[3] Ibid, 19.

[4] For an extensive overview, see Cedric Ryngaert, *Jurisdiction in International Law* (Oxford University Press, 2008).

them to. Importantly, the different forms of jurisdiction we discuss in this chapter must not be confused with the interpretation of various jurisdictional provisions in individual human rights conventions, such as the European Convention on Human Rights (ECHR).[5] There is no comprehensive convention regulating jurisdiction and the law is primarily derived from state practice. An influential Draft Convention on Jurisdiction with Respect to Crime was, however, published by a group of researchers at Harvard University in 1935.[6]

The overview is divided into two sections. We start in Section 5.2 with jurisdiction to prescribe before we examine jurisdiction to enforce in Section 5.3.

5.2 Jurisdiction to prescribe

5.2.1 Introduction

The jurisdiction to prescribe relates to the authority of a state to apply its national laws to any individual, property or event no matter where they may be located or occur. It is now well established that states are only entitled to exercise their legislative jurisdiction when it is supported by a permissive principle in international law.[7] Thus, the debate about the jurisdictional authorities of states revolves around identifying the limits of the established—but not always uncontroversial—categories of (potentially) permissible prescriptive jurisdiction.[8] A state is not generally entitled to exercise prescriptive jurisdiction over an individual or a particular matter if it is not somehow affected or deemed to have a reasonable interest in so doing.[9] Thus, there must be some sort of real link—a 'connecting factor'—between the acts or the behaviour that the state wants to prescribe and the legitimate interests of the state. In most cases, of course, it is unlikely that a state will take steps to prescribe acts it does not have any interest in.

---

[5] See also Marko Milanovic, *Extraterritorial Application of Human Rights Treaties* (Oxford University Press, 2011) 26. We will discuss the geographical reach of human rights law in Chapter 9.

[6] The draft convention is available in (1935) 29 *American Journal of International Law* 439.

[7] In *Lotus*, the PCIJ implied that there is a presumption against limiting a state's jurisdiction to apply its national law to matters abroad when it stated that international law leaves states 'a wide measure of discretion which is only limited in certain cases by prohibitive rules; as regards other cases, every State remains free to adopt the principles which it regards as best and most suitable'. See *Lotus* (n 2) 19. On this point, the Court went too far. See also *Arrest Warrant of 11 April 2000 (Congo v Belgium)*, Judgment, Separate Opinion of President Guillaume [2002] ICJ Rep 3, 43.

[8] See also *Barcelona Traction, Light and Power Co., Ltd (Belgium v Spain)*, Judgment, Separate Opinion of Judge Sir Gerald Fitzmaurice [1970] ICJ Rep 3, para. 70: 'It is true that ... international law does not impose hard and fast rules on States delimiting spheres of national jurisdiction in such matters (and there are of course others—for instance in the fields of shipping, "anti-trust" legislation, etc.), but leaves to States a wide discretion in the matter. It does however (a) postulate the existence of limits—though in any given case it may be for the tribunal to indicate what these are for the purposes of that case; and (b) involve for every State an obligation to exercise moderation and restraint as to the extent of the jurisdiction assumed by its courts in cases having a foreign element, and to avoid undue encroachment on a jurisdiction more properly appertaining to, or more appropriately exercisable by, another State.'

[9] Ryngaert (n 4) 31.

The power to prescribe is asserted according to five principles. While they have primarily been developed in relation to jurisdiction over criminal offences,[10] they are generally considered equally valid for claims in civil law. In the following, we visit each of the five principles in turn and start with the principles of territoriality (Section 5.2.2), nationality (Section 5.2.3), passive personality (Section 5.2.4), protective jurisdiction (Section 5.2.5) and universal jurisdiction (Section 5.2.6). Following that, Section 5.2.7 will briefly discuss the question of concurring/overlapping jurisdictions and Section 5.2.8 will provide an overview of jurisdiction over aircraft and on board ships.

5.2.2 Territorial jurisdiction

The most basic and uncontroversial basis of jurisdiction is the principle of territoriality derived from state sovereignty. In a sense, all other principles of jurisdiction can be considered 'extraterritorial'.[11] The territoriality principle holds that a state has jurisdiction over all acts, whether criminal or not, committed on its territory and over everyone located on the territory of that state.[12] Subject to limitations imposed under human rights law, a state can legislate as it pleases on whatever matter it so desires on its own territory. 'Territory' includes not only territory on land but also the territorial sea and the airspace above the land and sea territory.[13]

The practical application of the principle of territorial jurisdiction may occasionally cause problems. What does it mean that an act is committed or occurs on the territory of a state? Often, a sequence of events that cause an effect does not occur wholly within one state. A criminal offence, for example, may often be initiated or planned in one state but committed in another. International law has developed two approaches to deal with such 'cross-border' activities. 'Objective territoriality' focuses on the effects of an offence and holds that a state will have jurisdiction over an offence that is *completed* on its territory even though some of the elements of the offence took place abroad. 'Subjective territoriality', on the other hand, stipulates that a state has jurisdiction over all acts that are completed abroad as long as they are initiated or planned on the territory of the state in question. The subjective approach is of great practical importance in fighting transnational crime, such as international cybercrime. The distinction between objective and subjective territoriality can be illustrated by the 11 September 2001 terrorist attacks in the United States. As the attacks were completed on US territory, the Americans had jurisdiction over the attacks on the basis of objective territoriality. But since a substantial part of the planning and preparation of the attacks occurred elsewhere, most notably in Afghanistan and Germany, other states could derive a claim of jurisdiction on the basis of subjective territoriality.

---

[10] See, inter alia, Draft Convention on Jurisdiction with Respect to Crime (n 6).

[11] See also Rosalyn Higgins, *Problems and Process: International Law and How We Use It* (Oxford University Press, 1994) 73.

[12] See also Draft Convention on Jurisdiction with Respect to Crime (n 6) art. 3.

[13] As we will see in Section 5.2.8, special rules apply with regard to jurisdiction on board aircraft and vessels registered in the state.

It is doubtful whether a state can extend its legislation to acts committed abroad that only have an economic effect on the state. Antitrust legislation in the United States operates on a so-called 'effects doctrine', and in *Alcoa* a US Court of Appeals in 1945 found that 'any state may impose liabilities, even upon persons not within its allegiance, for conduct outside its borders that has consequences within its borders which the state reprehends; and these liabilities other states will ordinarily recognize'.[14] The legislation even prescribes acts that are lawful in the states they are committed.[15] European states have responded to the aggressive US jurisdictional claims by adopting 'blocking laws' prohibiting national companies from cooperating and complying with US authorities in antitrust cases.[16] US courts have since backed down from their most aggressive assertions of jurisdiction[17] with the result that jurisdictional relations have improved.[18] The United States is not alone in adopting an expansive interpretation of the reach of its competition laws. In the 1993 *Wood Pulp* case, the (then) European Court of Justice accepted legislative jurisdiction on the basis of what was essentially local effects/consequences of foreign conduct.[19]

5.2.3 Jurisdiction on the basis of nationality

States may extend their laws to their own nationals regardless of where they are located.[20] Indeed, as a basis for jurisdiction, this so-called 'active personality' principle has a longer history than any other principle of jurisdiction.[21] The state of nationality has traditionally enjoyed basically unlimited control over its nationals, and until the advent of international human rights law the manner in which a state treated its own citizens was of no interest to international law. States have a legitimate interest in the behaviour of their own citizens abroad and since they are reluctant to extradite their nationals to criminal prosecution in other states (see Section 5.3), preventing impunity for serious offences occasionally requires the state of nationality to prosecute its own nationals for crimes they have committed abroad.

---

[14] *United States v Aluminium Co. of America et al.*, 148 F.2d 416, 443 (2d Cir. 1945).

[15] See, inter alia, *Rio Tinto Zinc Corp. v Westinghouse Electric Corp.* (1978) 1 All ER 434 (HL).

[16] For an overview of the British 'blocking practice', see Vaughan Lowe, 'Blocking Extraterritorial Jurisdiction: The British Protection of Trading Interests Act, 1980' (1980) 75 *American Journal of International Law* 257. The laws were based on the principle that a state cannot require an individual to comply with an order if doing so would entail the violation of the laws in the territory where the potentially complying act must be done, see also *Société Internationale v Rogers*, 357 US 197, 205–206 (1958).

[17] See *Timberlane Lumber Co. v Bank of America*, 549 F.2d 597, § 67 (9th Cir. 1976). See also *Hartford Fire Insurance v California*, 529 US 764, 797–799 (1993) and *F. Hoffmann-La Roche Ltd v Empagran SA*, 542 US 155, 164–165 (2004).

[18] See, inter alia, Agreement on the Application of Positive Comity Principles in the Enforcement of their Competition Laws (European Community–United States) (adopted 4 June 1998), OJ L173/28.

[19] See Joined Cases 89, 104, 114, 116, 117 and 125–129/85 *Ahlström and Others v Commission* [1988] ECR 5193. The Court did not rely on an 'effects doctrine' but on an expansive interpretation of the territoriality principle and the fact that the relevant agreement was 'implemented' in the EU.

[20] Draft Convention on Jurisdiction with Respect to Crime (n 6) art. 5.

[21] Ryngaert (n 4) 42–47.

If an individual has dual nationality, both states of nationality may assert jurisdiction on the basis of nationality. States are generally free to decide who they consider to be their 'nationals' and under what circumstances an individual qualifies for citizenship.[22] In the *Nottebohm* case, however, the International Court of Justice (ICJ) stated that the exercise of rights associated with nationality may be challenged by other states and that nationality connotes a 'genuine connection' with the state that seeks to protect the rights of its citizens.[23]

5.2.4 **The passive personality principle**

According to the so-called 'passive personality' principle, a state can assert its jurisdiction over an offence committed abroad on the sole ground that the *victim* of the offence was a national of the state. As a principle of prescriptive jurisdiction, this has historically been controversial and Harvard Research in International Law did not include it in its 1935 Draft Convention on Jurisdiction with Respect to Crime because it found that it would only 'invite controversy without serving any useful objective'.[24] In the *Lotus* case, a number of the dissenting judges were also critical of the claim that Turkey could assert jurisdiction over the incident on the basis of the nationality of the drowned seaman.[25] The passive personality principle makes it practically impossible for a potential offender to anticipate which state's laws he or she may be subjected to and it creates uncertainty about acceptable behaviour within a state.

Passive personality has nevertheless become increasingly accepted in recent years, in particular in the context of international terrorism.[26] In the *Yunis* case, for example, the United States prosecuted a Lebanese citizen for hijacking a Jordanian civilian airliner in Beirut even though the only connection to the United States was the presence among the passengers of American citizens.[27] In addition to jurisdiction on the basis of the principle of universality and the 1970 Convention for the Suppression of Unlawful Seizure of Aircraft, the US court relied on the passive personality principle that it found was supported by international law 'at least where the state has a

---

[22] See also *Constitution of the Maritime Safety Committee of the Inter-Governmental Maritime Consultative Organization*, Advisory Opinion [1960] ICJ Rep 150. See also *Nationality Decrees Issued in Tunis and Morocco*, Advisory Opinion, 1923, PCIJ, Series B, No. 4, 24.

[23] *Nottebohm (Second Phase) (Liechtenstein v Guatemala)*, Judgment [1955] ICJ Rep 4, 23.

[24] Commentary to art. 10 in the Draft Convention on Jurisdiction with Respect to Crime (n 6) 579.

[25] See *Lotus* (n 2) Dissenting Opinion by M. Loder 36, Dissenting Opinion by Lord Finlay 57–58, Dissenting Opinion by M. Nyholm 62, Dissenting Opinion by Mr. Moore 91–93. Interestingly, the principle is not included as a jurisdictional basis in the International Convention on Certain Rules Concerning Civil Jurisdiction in Matters of Collision (adopted 10 May 1952, entered into force 14 September 1955), 439 UNTS 217 or the United Nations Convention on the Law of the Sea (LOSC, also known as UNCLOS) (adopted 10 December 1982, entered into force 16 November 1994) 1833 UNTS 2.

[26] Higgins (n 11) 66–69. See also Ryngaert (n 4) 94–96. See also the US Omnibus Diplomatic Security and Antiterrorism Act of 1986 and see Geoffrey R. Watson, 'The Passive Personality Principle' (1993) 28 *Texas International Law Journal* 1; John McCarthy, 'The Passive Personality Principle and Its Use in Combatting International Terrorism' (1989) 13 *Fordham International Law Journal* 298. See too *Arrest Warrant* (n 7) Joint Separate Opinion of Judges Higgins, Kooijmans and Buergenthal, para. 47.

[27] *United States v Fawaz Yunis, A/k/a Nazeeh, Appellant*, 924 F.2d 1086 (DC Cir. 1991).

particularly strong interest in the crime'. The United States also relied on the passive personality principle in relation to the 1985 *Achille Lauro* incident in which terrorists took control of an Italian cruise ship and caused the death of an American passenger.[28]

Jurisdiction on the basis of passive personality ought to be limited to serious offences (e.g. crimes of terrorism) that are prescribed in all states. This ensures that a state does not prosecute an individual for a crime that was lawful in the territory where it was committed and that potential offenders will know that their conduct constitutes a serious crime.[29] It would also appear sensible to argue that it ought to serve as a subsidiary means of jurisdiction in the sense that it is only asserted when the state in which the offence occurred does not intend to prosecute offender.

5.2.5 **Protective jurisdiction**

Jurisdiction on the basis of territory and nationality usually provides a state with sufficient jurisdictional means to protect its interests from potential harm. After all, most offences are committed by individuals physically located on the territory of the state or by the nationals of the state abroad. There are exceptions, however, and the 'protective principle' holds that a state may extend its jurisdiction over any matter that has a deleterious effect on it regardless of where the acts occur or who has committed it.[30] Protective jurisdiction is derived from the sovereign right of all states to conduct their affairs without outside interference.[31] The exercise of protective jurisdiction does require, however, the existence of a genuine threat to a *vital* state interest and it must not, therefore, be confused with the controversial effect doctrine visited earlier whereby a state extends its laws to acts that merely have a negative economic effect in the state. The classic example of the exercise of protective jurisdiction is the prohibition of falsification or counterfeiting of 'seals, currency, instruments of credit, stamps, passports, or public documents', issued by the state.[32] Another example was the prescription in the 1960s of so-called 'pirate radio broadcasting' emanating from unauthorized radio stations on ships on the high seas or from installations fixed to the seabed in areas outside the territorial sea of the coastal state.[33]

In 1935, Harvard Research in International Law argued for international agreement on limitations to relying on protective jurisdiction.[34] In general, however, protective

---

[28] For a brief overview, see Watson (n 26) 10–11.   [29] Ibid, 25.

[30] Draft Convention on Jurisdiction with Respect to Crime (n 6) arts 7–8.

[31] Ryngeart (n 4) 96–97. See also commentary to art 7 of the Draft Convention on Jurisdiction with Respect to Crime (n 6) 543–561.

[32] Draft Convention on Jurisdiction with Respect to Crime (n 6) art. 8. See also the commentary to art. 8 at 561–563.

[33] See, inter alia, Horace B. Robertson Jr, 'The Suppression of Pirate Radio Broadcasting: A Test Case of the International System for Control of Activities outside National Territory' (1982) 45 *Law and Contemporary Problems* 71.

[34] Commentary to art. 7 of the Draft Convention on Jurisdiction with Respect to Crime (n 6) 557–561. See also Manuel R. García-Mora, 'Criminal Jurisdiction over Foreigners for Treason and Offenses Against the Safety of the State Committed upon Foreign Territory' (1957–1958) 19 *University of Pittsburgh Law Review* 567, 588–589.

jurisdiction has not been a cause of great contention and states in most cases limit their reliance on this form of jurisdiction to serious offences that are not condoned by anyone.[35] Most recently, the principle has been relied on to combat drug smuggling and international terrorism. There are examples, though, where the principle seems to have been used in order to prescribe activity that cannot reasonably be said to have a serious negative impact on the prescribing state's vital interests. The seminal example is the so-called 'secondary boycott' laws adopted in the 1996 US Helms–Burton Act and the D'Amato Act. While the former sought to extend a long-existing US embargo on Cuba by penalizing foreign companies from trading in Cuban property confiscated from American citizens, the latter imposed penalties on persons who made certain investments in Iranian and Libyan oil and natural gas resources.[36] Since the legislation primarily seemed to serve as a tool for US foreign policy, it was met with protests from other states and both Canada and the EU enacted 'blocking legislation'.[37]

5.2.6 **Universal jurisdiction**

International law recognizes that certain offences are so serious and/or disruptive to international society that any state may claim jurisdiction over them no matter where they have been committed or by whom.[38] The lack of a direct link between the state and the offence makes so-called 'universal jurisdiction' stand out from other principles of jurisdiction. It was the crime of piracy that gave rise to the notion of universal juris-diction.[39] Since pirates roamed the high seas outside the territorial jurisdiction of any state it made good practical sense to allow all states to prosecute any pirate they could get their hands on and customary law thus established a right for all states to assert universal prescriptive jurisdiction over the crime.[40] Universal jurisdiction was thereby created to fulfil a potential jurisdictional vacuum.[41] Nowadays, universal jurisdiction is mostly applied in order to prevent impunity for perpetrators of particularly serious offences. The rationale was forcefully articulated by the District Court in Jerusalem in the 1961 *Eichmann* trial in Israel. As justification for prosecuting Eichmann under an Israeli law that gave Israeli courts jurisdiction to prosecute crimes committed outside Israel at a time when the State of Israel had not yet been established, the court stated that the 'abhorrent' crimes in question were not just crimes under Israeli law alone. According to the court:

> These crimes which offended the whole of mankind and shocked the conscience of nations are grave offences against the law of nations itself ('delicta juris gentium'). Therefore, so

---

[35] Ryngaert (n 4) 98–99.

[36] For more, see Stefaan Smis and Kim Van der Borght, 'The EU–US Compromise on the Helms Burton and D'Amato Acts' (1999) 93 *American Journal of International Law* 227.

[37] Ibid. In May 1998, the EU and the US reached an agreement according to which the latter would limit the application of the Acts on European companies and citizens.

[38] Draft Convention on Jurisdiction with Respect to Crime (n 6) art. 9.

[39] See Commentary to art. 9 in the Draft Convention on Jurisdiction with Respect to Crime (n 6) 563–572.

[40] See also the discussion in Chapter 15.

[41] See also LOSC (n 25), art. 105.

far from international law negating or limiting the jurisdiction of countries with respect to such crimes, in the absence of an International Court, the international law is in need of the judicial and legislative authorities of every country, to give effect to its penal injunctions and to bring criminals to trial. The jurisdiction to try crimes under international law is universal.[42]

Violations of norms of a peremptory character/*jus cogens*, such as genocide, crimes against humanity, serious war crimes and torture, are the most serious offences under international law and therefore constitute obvious candidates for being crimes under universal jurisdiction even in the absence of a treaty-based entitlement.[43]

In practice, universal jurisdiction is asserted in at least two situations. The first and 'purest' form is where a state asserts universal jurisdiction despite the fact that the alleged offender is not even present on its territory—also known as universal jurisdiction *in absentia*. In 1993, for example, Belgium adopted controversial legislation that granted its courts jurisdiction over a range of offences regardless of where they were committed, who the perpetrators or victims were or whether the alleged offender was present in Belgium. In the *Arrest Warrant* case, the Democratic Republic of Congo (DRC) brought a case against Belgium because Belgian authorities had issued an arrest warrant for the arrest of the acting minister of foreign affairs in the DRC pursuant to the new legislation.[44] The DRC claimed that the Belgian legislation violated international law. As we shall see in Chapter 6, the case was ultimately decided on the basis of immunity. But some of the judges also discussed the compatibility of this form of universal jurisdiction with international law. Their disagreement was noticeable.[45]

It is clear that the fight to end impunity for serious violations of international law speaks in favour of accepting even the purest form of universal jurisdiction as a basis for jurisdiction. But it is equally obvious that the peaceful and unimpeded conduct of international relations is strained by aggressive claims of universal jurisdiction and in particular by issuing an arrest warrant in the absence of the alleged offender's presence in the issuing state.[46] In 2003, Belgium gave in to substantial international pressure from, among others, the United States, and repealed its (controversial) legislation.

The second and more limited form of universal jurisdiction is tied to the obligation of a state in an increasing number of treaties to either prosecute or extradite—*aut dedere aut judicare*—an alleged offender of specific offences who is located on the territory of that state. As we shall see in Chapter 15, in practice the obligation requires a state to extend its prescriptive jurisdiction to certain individuals suspected of committing enumerated offences regardless of where the offence is committed and the nationality of the offender. It is a less controversial form of universal jurisdiction because the alleged offender is physically present in the state.[47] Since the legal basis for

---

[42] *Attorney General v Adolph Eichmann*, District Court of Jerusalem, Criminal Case No. 40/61, para. 12.

[43] Roger O'Keefe, *International Criminal Law* (Oxford University Press, 2015) 23–24 and 371.

[44] *Arrest Warrant* (n 7).

[45] See, inter alia, *Arrest Warrant* (n 7) Separate Opinion of President Guillaume, para. 16.

[46] For a discussion of universal jurisdiction *in absentia*, see Ryngaert (n 4) 119–125.

[47] See also the discussion of international criminal law in Chapter 15.

the obligation to prosecute or extradite is generally a treaty, non-state parties are not obliged to assert their (universal) jurisdiction over the offence in question.

The obligation to prosecute or extradite certain individuals found its way into treaty law in the early 1970s in relation to international terrorism. The 1970 Hague Convention for the Suppression of Unlawful Seizure of Aircraft, for example, specifies that a state must take the required measures to ensure that it can establish its jurisdiction over an offence covered by the Convention in relation to an individual who takes refuge on its territory. Similar provisions were introduced into the 1971 Montreal Convention for the Suppression of Unlawful Acts against the Safety of Civil Aviation, the 1979 Convention against the Taking of Hostages, the 1997 Convention for the Suppression of Terrorist Bombings and the 1999 Convention for the Suppression of the Financing of Terrorism. The obligation is also found in the 1984 UN Convention against Torture and Other Cruel, Inhuman or Degrading Treatment or Punishment.

5.2.7 Concurring/overlapping jurisdictions

Since states can rely on a number of principles in order to assert jurisdiction to prescribe a given person or matter, it is not uncommon for more than one state to be entitled to claim jurisdiction in a given case. If, say, a citizen of state A kills citizens of state B on the territory of state C, international law may potentially entitle all three states to assert jurisdiction over the offence. State A may assert jurisdiction on the basis of the offender's nationality while state C may rely on the principle of territoriality and the fact that the offence was committed on its territory. Depending on the circumstances, state B could also be entitled to assert jurisdiction on the basis of the nationality of the victims (at least to the extent that the offence in question could be characterized as an act of terrorism). In addition, the principle of universality may also entitle all states to exercise jurisdiction over an offence irrespective of a link between those states and the crime.

The issue of *concurrent jurisdiction* and the simultaneous exercise of jurisdiction by more than one state over the same matter may give rise to considerable international friction and it is therefore somewhat unfortunate that states are not under a legal obligation to exercise their jurisdiction in a particularly reasonable manner.[48] The aggressive jurisdictional assertions by US courts in antitrust cases and the Helms–Burton and D'Amato Acts illustrate the need for principles that help to solve jurisdictional conflicts in a mutually satisfactory manner. In a Separate Opinion in *Barcelona Traction* before the ICJ, Judge Fitzmaurice noted that states are obliged 'to exercise moderation and restraint as to the extent of the jurisdiction assumed by its courts in cases having a foreign element, and to avoid undue encroachment on a jurisdiction more properly exercised by another state'.[49] In most cases, the territorial state will claim that it has the closest link to a particular offence and therefore has a more privileged position compared to states with 'competing' claims of jurisdiction. In practical terms, it will be the

---

[48] Ryngaert (n 4) 128–129.
[49] *Barcelona Traction* (n 8) Separate Opinion of Judge Fitzmaurice, para. 70.

state with physical custody of the offender that determines which state will exercise jurisdiction over the individual. The principle *aut dedere aut judicare* discussed earlier can be perceived as a principle of resolving a potential jurisdictional dispute.

Attempts have been made to establish second-level discretionary principles for identifying the state with the strongest claim or interest in a given matter.[50] A principle of comity familiar to US lawyers suggests that a state should limit the reach of its laws and defer to other states if those states have a stronger link to a situation.[51] An example is the so-called jurisdictional 'rule of reason' in the 1987 *Restatement (Third) of the Foreign Relations Law of the United States* introduced in response to the contentious issue of jurisdiction in antitrust cases.[52] The purpose of the rule is to oblige the United States not to exercise its jurisdiction when it is deemed 'unreasonable'. It also lists a range of relevant factors, including 'the link of the activity to the territory of the regulating state', 'the character of the activity to be regulated', 'the extent to which another states may have an interest in regulating the activity' and 'the likelihood of conflict with regulation by another state'.[53] As noted earlier, US courts have become more sensitive to the jurisdictional concerns voiced by other states, in particular in the area of antitrust jurisdiction. European states are generally more reluctant to overtly balance interests in jurisdiction disputes and instead reach similar results by other means.

5.2.8 Jurisdiction over aircraft and ships

Jurisdiction over a state's airspace and aircraft is regulated in a number of conventions. The 1944 Chicago Convention on International Civil Aviation stipulates that all states have complete and exclusive sovereignty over the airspace above their territory, including the airspace over their territorial waters.[54] The 1963 Tokyo Convention on Offences and Certain Other Acts Committed on Board Aircraft specifies that the state of registration of an aircraft has authority to apply its laws to matters that occur on board its aircraft while in flight regardless of where it is located.[55] It also establishes the general rule that a contracting state which is not the state of registration may not interfere with an aircraft in flight in order to exercise its criminal jurisdiction over an offence committed on board.[56] The Tokyo

---

[50] Ryngaert (n 4), 136–153.

[51] Ibid, 136–142. See also the Harold G. Maier, 'Extraterritorial Jurisdiction at a Crossroads: An Intersection between Public and Private International Law' (1982) 76 *American Journal of International Law* 280. On the concept of comity in international law in general, see Joel R. Paul, 'Comity in International Law' (1991) 32 *Harvard International Law Journal* 1.

[52] Harold G. Maier, 'Resolving Extraterritorial Conflicts, or "There and Back Again"' (1984) 7 *Virginia Journal of International Law* 7.

[53] The American Law Institute, *Restatement (Third) of the Foreign Relations Law of the United States* (1988) para. 403.

[54] Convention on International Civil Aviation (Chicago Convention) (adopted 7 December 1944, entered into force 14 April 1947), 15 UNTS 295, arts 1–2.

[55] Convention on Offences and Certain Other Acts Committed on Board Aircraft (Tokyo Convention) (adopted 14 September 1963, entered into force 4 December 1969), 704 UNTS 219, art. 3(1).

[56] Ibid, art. 4.

Convention also provides the aircraft commander (the captain) with the authority to use reasonable force to deal with individuals who have committed or are about to commit a crime or acts that may jeopardize safety on board the aircraft.[57] In cases of hijacking of an aircraft, contracting states are obliged to 'take all appropriate measures to restore control of the aircraft to its lawful commander or to preserve his control of the aircraft'. The Tokyo Convention's regulation on the prevention of hijacking has since been supplemented by numerous other conventions including the 1970 Hague Convention for the Suppression of Unlawful Seizure of Aircraft according to which, as we saw earlier, contracting states are obliged to extradite or prosecute hijackers.

In Chapter 8 we will explore the issue of jurisdiction over ships on the high seas and the principles of innocent passage through a coastal state's territorial sea or exclusive economic zone (EEZ). In general, and as a point of departure, it is the flag state that has sole jurisdiction over a ship.

5.3 Jurisdiction to enforce

International law is clear when it comes to a state's physical enforcement of its laws. As the PCIJ stated in the *Lotus* case, the 'first and foremost restriction imposed by international law upon a state is that—failing the existence of a permissive rule to the contrary—it may not exercise its power in any form in the territory of another State'.[58] Thus, unless the territorial state gives its consent, a state cannot enter another state in order to secure the arrest of an alleged offender or confiscate stolen property.

In criminal law, the practical problems associated with the prohibition against physical enforcement in other states are solved by *extradition* where a state hands over an individual located on its territory who is wanted for criminal prosecution in another state.[59] In practice, states are very reluctant to extradite their own citizens to criminal prosecution abroad. In 2002, an EU framework decision—somewhat controversially—established a system for a European Arrest Warrant that generally obliges member states of the EU to surrender their own nationals to criminal prosecution for serious crimes in other member states.[60] All extraditions are generally governed by a number of principles. First, the principle of 'double criminality' stipulates that the offence involved must be a criminal offence in both states concerned. Secondly, the principle of 'double jeopardy' (*ne bis in idem*) specifies that an individual should not be punished twice for the same offence. In addition, extraditing states are bound by obligations in human rights conventions. The most important of these is the

---

[57] Ibid, arts 6–7.   [58] *Lotus* (n 2) 18–19.

[59] In general, see Ivan Anthony Shearer, *Extradition in International Law* (Manchester University Press, 1971).

[60] Council of the European Union, Council Framework Decision of 13 June 2002 on the European arrest warrant and the surrender procedures between Member States (2002/584/JHA), OJ L190/1.

obligation not to extradite an individual to another state if there is a risk that the individual may be subjected to inhuman or degrading treatment in the receiving country or in a third state to which the individual may subsequently be transferred.[61] The obligation is contained in article 3 of the ECHR,[62] article 7 of the UN Covenant on Civil and Political Rights[63] and in article 3 of the UN Convention against Torture and Other Cruel, Inhuman or Degrading Treatment or Punishment.[64] In the *Niels Holck* case in June 2011, a Danish court of second instance concluded that the ECHR prevented the extradition of a Danish national to India.[65] Human rights law may also bar extradition to state where there is a risk of the death penalty being imposed[66] or of a trial that constitutes a 'flagrant denial of justice'.[67] In 1990, the UN General Assembly adopted a 'model treaty for extradition' to serve as a guide for the establishment of bilateral extradition treaties.[68]

A state can give its consent to another state's enforcement of jurisdiction on its territory. Under a so-called 'Status of Forces Agreement' (SOFA), for example, a host state consents to the presence of foreign troops on its territory.[69] Parties to the Schengen Treaty have accepted that law enforcement officers from other state parties may in certain circumstances continue the active pursuit of a suspected criminal into their territories without prior authorization.[70]

History is full of examples where state officials have enforced jurisdiction in another state without permission from the host state. A well-known case was Israeli agents' apprehension and subsequent transfer in 1960 from Argentina to Israel of the former high-ranking Nazi officer Adolph Eichmann.[71] In Israel, Eichmann

[61] See also the overview in Chapter 9.
[62] See also ECtHR, *Soering v UK*, App. no. 14038/88, 7 July 1989, para. 91. For case law on a risk to transfer to third countries, see *TI v UK*, App. no. 43844/98, Admissibility, 7 March 2000.
[63] For case law from the Human Rights Committee on the prohibition on transfer to a risk of ill-treatment, see *Kindler v Canada* (Communication No. 470/1991, CCPR/C/48/D/470/1991, 11 November 1993); *Chitat Ng v Canada* (Communication No. 469/1991, CCPR/C/49/D/469/1991, 7 January 1994).
[64] For relevant case law from the Committee Against Torture, see *Mutombo v Switzerland* (Communication No. 13/1193, CAT/C/12/D/13/1993, 27 April 1994) and *Haydin v Sweden* (Communication No. 101/1997, CAT/C/21/D/101/1997, 20 November 1998). See also Committee Against Torture, 'General Comment No. 1: Implementation of article 3 of the Convention in the context of article 22' (21 November 1997), UN Doc. A/53/44, annex IX, para. 2.
[65] U.2011.2904Ø.
[66] In the ECHR, the death penalty is proscribed under the 1983 Protocol No. 6 to the ECHR concerning the abolition of the death penalty and the 2002 Protocol No. 13 to the ECHR concerning the abolition of the death penalty in all circumstances. For transfer to a state where there is a risk thereof, see *Nivette v France*, App. no. 44190/98, Admissibility, 3 July 2001, 3.
[67] For case law from the ECtHR, see *Mamatkulov and Askarov v Turkey*, App. nos 46827/99 and 46951/99, 4 February 2005, para. 91. See also *Mohammed Ali Hassan Al-Moayad v Germany*, App. no. 35865/03, Admissibility, 20 February 2007, para. 100.
[68] GA Res. 45/116 (14 December 1990), UN Doc. A/RES/45/116.
[69] Paul J. Conderman, 'Status of Armed Forces on Foreign Territory Agreements (SOFA)' in Rüdiger Wolfrum (ed.), *Max Planck Encyclopedia of Public International Law* (Oxford University Press, 2013).
[70] Convention Implementing the Schengen Agreement of 14 June 1985 between the Governments of the States of the Benelux Economic Union, the Federal Republic of Germany and the French Republic, on the Gradual Abolition of Checks at their Common Borders, OJ L239/19, 19 June 1990, art. 41.
[71] See, inter alia, J. E. S. Fawcett, 'The *Eichmann* Case' (1963) 38 *British Yearbook of International Law* 181.

was convicted and executed for atrocities committed during the Second World War. The UN Security Council responded to the unlawful Israeli incursion into Argentina by requesting Israel to offer compensation.[72] A more recent example of a potentially unlawful exercise of enforcement jurisdiction was the extraordinary rendition programme initiated by the United States after the terrorist attacks on 9/11.[73]

In its Draft Convention on Jurisdiction with Respect to Crime, Harvard Research in International Law stipulated that a state should refrain from prosecuting an individual brought into the state through measures that violated international law.[74] In practice, however, most states follow the maxim of *mala captus, bene detentus* whereby a state can try an individual even if the state believes that the defendant was brought there by irregular means. In the *Eichmann* case, for example, the District Court of Jerusalem stated that a state must only abstain from prosecution if the defendant is tried for an offence different from that for which he or she was extradited.[75] In *Stocke*, the German Federal Constitutional Court similarly concluded that national courts should generally only refuse jurisdiction if another state has protested about the abduction of an individual and requested that the person be returned.[76] US courts are notorious for their refusal to be influenced by the potentially unlawful manner in which a defendant is brought before court.[77] In *Alvarez-Machain*, the US Supreme Court did not find that the kidnapping and subsequent transport to the United States of a Mexican citizen in Mexico was a bar to prosecuting him for participating in the murder of a US official and a local pilot in Mexico.[78] Courts in other common law countries are more reluctant, though. In *R v Horseferry Road Magistrates' Court*, the UK House of Lords refused to allow the criminal trial of an individual who was abducted from South Africa to England in disregard of the established extradition procedures in place between the two states.[79]

---

[72] SC Res. 138 (23 June 1960), UN Doc. S/RES7138.

[73] It must be noted that at least some states have actively cooperated with the United States, see, inter alia, ECtHR, *Husayn (Abu Zubaydah) v Poland*, App. no. 7511/13, 24 July 2914; *Al Nashiri v Poland*, App. no. 28761/11, 24 July 2014.

[74] Draft Convention on Jurisdiction with Respect to Crime (n 6) art. 16. See also the commentaries to the article at 623–632. See also the debate in, inter alia, Higgins (n 11) 71–73 and F. A. Mann, 'Reflections on the Prosecution of Persons Abducted in Breach of International Law' in Yoram Dinstein (ed.), *International Law at a Time of Perplexity* (Springer, 1989) 407.

[75] *Adolph Eichmann*, District Court of Jerusalem, Criminal Case No. 40/61, paras 41–52.

[76] Decision of 17 July 1985, AZ: 2 BvR 1190/84. Bundesverfassungsgericht (Federal Constitutional Court), see § 1 c. For similar French practice, see the Klaus Barbie case, *Federation Nationale des Desportes et Internes Resistants et Patriotes and Others v Barbie*, Court of Cassation, 6 October 1983.

[77] The classic case is *Ker v Illinois*, 119 US 436, 438 (1866).

[78] *United States v Alvarez-Machain*, 504 US 655 (1992) (US Supreme Court). Remarkably, the Court did not find the abduction of the defendant from Mexican territory incompatible with an existing extradition treaty between the United States and Mexico because that treaty did not expressly prohibit such abductions, see at 664.

[79] *R v Horseferry Road Magistrates' Court, ex p. Bennett* [1994] 1 AC 42, 62. See also *R v Hartley* [1978] 2 NZLR 199, 216 (New Zealand Court of Appeals).

Summary

In international law, jurisdiction is concerned with the authority of a state to exert its influence and power over individuals or property. The rules can be divided into three forms of jurisdiction: jurisdiction to prescribe, jurisdiction to enforce and jurisdiction to adjudicate. The purpose of the rules is to strike a balance between the rights of a sovereign state to exert its influence on matters of interest to it and the interests of other sovereign states that may be at risk of undue encroachments on their own right to conduct their affairs as they please. International law generally operates with five bases for the exercise of prescriptive jurisdiction. These are jurisdiction on the basis of territoriality, nationality, universality, protective principles and so-called passive personality. While the first three are well accepted, the latter basis of jurisdiction—passive personality—is particularly controversial. International law prohibits a state from physically enforcing its jurisdiction on the territory of another state unless the latter gives its consent. In practice, however, this has not generally precluded national courts from bringing criminal proceedings against an individual who has been brought before the court in violation of that principle.

Recommended reading

For a broad overview of jurisdiction in international law, see Cedric Ryngaert, *Jurisdiction in International Law* (Oxford University Press, 2008). See also Rosalyn Higgins, *Problems and Process: International Law and How We Use It* (Oxford University Press, 1994) 56–77 and Frederick A. Mann, 'The Doctrine of Jurisdiction in International Law' (A. W. Sijthoff, 1964).

For an overview of the concept of 'blocking legislation', see Vaughan Lowe, 'Blocking Extraterritorial Jurisdiction: The British Protection of Trading Interests Act, 1980' (1980) 75 *American Journal of International Law* 257.

On the protective principle, Manuel R. García-Mora, 'Criminal Jurisdiction over Foreigners for Treason and Offenses Against the Safety of the State Committed upon Foreign Territory' (1957) 19 *University of Pittsburgh Law Review* 567.

On passive personality, see John McCarthy, 'The Passive Personality Principle and Its Use in Combatting International Terrorism' (1989) 13 *Fordham International Law Journal* 298; Geoffrey R. Watson, 'The Passive Personality Principle' (1993) 28 *Texas International Law Journal* 1.

Other works include Harold G. Maier, 'Extraterritorial Jurisdiction at a Crossroads: An Intersection between Public and Private International Law' (1982) 76 *American Journal of International Law* 280, and the same author in 'Resolving Extraterritorial Conflicts, or "There and Back Again"' (1984) 7 *Virginia Journal of International Law* 7.

As for the different approaches to jurisdictional conflicts in various states, see Hannah L. Buxbaum, 'Territory, Territoriality, and the Resolution of Jurisdictional Conflict' (2009) 57 *American Journal of International Law* 631.

Questions for discussion

1. What does it mean that jurisdiction flows from sovereignty and not from international law?

2. State sovereignty may speak in favour of both a wide and a narrow authority to assert jurisdiction. Why?

3. Why is the 'effects doctrine' in the area of prescriptive jurisdiction controversial?

4. Can you think of some examples where a state's assertion of prescriptive jurisdiction on the basis of the protective principle would be problematic?

5. What do you think is the best way to handle cases of concurring jurisdiction?

6. Why is the maxim of *mala captus, bene detentus* problematic from the point of view of international law?

6

Immunity from national jurisdiction and diplomatic protection

CENTRAL ISSUES

1. This chapter discusses the different forms of immunity from national jurisdiction enjoyed by a state and its representatives.

2. It presents state immunity and the complicated distinction between sovereign (*jure imperii*) and commercial (*jure gestionis*) acts. It discusses the exception to state immunity for commercial acts and provides an overview of some of the additional exceptions to state immunity.

3. The chapter also discusses the immunities of state representatives and introduces the distinction between immunity *ratione personae* and immunity *ratione materiae*. It also discusses how the distinction is applied to different state representatives.

4. It also briefly discusses the immunities and protection of diplomatic representatives and diplomatic missions as well as the issue of consular protection and the immunities enjoyed by so-called special missions.

6.1 Introduction

We saw in the previous chapter that a state has full and absolute jurisdiction within its own territory. So, not only can the territorial state prescribe as it pleases, it can also generally enforce its laws and regulations over all matters and individuals. In some circumstances, however, the territorial state will be obliged to refrain from exercising its jurisdiction. Most importantly, under the principles of sovereign immunity a foreign state and its representatives are entitled to certain immunities from the exercise of jurisdiction by other states and a violation of these immunities will give rise to international responsibility. The principles of immunity from national jurisdiction are applied by national courts pursuant to national law.

Importantly, respect for sovereign immunity is mandated by international law and not simply a matter of expediency or comity on behalf of the host state.[1] In its 2012

---

[1] *Jurisdictional Immunities of the State (Germany v Italy: Greece intervening)*, Judgment [2012] ICJ Rep 99, paras 53–57. But see practice from US courts: a classic example is *The Schooner Exchange v McFaddon*, 11 US (7 Cranch) 116, 136–137 (1812).

judgment in *Jurisdictional Immunities of the State*, the International Court of Justice (ICJ) stated that the obligation of a host state—or the 'forum' state—to refrain from exercising its jurisdiction over another state derives from the sovereign equality of states.[2] A state cannot require another sovereign state to submit to its national courts. The immunities enjoyed by state representatives can be said to derive from state immunity in the sense that such representatives—and in particular high-ranking officials—can be conceived of as 'personifying' the state on whose behalf they act. Alongside this 'representational' rationale for the immunity of state representatives are more functional considerations. As the ICJ noted in *Arrest Warrant*, a foreign minister can only perform his or her official functions if the individual can travel freely and remain in constant communication with not only the home government but also with diplomatic missions and representatives of other states.[3] The functional rationale is particularly relevant for understanding the rights and privileges of diplomatic missions and representatives.

The discussion of state immunity and diplomatic protection in this chapter is divided into three sections. We begin in Section 6.2 with the immunity of *the state and its property*. Since a state cannot be found criminally liable, the discussion concerns immunity from civil claims. Section 6.3 then discusses the immunities of state representatives that may involve questions of immunity from both civil and criminal jurisdiction. Section 6.4 examines the right and privileges accorded to envoys of a foreign state in a 'host state'—generally known as *diplomatic and consular immunity*.

Although the present chapter focuses on the immunities of states, it is worth noting that international organizations and their representatives also enjoy certain immunities from national jurisdiction. An international organization enjoys the immunities that are required for it to fulfil its functions without interference from local authorities.[4] In relation to the UN, this is reflected in article 105 of the UN Charter. For the UN, a particularly important convention is the 1946 Convention on the Privileges and Immunities of the United Nations that governs the immunity and inviolability of UN property, funds and assets,[5] communications[6] and representatives and officials.[7] The relations between an international organization and the state on which territory the organization is located are often governed by a headquarters agreement.

---

[2] *Jurisdictional Immunities* (n 1) para. 57. See also ECtHR, *Al-Adsani v UK*, App. no. 35763/97, 21 November 2001, para. 54. See also *Arrest Warrant of 11 April 2000 (Congo v Belgium)*, Joint Separate Opinion of Judges Higgins, Kooijmans and Buergenthal [2002] ICJ Rep 3, para. 72. For a—critical—analysis of the basis of state immunity, see Xiaodong Yang, *State Immunity in International Law* (Cambridge University Press, 2012) 44–58.

[3] *Arrest Warrant of 11 April 2000 (Congo v Belgium)*, Judgment [2002] ICJ Rep 3, para. 53.

[4] *Difference Relating to Immunity from Legal Process of a Special Rapporteur of the Commission on Human Rights*, Advisory Opinion [1999] ICJ Rep 62, para. 66. On the immunity of international organizations, see August Reinisch (ed.), *The Privileges and Immunities of International Organizations in Domestic Courts* (Oxford University Press, 2013) and Cedric Ryngaert, 'The Immunity of International Organizations Before Domestic Courts: Recent Trends' (2007) 7 *International Organizations Law Review* 121.

[5] Art. II.   [6] Art. III.   [7] Arts IV–VI.

6.2 State immunity

6.2.1 Introduction and concepts

State immunity is a principle of customary international law and its modalities have primarily been developed through national legislation and the jurisprudence of national courts.[8] Two conventions regulate state immunity. In 1972, the European Convention on State Immunity was adopted by the Council of Europe and entered into force in 1976. By July 2016, though, only eight states had ratified it.[9] More importantly, the UN Convention on Jurisdictional Immunities of States and Their Property was adopted by the General Assembly in 2004. The Convention was prepared by the International Law Commission (ILC) and while it is not yet in force, many of its provisions reflect customary international law.

At the outset it is important to understand an important distinction between pleas of immunity for, respectively, *adjudicative* and *enforcement* jurisdiction. While the former relates to the jurisdiction of a court to render a judgment in a matter that involves a foreign state, the latter concerns the administrative and executive powers by whatever measures or procedures and by whatever authorities of the forum state. The question of immunity from enforcement only arises after the issue of jurisdictional immunity has been dealt with and decided against granting the foreign state immunity. The imposition of coercive measures is more intrusive than court proceedings and, as we shall see in later in the chapter, states are almost completely protected from enforcement.

In practice, state immunity from adjudication means that a state cannot be sued before a foreign court unless it gives its consent. It is a procedural matter and must therefore be dealt with *prior* to an inquiry into the merits of the case. Since it is unrelated to the substantive legal issues of the case, a finding by a national court that it must refrain from exercising its jurisdiction therefore says nothing about the extent to which the foreign state has breached its legal obligations.[10] In reality, of course, the decision not to exercise jurisdiction will often mean that the substantive legal issues of the case are not dealt with. If the foreign state waives its immunity and consents to the national court's exercise of jurisdiction, the court can move forward with the case and deal with its merits.[11] As we shall see later, immunity from execution requires an additional and separate waiver.

---

[8] See, inter alia, UK State Immunity Act 1978 and US Foreign Sovereign Immunities Act 1976; Yang (n 2) 27–29. See also the discussion in Hazel Fox, *The Law of State Immunity* (2nd edn, Oxford University Press, 2008) 20–25.

[9] Council of Europe, 'Chart of signatures and ratifications of Treaty 074: European Convention on State Immunity' www.coe.int/en/web/conventions/full-list/-/conventions/treaty/074/signatures?p_auth=n6lNcTH9 (accessed 30 October 2015).

[10] *Jurisdictional Immunities* (n 1) para. 58. See also *Arrest Warrant* (n 3) para. 60.

[11] United Nations Convention on Jurisdictional Immunities of States and Their Property (adopted 2 December 2004), UN Doc. A/RES/59/38 (UN Convention on Jurisdictional Immunities), art. 7.

State immunity must be granted whenever the circumstances of a case show that a state is entitled to immunity and it is not necessary for the foreign state to appear before the court and claim immunity. The UN Convention specifies that a state 'shall ensure that its courts determine on their own initiative' if the immunity of a foreign state is respected.[12]

Immunity is just one of the ways by which a national court may find that it lacks the competence to deal with a matter that involves the interests of a foreign state.[13] In common law jurisdictions, a national court may also find that an issue ought to be dealt with by another branch of government, usually the executive.[14] A common law court may also rely on the doctrine of 'acts of state' and find that it lacks the competence to rule on acts by foreign governments in its own territory and reject the case as *non-justiciable*.[15] In civil law jurisdictions, sensitive issues relating to the effects of laws in foreign states will usually be dealt with pursuant to principles of private international law and the doctrine of '*ordre public*'. This section deals only with immunity.

Only independent and sovereign states can assert state immunity. If there is doubt about an entity's statehood, national courts will usually follow instructions from the executive branch, often a ministry of foreign affairs. For the purposes of state immunity, the term 'state' includes the state and its various organs of government— ministries, diplomatic missions, armed forces etc.—as well as any other instrumentality that perform acts in the exercise of sovereign authority.[16] So, if an entity that would otherwise qualify as being 'private', for whatever reason, performs official sovereign acts, it may be entitled to assert state immunity.

We begin the discussion in Section 6.2.2 with the principles of adjudicative jurisdiction and the importance of the distinction between official acts—acts *jure imperii*—and commercial acts—acts *jure gestionis*. We then discuss exceptions to state immunity in Section 6.2.3 and the relationship between state immunity from adjudicative jurisdiction and violations of international law in Section 6.2.4. We conclude in Section 6.2.5 with an overview of the principles on immunity from enforcement.

6.2.2 The distinction between sovereign and commercial acts in adjudicative jurisdiction

6.2.2.1 Background

Historically, the international law of state immunity from adjudication has progressed from a doctrine of absolute immunity to one of restrictive immunity according to

---

[12] Art. 6(1). See also art. 23(1)(c).   [13] For an overview, see Fox (n 8) 100–138.

[14] From US practice, see *Baker v Carr*, 639 US 186, 217 (1962) and more recently *Sarei v Rio Tinto plc*, 456 F.3d 1069 (2006).

[15] See, inter alia, *Banco National de Cuba v Sabbatino*, 376 US 398, 428 (1964). For UK practice, see *Buttes Gas and Oil Co. v Hammer* [1982] AC 888, 938 (HL). For a more narrow conception of 'acts of state', see *Kuwait Airways Corp. v Iraqi Airways Co.* [2002] UKHL 19, [2002] 2 AC 883, [29], [114], [140], [149].

[16] UN Convention on Jurisdictional Immunities (n 11) art. 2(b). See also ILC, Draft Articles on Jurisdictional Immunities of States and Their Property, with commentaries, *Yearbook of the International Law Commission*, 1991, vol. II, Part Two, pp. 14–18, paras 5–19.

which immunity is only granted in relation to *certain acts* of a state. Until the middle of the 20th century, it was well-established practice that a foreign state was entitled to immunity before national courts in relation to any subject matter and therefore could not be sued unless it consented.[17] The only general exception related to immovable/ 'real' property, such as land or houses that has always been considered as an integral part of the territorial state and not subject to any other laws.[18] The practical effect of absolute immunity was that a national court had to refrain from exercising jurisdiction over a matter on the sole ground that one of the parties to the dispute was a state. It is therefore also referred to as immunity *ratione personae*.

But as states became increasingly involved in commercial and economic activities at the end of the 19th and the early parts of the 20th centuries, national courts began to move towards a more nuanced approach to state immunity.[19] After the end of the Second World War, states introduced a restrictive approach to immunity from adjudicative jurisdiction.[20] In 1950 in *Hoffmann Dralle v Czechoslovakia*, the Austrian Supreme Court found that a foreign state was only exempted from Austrian jurisdiction for acts of a sovereign character. In *Empire of Iran* in 1963, the German Federal Constitutional Court concluded that absolute immunity was no longer a rule of customary international law. The court also introduced a vital distinction between acts of a sovereign nature—*jure imperii*—and those of a non-sovereign character—*jure gestionis*.[21] In treaty law, restrictive immunity was introduced in both the 1972 European Convention on State Immunity[22] and the 2004 UN Convention on the Jurisdictional Immunities of States and Their Property.[23] In addition, in 2013 the European Court of Human Rights (ECtHR) concluded that Russia—a signatory state to the 2004 UN Convention—had violated its obligations under the European Convention on Human Rights by effectively reintroducing and relying on absolute immunity (immunity *ratione personae*).[24] Today, it is well established that a foreign state only enjoys immunity from a territorial state's exercise of adjudicative jurisdiction in relation to sovereign or governmental acts (acts *jure imperii*) and not with regard to commercial or private acts (acts *jure gestionis*). Unlike during the era of absolute immunity, then, a claim of immunity is no longer solely dealt with on the basis of the identity of the defendant—*ratione personae*—but at times also due to the subject matter of the case— *ratione materiae*.

[17] For US practice, see, inter alia, *The Schooner Exchange v McFaddon* (n 1) but more to the point *Berizzi Bros Co. v The Pesaro*, 271 US 562, 574 (1926). From UK case law, see *Compania Naviera Vascongada v The Cristina* [1938] AC 485, 490 (HL) and *The Porto Alexandre* [1920] P 30 (CA).

[18] Yang (n 2) 10–11.

[19] For a historical overview, see Draft Articles on Jurisdictional Immunities (n 16) pp. 36–40, paras 14–25.

[20] For developments in the US, see 'The Tate Letter' (1952) 26 *Department of State Bulletin* 984. For subsequent case law, see, inter alia, *Alfred Dunhill of London, Inc. v Republic of Cuba*, 425 US 682 (1976).

[21] *Empire of Iran* (1963) 45 ILR 57, 79–81. Only later did courts in the UK begin to abandon absolute immunity, see *Owners of the Philippine Admiral v Wallem Shipping (Hong Kong) Ltd (The Philippine Admiral)* [1977] AC 373 (Privy Council).

[22] Art. 7(1).   [23] See Part III of the Convention.

[24] ECtHR, *Oleynikov v Russia*, App. no. 36703/04, 14 March 2013, paras 60–61. See also *Al-Adsani v UK* (n 2) para. 54.

6.2.2.2 Jure imperii v jure gestionis acts

The underlying purpose of refusing state immunity from adjudicative jurisdiction for commercial activities is clear: when a state engages in commercial activities and competes with private individuals or corporations, it should not be immune from scrutiny by the courts of the state in which it conducts those activities. If a state participates in commercial activities, it no longer acts in a public capacity but in the capacity of a trader/merchant and that should be reflected in the laws of immunity. In practice, however, it has turned out to be difficult for legislators and national courts to develop a workable definition of a commercial act.[25] The classic method of differentiating between sovereign and commercials acts is to apply a 'private individual test' and ask if the activity is one that can be performed by a private individual. If the answer is yes, the activity is deemed to be commercial and thus a not immune.[26]

In order to further assist in the determination, legislators and national courts have relied on both the purpose and the nature of the act in question. An approach that focuses on the *purpose* of the activity means that an activity is deemed to be sovereign and thus immune if it is performed for public/governmental purposes. The problem is, however, that states generally act for public purposes and for that reason a purpose test ends up excluding a very wide range of acts from adjudication. In *Empire of Iran*, the German Federal Constitutional Court therefore rejected the purpose test[27] and instead focused on the *nature* of the activity.[28] Thus, if the *type* of action is one in which a private individual could participate, it is a commercial and thus a non-immune act. According to that logic, since private individuals can purchase goods and commodities all contracts for purchases and acquisitions entered into by states must be deemed to be commercial and thus non-immune acts. In 1999, the Danish Supreme Court also concluded that an embassy's purchase of airline tickets as a private law transaction was a non-immune activity.[29] But while the purpose test may be over-inclusive, a nature test may turn out to be the exact opposite because it effectively ignores the fact that states sometimes exercises their sovereignty through seemingly commercial activities. In practice, therefore, distinguishing between commercial and non-commercial acts often requires a more nuanced and *contextual* approach that take account of both the purpose and the nature of the activity.[30] The 2004 UN Convention specifies that the determination 'should be made primarily to the nature of the contract or transaction, but its purpose should also be taken into account if the parties to the contract or transaction have so agreed, or if, in the practice of the State of the forum, that

---

[25] For an overview, see Fox (n 8) 502–532; Yang (n 2) 75–132.

[26] In France, the private person test resonates with the internal division of adjudicative competences between commercial and administrative courts, see the discussion in Fox (n 8) 507–508. See also, from the UK, *I Congreso del Partido* [1983] AC 244, 262, from the US, *Argentina v Weltover*, 504 US 607, 614–617 (1992) and, from Austria, *Holubek v The Government of the United States*, Austrian Supreme Court, 10 February 1961.

[27] *Empire of Iran* (n 21) 27. See also *Argentina v Weltover* (n 26) 614.

[28] *Empire of Iran* (n 21) 80. US Foreign Sovereign Immunities Act 1976, § 1603(d).

[29] U.1999.939H. See also *Argentina v Weltover* (n 26) 615.

[30] See, inter alia, Lord Wilberforce's judgment in *Owners of Cargo Lately Laden on Board the Playa Larga v Owners of the I Congreso del Partido* [1983] 1 AC 244, 257 (HL).

purpose is relevant to determining the non-commercial character of the contract or transaction'.[31]

The UK House of Lords decision in *Holland v Lampen-Wolfe* adopted a contextual approach. The case concerned proceedings for defamatory damages in the UK against a US official, and the claim related to statements made by the official in his capacity as an educational officer at a US base in the UK. Although the act in question—the writing of a memorandum by a civilian educational services officer in connection with an educational programme provided by civilian staff employed by a university—did not appear at first sight to be a sovereign act (*jure imperii*), the court nevertheless concluded that the statement fell within the area of sovereign activity. In reaching its decision, the court referred to the broader context of the statement, including where and to whom the educational programme was provided and whom it was designed to benefit. Among other things, the court noted that the 'whole activity was designed as part of the process of maintaining forces and associated civilians on the base by U.S. personnel to serve the needs of the U.S. military authorities'.[32]

Some states try to overcome the difficulties of distinguishing between sovereign and commercial activities by enacted legislation that lists acts deemed of a non-sovereign and thus non-immune character.[33] The 2004 UN Convention adopts a similar approach. Thus, according to article 2(1)(c) of the Convention, commercial transactions are: (i) any commercial contract or transaction for the sale of goods or supply of services; (ii) any contract for a loan or other transaction of a financial nature, including any obligation of guarantee or of indemnity in respect of any such loan or transaction; (iii) any other contract or transaction of a commercial, industrial, trading or professional nature, but not including a contract of employment of persons.

6.2.3 Exceptions to state immunity in the UN Convention on the immunities of states and their property

In the UN Convention on the Immunities of States and Their Property, the substantive exception to state immunity for commercial activities is found in article 10. But commercial activities are not the only exception to state immunity in the Convention. According to article 5, a state enjoys immunity from the jurisdiction of the courts of another state unless the activity in question falls under a number of exceptions contained in articles 10–17 of the Convention. Articles 11–17 supplement the general exception for commercial activities by listing the most important examples of activities that may (also) be deemed to be of a non-immune character.

One of the exceptions relates to *employment contracts*.[34] Such contracts merit specialized treatment because the traditional way of distinguishing between *jure imperii*

---

[31] Art. 2(2). See also Draft Articles on Jurisdictional Immunities (n 16) para. 27.

[32] *Holland v Lampen-Wolfe* [2000] 1 WLR 1573, 1576ff, 1581ff (HL).

[33] See UK State Immunity Act 1978, ss 2–11. See also US Foreign Sovereign Immunities Act 1976, §§ 1604, 1605 and 1607.

[34] For an overview of the rules, see Fox (n 8) 547–563 and Yang (n 2) 132–198.

and *jure gestionis* activities is of little assistance. Since private individuals and companies hire people all the time and there is nothing inherently 'governmental' about the simple act of employing someone, a nature test would dictate that all issues in relation to employment contracts are acts of a *jure gestionis* character and thus non-immune. This, however, is not acceptable to states and state practice illustrates that national courts grant extensive immunity to states in relation to proceedings that concern employment contracts. The main rule is found in article 11 whereby a foreign state cannot invoke immunity from adjudicative jurisdiction in relation to an employment contract for work performed on the territory of the forum state unless the dispute falls within a number of listed exceptions. An important exception stipulates that a foreign state remains immune if the employee has 'been recruited to perform functions in the *exercise of governmental authority*'.[35] As a general rule, state immunity is also maintained in relation to *diplomatic missions*.[36]

Another important exception is found in article 12 of the 2004 UN Convention that excludes immunity:

> in a proceeding which relates to pecuniary compensation for death or injury to the person, or damage to or loss of tangible property, caused by an act or omission which is alleged to be attributable to the State, if the act or omission occurred in whole or in part in the territory of that other State and if the author of the act.

The 1972 European Convention on State Immunity contains a similar provision.[37] The exception is first and foremost meant to apply to insurable risks from injuries and damage caused by traffic accidents. It does not cover cases where there is no physical damage thus proceedings relating to allegedly false or defamatory statements are covered by immunity unless the foreign state gives its consent.[38] It is also worth noting that the exception only covers wrongful conduct that has occurred or been committed in the territory of the forum state where the author of the act or omission is also present in the forum state. It does not, therefore, justify refusing immunity in the more likely event that the injury or damage was inflicted abroad, such as in the territory of the foreign state itself.[39] It has been a particular matter of contention whether the exception in article 12 includes acts committed by a state on the territory of the forum state *in times of armed conflict*. A traditional reading of international law holds that claims arising out of conduct in times of armed conflict are governed by the law of armed conflict (international humanitarian law) and for that reason are not covered by article 12.[40] This is also supported by the *travaux*

---

[35] Art. 11(2)(a).

[36] Art. 11(2)(b). Relevant rules are also found in the Vienna Convention on Diplomatic Relations (VCDR) (adopted 18 April 1961, entered into force 24 April 1964), 500 UNTS 95 and the Vienna Convention on Consular Relations (VCCR) (adopted 24 April 1963, entered into force 19 March 1967), 596 UNTS 261 See also ECtHR, *Fogarty v UK*, App. no. 37112/97, 21 November 2001, paras 37–38.

[37] See art. 11.   [38] Draft Articles on Jurisdictional Immunities (n 16) para. 5.

[39] The practical application of the exception in art. 12 is not uniform and a number of issues remain unsolved. For ECtHR practice, see *McElhinney v Ireland*, App. no. 31253/96, 21 November 2001.

[40] See also the debate in Fox (n 8) 582–583. See also art. 31 of the European Convention on State Immunity (adopted 16 May 1972, entered into force 11 June 1976), ETS No. 074.

préparatoires.[41] Courts in Greece and Italy nevertheless found that Germany was *not* entitled to state immunity in relation to claims for compensation concerning atrocities committed by German armed forces during the Second World War.[42] In *Jurisdictional Immunities of the State*, the ICJ concluded that customary international law (still) requires a state to be afforded immunity in relation to *jure imperii* acts allegedly committed on the territory of another state by its armed forces and other organs of the state during the course of armed conflict.[43] It bears mentioning, however, that a number of the ICJ judges dissented;[44] and this is one area of the law of immunity that may change in the future.

The third and final exception to state immunity mentioned here concerns the issue of immovable property located on the territory of the forum state. As we saw earlier, even in the age of absolute immunity it was well established that an exception from immunity was made in relation to immovable/'real' property situated in the forum state. Immovable property forms an integral part of the forum state and is therefore not subject to other laws—also known in Latin as the *lex situs* rule.[45] This rule is reflected in article 13(a) of the 2004 UN Convention. It is important to note, however, that the exception for immovable property does not alter the privileges and immunities a foreign state enjoys under other parts of international law with regard to its diplomatic missions and other representative offices.[46] However, premises used as a private residence by a member of a diplomatic mission are covered by the exception from immunity and there is also practice to support the conclusion that a national court may exercise jurisdiction over the premises of the diplomatic mission itself when it is purely the ownership or title that is in issue if there is no interference with the performance of diplomatic duties.[47]

6.2.4 State immunity and violations of international law

Since state immunity serves as a procedural bar to the exercise of jurisdiction by a national court, the court must dismiss a case against a state that is entitled to state immunity, regardless of the nature of the allegations against the state. There is, in other words, a clear tension between state immunity and more overarching notions of justice.[48] In recent decades, a limited number of national courts have adopted the

[41] See, inter alia, Gerhard Hafner, Chairman of the Ad Hoc Committee on Jurisdictional Immunities of States and Their Property, 'Remarks to the United Nations General Assembly Sixth Committee', Summary Record of the 13th Meeting (22 March 2005), UN Doc. A/C.6/59/SR.13.

[42] For practice in Greece, see *Prefecture of Voiotia v Federal Republic of Germany*, Supreme Court (Areios Pagos) case No. 11/2000, 4 May 2000. But see also *Margellos v Federal Republic of Germany*, case No. 6/2002, Supreme Court of Greece, 17 September 2002. For Italian practice, see *Ferrini v Federal Republic of Germany*, Corte di Cassazione (Sezioni Unite), judgment No. 5044 of 6 November 2003, registered 11 March 2004 (2004) 87 *Rivista diritto internazionale* 539.

[43] *Jurisdictional Immunities* (n 1) paras 72–78.

[44] See, inter alia, the Dissenting Opinions of Judge ad hoc Gaja and Judge Yusuf. See also the discussion in the Separate Opinion of Judge Bennouna. See also Separate Opinion of Judge Koroma, para. 7.

[45] See also European Convention on State Immunity (n 40) art. 9. For an overview, see Fox (n 8) 591–597.

[46] See UN Convention on Jurisdictional Immunities (n 11) art. 3.   [47] Fox (n 8) 594–595.

[48] See, inter alia, the remarks by the ECtHR in *Kalogeropoulou and Others v Greece and Germany*, App no. 59021/00, 12 December 2002, 9 (on crimes against humanity) and those of Lord Bingham of Cornhill in *Jones v Ministry of Interior of Kingdom of Saudi Arabia et al.* [2006] UKHL 26, [2007] 1 AC 270, [26].

view that a foreign state should not be able to assert state immunity in relation to violations of *international* law, including human rights violations. While the issue of state
immunity and individual criminal responsibility for crimes in international law for
heads of state and other state representatives are discussed in Section 6.3, the issue of
immunity for civil suits for alleged violations of international law against a state need
to be covered here.[49]

The 2004 UN Convention on Jurisdictional Immunities of States and Their Property
does not include any exceptions to state immunity for breaches of international law
and the last Working Group under the ILC refused to discuss the feasibility of including such an exception. But in 2000, in *Distomo*, the Supreme Court of Greece nevertheless held that Germany was not protected by state immunity in relation to a claim
for compensation by the successors of the victims of a massacre committed by German
armed forces during the German occupation of Greece in the Second World War.[50]
And in 2004, in *Ferrini v Federal Republic of Germany*, an Italian court similarly held
that Germany could not claim state immunity in relation to certain acts committed
by German troops during the Second World War because the acts constituted international crimes.[51]

The relationship between state immunity and violations of international law was
discussed extensively by the ICJ in its 2012 decision in the *Jurisdictional Immunities
of the State* case. In response to, among others, the *Ferrini* case, Germany argued that
Italy had violated its obligations under state immunity by allowing civil claims to
be brought against it in Italian courts and by declaring that decisions by Greek civil
courts rendered against Germany on the basis of acts similar to those which gave rise
to the claims brought before Italian courts could be enforced in Italy. It was clear that
the acts of the German armed forces constituted acts of a *jure imperii* character but
Italy argued that Germany was not entitled to immunity because the acts involved the
most serious violations of rules of international law of a peremptory character (*jus
cogens*).[52] Although the ICJ stated that there was no doubt that the acts of the German
armed forces that gave rise to the proceedings in the Italian courts were serious violations of the laws of armed conflict and constituted crimes under international law, it
rejected the Italian argument.[53] The Court could not find any practice that supported
the claim that state immunity could be limited in cases of serious violations of international law and it concluded that a state's entitlement to immunity does not depend
upon the 'gravity of the act … or the peremptory nature of the rule which it is alleged to
have violated'.[54] Among others things, the Court referred to case law from the ECtHR
according to which a state is not 'deprived of immunity by reason of the fact that it is
accused of serious violations of international human rights law or the international
law of armed conflict'.[55] The ICJ rejected the notion that upholding state immunity

---

[49] For an overview, see Fox (n 8) 139–166.
[50] *Prefecture of Voiotia v Federal Republic of Germany* (n 42).   [51] See n 42.
[52] *Jurisdictional Immunities* (n 1) para. 61.   [53] Ibid, para. 81.   [54] Ibid, para. 84.
[55] Ibid, para. 90. For ECtHR case law, see *Al-Adsani v UK* (n 2) para. 66 (regarding alleged torture). See
also *Kalogeropoulou v Greece and Germany* (n 48) 9.

conflicted with the existence of *jus cogens* rules from which no derogation is permitted. Indeed, the rules that 'determine the scope and extent of jurisdiction and when that jurisdiction may be exercised do not derogate from those substantive rules which possess *jus cogens* status'.[56] The UK House of Lords reached a similar conclusion in its 2006 judgment in *Jones v Ministry of Interior of Kingdom of Saudi Arabia et al.*, where the court found that Saudi Arabia was entitled to state immunity in relation to alleged violations of the prohibition against torture in the UN Convention against Torture.[57]

6.2.5 Immunity from enforcement

As mentioned in the introduction to this section, a distinction exists between state immunity from adjudicative jurisdiction and immunity from subsequent enforcement measures of the orders of a court by the host state. Since the issue of immunity from enforcement only arises after jurisdictional immunity has been dealt with and a national court has decided the case against the foreign state, immunity from enforcement constitutes 'the last bastion of State immunity'.[58]

The different treatment of the two kinds of jurisdiction means that the principles of state immunity are distinct and must be so applied. A number of consequences flow from this. First, as already noted, a waiver of immunity from execution must be expressed separately. This is also reflected in article 20 of the 2004 UN Convention. Secondly, unlike immunity from adjudication, immunity from enforcement is by and large absolute and it may very well be that a national court concludes that a foreign state is not immune from proceedings but is immune from any enforcement measures. The separate application of the principles of immunity from, respectively, adjudication and enforcement was noted by the ICJ in *Jurisdictional Immunities of the State* where the Court stated that it could rule on whether a measure of constraint on property owned by the German state in Italy violated Germany's immunity from enforcement without determining if the underlying decision by a Greek court against Germany that formed the basis for the constraint was in itself a breach of the rules on jurisdictional immunity.[59]

Historically, states have been very reluctant to accept limitations on immunity from enforcement.[60] However, in response to the introduction of restrictive adjudicative jurisdiction a number of continental European states slowly began to permit enforcement measures against property located in the forum state that was used for commercial activities.[61] That development later matured and international law now contains a clear distinction between property located in the forum state that is used for public purposes and local property used for commercial purposes. Only the former category of property is protected from enforcement.[62]

---

[56] Ibid, para. 95.   [57] *Jones v Ministry of Interior of Kingdom of Saudi Arabia et al.* (n 48) [33].
[58] Draft Articles on Jurisdictional Immunities (n 16) para. 2.
[59] *Jurisdictional Immunities* (n 1) para. 114.   [60] For an overview, see Fox (n 8) 600–609.
[61] See, inter alia, *Socobelge v The Hellenic State*, Tribunal civil de Bruxelles (1951) and *The Philippine Embassy*, 46 BVerfGE, 342. See also the overview in August Reinisch, 'European Court Practice Concerning State Immunity from Enforcement Measures' (2006) 17 *European Journal of International Law* 803.
[62] See also *The 'Ara Libertad' (Argentina v Ghana)*, Provisional Measures, Order of 15 December 2012, ITLOS Rep 21.

The 2004 UN Convention on the Immunities of States and Their Property covers immunity from enforcement in Part IV—articles 18–21. While article 18 concerns pre-judgment measures, article 19 deals with immunity for measures of constraint after a judgment against a foreign state has been rendered. In both instances, the Convention stipulates that enforcement measures require that the foreign state has either expressly consented to such measures or has allocated or earmarked property for the satisfaction of the particular claim. In addition, post-judgment measures of enforcement can be taken if the property in question is based in the forum state and is specifically used or intended to be used by the foreign state for commercial purposes, and the enforcement measure is taken against property that 'has a connection with the entity against which the proceeding was directed'.[63] With regard to the use of the property, then, it is purpose and not nature that is decisive. Article 21 then lists a number of types of property which due to their purpose or use are considered to be non-commercial and thus immune. These include bank accounts for use in the performance of functions of a diplomatic mission or consular post, military property, property of a central bank or other monetary authority, property that is part of the cultural heritage of the state or part of its archives and property that form part of an exhibition of objects of scientific, cultural or historical interest.

The issue of enforcement of a local judgment against real property used partly for diplomatic purposes was discussed by the Swedish Supreme Court in 2011. In *Sedelmayer v Russian Federation*, the court concluded that state immunity did not preclude execution against a multi-unit building owned by the Russian state whose units were for the most part rented out to either individuals employed at the Russian embassy or trade mission or otherwise used in connection with Swedish–Russian scientific exchanges of other governmental activities.[64] Since the building was only used for official purposes to a limited extent, the court found that the property was not immune. In *Jurisdictional Immunities of the State*, the ICJ concluded that the measures of constraint taken by the Italian authorities against property owned by the German state in the absence of express German consent violated international law. The Court noted that the property in question—a cultural centre intended to promote cultural exchanges between Germany and Italy—was used for governmental non-commercial purposes and thus for sovereign purposes.[65]

6.3 The immunities of state representatives

6.3.1 Introduction

State representatives enjoy certain immunities from national jurisdiction because they 'personify' the state on whose behalf they act and because they need protection

---

[63] UN Convention on Jurisdictional Immunities (n 11) art. 19(c).

[64] *Sedelmayer v Russian Federation*, No. O 170-10. 2011, see the discussion in Pål Wrange, '*Sedelmayer v Russian Federation*' (2012) 106 *American Journal of International Law* 347.

[65] *Jurisdictional Immunities* (n 1) paras 119–120.

from national jurisdiction in order to fulfil their functions as state representatives.[66] As the ICJ noted in *Arrest Warrant*, a foreign minister can only perform his or her official functions if the individual can travel freely and remain in constant communication with not only the home government but also with diplomatic missions and representatives of other states.[67] The immunities are therefore not granted for the personal benefit of the representative but so that the individual can fulfil his or her official functions.[68]

At the outset, a few important points must be noted. First, the extent of immunity offered to various representatives differs substantially. While some representatives enjoy almost absolute immunity, others enjoy more limited protection. Thus, when determining what immunity a particular state representative is entitled to it is of crucial importance to identify the category of state representatives to which the representative belongs.

The second important point to note is that the extent of immunity offered to state representatives revolves around an important distinction between immunity *ratione personae*—or 'personal immunity'—and immunity *ratione materiae*—'functional immunity'. Immunity *ratione personae* flows from the *position* a representative holds in a state and (as we shall see in Section 6.3.2) is only enjoyed by a very small group of individuals with certain high-level governmental position as well as by diplomatic agents and by representatives on 'special missions'. As a form of immunity, it applies to both *official* and *private* acts as well as to acts committed both *before* and *while* the representative occupied his or her public position. Immunity *ratione materiae*, on the other hand, relates to the functions the representative performs and is enjoyed by all state representatives. It does not apply to private acts but applies after the representative leaves his or her position for public acts committed while in public service.

We begin the overview with the immunities of high-ranking state representatives in Section 6.3.2 before we examine the immunity of other state representatives in Section 6.3.3.

6.3.2 The immunity of certain high-ranking representatives

6.3.2.1 Introduction

A limited number of state representatives are so closely tied to the sovereignty of the state that they enjoy particularly extensive legal protection.[69] These few representatives

---

[66] For an overview of the different rationales for immunity for state representatives, see Roman Anatolevich Kolodkin, 'Preliminary Report on immunity of State officials from foreign criminal jurisdiction' (ILC, 2008), UN Doc. A/CN.4/601, paras 84–97. See also Hazel Fox, *The Law of State Immunity* (Oxford University Press, 2015) 547.

[67] *Arrest Warrant* (n 3) para. 53.   [68] Ibid.

[69] This appears to be accepted everywhere apart from in the United States where immunity for heads of state seemingly remains 'a matter of grace and comity, rather than a matter of right'. See, inter alia, *Lafontant v Aristide*, 844 F.Supp. 128, 132 (1994) and *Flatow v Islamic Republic of Iran et al.*, 999 F.Supp. 1, 24 (DDC 1998). For a persuasive presentation, see Astrid Kjeldgaard-Pedersen, *Statsrepræsentanters immunitet* (Forlaget Thomson, 2005).

hold a very special position and enjoy immunity *ratione personae*/personal immunity. First of all, *heads of state* have always had a privileged status in international law and in earlier periods of international law there was a tendency to consider the ruler of a state as the embodiment of the latter.[70] In *Questions of Mutual Assistance in Criminal Matters*, the ICJ stated that the immunity of heads of state is derived from customary international law.[71] Heads of state are not the only high-ranking state officials with personal immunity. In *Arrest Warrant*, the Court found it 'well-established that certain holders of high-ranking office in a State, such as the Head of State, Head of Government and Minister for Foreign Affairs, enjoy immunities from jurisdiction in other States, both civil and criminal'.[72] In the light of the representative powers these representatives possess, this is not surprising. For example, as we saw in Chapter 3, these few representatives may enter into legally binding commitments on behalf of their states without having to produce full powers.[73] In 2001, a French court adopted a *de facto* assessment and concluded that Muammar Gaddafi was to be considered the 'head of state' of Libya even though he did not formally appear to qualify under the Libyan constitution.[74]

The extent to which other high-ranking representatives enjoy immunity *ratione personae* is unclear.[75] UK courts have found that an Israeli minister of defence and a Chinese minister for commerce and international trade benefitted from personal immunity.[76] The ICJ, on the other hand, came to the opposite result in relation to a state prosecutor and a head of national security. In *Khurts Bat*, a court in the UK similarly denied personal immunity to the head of an office of national security who Germany had requested to be extradited.[77]

6.3.2.2 The protection offered

Personal immunity offers high-ranking state officials widespread protection from both civil and criminal prosecutions and in relation to official as well as private acts. Protection from *civil jurisdiction* is less extensive, however, and certain acts performed in a private capacity do not seem to be immune from adjudicative

---

[70] See also Lord Millett in *R v Bow Street Metropolitan Stipendiary Magistrate, ex p. Pinochet Ugarte (No. 3)* [2000] 1 AC 147, 269 (HL).

[71] *Certain Questions of Mutual Assistance in Criminal Matters (Djibouti v France)*, Judgment [2008] ICJ Rep 177, para. 174.

[72] *Arrest Warrant* (n 3) para. 51.

[73] Vienna Convention on the Law of Treaties (adopted 23 May 1969, entered into force 27 January 1980), 1155 UNTS 331, art. 7(2).

[74] *Arrêt* of the Cour de Cassation, 13 March 2001, No. 1414.

[75] See also Concepción Escobar Hernández, 'Second Report on the immunity of State officials from foreign criminal jurisdiction' (ILC, 2013), UN Doc. A/CN.4/661, paras 56–68.

[76] See, respectively, the ruling of 12 February 2004 in the case regarding General Shaul Mofaz, and the ruling of 8 November 2005 in the case regarding Re Bo Xilai, quoted Kolodkin, 'Preliminary Report on immunity of State officials from foreign criminal jurisdiction' (n 66) para. 118. See also the debate in paras 118–121.

[77] *Khurts Bat v Investigating Judge of the German Federal Court* [2011] EWHC 2029 (Admin). For an extensive overview and debate, see Andrew Sanger, 'Immunity of State Officials from the Criminal Jurisdiction of a Foreign State' (2013) 62 *International and Comparative Law Quarterly* 193.

jurisdiction. For practical purposes, the protection offered may be parallel to that enjoyed by diplomatic agents.[78] It would thereby follow that protection is unavailable for certain acts relating to private immovable property, succession in which the official is involved as an executor, administrator, heir or legatee as a private person or professional or commercial activities exercised outside their official functions.[79]

Immunity *ratione personae* from *criminal jurisdiction* applies to both acts done in an official as well as in a private capacity and in relation to conduct performed both before and during the period in office.[80] And unlike the situation that applies to civil claims, there is no need to distinguish between immunity from jurisdiction and immunity from execution with regard to criminal jurisdiction. Criminal jurisdiction refers to *all* criminal procedural measures in respect of a foreign representative. In *Arrest Warrant*, the ICJ stated that the protection extends to 'any act of authority of another State which would hinder' the representative in performing his or her duties.[81] In *Certain Questions of Mutual Assistance in Criminal Matters*, the Court found that the 'determining factor in assessing whether or not there has been an attack on the immunity of the Head of State lies in the subjection of the latter to a constraining act of authority'.[82] It seems, in other words, that immunity is breached when an obligation is imposed on the official.[83] The state that is considering exercising criminal jurisdiction against a foreign head of state, head of government or a minister for foreign affairs is under an obligation to consider the issue of immunity and make its own determination of whether or not immunity bars the proceedings.[84]

Personal immunity does not offer absolute protection from criminal jurisdiction. In *Arrest Warrant*, the Court stated that criminal prosecution of a minister for foreign affairs is possible in four circumstances.[85] First, the minister can be criminally prosecuted by courts in his or her own 'home state'. Secondly, prosecution in the forum state is possible if the 'home state' agrees to the prosecution by waiving immunity. A waiver of immunity must, however, be express.[86] The third option for prosecution mentioned by the court was criminal prosecution before international courts. We shall return to this option in Chapter 15. As a fourth option for possible criminal prosecution, the Court stated that a foreign minister can be prosecuted *after* his or her term expires for acts committed either *prior* or *subsequent* to the

---

[78] See generally *Certain Questions of Mutual Assistance* (n 71) para. 174   [79] VCDR art. 31(1).

[80] *Arrest Warrant* (n 3) para. 55. See also *Prosecutor v Omar Hassan Ahmad al-Bashir*, Decision on the Cooperation of the Democratic Republic of the Congo Regarding Omar al-Bashir's Arrest and Surrender to the Court, ICC-02/05-01/09 (9 April 2014), para. 25. In *Certain Questions of Mutual Assistance* (n 71) the ICJ also concluded that the rules on the inviolability of diplomatic agents in art. 29 of the VCDR are equally applicable to heads of state, see para. 174.

[81] *Arrest Warrant* (n 3) para. 54.   [82] *Certain Questions of Mutual Assistance* (n 71) para. 170.

[83] See also Roman Anatolevich Kolodkin, 'Second Report on immunity of State officials from foreign criminal jurisdiction' (ILC, 2010), UN Doc. A/CN.4/631, para. 41.

[84] Roman Anatolevich Kolodkin, 'Third Report on immunity of State officials from foreign criminal jurisdiction' (ILC, 2011), UN Doc. A/CN.4/646, para. 19.

[85] *Arrest Warrant* (n 3) para. 61.   [86] Ibid, para. 41.

period of office or for *private acts* committed during the period in office. The Court thereby implied that immunity remains in relation to all official acts performed during the period in office. As we shall see in Section 6.3.3.2, however, this is a statement not everyone agrees with.

6.3.3 The immunity of other state representatives who perform official acts

6.3.3.1 Introduction

As we have just seen, it is only a limited number of certain state representatives who enjoy immunity for both official and private acts—immunity *ratione personae*. All other state representatives are merely protected by immunity in relation to the acts they perform on behalf of the state they represent—immunity *ratione materiae* (functional immunity). Functional immunity is derived from the conceptual understanding that it is not the representative but the state that he or she represents that is the real object of the proceedings. The grant of immunity therefore prevents an applicant from circumventing state immunity by bringing a case against the representative of the state. Like immunity *ratione personae*, functional immunity can therefore also be waived by the state on whose behalf the state official has acted.

The determination of whether conduct is 'official' or 'personal' is made according to the general rules and principles on state responsibility and attribution of conduct.[87] While state responsibility is dealt with more extensively in Chapter 7, a few points must be made here. First, the motives of the state representative are immaterial. As long as an act is performed by an individual with official authority ('under the colour of authority') it is an 'official' act. Secondly, acts that fall outside the official functions of a state representative—conduct *ultra vires*—are still deemed to be official acts if they are performed in a public capacity.[88] The same logic applies to illegal acts carried out by a state representative. Indeed, since it is precisely in cases of suspicion of unlawful conduct that the question of jurisdiction arises, it would run counter to the whole idea of immunity to exclude illegal acts from immunity *ratione materiae*.[89] As we shall see in the following section, however, it is hotly debated whether exceptions to criminal immunity can be made in cases of certain international crimes. It is also worth noting that the distinction between acts *jure imperii* and *jure gestionis* is irrelevant for the purposes of attribution and that nothing precludes classifying a commercial act as an official act. In practice, then, a representative who performs a commercial act on behalf of a state enjoys immunity whereas the state does not (due to the commercial character of the act).

---

[87] See also Eileen Denza, *Diplomatic Law: A Commentary on the Vienna Convention on Diplomatic Relations* (2nd edn, Oxford University Press, 1998) 363.

[88] See also Draft Articles on Jurisdictional Immunities (n 16) art. 7.

[89] See the overview and discussion in Kolodkin, 'Second Report on immunity of State officials from foreign criminal jurisdiction' (n 83) para. 31.

6.3.3.2 **The protection offered**

Immunity *ratione materiae* protects all state officials from *civil proceedings* in respect of their official acts. If it was otherwise, an applicant would be able to circumvent state immunity by bringing a case against the representative who represents the state. This is also reflected in the 2004 United Nations Convention on Jurisdictional Immunities of States and Their Property according to which the concept of a 'state' for the purposes of immunity includes 'representatives of the State acting in that capacity'.[90] Similar conclusions were reached by the UK House of Lords in *Jones v Ministry of Interior of Kingdom of Saudi Arabia et al.*[91] and by a Canadian appeals court in *Bouzari v Islamic Republic of Iran.*[92] In both cases, the courts rejected the claim that an exception to immunity from civil proceedings could be made in relation to allegations of the (*jus cogens*) prohibition against torture.

Functional immunity from *criminal proceedings* for non-high-ranking state representatives differs from that applied to *civil proceedings* and *criminal proceedings against high-ranking state officials*. In contrast to the situation that applies in relation to the criminal immunity of high-ranking state officials, the forum state does not appear to be obliged to consider the immunity of other state representatives unless the foreign state invokes it.[93] So if the state of a non-high-ranking representative wants to protect its own official from foreign criminal prosecution it must notify the forum state and assert that the representative acted in an official capacity and should thus enjoy immunity. If not, the forum state may proceed with the case. In *Certain Questions of Mutual Assistance in Criminal Matters*, the ICJ concluded that the head of national security in Mongolia was not entitled to immunity *ratione materiae* and that this was partly because his home state had never invoked it.[94]

Unlike the circumstances with regard to the functional immunity of non-high-ranking officials in civil proceedings, it is not clear if state representatives are always immune in relation to criminal prosecution. As we saw earlier, in *Arrest Warrant* the ICJ concluded that a high-ranking state representative may be prosecuted before international courts where those courts have jurisdiction. We will return to such prosecutions in Chapter 15. With regard to prosecution before national courts, the ICJ also indicated that a high-ranking state representative (in the absence of a waiver of immunity) remains immune after the end of his or her term for *official* acts committed during their period in office. National case law is not, however, exactly in line with that statement. Two potential exceptions to immunity *ratione materiae* are currently under debate.

First, a number of national cases indicate that functional immunity from criminal jurisdiction may not always apply in relation to official acts committed *on the territory*

---

[90] Art. 2(1)(b)(iv).   [91] *Jones v Ministry of Interior of Kingdom of Saudi Arabia et al.* (n 48).
[92] *Bouzari v Islamic Republic of Iran*, 71 OR (3d) 675, para. 91.
[93] Kolodkin, 'Third Report on immunity of State officials from foreign criminal jurisdiction' (n 84) para. 18. See also Ingrid Wuerth, 'Pinochet's Legacy Reassessed' (2012) 106 *American Journal of International Law* 731, 745–747.
[94] *Certain Questions of Mutual Assistance* (n 71) para 196.

of the forum state. The existence of a territorial exception to criminal immunity seems to be supported by the ILC's first Special Rapporteur.[95] The rationale for refusing criminal immunity in such circumstances would be the jurisdictional priority of the forum state on its own territory. It would also correlate with article 12 of the UN Convention whereby a state cannot invoke immunity from civil jurisdiction in relation to pecuniary compensation for death or injury to the person, or damage to or loss of tangible property, caused by an act or omission that occurred in whole or in part on the territory of that other state.

The second possible exception to immunity *ratione materiae* from criminal jurisdiction relates to international crimes.[96] In 1999, the House of Lords in the UK concluded that immunity did not protect the former head of state of Chile—August Pinochet—from extradition to criminal prosecution in Spain for acts of torture.[97] A majority of the law lords found that Pinochet was not immune after his official term had ended in relation to an established international crime where both the forum and the home states had accepted that they were under an obligation to prosecute. The House of Lords limited the conclusion to torture. After *Pinochet*, a number of arguments have been advanced in support of the general conclusion that functional immunity from criminal jurisdiction cannot be asserted in relation to international crimes.[98] According to one argument, international crimes cannot be considered official acts that are protected by immunity. It is, however, difficult to see how the gravity of a criminal offence alters the attribution of the act. In most cases, it is precisely the presence of a complete state apparatus that enables the perpetration of the worst atrocities. Most international crimes are actually carried out in furtherance of some sort of public policy, however reprehensible. Another argument holds that the prohibition against the commission of certain core international crimes, including torture, is of a peremptory/*jus cogens* nature and therefore overrides any claim of immunity *ratione materiae*.[99] This, however, is also a dubious claim. In *Jurisdictional Immunities of the State*, the ICJ did not find that immunity depended upon the 'gravity of the act ... or the peremptory nature of the rule which it is alleged to have violated'.[100] Although it was a case of immunity from civil and not criminal jurisdiction, it is hard to see why the outcome would revolve around the type of jurisdiction. In addition, the peremptory nature of some

---

[95] Kolodkin, 'Second Report on immunity of State officials from foreign criminal jurisdiction' (n 83) paras 82 and 94. But see also *Pinochet* (n 70) and the discussion of that judgment in Sanger (n 77) 207–209.

[96] See also the overview and discussion in Kolodkin, 'Second Report on immunity of State officials from foreign criminal jurisdiction' (n 83) para. 31 and Lee M. Caplan, 'State Immunity, Human Rights, and *Jus Cogens*: A Critique of the Normative Hierarchy Theory' (2003) 97 *American Journal of International Law* 741.

[97] *Pinochet* (n 70). See also Hazel Fox, Colin Warbrick and Dominic McGoldrick, 'The Pinochet Case No. 3' (1999) 48 *International and Comparative Law Quarterly* 687.

[98] See, inter alia, Antonio Cassese et al., *Cassese's International Criminal Law* (3rd edn, Oxford University Press, 2013) 242–246 and 320. See also Andrea Bianchi, 'Immunity versus Human Rights: The Pinochet Case' (1999) 10 *European Journal of International Law* 237.

[99] *Arrest Warrant* (n 3) Dissenting Opinion of Judge Al-Khasawneh, para. 7.

[100] Ibid, para. 84. See also *Al-Adsani v UK* (n 2) para. 66 and *Jones v Ministry of Interior of Kingdom of Saudi Arabia et al.* (n 48) para. 33.

international crimes relate to the *commission* of the crime and not to the obligation to *prosecute*. Thus, it is the state that perpetrates the crime of, say, genocide
or torture, that violates an obligation of a *jus cogens* nature and not the state that
fails to prosecute.[101] A further argument bases the rejection of immunity *ratione
materiae* on case law from national courts and the emergence of a customary law-
based exception to immunity. National cases are not, however, as clear-cut as their
proponents would like to portray them. In many cases, immunity is not even discussed by the courts, and while this could be due to an understanding that a plea
of immunity would be unsuccessful, it could also be explained by the absence of an
assertion of immunity on behalf of the foreign state or by the existence of a waiver of
immunity—either explicit or implicit—by that state.[102]

The law appears to be unclear and it may well be that international law is not yet
able to deliver on the high expectations of those who would like to see functional
immunity limited in relation to the worst international offences.[103] A tentative conclusion holds that functional immunity is unavailable with regard to certain of those
international crimes that both the foreign as well as the forum state are under a treaty-
based obligation to criminalize and prosecute in their national systems unless the
foreign state explicitly invokes it.[104] Such an exception would be based on the fact,
discussed in Chapter 15, that some international crimes are no longer only attributed
to the state on whose behalf they are committed but also to the individual officials who
perpetrate them. Here, the rules on universal jurisdiction may in effect be said to remove immunity *ratione materiae*.[105]

6.4 Diplomatic immunities and protection

6.4.1 Introduction

In day-to-day relations, the majority of interstate communication is conducted
through the many diplomatic missions that most states have established around the
world. Due to their physical location on the territory of another state, diplomatic
premises and diplomatic staff find themselves in a particularly vulnerable situation
and in need of extensive international protection. The rules that govern the rights
and privileges of diplomatic missions and representatives are primarily derived from
functional needs and the understanding that state representatives must enjoy certain
privileges in order to perform their official functions. Accordingly, the purpose of

---

[101] See also Dapo Akande and Sangeeta Shah, 'Immunities of State Officials, International Crimes, and
Foreign Domestic Courts' (2011) 21 *European Journal of International Law* 815, 835–836.

[102] For a critical discussion, see Kolodkin, 'Second Report on immunity of State officials from foreign
criminal jurisdiction' (n 83) paras 68–71. See also Wuerth (n 93).

[103] Kolodkin, 'Second Report on immunity of State officials from foreign criminal jurisdiction' (n 83)
para. 90.

[104] Fox (n 66) 560–561. See also Akande and Shah (n 101) 842–846. For an overview of the crimes, see
the discussion in Chapter 15.

[105] Akande and Shah (n 101) 840–841.

diplomatic law is not to benefit the state representative in his or her personal capacity but the state he or she represents. The relevant rules are found in the 1961 Vienna Convention on Diplomatic Relations (VCDR) that has been ratified by the majority of states and the provisions of which generally reflect customary international law.[106] In *Tehran Hostages*, the ICJ noted the 'the extreme importance' of the law of diplomatic protection, 'carefully constructed by mankind over a period of centuries, the maintenance of which is vital for the security and well-being of the complex international community of the present day'.[107]

The purpose of diplomatic law is to strike a balance between the legitimate concerns of the sending state and the state in which the representatives and the diplomatic mission are based. Conceptually, diplomatic relations are always based on mutual consent and states are not obligated to enter into diplomatic relations with each other. The presence of a diplomatic mission of a foreign state is therefore based on the consent of the host state and the latter is always free to revoke its consent without having to offer any justification.[108] In addition, the host state must accept the appointment of the head of the mission (and the military attaché) by 'accreditation'.[109] The host state may at any time and without justification declare that the head of the mission or any other member of the diplomatic mission is not welcome on its territory—'*persona non grata*'—in which event the sending state must recall the person or terminate his or her functions with the mission.[110] If the sending state does not honour its obligations in this regard 'within a reasonable time', the host state may refuse to recognize the individual concerned as a member of the mission.

In this section we examine both the immunity from national jurisdiction offered by international law to diplomats as well as the inviolability of diplomats and diplomatic premises and communications. We begin with an overview of the immunities and protections offered to diplomatic agents (Section 6.4.2). We then examine the protection offered to diplomatic premises (Section 6.4.3) and diplomatic communication (Section 6.4.4). Brief attention is then turned to the obligations of the sending state (Section 6.4.5). To supplement the treatment of diplomatic protection, we will also briefly discuss consular relations (Section 6.4.6) and so-called 'special missions' or 'ad hoc diplomacy' (Section 6.4.7).

6.4.2 **Immunity and protection of diplomatic agents**

The relevant rules concerning the protection and immunities of diplomatic staff are found in articles 29–39 of the VCDR. The extent of protection differs according to the status and functions of the staff. According to article 29, a *diplomatic agent* is inviolable and shall not be liable to any form of arrest or detention and all attacks on his person, freedom and liberty must be prevented by the host state. The private residence of the diplomat benefits from the same extensive protection as that offered to the premises

---

[106] *United States Diplomatic and Consular Staff in Tehran (United States v Iran)*, Judgment [1980] ICJ Rep 3, para. 62.
[107] Ibid, para. 92.   [108] See also VCDR art. 2.   [109] Art. 4.   [110] Art. 9(1).

of the diplomatic mission (see Section 6.4.3).[111] Article 31 is the key provision when it comes to jurisdictional protection. The article stipulates that a diplomatic agent enjoys immunity *ratione personae* and has (full) immunity from the criminal jurisdiction of the host state. Diplomatic agents also benefit from civil and administrative immunity, except in proceedings that relate to one of the following:

(a) A real action relating to private immovable property situated in the territory of the receiving State, unless he holds it on behalf of the sending State for the purposes of the mission;

(b) An action relating to succession in which the diplomatic agent is involved as executor, administrator, heir or legatee as a private person and not on behalf of the sending State;

(c) An action relating to any professional or commercial activity exercised by the diplomatic agent in the receiving State outside his official functions.

Article 31 also specifies that a diplomatic agent is not obliged to give evidence as a witness.

With regard to immunity from enforcement jurisdiction, no such measures can be taken unless they relate to the three exception mentioned above and provided the measures taken do not infringe the inviolability of the diplomatic agent or his or her residence.[112] In general, and with a few exceptions, diplomatic agents are also exempt from all dues and taxes[113] as well as all personal services and from military obligations.[114] The diplomat's family—unless they are nationals of the host state—enjoy the same immunities and protections.[115] Provided they are not nationals or permanently residing in the host state, members of the administrative and technical staff of a mission, as well as their families, are afforded similar immunities to those of diplomatic agents, except that they only enjoy immunity from civil and administrative jurisdiction in relation to official—and not private—acts (immunity *ratione materiae*).[116] Other members of the staff are offered progressively less protection.[117]

Since the immunity from jurisdiction enjoyed by diplomatic staff is not granted for the personal benefit of the representatives but to enable them to perform their functions, it can be waived by the sending state.[118] A waiver must, however, be explicit.[119] In addition, a waiver from jurisdiction in relation to civil and administrative proceedings does not imply a waiver from execution. Here, a separate waiver is required.[120]

6.4.3 Protection of diplomatic premises and property

Article 22 of the VCDR stipulates that the 'premises of the mission shall be inviolable' and 'agents of the receiving state may not enter them, except with the consent of the head of the mission'. In addition, the host state is under 'a special duty to take all appropriate steps to protect the premises of the mission, including its means of transport, against any intrusion or damage and to prevent any disturbance of the peace of the mission or impairment of its dignity'. Also inviolable are the archives and documents of the mission no matter where they are located.[121] While violations

---

[111] Art. 30.   [112] Art. 31(3).   [113] Art. 34.   [114] Art. 35.   [115] Art. 37.
[116] Art. 37(2).   [117] Art. 37(3) and (4).   [118] Art. 32(1).   [119] Art. 32(2).
[120] Art. 32(4).   [121] Art. 24.

of the obligation to protect foreign diplomatic missions are rare, they are not un-heard of. In *Tehran Hostages*, for example, the ICJ concluded that Iran violated its obligations under the VCDR by failing to protect, *inter alia*, the US embassy in Tehran from local protesters who stormed the diplomatic premises in 1979 and took the staff hostage.[122] A more recent example of disregard for the obligations under article 22 of the VCDR includes the passivity of local authorities in relation to the attacks and torching by local crowds of the Danish embassies in Lebanon and Syria following the publication in a Danish newspaper in 2005 of cartoons depicting the Prophet Muhammed.

6.4.4 Protection of communication

Article 26 of the VCDR specifies that the host state shall ensure that members of a dip-lomatic mission can move and travel freely in its territory and exceptions can only be made for reasons of national security in relation to certain zones. According to article 27, the host state shall permit and protect 'free communication on the part of the mis-sion for all official purposes' and the diplomatic mission is generally free to employ all appropriate means of communicating including 'diplomatic couriers and messages in code or cipher'. The article also stipulates that all correspondence relating to the mission and its functions 'shall be inviolable'.[123] Extensive protection is additionally offered to the so-called 'diplomatic bag' that may be neither opened nor detained. The courier of the bag also enjoys inviolability and will not be liable to any form of arrest or detention.[124] The 'bag' can vary in size but must bear visible external marks. In 1989, the ILC issued a set of Draft Articles on the Status of the Diplomatic Courier and the Diplomatic Bag not accompanied by Diplomatic Courier.

6.4.5 Obligations of the sending state and abuse of privilege

Despite the widespread protection offered to diplomatic agents by international law, diplomats of the sending states are not above the laws of the host state. Article 41 of the VCDR explicitly states that all persons protected by the Convention must respect the local laws and regulations. The representatives are also obliged not to 'interfere in the internal affairs' of the host state.[125] The premises of the diplomatic mission must not be used in any manner incompatible with the functions of the mission.[126] If a sending state abuses its rights and privileges, the VCDR offers the host state a number of remedies. First of all, as mentioned in Section 6.4.1, under article 9 of the Convention it can withdraw its consent in respect of a member of the mission by declaring the representative *persona non grata* in which cases the send-ing state must recall the individual or terminate his or her functions.[127]

---

[122] *Tehran Hostages* (n 106) para. 63.   [123] Art. 27(2).   [124] Art. 27(3)–(7).
[125] Art. 41(1).   [126] Art. 41(3).   [127] *Tehran Hostages* (n 106) para. 85.

Secondly, in a particularly serious case of abuse the host state may break off diplomatic relations. But, even in cases of abuse, diplomatic protections and immunities and the inviolability of the diplomatic premises remain intact. In *Tehran Hostages*, the Iranian government argued that its (unlawful) occupation of the US embassy should be considered in the light of more than '25 years of continual interference by the United States in the internal affairs of Iran, the shameless exploitation of our country, and numerous crimes perpetrated against the Iranian people, contrary to and in conflict with all international and humanitarian norms'. The ICJ responded, however, by noting that the rules of diplomatic law are a 'self-contained régime which specifies the means at the disposal of the receiving State to counter any such abuse'. The inviolability of diplomatic premises was confirmed in the so-called 1984 'St James's Square Incident' during which shots fired from inside the Libyan embassy in London killed a British policewoman. Despite a public outcry, the UK authorities refrained from entering the embassy. More recently, the British authorities have respected the inviolability of the premises of the Ecuadorian embassy even though the premises are being (ab)used to shield the founder of WikiLeaks, Julian Assange, from arrest and subsequent extradition to Sweden in relation to charges of sexual assault.

6.4.6 **Consular protection**

Unlike diplomatic agents, the functions of consular agents are generally limited to offering assistance in relation to more technical, commercial and/or private matters to the nationals of the sending state, including in situations where nationals in one way or another find themselves in difficulty.[128] In the *LaGrand* case, the ICJ concluded that the United States had violated its obligations under consular law when the authorities of the State of Arizona tried and sentenced to death two German nationals without informing them of their rights to consular assistance.[129] The main body of rules are found in the 1963 Vienna Convention on Consular Relations the structure of which in many ways resembles that of the Vienna Convention on Diplomatic Relations. Like diplomatic premises, consular premises are inviolable and the authorities of the host state are not allowed to enter the premises without consent.[130] The less 'political' role traditionally played by consuls is reflected in the extent of protection from the jurisdiction of the host state that international law offers to consular agents. In contrast to diplomats, consular officers only enjoy immunity *ratione materiae* in relation to functions performed in the exercise of their official functions.[131]

---

[128] For an overview of normal functions, see art. 5 of the Vienna Convention on Consular Relations.

[129] *LaGrand (Germany v United States)*, Judgment [2001] ICJ Rep 466. See the rights under art. 36 of the Vienna Convention on Consular Relations.

[130] Art. 31.   [131] Art. 43.

6.4.7 **Immunity for representatives on 'special missions'**

As an alternative—or a supplement—to the creation of more permanent diplomatic and consular relations, a state may conduct so-called 'ad hoc diplomacy' and send state representatives on 'special missions' to other states. In essence, a special mission should be conceived of as a temporary diplomatic mission with the features of a regular diplomatic mission, but for a limited period of time. A 1969 Convention on Special Missions has entered into force but has yet to be widely ratified. Its status under customary international law is unclear. It is, however, well established that members of a special mission enjoy immunity *ratione personae* and are immune from the jurisdiction of the national courts of the host state.[132] But since the immunities of a representative on a special mission derive from the consent of the forum state to the presence of the mission on its territory, the foreign state must obtain the prior consent of the host state. In October 2011, authorities in the UK declined to issue an arrest warrant for an Israeli politician in relation to alleged war crimes because the British government had consented to her presence on a special mission. In contrast, in *Khurts Bat*, a Mongolian state official could not claim the protections of a special mission because the local authorities had not consented to his presence prior to his arrival in the UK.[133]

Summary

Respect for the sovereign equality of states generally requires that a territorial state refrains from exercising its jurisdiction—whether adjudicative or in relation to enforcement—over another state and its representatives. Immunity is a procedural matter and must therefore be dealt with *prior* to an inquiry into the merits of the case. It is now well established that foreign states only enjoy immunity from a territorial state's exercise of adjudicative jurisdiction in relation to sovereign or governmental acts (acts *jure imperii*) and not with regard to commercial or private acts (acts *jure gestionis*). Thus, immunity is denied when a state engages in commercial activities and competes with private individuals or corporations. State immunity also applies in cases of serious violations of international law. The immunity offered to state representatives revolves around the distinction between immunity *ratione personae*—or 'personal immunity'—and immunity *ratione materiae*—'functional immunity'. The former is derived from the *position* a representative holds and the latter relates to the functions the representative performs. Personal immunity is more extensive than functional immunity. It is at present unclear if functional immunity can be limited in cases of international crimes. Foreign diplomats and diplomatic premises enjoy widespread protection under international law.

---

[132] For discussion, see Sanger (n 77).
[133] *Khurts Bat v Investigating Judge of the German Federal Court* (n 77).

Recommended reading

A seminal work on state immunity is Hazel Fox, *The Law of State Immunity* (Oxford University Press, 2008). See also Xiaodong Yang, *State Immunity in International Law* (Cambridge University Press, 2012) and the elaborate work in Roger O'Keefe and Christian J. Tams (eds), *The UN Convention on Jurisdictional Immunities of States and Their Property: A Commentary* (Oxford University Press, 2013).

A good—and shorter overview—is contained in Hazel Fox, 'International Law and Restraints on the Exercise of Jurisdiction by National Courts of States' in Malcolm D. Evans (ed.), *International Law* (4th edn, Oxford University Press, 2014). See also James Crawford (ed.), 'Privileges and Immunities of Foreign States' in *Brownlie's Principles of Public International Law* (8th edn, Oxford University Press, 2012).

For the distinction between sovereign and commercial acts, see James Crawford, 'Foreign Sovereigns: Distinguishing Immune Transactions' (1983) 54 *British Yearbook of International Law* 75.

On practice in relation to immunity from enforcement, see August Reinisch, 'European Court Practice Concerning State Immunity from Enforcement Measures' (2006) 17 *European Journal of International Law* 803.

A good introduction and discussion of immunity for state representatives is Chanaka Wickremasinghe, 'Immunities Enjoyed by Officials of States and International Organizations' in Malcolm D. Evans (ed.), *International Law* (4th edn, Oxford University Press, 2014). See also the latest edition of Hazel Fox, *The Law of State Immunity* (Oxford University Press, 2015).

There is a vast literature on the immunities from criminal jurisdiction of state representatives, see inter alia, Dapo Akande and Sangeeta Shah, 'Immunities of State Officials, International Crimes, and Foreign Domestic Courts' (2011) 21 *European Journal of International Law* 815. See also Andrew Sanger, 'Immunity of State Officials from the Criminal Jurisdiction of a Foreign State' (2013) 62 *International and Comparative Law Quarterly* 193.

On diplomatic law, see the seminal work of Eileen Denza, *Diplomatic Law: A Commentary on the Vienna Convention on Diplomatic Relations* (2nd edn, Oxford University Press, 1998).

Questions for discussion

1. How would you justify state immunity?
2. Can you identify some of the tensions that respect for state immunity creates in relation to other considerations in international law?
3. Why has it proven to be difficult to introduce a workable definition of, respectively, a sovereign (*jure imperii*) and a commercial (*jure gestionis*) act?
4. In the *Arrest Warrant* case, the ICJ stated that immunity from criminal jurisdiction for a foreign minister is not the same as impunity. What did the Court mean by that?

5. How would you justify limiting immunity *ratione materiae* in relation to international crimes?

6. Why are there generally more exceptions to immunity in relation to civil proceedings than with regard to criminal jurisdiction?

7. Where is the consensual character of diplomatic relations reflected in diplomatic law?

8. What options does a forum state have in relation to criminal activities emanating from a foreign diplomatic mission located on its territory?

7

State responsibility

CENTRAL ISSUES

1. This chapter discusses the international law of responsibility as primarily reflected in the 2001 International Law Commission's Articles on the Responsibility of States for Internationally Wrongful Acts.

2. It discusses the core principles of state responsibility, including the dual requirements of wrongful conduct and state attribution.

3. The chapter provides an overview of the different means by which a state will be held to be internationally responsible for wrongful conduct (attribution) and it discusses the different circumstances that may preclude the wrongfulness of conduct that may otherwise constitute a violation of an international obligation.

4. It also analyses the primary consequences that flow from international responsibility for wrongful conduct and discusses when a state may invoke the international responsibility of another state.

7.1 Introduction

All systems of law must deal with the issue of responsibility for breaches of the obligations contained in the system. To supplement the rules that identify the concrete rights and obligations, a legal system must have rules specifying what happens when one of the subjects violates its obligations and how an aggrieved party can vindicate its rights. In international law, these rules are primarily found within the field of state responsibility, supplemented by the rules on the responsibility of international organizations. It is an area of international law that is indispensable for the well functioning of international law and the international society that the law regulates.

The laws on responsibility contain rules of a so-called secondary nature. Conceptually, there is merit to distinguishing between primary and secondary rules of international law.[1] Primary rules are those that define the particular obligations

---

[1] The distinction was introduced by Roberto Ago in his capacity as the second Special Rapporteur, see also the discussion in James Crawford, *State Responsibility* (Cambridge University Press, 2013) 64–66.

that may generate responsibility if they are violated. Secondary rules, on the other hand, determine the consequences of violating the primary rules. The rules on immunity from national jurisdiction we visited in the previous chapter, for example, are primary rules because they contain the substantive rules that identify the extent to which a territorial state is obliged to refrain from exercising its jurisdiction in a case that involves a foreign state and the representatives of a foreign state. The purpose of the secondary rules on state responsibility is to determine what the legal consequences are in cases of a breach of those substantive obligations. It also bears emphasizing that the issue of responsibility is distinct from treaty law and the question of whether or not a treaty obligation is binding. The law of treaties determines if a treaty is in force, how it must be interpreted or if it has been suspended but it is the rules on responsibility that deal with the issue of whether or not a breach of an (existing) treaty obligation involves the responsibility of the breaching actor and what the consequences of a breach may be.[2]

This chapter primarily focuses on the responsibility of states and the most relevant rules and principles are found in a series of Articles on Responsibility of States for Internationally Wrongful Acts prepared by the International Law Commission (ILC) on the basis of the prior work carried out by a number of Special Rapporteurs. State responsibility was one of the first issues taken up by the Commission but it was not until May 2001 that the final set of articles was adopted.[3] In December 2001, the UN General Assembly recommended the articles.[4] Though the articles have yet to be developed into a treaty (which is currently unlikely),[5] they have been referred to in a large number of cases and are generally considered to reflect customary international law.[6]

The structure and discussion in this chapter takes as its point of departure the structure of the ILC articles. It therefore opens in Section 7.2 with an overview of some of the core principles and elements of state responsibility for wrongful acts. Section 7.3 discusses the issue of state attribution of conduct before Section 7.4 examines the various circumstances that may preclude the wrongfulness of conduct otherwise in violation of a (primary) legal obligation. Section 7.5 looks into the consequences of state responsibility for wrongful conduct before Section 7.6 discusses who may be entitled to invoke state responsibility. Section 7.7 will provide a brief overview of the responsibility of international organizations.

Currently, the only international legal rules relating to the responsibility of individuals are those found in international criminal law. Those rules are covered in Chapter 15. As noted in Chapter 4, international corporations do not yet hold responsibilities under international law.

---

[2] See also *Gabčíkovo-Nagymaros Project (Hungary v Slovakia)*, Judgment [1997] ICJ Rep 7, para. 47.
[3] For an overview of the process, see Crawford (n 1) 35–44.
[4] GA Res. 56/83 (12 December 2001).   [5] Crawford (n 1) 42–44.
[6] See, inter alia, *Application of the Convention on the Prevention and Punishment of the Crime of Genocide (Bosnia and Herzegovina v Serbia and Montenegro)*, Judgment [2007] ICJ Rep 43, para. 401.

7.2 The core principles and elements of state responsibility

The fundamental principle of state responsibility is reflected in article 1 of the ILC articles according to which 'Every internationally wrongful act of a State entails the international responsibility of that State.' The article illustrates that as a main rule each state is responsible for its own conduct. In certain instances, however, conduct may be attributable to more than one state at the same time and therefore activate the responsibility of a number of states.[7] On some occasions, a state may 'share' its international legal responsibility with an international organization.[8] The issue of shared responsibility is not covered in the present chapter.

Article 2 of the ILC articles specifies that state responsibility consists of two elements: (1) conduct must be a breach of an international obligation and (2) that conduct must be attributable to a state. In practice, of course, there is an additional initial element to state responsibility that is often overlooked in the treatment of the topic: the existence of an international obligation. If a state is free to act within a given area, its acts cannot give rise to state responsibility. The International Court of Justice (ICJ) referred to the two main elements of a breach of an obligation and attribution of conduct in reverse order in the *Tehran Hostages* case, where Iranian citizens overran US diplomatic installations in Iran including the US embassy in Tehran, in a prelude to a lengthy state-sanctioned occupation of the premises. The Court had to determine, first, 'how far, legally, the acts in question may be regarded as imputable to the Iranian State' and, secondly, 'their compatibility or incompatibility with the obligations of Iran'.[9] As noted in the introduction, it is within the primary rules of international law and not the (secondary) rules on state responsibility that one decides if conduct violates an existing international obligation, whether in a treaty or in any other legal source. Depending on the primary rule, both action as well as omissions may constitute wrongful conduct. This is also reflected in article 2 of the ILC articles. In *Tehran Hostages*, the ICJ found that Iran breached its international obligations under the Vienna Convention on Diplomatic Relations (the primary rules) due to the failure of the local Iranian authorities to offer protection to the US premises from Iranian citizens.[10]

National legal systems generally operate with different forms of liability depending on the primary obligation. Thus, there is usually one standard for liability for contracts, another for torts and yet another standard in criminal law. In international law, however, there is no similar distinction. Thus, according to article 12 of the ILC

---

[7] See chapter IV of the ILC articles.

[8] Draft Articles on Responsibility of International Organizations, arts 14–18. For more information, see André Nollkaemper and Ilias Plakokefalos (eds), *Principles of Shared Responsibility in International Law: An Appraisal of the State of the Art* (Cambridge University Press, 2017).

[9] *United States Diplomatic and Consular Staff in Tehran (United States v Iran)*, Judgment [1980] ICJ Rep 3, para. 56.

[10] Ibid, para. 67. See also *Corfu Channel (UK v Albania)*, Judgment of 9 April 1949 [1949] ICJ Rep 4, 22–23.

articles, an international obligation is breached by a state 'when an act of that State is not in conformity with what is required of it by that obligation, regardless of its origin or character'.[11] In sum, the standard of liability depends on the primary legal source. As we shall see in Chapter 10, particularly strict liability regimes (often without fault) have been introduced in international environmental law in relation to, for example, nuclear energy and oil pollution.[12] It is also worth noting that the law on state responsibility does not distinguish between 'civil' and 'criminal' illegality. In fact, an attempt to introduce the concept of an 'international crime' into the ILC articles on state responsibility was not supported by states. As discussed in Chapter 6, however, this does not mean that individual state representatives cannot be held *criminally* accountable for violating international law.[13] It must also be noted that the absence in international law of a formal differentiation between various forms of legal obligations does not prevent the law from treating some breaches of existing obligations as more serious than others. As we shall see in Section 7.5, certain consequences flow from a breach of a peremptory/*jus cogens* norm.[14] In addition, the overview in Section 7.6 will illustrate that respect for some legal obligations (*erga omnes*) is deemed to be of concern to not only an injured state but to all states.

State responsibility does not necessarily require that actual damage in the form of material or other actual loss must follow from wrongful conduct. It all depends on the primary obligation and while some primary rules—such as those relating to marine pollution—require that actual damage has been caused, other may not.[15] In fact, there is a substantial part of international law that establishes standards of conduct that must be adhered to by states regardless of tangible effects on other states. In such instances, responsibility exists as soon as a state's conduct is at variance with the legal obligation. Two things must be noted, however. First, as we shall see in Section 7.5, the existence of actual damage, such as financial losses, may be relevant for determining

---

[11] See also *Rainbow Warrior (New Zealand v France)* (1990) XX RIAA 217, para. 75.

[12] See Pierre-Marie Dupuy and Jorge E. Viñuales, *International Environmental Law* (Cambridge University Press, 2015) 259–264. Within the field of nuclear energy, relevant conventions include the 1960 OECD (Paris) Convention on Third Party Liability in the Field of Nuclear Energy and the 1963 supplementary convention to the Paris Convention, the 1963 International Atomic Energy Agency (IAEA) Convention on Civil Liability for Nuclear Damage (the Vienna Convention) and the 1997 Protocol to amend the Vienna Convention and the 1997 Convention on Supplementary Compensation for Nuclear Damage. See also the 1988 Joint Protocol Relating to the Application of the Vienna Convention and the Paris Convention. For oil pollution, see the 1969 International Maritime Organization (IMO) Convention on Civil Liability and the 1992 Protocol amending the convention and the International Convention on the Establishment of an International Fund for Compensation for Oil Pollution Damage (the FUND Convention) and the, respectively, 1992 and 2003 Protocols to amend the FUND Convention. See also the 2001 International Convention on Civil Liability for Oil Pollution Damage. For hazardous waste, see the 1996 International Convention on Liability and Compensation for Damage in Connection with the Carriage of Hazardous and Noxious Substances and the 2003 Protocol on Civil Liability and Compensation for Damage Cause by the Transboundary Effects of Industrial Accidents on Transboundary Waters.

[13] International criminal law is discussed in Chapter 15.

[14] See also the overview in the Draft Articles on the Responsibility of States for Internationally Wrongful Acts, with commentaries, *Yearbook of the International Law Commission*, 2001, vol. II, Part Two, pp. 112–116.

[15] See also the discussion in Crawford (n 1) 54–60.

what form reparations for wrongful conduct should take. Secondly, Section 7.6 will illustrate that the existence of actual damage may be relevant to the question of who may invoke the responsibility of the state that is in breach of its obligations.

Article 3 of the ILC articles contains the well-known international principle that the characterization of an act of a state as internationally wrongful is governed solely by international law and that it is immaterial if the same act is considered lawful by a state's own internal laws. Thus, a state cannot justify a breach of its international legal obligations by invoking its national laws and a state must also comply with international obligations even if it requires breaching its national laws.[16]

7.3 Attribution of conduct

7.3.1 Introduction

One of the core elements of state responsibility is that the wrongful conduct can be attributed to a state. The issue of attribution is dealt with in articles 4–11 in Chapter III of the ILC articles and the provisions are based on the overall premise that a state is solely internationally responsible for its own acts. Thus, only the conduct of a state's own organs or of other individuals or actors who have acted under the direction, instigation or effective control of such organs is attributable to the state. As a main rule, then, acts of private individuals are not attributable to a state. But as *Tehran Hostages* illustrates, this does not mean that a state cannot breach its international obligations in relation to acts of private individuals if a state is under a (primary) legal obligation to offer effective protection from such private acts. The existence of a more general due diligence obligation was implied in the *Corfu Channel* case where the ICJ stated that a state may not 'allow knowingly its territory to be used for acts contrary to the rights of other States'.[17] As we shall see in Chapter 10, the due diligence obligation plays a prominent role in international environmental law where it is translated into a state's obligation to use all means 'to avoid activities which take place in its territory, or in any area under its jurisdiction, causing significant damage to the environment of another State'.[18] More recently, due diligence has been brought up in relation to the activities of private individuals in cyberspace.[19]

---

[16] See, inter alia, *SS 'Wimbledon'*, 1923, PCIJ Series A, No. 1, 15, see 29–30, and *Reparations for Injuries Suffered in the Service of the United Nations*, Advisory Opinion of 11 April 1949 [1949] ICJ Rep 174, 180. See also art. 26 of the Vienna Convention on the Law of Treaties according to which a state party may not invoke its national laws as justification for a failure to perform a treaty-based obligation.

[17] *Corfu Channel* (n 10) 20. On the concept of due diligence more generally, see also the International Law Association's Study Group on Due Diligence in International Law, First report, Duncan French and Tim Stephens, 7 March 2014 available at http://www.ila-hq.org/en/committees/study_groups.cfm/cid/1045 (accessed 15 January 2016).

[18] *Pulp Mills on the River Uruguay (Argentina v Uruguay)*, Judgment [2010] ICJ Rep 14, para. 101. See also *Trail Smelter (United States v Canada)* (1938 and 1941) III RIAA 1905.

[19] See, inter alia, *Tallinn Manual on the International Law Applicable to Cyber Warfare* (Cambridge University Press, 2013) 26 and rule 5 and the discussion of the obligation to respect the sovereignty of another state in relation to cyber infrastructure.

In this section, we examine the principles governing when the conduct of state organs, as well as private groups and individuals, is attributable to a state as those principles appear in the ILC articles. It bears mentioning, however, that a state may also in certain rare circumstances be internationally responsible for the wrongful acts of other states. The issue of such collaborative responsibility is covered in Chapter IV of the ILC articles and will not be examined further here. We begin with the general principle of attribution (Section 7.3.2).

7.3.2 Attribution for acts performed by the state and its organs

The first principle of state attribution is straightforward and uncontroversial.[20] According to article 4 of the ILC articles, all conduct of state organs is considered an act of the state regardless of whether the organ in question 'exercises legislative, executive, judicial or any other functions'. Thus, all three branches of power may act in a manner that implicates the international responsibility of the state. It is also immaterial what position the organ holds within the state and if it is an organ of the central government or of a territorial unit of the state. In addition, the term 'organ' is interpreted broadly to include 'any person or entity which has that status in accordance with the internal law of the State'. Attribution is established even if the conduct in question is performed by low-level state officials, provided they act in an official capacity. Furthermore, while a state 'organ' includes any entity or individual with that status under the national laws of the state—*de jure* state organs—a state cannot avoid responsibility for the acts or omission of an entity that in practice acts as a state organ—*de facto*—by denying it an official status in its national laws. This was also noted by the ICJ in the *Genocide (Bosnia and Herzegovina v Yugoslavia)* case, where the Court had to determine if the Federal Yugoslavian government could be held internationally responsible for the 1995 Srebrenica massacres in Bosnia that were perpetrated by Bosnian Serb forces who were not officially state organs in Yugoslavia.[21] The Court rejected the notion that the forces in question could be considered to be organs of the Federal Yugoslavian state[22] and noted that this would require that the group act in 'complete dependence on the State, of which they are ultimately merely the instrument'.[23] And that could not be established. The Court also stated that 'to equate persons or entities with State organs when they do not have that status under internal law must be exceptional'.[24] As a main rule, conduct by the authorities of subunits in a federal state is also attributable to the state and in the *LaGrand* case, the United States was held internationally responsible for the conduct of federal authorities in the state of Arizona and acts that fell within the jurisdiction of the governor

---

[20] *Application of the Convention on the Prevention and Punishment of the Crime of Genocide* (n 6) 43, para. 385.

[21] Ibid, para. 392.   [22] Ibid, para. 388.

[23] Ibid, para. 392. See also *Military and Paramilitary Activities in and against Nicaragua (Nicaragua v United States)*, Merits [1986] ICJ Rep 14, para. 109.

[24] *Genocide* (n 20) para. 393.

of that US state.[25] Limited exceptions may apply, however, in relation to the acts of certain constituent units of a federation.[26]

7.3.3 Attribution of acts performed by organs exercising governmental authority

Article 5 of the ILC articles is concerned with state responsibility for individuals and entities that exercise governmental authority in the absence of their status as a state organ in the formal sense. To an increasing extent, private corporations have begun to fulfil functions that are normally exercised by the organs and institutions of the state, and article 5 of the ILC articles stipulates that the conduct of individuals and entities that have been empowered to exercise governmental authority are attributable to the state when the individual or entity acts in that capacity. Thus, the point is that the state cannot avoid its responsibility by privatizing/outsourcing what are properly governmental functions. Article 5 is of relevance, therefore, to the privatization of certain military and police functions, matters relating to the running of detention and prison facilities and the delegation of powers relating to immigration and border control to private airlines or ships. Attribution under article 5 is limited, however, to cases where conduct of governmental authority flows from the internal laws of the state and it should therefore not be conflated with the issue of attribution for the conduct of private individuals who act under the direction or control of a state. That falls under article 8 (see Section 7.3.6).

It may be difficult to determine if an activity should be considered as an exercise of 'governmental authority' and the assessment may differ from state to state. The commentary to article 5 notes that the content of the powers granted as well as 'the way they are conferred on an entity, the purposes for which they are to be exercised and the extent to which the entity is accountable to government for their exercise' is of interpretative importance.[27]

7.3.4 Attribution for acts by organs on 'loan' from another state

Article 6 of the ILC articles covers the rather exceptional situation where a state places one of its organs at the disposal of another state. Examples include health service units in crisis situations and the occasional appointment of judges. The article stipulates that the acts of the 'loaned' organ are attributed to the receiving and not the sending state. This, however, requires that the organ in question is actually placed under the authority or structure of the receiving state and does not retain its autonomy and that the organ exercises governmental authority.[28] In *Jaloud v Netherlands*, the European

---

[25] *LaGrand (Germany v United States)*, Order, Request for the Indication of Provisional Measures) [1999] ICJ Rep 9, para. 28.

[26] See the Draft Articles on the Responsibility of States for Internationally Wrongful Acts, with commentaries, *Yearbook of the International Law Commission*, 2001, vol. II, Part Two, p. 42, para. 10.

[27] Ibid, p. 43, para. 6.   [28] See also *Genocide* (n 20) para. 389.

Court of Human Rights did not find that Dutch troops stationed in an area in south-eastern Iraq in 2004, where all relevant forces were under the command of an officer from the UK, were placed 'at the disposal' of, inter alia, the UK.[29] The Netherlands was responsible for providing security in the area, to the exclusion of other troop-partici-pating states, and retained full command over its contingent.[30]

7.3.5 Responsibility for acts *ultra vires*

A state remains responsible for conduct performed by its organs and officials in cases where the organ or official acted contrary to orders and instructions or in excess of authority—conduct *ultra vires*. This is reflected in article 7 of the ILC articles. As the Inter-American Court of Human Rights stated in *Velásquez Rodriguez*, which con-cerned the disappearance of a student at the hands of the armed forces of Honduras, the determination of whether a state has breached its obligations under international law is 'independent of whether the organ or official has contravened provisions of internal law or overstepped the limits of his authority'. A state is 'responsible for the acts of its agents undertaken in their official capacity and for their omissions, even when those agents act outside the sphere of their authority or violate internal law'.[31] Responsibility is a fact as long as an organ or official has acted with 'apparent authority'.[32]

7.3.6 Attribution for acts performed by private individuals

We have already seen that states are generally not responsible for the acts of private individuals. Exceptions do exist, however, and one of the more contentious issues within the field of state responsibility concerns the responsibility of a state for the acts committed by private persons or private organizations that are somehow linked to or supported by the state. The issue was brought to the fore in connection with the 11 September 2001 terrorist attacks on the United States that were perpetrated by the al Qaida network, at the time based in Afghanistan where it was provided sanctuary by the Taleban regime. The relationship between al Qaida and the Taleban led to a debate about how closely related a state must be to a private terrorist organization before the acts of the terrorists can be attributed to the state.

Article 8 of the ILC articles specifies that a state is only responsible for the conduct of a person or a group of persons if they are 'in fact acting on the instructions of, or under the direction or control of, that state in carrying out the conduct'. State respon-sibility therefore only exists in two situations. Either the private individuals must be *acting on the instructions or orders* of the state or they must *act under the direction*

---

[29] *Jaloud v the Netherlands*, App. no. 47708/08, 20 November 2014, para. 151.

[30] Ibid, para. 149. As noted earlier, the issue of shared responsibility is covered in chapter IV of the ILC articles.

[31] *Velasquez Rodriguez*, Judgment of 29 July 1988, Inter-AmCtHR, Series C, No. 4 (1988), see paras 169–170.

[32] Draft Articles on the Responsibility of States for Internationally Wrongful Acts, with commentaries, *Yearbook of the International Law Commission*, 2001, vol. II, Part Two, p. 46, para. 8.

or control of the state. While it is fairly obvious that a state should be responsible for acts that it instructs someone to do on its behalf, it has proven more difficult to reach agreement on what is contained in the concept of 'direction and control'. The seminal case is the *Nicaragua* case where the ICJ, among other things, had to determine if the United States were internationally responsible for violations of the laws of armed conflict committed by a paramilitary force—the *contras*—in Nicaragua. Although the *contras* were heavily subsidized and supported by the US government, the Court did not find that their acts could be attributed to the United States. That would only be the case if it could be proven that the United States 'had effective control of the military or paramilitary operations in the course of which the alleged violations were committed'.[33] The key, in other words, was the concept of 'effective control'.

In *Tadić*, the Appeals Chamber of the International Criminal Tribunal for the former Yugoslavia (ICTY) in 1999 criticized the high threshold for attribution in *Nicaragua* and concluded that the required degree of control over the private actors 'vary according to the factual circumstances of each case'.[34] Thus, according to the Chamber, the exercise of 'overall control' may in some circumstances suffice in relation to the acts of militarily organized groups.[35] It must be noted, however, that the ICTY was not concerned with attribution under the principles of state responsibility but rather for the purpose of classifying an armed conflict as one of an international or a non-international character. In the 2007 *Genocide* case, the ICJ had to determine if the Federal Yugoslavian government could be held internationally responsible for, among other things, the 1995 Srebrenica massacres perpetrated by Bosnian Serb forces supported by the Yugoslavian government. The Court rejected the ICTY's arguments for lowering the threshold for control and stated that the standard in *Nicaragua* still reflected customary international law.[36] To the Court, an 'overall control' threshold 'stretches too far, almost to breaking point, the connection which must exist between the conduct of a State's organs and its international responsibility'.[37] Thus, attribution (still) requires that effective control can be established 'in respect of each operation in which the alleged violations occurred, not generally in respect of the overall actions taken by the persons or groups of persons having committed the violations'.[38] The Court did not find that was established in relation to the Srebrenica massacre. To the Court, all indications were that the decision to kill the adult male population of the Muslim community in Srebrenica was taken by the Bosnian Serbs without instructions from or effective control by the Yugoslavian state.[39] The Court also rejected the notion that the particular (reprehensible) nature of the conduct—in this case, the crime of genocide—justified lowering the threshold for attribution in the absence of a clearly expressed *lex specialis*.[40] This, of course, would also seem to rule out that the standard for attribution should be lower in relation to,

---

[33] *Nicaragua* (n 23) para. 115.
[34] ICTY, *Tadić*, Appeals Chamber, Judgment, para. 117. See also para. 137.   [35] Ibid, para. 145.
[36] *Genocide* (n 6) paras 404–406. It did leave open, however, the possibility that an 'overall control' test could be applied in relation to determining whether or not an armed conflict is international, see para. 404.
[37] Ibid, para. 406.   [38] Ibid, para. 400.   [39] Ibid, para. 413.   [40] Ibid, para. 401.

for example, international terrorism. Since there is no indication that the Taleban regime exercised effective control over the al Qaida terrorists who perpetrated the 9/11 attacks, the conclusion therefore also seems to be that the terrorist acts could not be attributed to Afghanistan. As we will see in the discussion on the use of force in Chapter 13, the 9/11 attacks helped to pave the way for the introduction of an 'unable or unwilling' doctrine whereby a state may be entitled to resort to measures of self-defence against a private actor, such as a terrorist organization, located in another state if the host state does not have the ability or willingness to stop the private actor's activities. Importantly, however, the doctrine does not hold that the host state is internationally responsible for the acts of the private actor and thus does not constitute a lowering of the standard for attribution.

An additional point must be noted at this stage. We saw earlier that a state is responsible for conduct that is contrary to or in excess of directions of the state—*ultra vires*—by its own organs. The same does not hold in relation to *ultra vires* acts performed by persons or groups of persons who merely operate under the direction or effective control of the state.[41]

7.3.7 **Acts of an insurrectional movement**

It is a well-established principle that the acts of insurrectional movements are not attributable to the state.[42] If, however, the movement succeeds in assuming power and establishes itself as the new government of the state, or manages to form a new state in part of the territory of the pre-existing state, article 10 of the ILC articles stipulates that the state will be responsible for the acts of the movement. Theoretically, attribution can be justified by adopting the position that the movement can be considered as the continuity of the former government.

7.3.8 **Responsibility for acts subsequently acknowledged and adopted**

Article 11 of the ILC articles specifies that a state may become responsible for conduct that was not attributable to the state when it was committed if the state *subsequently* acknowledges the conduct and adopt it as its own. The best example is the *Tehran Hostages* case, where the ICJ concluded that the acts of the Iranian government subsequent to the storming and occupation of the US embassy by private Iranian citizens meant that the conduct became acts of the Iranian state. Not only did the Iranian government give their approval to the occupation of the embassy and the taking of its staff as hostages, it decided to perpetrate it and use it as a means of exerting pressure on the US government. From then on, the 'militants, authors of the invasion and jailers of the hostages, had now become agents of the Iranian State for whose acts the State itself was internationally responsible'.[43] But conduct will only be attributed to the state

---

[41] Draft Articles on the Responsibility of States for Internationally Wrongful Acts, with commentaries, *Yearbook of the International Law Commission*, 2001, vol. II, Part Two, p. 48, para. 8.
[42] Ibid, p. 50, para. 3.   [43] *Tehran Hostages* (n 9) para. 74.

under article 11 if the state somehow acknowledges and adopts the conduct as *that of its own*. The state must show a willingness to assume responsibility for the acts in question and mere statements of support or sympathy or general acknowledgements of factual circumstances are not in themselves sufficient. For example, the fact that the Taleban regime refused to cooperate with the United States and surrender those deemed responsible for the 9/11 attacks was not enough to make Afghanistan internationally responsible for the attacks.

7.4 Circumstances precluding wrongfulness

7.4.1 Introduction

Chapter V of the ILC articles lists a number of circumstances the existence of which individually will preclude the international wrongfulness of an act otherwise in breach of international law. In practice, then, the circumstances listed serve as justifications for not complying with an international obligation. They are general in the sense that they will apply to any wrongful act regardless of whether it constitutes a breach of a treaty or any other source of international law. The existence of a circumstance precluding wrongfulness does not, however, terminate the underlying legal obligation. As the ICJ stated in the *Gabčíkovo-Nagymaros Project*, in relation to a claim of a state of necessity that even if 'found justified, it does not terminate a Treaty ... As soon as the state of necessity ceases to exist, the duty to comply with treaty obligations revives.'[44]

7.4.2 Consent

The first of the circumstances precluding wrongfulness that is mentioned in the ILC articles is *consent*. According to article 20, valid consent by a state to the commission of an act precludes the wrongfulness of that act as long as the act does not exceed the limits of that consent. As the article illustrates, consent must be 'valid' and in some cases this may require a determination of whether the individual who gave the consent was actually authorized to do so by his or her state and if an alleged excess of authority was known or should have been known to the state that relies on the consent.[45] Different officials may be authorized to give their consent to different conduct. Consent must be given freely without coercion and it must be clearly expressed. It must, furthermore, be given either beforehand or at the time otherwise wrongful conduct occurs.

Consent plays an important practical role in everyday international relations (overflight of aircraft, disaster assistance, rescue operations etc.) and is usually not a cause of great controversy. There are also many uncontroversial instances when the use of international force is justified on the basis of consent from the host state. Notable

---

[44] *Gabčíkovo-Nagymaros Project* (n 2) para. 101.

[45] On this issue, see inter alia the Vienna Convention on the Law of Treaties, arts 27 and 46. See also the discussion in Crawford (n 1) 284–289.

examples include the military presence of the North Atlantic Treaty Organization (NATO) in Afghanistan from December 2001 onwards and the existing international military campaign against the so-called Islamic State in Iraq. There are cases, however, where the reliance on consent as a justification for using force is controversial.[46] For example, some argue that consent cannot be relied upon as a justification for intervening in widespread civil wars as there may doubt about which party among the contending parties is in a position to give valid consent to the intervention.[47] On that view, the Russian military presence in the Syrian civil war, which is current at the time of writing, is controversial.[48] The role of consent has also been debated in relation to the US programme for targeted killings of alleged terrorists—often with the use of remotely piloted vehicles (drones)—in states that may or may not have given valid consent to the US operations.[49]

7.4.3 Self-defence

Article 21 of the ILC articles specifies that the wrongfulness of an otherwise unlawful act is precluded if it is *in conformity with the inherent right to self-defence* in article 51 of the UN Charter. The two articles must therefore be interpreted together and conduct that does not comport with article 51 of the Charter cannot be justified under article 21.[50] Article 21 does not preclude the wrongfulness of conduct that is in breach of the international obligations that are meant to apply in times of armed conflict.[51]

7.4.4 Lawful countermeasures

The third circumstance that may preclude the wrongfulness of an otherwise unlawful act springs from the recognition that a state must be allowed to respond to another state's international wrongful acts by taking certain *countermeasures* in order to bring the wrongful acts to an end.[52] Thus, according to article 22 of the ILC

---

[46] See also Ashley S. Deeks, 'Consent to the Use of Force and International Law Supremacy' (2013) 54 *Harvard International Law Journal* 1.

[47] See, inter alia, the debate in Louise Doswald-Beck, 'The Legal Validity of Military Intervention by Invitation of the Government', *British Yearbook of International Law 1985* (1986) 189–253.

[48] TASS, 'Lawmakers authorize use of Russian military force for anti-IS airstrikes in Syria', 30 September 2015.

[49] See, inter alia, Sean D. Murphy, 'The International Legality of US Military Cross-Border Operations from Afghanistan into Pakistan' in Michael N. Schmitt (ed.), *The War in Afghanistan: A Legal Analysis*, International Law Studies, vol. 85 (Naval War College Press, 2009) 109 and Anders Henriksen, '*Jus ad bellum* and American Targeted Use of Force to Fight Terrorism Around the World' (2014) 1 *Journal of Conflict and Security Law* 1.

[50] The content of the right to self-defence is discussed in Chapter 13.

[51] In general, see also *Legality of the Threat or Use of Nuclear Weapons*, Advisory Opinion [1996] ICJ Rep 226.

[52] *Gabčíkovo-Nagymaros Project* (n 2) para. 83. For an overview, see also Nigel White and Ademola Abass, 'Countermeasures and Sanctions' in Malcolm D. Evans (ed.), *International Law* (Oxford University Press, 2010) 531–545.

articles, a state is entitled to breach its international obligations towards another state 'if and to the extent that the act constitutes a countermeasure taken against the latter State'. As the tribunal in the *US–French Air Services Arbitration* case stated: 'If a situation arises, which in one State's view, results in the violation of an international obligation by another State, the first State is entitled ... to affirm its right through "countermeasures".'[53]

The specific modalities that govern countermeasures are contained in articles 49–54 of the ILC articles. It follows that the purpose of a countermeasure must be to induce the other state to comply with its international obligations and that it should therefore be of a temporary nature and applied in a way that permits the resumption of performance of the obligations in question.[54] The measure must be lifted as soon as the internationally wrongful acts on the part of the other state has ceased.[55] Some obligations are of such importance that they cannot be the object of countermeasures.[56] The first of these is the obligation to refrain from the threat or use of force contained in the UN Charter. A state is therefore not allowed to respond to a wrongful act by resorting to a measure that would constitute a use of force as that concept is interpreted under article 2(4) of the Charter.[57] Secondly, countermeasures may not infringe 'obligations for the protection of fundamental human rights'. It is not clear which human rights are considered 'fundamental' but they would seem to include at least those that cannot be derogated from even in times of war or other public emergency.[58] The third type of obligations that cannot be the object of a countermeasure are those of a 'humanitarian character prohibiting reprisals' and the fourth are peremptory/*jus cogens* norms. The right to resort to countermeasures does not relieve a state from fulfilling its obligations under a relevant 'dispute settlement' or to respect the inviolability of diplomatic or consular agents, premises, archives and documents.[59] To be lawful, countermeasures must be proportionate and strike a fair balance between the initial breach of international law and the measures taken.[60] If not, they may be interpreted as a reaction aimed at exerting revenge or punishment on the targeted state and therefore fall outside the boundaries of lawful countermeasures. There is, however, no requirement that a countermeasure must be reciprocal in nature and a state may be justified in responding to another state's breach of international law by adopting measures that are different in kind.[61] In practice, assessments of proportionality are usually very difficult.[62] In the *Gabčíkovo-Nagymaros Project* case, the ICJ concluded that a Czechoslovakian project aimed at diverting part of the Danube in response to Hungary's failure to comply with a treaty on

---

[53] *Air Services Agreement (US v France)*, Arbitral Award, 9 December 1978, XVIII RIAA 337.

[54] Art. 49. *Gabčíkovo-Nagymaros Project* (n 2) para. 87.   [55] Arts 52(3) and 53.

[56] Art. 50(1).   [57] See also the discussion in Chapter 13.

[58] But see also Economic and Social Council, Committee on Economic, Social and Cultural Rights, 'General Comment No. 8: The Relationship between economic sanctions and respect for economic, social and cultural rights' (12 December 1997), para. 4.

[59] Art. 50(2).   [60] Art. 51.   [61] See also White and Abass (n 52) 535.

[62] Thomas Franck, 'On Proportionality of Countermeasures in International Law' (2008) 102(4) *American Journal of International Law* 763.

the construction of a dam was not proportionate.[63] A countermeasure can only be directed against the state that has breached its international obligations and before initiating countermeasures a state must take every possible measure to avoid affecting a third party.[64] A state must call upon the responsible state to fulfil its international obligations before it can initiate a countermeasure[65] and it must also notify the other state of the initiation of countermeasures and offer a chance to negotiate. In urgent circumstances, however, the state may 'take such urgent countermeasures as are necessary to preserve its rights'.[66]

7.4.5 *Force majeure*

The fourth circumstance that may preclude the wrongfulness of otherwise unlawful conduct is *force majeure*. According to article 23 of the ILC articles, a state may justify non-performance of an obligation in the case of the 'occurrence of an irresistible force or of an unforeseen event, beyond the control of the State' that makes it 'materially impossible in the circumstances' to perform the obligation. A plea of *force majeure* is not available, however, if the state that invokes it has contributed to the situation or if it has 'assumed the risk' of the situation occurring.[67] In the *Rainbow Warrior* case, the Permanent Court of Arbitration (PCA) stated that *force majeure* requires 'absolute or material impossibility' and that circumstance that merely render performance of the obligation more difficult or burdensome does not suffice.[68] The Court also noted that *force majeure* is generally relied upon in relation to involuntary or at least unintentional conduct and that it is based on the premise that no one can be required to do the impossible.[69]

7.4.6 Distress

The fifth circumstance precluding wrongfulness is *distress* according to which an agent of a state may be justified in not performing an international obligation if it has no other reasonable way of saving the agent's life or that of other persons in the agent's care. It is covered by article 24 of the ILC articles. As the PCA noted in *Rainbow Warrior*, distress differs from *force majeure* in the sense that it can be relied upon in a situation where the state could in theory fulfil its international obligation but where it would require a sacrifice that it was unreasonable to demand.[70] According to article 24(2), distress cannot be invoked if the situation of distress is due to the state's own

---

[63] *Gabčíkovo-Nagymaros Project* (n 2) para. 87.

[64] See also Draft Articles on the Responsibility of States for Internationally Wrongful Acts, with commentaries, *Yearbook of the International Law Commission*, 2001, vol. II, Part Two, p. 130, para. 4.

[65] Art. 52(1). See also *Gabčíkovo-Nagymaros Project* (n 2) para. 84.　　[66] Art. 52(2).

[67] Art. 23(2).　　[68] *Rainbow Warrior* (n 11) para. 77.

[69] Ibid. See also Draft Articles on the Responsibility of States for Internationally Wrongful Acts, with commentaries, *Yearbook of the International Law Commission*, 2001, vol. II, Part Two, p. 76, para. 2.

[70] *Rainbow Warrior* (n 11) para. 78.

conduct or if the act that constitutes a breach of the international obligation 'is likely to create a comparable or greater peril'.

7.4.7 Necessity

The final circumstance precluding wrongfulness mentioned in the ILC articles is *necessity*, contained in article 25. It relates to those rare cases where the only way for a state to safeguard an 'essential interest' that is threatened by 'a grave and imminent peril' is, for the time being, to refrain from performing another international obligation that is considered to be of a lesser weight or urgency.[71] In *Gabčíkovo-Nagymaros Project*, the ICJ stated that a plea of necessity can only be accepted 'on an exceptional basis'[72] and the ILC Special Rapporteur James Crawford has described necessity as being 'at the outer edge of the tolerance of international law for otherwise wrongful acts'.[73] As already noted, an 'essential interest' must be at stake and the international obligation that is not performed must be of a lesser value. In addition, the wrongful act must be 'the only way' for the state to safeguard its vital interest. In its advisory opinion in *The Wall* case, the ICJ concluded that Israel's construction of a security barrier on Palestinian territory violated its obligations under international law and that a plea of necessity could not preclude the wrongfulness of Israel's conduct. While the Court noted the existence of 'indiscriminate and deadly acts of violence against its civilian population' and that Israel had both the right and duty to protect the life of its citizens, it was not convinced that the construction of the wall along the route chosen was the only means to safeguard the interests of Israel against that peril.[74] According to article 25(2), when invoking necessity a state may not 'seriously impair an essential interest of the State or States towards which the obligation exists, or of the international community as a whole'.[75] It also follows from the article that necessity is unavailable if the 'international obligation in question excludes the possibility of invoking necessity', or if the state has contributed to the situation of necessity. Importantly, even if a state of necessity exists, it will only justify a state not performing a treaty-based obligation for as long as that state of necessity lasts. The underlying obligation and the treaty are not terminated and as soon as the state of necessity ceases to exist, the state is under a duty to resume compliance with its treaty obligations.[76]

---

[71] See also the discussion in Crawford (n 1) 305–315.

[72] *Gabčíkovo-Nagymaros Project* (n 2) para. 51. See also the general scepticism displayed in *Rainbow Warrior* (n 11) para. 78 and in the Draft Articles on the Responsibility of States for Internationally Wrongful Acts, with commentaries, *Yearbook of the International Law Commission*, 2001, vol. II, Part Two, p. 80, para. 2 and p. 83, para. 14.

[73] Report of the International Law Commission on its work of its 51st Session (1999), UN Doc. A/54/10, para. 378.

[74] *Legal Consequences of the Construction of a Wall in the Occupied Palestinian Territory*, Advisory Opinion [2004] ICJ Rep 136, paras 140–141.

[75] Art. 25(1).   [76] *Gabčíkovo-Nagymaros Project* (n 2) para. 101.

A plea of necessity does not cover conduct regulated by a primary rule. It follows, therefore, that it does not cover an assertion of military necessity that is subject to regulation in the substantive provisions in the laws of armed conflict. According to ILC commentaries to article 25, the same conclusion applies to the issue of humanitarian intervention regulated by the UN Charter.[77] Article 59 of the ILC articles explicitly states that they are without prejudice to the UN Charter.[78] Some have nevertheless argued that necessity may justify the use of force in another state for humanitarian purposes in violation of the prohibition on the use of force in article 2(4) of the UN Charter.[79] In *Legality of Use of Force*, for example, Belgium relied, in part, on an alleged state of necessity to justify its participation in the unilateral humanitarian intervention in Kosovo in 1999. According to Belgium, the alleged violation of the prohibition on the use of force in article 2(4) of the UN Charter was justified because the intervention attempted to safeguard 'rights of *jus cogens*'.[80] It is doubtful whether necessity can justify breaching the prohibition on the use of force in the Charter.[81] As mentioned above, necessity cannot be invoked if the actions taken 'seriously impair an essential interest of the State or States to which the obligations exists' and it is difficult to imagine a more essential interest to a state than its territorial sovereignty.[82] It also bears reiterating that necessity cannot be resorted to if the international obligation in question 'excludes the possibility of invoking necessity'. Although the Charter does not explicitly mention necessity, it seems logical to conclude that the Charter is the *exclusive* source on the international legal regulation of interstate force in the sense that it rules out the invocation of necessity.[83]

7.4.8 Circumstances precluding wrongfulness and *jus cogens*

Articles 20–25 of the ILC articles must all be read in conjunction with article 26, according to which a state cannot preclude the wrongfulness of any act that violates a peremptory norm/*jus cogens*. As we saw in Chapter 2, it is not clear what norms can be said to be of a peremptory character, but it appears to include, at a minimum, the crime of genocide, the prohibition on torture, the ban on slavery, the aggressive use of force, crimes against humanity and the prohibition of apartheid and other forms of gross racial discrimination.

---

[77] Draft Articles on the Responsibility of States for Internationally Wrongful Acts, with commentaries, *Yearbook of the International Law Commission*, 2001, vol. II, Part Two, p. 84, para. 21.
  [78] Art. 59.   [79] On the regulation of the use of force, see Chapter 13.
  [80] *Legality of Use of Force (Serbia and Montenegro v Belgium)*, Public sitting, 10 May 1999, 13–14. See also Ole Spiermann, 'Humanitarian Intervention as a Necessity and the Threat or Use of *Jus Cogens*' (2002) 71 *Nordic Journal of International Law* 543; http://justsecurity.org/2013/10/02/koh-syria-part2/ (accessed 10 January 2016).
  [81] Anders Henriksen and Marc Schack, 'The Crisis in Syria and Humanitarian Intervention' (2014) 1(1) *Journal on the Use of Force and International Law* 122.
  [82] See also Jens Elo Rytter, 'Humanitarian Intervention without the Security Council: From San Francisco to Kosovo—and Beyond' (2001) 70 *Nordic Journal of International Law* 134.
  [83] James Crawford, 'Second Report on State Responsibility' (1999), UN Doc. A/CN.4/498/Add.2, para. 287.

7.5 Consequences of wrongful conduct

7.5.1 Introduction

In this section we examine the *consequences* that flow from a conclusion that a state is found to be internationally responsible. The two most important consequences are the obligations of the state to cease the wrongful conduct and the obligation to make reparations. These dual obligations are listed in articles 30 and 31 respectively. At the outset it is important to note, however, that the obligations to cease wrongful conduct and make reparations do not affect the duty of the responsible state to perform the obligation that it has breached. The pre-existing legal obligation continues.[84] In the *Gabčíkovo-Nagymaros Project* case, the ICJ noted that the treaty for the construction of a dam on the Danube entered into by Czechoslovakia and Hungary was still in force even though both states had materially breached the provisions of the treaty.[85] Regardless of their wrongful conduct, both parties remained under an obligation to consider how the 'multiple objectives of the Treaty could best be served, keeping in mind that all of them should be fulfilled'.[86]

7.5.2 The cessation of wrongful conduct

It is almost banal to point out that the first and primary obligation incumbent on a state that is responsible for an internationally wrongful act is to cease the act in question. Thus, in its opinion in *The Wall*, after having concluded that Israel had violated its international obligations by constructing a security barrier on occupied Palestinian territory, the ICJ concluded that Israel must put an end to the violations that flowed from the construction of the barrier.[87] The duty of cessation is contained in article 30(1) of the ILC articles. Paragraph (2) of the article stipulates that the responsible state may be obliged to 'offer appropriate assurances and guarantees of non-repetition' if that is required by the circumstances. The issue of a guarantee of non-repetition was discussed in the *LaGrand* case, where the United States was found to be in violation of its obligations under the Vienna Convention on Consular Relations for not notifying foreign nationals in their custody of their rights to consular assistance. Germany wanted an assurance from the United States that it would in future comply with the Convention. To the Court, however, the commitment expressed by the United States to ensure future compliance was deemed to be sufficient assurance.[88]

---

[84] See also art. 29 of the ILC articles.

[85] *Gabčíkovo-Nagymaros Project* (n 2) paras 114 and 132. See also the Vienna Convention on the Law of Treaties, art. 60.

[86] *Gabčíkovo-Nagymaros Project* (n 2) para. 139.   [87] *The Wall* (n 74) paras 149–150.

[88] *LaGrand* (n 25) para. 124.

7.5.3 **The duty to make reparation**

A responsible state is under an obligation to 'make full reparation for the injury cause by the internationally wrongful act'. This general principle of international law is reflected in article 31 of the ILC articles.[89] Thus, since both parties in the *Gabčíkovo-Nagymaros Project* case had committed an international wrong, both were in theory entitled to compensation.[90] The seminal case on the concept of 'reparation' is the decision by the Permanent Court of International Justice (PCIJ) in the *Factory in Chorzów* case where the PCIJ articulated the fundamental principle that the 'breach of an engagement involves an obligation to make reparation in an adequate form' and that reparation is the indispensable complement to a failure to apply a convention.[91] The Court also stated that the purpose of reparation must be to 'as far as possible, wipe out all the consequences of the illegal act and re-establish the situation which would, in all probability, have existed if that act had not been committed'.[92] As we shall see in Chapter 11, the issue of the proper standard of reparation and compensation has been debated in relation to the expropriation of foreign property. During the Cold War in particular, Communist states and states in the developing world sought to lower the standard of compensation from that of 'full' to 'appropriate' compensation.

The concept of 'injury' includes not just material but also moral damage, and article 31 leaves it to the primary rule to identify what is required. Material damage relates to losses etc. that are measurable in financial terms while moral damage includes more intangible losses, including issues such as pain and suffering. In Chapter 10, we will see that the usual approach to reparation for damage is not very well suited to environmental damage. This is due both to the difficulties of drawing causal links between an act or omission and damage to the environment and to determining the appropriate compensation for environmental damage that may be irreversible. As alluded to in the introduction, there is no general requirement of material harm or damage suffered before a state can seek reparation. In *Rainbow Warrior*, the PCA concluded that the French breach of its obligations towards New Zealand had been an 'affront to the dignity and prestige of New Zealand' and led to damage 'of a moral, political and legal nature'.[93] The different forms that reparation can take are listed in articles 34–38, and the enumeration includes restitution, compensation, satisfaction and interest. Of these, compensation is the most relevant means of reparation and it is well established that a court or tribunal with jurisdiction over a case may award compensation for damage suffered.[94]

---

[89] See also *Factory at Chorzów*, 1928, PCIJ, Series A, No. 17, 21.
[90] *Gabčíkovo-Nagymaros Project* (n 2) para. 152.   [91] *Factory at Chorzów* (n 89) 21.
[92] Ibid, 47. See also *Gabčíkovo-Nagymaros Project* (n 2) para. 150.
[93] *Rainbow Warrior* (n 11) para. 110.
[94] See also Draft Articles on the Responsibility of States for Internationally Wrongful Acts, with commentaries, *Yearbook of the International Law Commission*, 2001, vol. II, Part Two, p. 99, para. 2.

7.5.4 **Obligations of third states**

International law recognizes that some legal norms are of greater normative import-ance than others. Chapter 2 noted, for example, that the Vienna Convention on the Law of Treaties requires that norms of a *jus cogens* or peremptory nature cannot be derogated from by contracting parties.[95] In the law on state responsibility, the special status of such norms is reflected in articles 40 and 41 whereby the violation of per-emptory/*jus cogens* norms has a consequence for all states. According to article 41, all states are under an obligation to 'cooperate to bring to an end through lawful means any serious breach' by a state of a *jus cogens* norm as well as to refrain from recogniz-ing 'as lawful a situation created by a serious breach' of a peremptory norm nor can a state 'render aid or assistance in maintaining that situation'.[96] The breach of the per-emptory norm must, however, be serious.[97] The obligation not to recognize a situation that has been created by a serious breach of a *jus cogens* norm is reflected in the ICJ's Advisory Opinion on *Namibia*,[98] the General Assembly's Declaration on Friendly Relations[99] and in the international reaction to the Iraqi invasion and attempt at an-nexation of Kuwait in 1990.[100] And in *The Wall* case, the ICJ concluded that all states are obliged not to 'recognize the illegal situation resulting from the construction of the wall in the Occupied Palestinian Territory, including in and around East Jerusalem' just as all states are 'under an obligation not to render aid or assistance in maintaining the situation created by such construction'.[101] In March 2014, the General Assembly also responded to Russia's annexation of Crimea by calling upon states, international organizations and specialized agencies not to recognize any alteration of the status of Crimea and to 'refrain from any action or dealing that might be interpreted as recog-nizing any such altered status'.[102]

7.6 Who may invoke a breach of international law?

7.6.1 **Introduction–the injured state**

It is a fundamental principle of state responsibility that it is the state whose individual rights have been violated or denied by the internationally wrongful act of another state—the 'injured state'—that is entitled to invoke the responsibility of the responsible state and demand cessation and reparation.[103] It may be difficult to determine when a state can reasonably be considered to be 'injured' by the wrongful act of another

---

[95] See art. 53 of the VCLT.   [96] Art. 41(1) and (2).
[97] See also the overview in Draft Articles on the Responsibility of States for Internationally Wrongful Acts, with commentaries, *Yearbook of the International Law Commission*, 2001, vol. II, Part Two, pp. 112–116.
[98] *Legal Consequences for States of the Continued Presence of South Africa in Namibia (South West Africa) notwithstanding Security Council Resolution 276 (1970)*, Advisory Opinion [1971] ICJ Rep 16, para. 126.
[99] GA Res. 2656 (XXV) (24 October 1970), UN Doc. A/25/2625.
[100] SC Res. 662 (9 August 1990), UN Doc. S/RES/662.   [101] *The Wall* (n 74) para. 159.
[102] GA Res. 68/262 (27 March 2014), UN Doc. A/68/L.39 and Add.1, para. 6.   [103] Art. 42.

state but article 42 lists a number of circumstances.[104] First, under the article, a state is injured if the obligation breached was owed to it individually. That, of course, will be the case in relation to breaches of bilateral treaties and other obligations that directly concern the state.[105] But a state will also be deemed to be 'injured' if the obligation is not owed to it individually but instead to a group of states and the breach 'specially affects' the state or if the obligation breached radically changes the position of all other states to which the obligation is owed.[106]

7.6.2 Obligations *erga omnes*

According to article 48 of the ILC articles, a state does not always have to be considered 'injured' to be entitled to invoke the responsibility of another state. Under article 48(1)(a), a non-injured state may invoke the responsibility of another state 'if the obligation breached is owed to a group of States including that State, and is established for the protection of a collective interest of the group'.[107] This category—sometimes referred to obligations *erga omnes partes*—includes, inter alia, obligations under multilateral human rights treaties. In *Certain Questions Relating to the Obligation to Prosecute or Extradite*, the ICJ stated that obligations under the UN Torture Convention 'are owed by any State party to all the other States parties to the Convention' and that 'each State party has an interest in compliance with them in any given case'.[108]

The most interesting part of article 48 is the concept of so-called *erga omnes* obligations listed in paragraph (1)(b). As an international legal concept, *erga omnes* was introduced by the ICJ in the *Barcelona Traction* case. Here, the Court did not find that Belgium possessed legal standing on behalf of shareholders in Belgium in a Canadian company against Spain. According to the Court:

> ... an essential distinction should be drawn between the obligations of a State towards the international community as a whole, and those arising vis-à-vis another State in the field of diplomatic protection. By their very nature the former are the concern of all States. In view of the importance of the rights involved, all States can be held to have a legal interest in their protection; they are obligations *erga omnes*.[109]

Due to their fundamental character, 'the obligation breached is owed to the international community as a whole' and can be invoked not only by an 'injured' state but by any state.[110] As the quote above illustrates, *all* states can be said to have a legal interest in the respect for and fulfilment of such rights.[111] The category of *erga omnes* is therefore broader than that of *erga omnes partes*. As we saw in Chapter 2, it is logical

---

[104] The article borrows heavily from art. 60(2) of the Vienna Convention on the Law of Treaties.

[105] Art. 42(a).   [106] Art. 42(b).   [107] Art. 48(1)(a).

[108] *Certain Questions of Mutual Assistance in Criminal Matters (Djibouti v France)*, Judgment [2008] ICJ Rep 177, para. 68.

[109] *Barcelona Traction, Light and Power Co., Ltd*, Judgment [1970] ICJ Rep 3, para. 33.

[110] Art. 48(1)(b).

[111] See also 'Fragmentation of International Law: Difficulties Arising from the Diversification and Expansion of International Law', Report of the Study Group of the International Law Commission (13 April 2006), UN Doc. A/CN.4/L.682, paras 380–409.

to conclude that the *erga omnes* obligations are somewhat identical to those norms that are deemed to be of a peremptory/*jus cogens* nature.[112] In *Barcelona Traction*, the ICJ listed the outlawing of aggression, and genocide, as well as the principles and rules concerning the basic rights of the human person, including protection from slavery and racial discrimination, as examples of *erga omnes* obligations.[113] In *East Timor*, the ICJ also referred to the right of peoples to self-determination as having a similar character[114] and in its advisory opinion in *The Wall* case, the Court concluded that Israel's construction of a security barrier on occupied Palestinian territory violated the *erga omnes* obligation 'to respect the right of the Palestinian people to self-determination, and certain of its obligations under international humanitarian law'.[115] Recently, the principles of *erga omnes* have also been brought up as being of relevance in international environmental law.

Even though all states are entitled to invoke breaches of *erga omnes* obligations, fewer rights are attached to the invocation of collective rights than to those afforded to an injured state under article 42. According to article 48(2), the rights are limited to claiming cessation of the wrongful act, seeking assurances and guarantees of non-repetition[116] and claiming compensation in the interest of an injured state.[117] Since the invoking state is not injured, it cannot claim compensation in its own right.

7.7 The international responsibility of international organizations

The 2002 ILC Articles on the Responsibility of States explicitly state that they do not apply to the responsibility of international organizations.[118] Instead, that falls within a series of Draft Articles on Responsibility of International Organizations adopted by the ILC in 2011. The articles are largely based on the articles on state responsibility and in the following only a limited number of issues will be dealt with.

Article 2(a) defines an international organization as 'an organization established by a treaty or other instrument governed by international law and possessing its own international legal personality'. Article 3 stipulates the basic principle whereby 'Every internationally wrongful act of an international organization entails the international responsibility of that organization.'[119] In addition, under article 4, an international wrongful act of an international organization exists when conduct attributable to that

---

[112] See also M. Cherif Bassiouni, 'International Crimes: "*Jus Cogens*" and "*Obligatio Erga Omnes*"' (1996) 59(1) *Law and Contemporary Problems* 72.

[113] *Barcelona Traction* (n 109) para. 34.

[114] *East Timor (Portugal v Australia)*, Judgment]1995] ICJ Rep 90, para. 29.

[115] *The Wall* (n 74) paras 155 and 157.   [116] Art. 48(2)(a).   [117] Art. 48(2)(b).

[118] See art. 57.

[119] See also *Difference Relating to Immunity from Legal Process of a Special Rapporteur of the Commission on Human Rights*, Advisory Opinion [1999] ICJ Rep 62, para. 66. The international responsibility of individuals is covered in the treatment of international criminal law in Chapter 15.

organization 'constitutes a breach of an international obligation of that organization'. Conduct may cover both acts and omissions.

One of the most interesting issues relates to that of attribution of conduct. An international organization is, after all, unlike a state in the sense that it does not have any territory and merely exists in order to fulfil certain functions assigned to it by the creating states.[120] According to article 6, conduct is attributable to an international organization when performed by an organ or an agent of the organization, regardless of the position held by that organ or agent. Importantly, the term 'agent' is given a wide application and it includes an individual who does not hold any official position in the organization as long as the conduct performed by the individual is done on the instruction or under the direction or control of the organization.[121]

Article 7 concerns the important question of responsibility for conduct performed by an actor (or agent) that has been 'loaned' to an international organization by a state or another international organization. The issue is particularly relevant to UN peacekeeping operations. The UN does not have its own 'UN forces' and instead relies on forces put forward by the member states that generally retain certain powers, such as the power to discipline and criminally prosecute individual soldiers. According to article 7, the UN is responsible for the conduct of the forces it lends when it exercises 'effective control' over their conduct. It is, however, not entirely clear what 'effective control' means.

In 2007 in *Behrami and Behrami v France*, the Grand Chamber of the European Court of Human Rights held that acts committed by the UN Kosovo Force (KFOR) troops in Kosovo were attributed to the UN and not the troop-contributing NATO states because the UN Security Council had retained 'ultimate authority and control' and only delegated operational control to the states.[122] The decision was, however, widely (and justifiably) criticized for allowing states to escape their international responsibilities,[123] and in *Al-Jedda* the Court seemed to backtrack somewhat from its controversial conclusions in *Behrami*.[124] In its 2011 commentary to article 7, the ILC noted that the decisive issue is the element of 'factual control' and that ' "operational" control would seem more significant than "ultimate" control, since the latter hardly implies a role in the act in question'.[125] Thus, what is decisive according to the ILC is

---

[120] See also ILC, Draft articles on the responsibility of international organizations, with commentaries, *Yearbook of the International Law Commission*, 2011, vol. II, Part Two, p. 3.

[121] See also *Reparations* (n 16) 177. See also ILC, Draft Articles on the Responsibility of International Organizations, with commentaries (2011), *Yearbook of the International Law Commission*, 2011, vol. II, Part Two, commentary to art. 6, paras 10–11.

[122] *Behrami and Behrami v France*, App. no. 71412/01 and *Saramati v France, Germany and Norway*, App. no. 78166/01 (Grand Chamber), Admissibility, 2 May 2007, paras 57–61.

[123] See, inter alia, Marko Milanovic and Tatjana Papic, 'As Bad as it Gets: The European Court of Human Rights's *Behrami and Saramati* Decision and General International Law' (2009) 58(2) *International and Comparative Law Quarterly* 267.

[124] *Al-Jedda v UK*, App. no. 27021/08 (Grand Chamber), Judgment, 7 July 2011, paras 83–84.

[125] Commentary to art. 7, p. 23, para. 103. See also the 2007 decision by the UK House of Lords in *R (on the application of Al-Jedda) (FC) v Secretary of State for Defence* [2007] UKHL 58, see e.g. the judgment of Lord Bingham of Cornhill, [22]–[24].

not who holds ultimate responsibility over a military operation but instead who—the organization or the state—actually directs the forces when the relevant conduct occurs. In a 2013 decision, the Supreme Court of the Netherlands concluded that 'all factual circumstances and the special context of the case must be taken into account'[126] and upheld a decision from a lower court that had held that conduct performed by a Dutch battalion deployed in Bosnia under the UN Protection Force (UNPROFOR) could be attributed to the Netherlands.[127] The Court limited its decisions to the responsibility of the Netherlands and left open the possibility that the conduct by the Dutch forces could *also* have been attributed to the UN.[128] The case therefore illustrates the important point that article 7 does not rule out that conduct can be attributed to both the international organization and the lending state or organization.[129]

Summary

The international law on state responsibility specifies what happens when a state violates its obligations under international law. The most relevant rules are found in a set of 2001 articles on state responsibility adopted by the ILC. State responsibility generally arises when conduct is in breach of an international obligation and the conduct can be attributed to a state. As a main rule, a state is only internationally responsible for its own acts and not for the acts of private actors. International law recognized that the existence of one of a number of circumstances precludes the international wrongfulness of an act otherwise in breach of international law. The circumstances in question may justify not complying with an international obligation. The two most important consequences that follow from wrongful conduct are the obligations of the responsible state to cease the wrongful conduct and the obligation to make reparations. Some breaches of international law are so serious that it will trigger obligations for third parties. Although a state that is injured by another state's breach of international law may always invoke the responsibility of the latter, non-injured states may also be entitled to invoke breaches of international law.

Recommended reading

On the topic of state responsibility in general, see the seminal work by James Crawford, *State Responsibility* (Cambridge University Press, 2013). Another helpful source is the commentaries to the 2001 Articles on the Responsibility of States for Internationally Wrongful Acts, see *Yearbook of the International Law Commission*, 2001, vol. II, Part Two. For a more concise overview and discussion of state responsibility, see James Crawford and

---

[126] Supreme Court of the Netherlands, *The State of the Netherlands v Hasan Nuhanovic*, Case 12/03324, 6 September 2013. For the particular circumstances, see para. 3.12.2.

[127] Ibid, paras 3.11.3 and 3.12.3.   [128] Ibid, para. 3.9.4.

[129] See also ILC, Draft Articles on the Responsibility of International Organizations, with commentaries (2011), *Yearbook of the International Law Commission*, 2011, vol. II, Part Two, p. 16, para. 4. See also Supreme Court of the Netherlands, *Hasan Nuhanovic* (n 126) paras. 3.11.2–3.11.3.

Simon Olleson, 'The Character and Forms of International Responsibility' in Malcolm D. Evans (ed.), *International Law* (4th edn, Oxford University Press, 2014) 443–476.

A good presentation of the issue of consent as a circumstance precluding wrongfulness and its role in relation to the use of force, is Ashley S. Deeks, 'Consent to the Use of Force and International Law Supremacy' (2013) 54 *Harvard International Law Journal* 1.

For the topic of countermeasures, see Nigel White and Ademola Abass, 'Countermeasures and Sanctions' in Malcolm D. Evans (ed.), *International Law* (Oxford University Press, 2010) 531–545 and Thomas Franck, 'On Proportionality of Countermeasures in International Law' (2008) 102(4) *American Journal of International Law* 715.

The issue of necessity is covered in Ole Spiermann, 'Humanitarian Intervention as a Necessity and the Threat or Use of *Jus Cogens*' (2002) 71 *Nordic Journal of International Law* 543.

The concept of *erga omnes* is discussed in M. Cherif Bassiouni, 'International Crimes: "*Jus Cogens*" and "*Obligatio Erga Omnes*"' (1996) 59(1) *Law and Contemporary Problems* 63.

Questions for discussion

1. Why are the rules on state responsibility classified as secondary rules of international law?

2. Can a state be in breach of its international obligations due to acts of private individuals?

3. What is the relationship between treaty law and state responsibility?

4. What are the conceptual differences between peremptory norms/*jus cogens* and *erga omnes* obligations?

5. Why was the 2007 *Behrami* decision from the European Court of Human Rights criticized?

6. When may a state invoke the responsibility of another state?

8

The international law of the sea

CENTRAL ISSUES

1. This chapter discusses the main principles and rules that make up the international legal regulation of the seas.

2. It presents the rationale behind the division of the sea into a set of different jurisdictional zones in which states hold various rights and obligations.

3. The chapter discusses the regulation of the different maritime zones and the question of how overlapping zones are delimited.

4. The chapter also discusses a number of issues related to the conservation of marine life and marine protection and the different means by which disputes about the proper interpretation of the law of the sea can be adjudicated peacefully.

8.1 Introduction

The international law of the sea is one of the oldest disciplines of public international law. In fact, the identification and application of principles for governing the roughly 70 per cent of the earth's surface that consists of water has been a topic of interest for centuries. A substantial part of the modern interest in the regulation stems from the age of the explorers where the extent to which the oceans could be traversed without obstacles was of crucial importance to powerful maritime powers and their 'colonial companies', such as the British and the Dutch. It is therefore within the international law of the sea that some of the most noteworthy contributions to international law were published. A notable example is that of Hugo Grotius's *Mare Liberum* (1609) that offered a strong defence of the principle of the freedom of the seas.[1]

The identification of the balance between the needs and sovereign concerns of coastal states and the interest of other states that wish to enjoy the benefits of the seas is, of course, vital to the maintenance of peaceful international relations, and the basic principles of the law of the sea form part of the international law of coexistence. In

---

[1] Hugo Grotius, *Mare Liberum* (1609).

contemporary international law, the competing interests between coastal states and other states is primarily reflected in a spatial partitioning of the sea into jurisdictional zones. This 'zonal system' is based on the premise that the rights of coastal states decrease the further away one moves from the shore. More recently, by classifying the deep seabed and the resources of its subsoil as the 'common heritage of mankind', the law of the sea recognizes collective rights alongside the rights of individual states. Not all concerns and interests can be accommodated through a spatial division of the sea, however, and the law of the sea also seeks to facilitate international cooperation on matters of concern to all states, such as the preservation of marine life and the limitation of marine pollution.

We begin in Section 8.2 with the most important legal sources in the law of the sea, including the 1982 United Nations Law of the Sea Convention (LOSC). Section 8.3— which constitutes the bulk of the chapter—discusses the spatial partitioning of the sea and the different maritime zones that exist in the law of the sea. Section 8.4 examines a number of selected issues relating to the conservation of marine life and Section 8.5 discusses the protection of the marine environment. Section 8.6 contains a short introduction to dispute settlement in the law of the sea.

8.2 The sources of the international law of the sea

The most important legal source in the international law of the sea is the 1982 United Nations Convention on the Law of the Sea (LOSC) that entered into force in November 1994. LOSC is a massive document and its 320 articles cover the vast majority of issues in the law of the sea. It is built on a holistic understanding of the challenges associated with regulating the oceans[2] and the mandate for the 1973–1982 Third UN Conference on the Law of the Sea (LOSC III) that adopted the Convention was to reach agreement on 'all matters relating to the law of the sea'.[3] It is therefore an integral legal instrument—a 'package deal'—that disallows reservations unless expressly permitted.[4] By July 2016, 167 states had become parties to the Convention. Some important maritime states, including the United States and Turkey, remain outside.

The LOSC is the impressive result of years of complicated negotiations.[5] It builds upon already existing treaty-based regulation, most notable four conventions adopted at the First UN Conference on the Law of the Sea in 1958 in Geneva. Unlike the 1958 Conventions, however, the Third UN Conference managed to reach agreement on a host of contentious issues, most notably the maximum breadth of the territorial sea and the extent to which coastal states possess exclusive rights to the natural resources of the sea adjacent to their shores. The Conference also managed to take account of more recent technological advances that enabled mining of the deep seabed. After

---

[2] LOSC Preamble.   [3] See GA Res. 3067 (XXVIII) (16 November 1973).   [4] LOSC art. 309.
[5] For an overview of the process, see James Harrison, *Making the Law of the Sea: A Study in the Development of International Law* (Cambridge University Press, 2013) 27–61.

tough negotiations and a noticeable delay, it established a system that seeks to balance the interests of states willing to exploit the deep seabed with a fair distribution of the wealth thereof. Other notable accomplishments in LOSC include the creation of the International Tribunal for the Law of the Sea (ITLOS).

Customary international law remains an important legal source in the international law of the sea. In fact, some of the most important statements by the International Court of Justice (ICJ) on customary international law are found in decisions that deal with the law of the sea.[6] As we saw in Chapter 2, the ICJ has also made extensive resort to 'principles of equity' as a general principle of international law when settling maritime delimitation disputes or when dividing a shared continental shelf.

8.3 The spatial partitioning of the sea

8.3.1 Introduction

As noted already, it is a prime concern of international law to find a reasonable balance between the legitimate interests of coastal states that wish to extend their sovereignty to the waters that run adjacent to their shores and the often equally legitimate interests of other states that want to utilize the sea for a myriad of purposes. The result of the balancing act is a finely marked legal system that divides the sea into a number of maritime zones in which coastal and other states hold a variety of rights and obligations. Since the aim is to balance the rights of a coastal state with the freedom of other states, it is not surprising that the rights of the former decrease with the distance from the shore.

Conceptually, there is merit to distinguishing between those marine spaces that lie *within the national jurisdiction of a coastal state* (internal waters, territorial sea, archipelagic waters, international straits, the contiguous zone, the exclusive economic zone (EEZ) and the continental shelf) and those spaces that lie *beyond the jurisdiction of a coastal state* (the high seas and the seabed and subsoil thereof, also known as the Area). The first category—the zones of national jurisdiction—can be subdivided into two additional sorts of 'spaces'. The first consists of spaces that fall *within the territorial sovereignty of a coastal state* and where the state has the exclusive right to enforce its laws and regulations. These areas include the internal waters, the territorial sea, the archipelagic waters and international straits. The second type of spaces are those situated *beyond the territorial sovereignty of a coastal state* where the state may only assert certain jurisdictional powers. These areas include the contiguous zone, the EEZ and the continental shelf. For the purposes of the international law of the sea, the 'sea' consists of three elements: the atmosphere above the sea, the water in the sea and the seabed and subsoil.

---

[6] See, inter alia, *North Sea Continental Shelf Cases*, Judgment [1969] ICJ Rep 53, para. 63 and *Norwegian Fisheries (UK v Norway)*, Judgment [1951] ICJ Rep 116, 131.

Our overview of the zonal system starts with the concept of the baseline (Section 8.3.2). We then discuss the regulation of internal waters and the territorial sea (Section 8.3.3), the contiguous zone (Section 8.3.4), and the EEZ (Section 8.3.5). Attention is then turned to the exploitation of the continental shelf (Section 8.3.6) and the deep seabed (Section 8.3.7), before we examine the regulation of the high seas (Section 8.3.8). The final section is devoted to delimitation of overlapping maritime zones (Section 8.3.9).

8.3.2 **The concept of baselines**

To measure the breadth of the various maritime zones one must identify the exact physical point from where the breadth of the zone is measured.[7] This point is the *baseline*. It practical terms, a baseline serves two purposes. First, as already mentioned, it is the point from where the breadth of the various maritime zones is measured. Secondly, a baseline also delimits the internal waters of a state from that of its territorial sea. For obvious reasons, then, a coastal state has an interest in pushing its baseline as far as possible out into the sea. The practical drawing of baselines is governed by certain principles developed to take account of the different physical configurations of coastlines.

The main rule is found in article 5 of LOSC whereby the 'normal baseline … is the low-water line along the coast as marked on large-scale charts officially recognized by the coastal State'.[8] In the *Anglo-Norwegian Fisheries* case, however, the ICJ accepted that Norway could draw *straight baselines* between fixed points on the mainland and on islands or rocks where the coast 'is deeply indented and cut into' or where there is a fringe of islands along the coast in its immediate vicinity.[9] Article 7(1) of LOSC accepts straight baselines as an exception to a normal baseline.[10] Straight baselines are drawn across the water with the practical effect that the water on the landward side of the line becomes internal waters. Article 8(2) specifies that other states enjoy a right of innocent passage (see more in Section 8.3.3) in such territorial waters.

Article 7(3) contains a number of conditions for drawing straight baselines.[11] First, the baseline may not depart 'to any appreciable extent from the general direction of the coast'. Secondly, the 'sea areas lying within the lines must be sufficiently closely linked to the land domain to be subject to the regime of internal waters'. In the *Anglo-Norwegian Fisheries* case, the ICJ also noted that 'certain economic interests peculiar to the region, the reality and importance of which are clearly evidenced by a long

---

[7] For an overview, see Yoshifumi Tanaka, *The International Law of the Sea* (2nd edn, Cambridge University Press, 2015) 44–74.

[8] See also the 1958 Geneva Convention on the Territorial Sea and the Contiguous Zone (TSC), art. 3 and *Fisheries* (n 6) 128.

[9] *Fisheries* (n 6) 128–129. See also LOSC art. 7(1) and *Maritime Delimitation and Territorial Questions between Qatar and Bahrain*, Merits, Judgment [2001] ICJ Rep 40, 103, para. 212.

[10] See also TSC art. 4. All of the Scandinavian states have drawn straight baselines.

[11] See also *Fisheries* (n 6) 133.

usage' may be a relevant factor when determining if a straight baseline is called for.[12] In either case, a coastal state has a fairly wide discretion in drawing its baseline.[13]

Article 10 of LOSC concerns *bays* on coastal lines belonging to a single state. A 'bay' is defined as a 'well-marked indentation whose penetration is in such proportion to the width of its mouth as to contain land-locked waters and constitute more than a mere curvature of the coast'. An indentation is not a bay, however, if its area is smaller than that of a 'semi-circle whose diameter is a line drawn across the mouth of that indentation'.[14] If an indention fulfils the conditions for constituting a 'bay', a coastal state may draw the baseline across the mouth of the bay and turn the water inside the bay into internal waters. But a bay cannot be closed by a baseline if the distance between the two sides of the mouth exceeds 24 nautical miles.[15] The ICJ has indicated that the provisions on bays in LOSC reflect customary international law.[16] Special rules apply to large *historic bays* over which a coastal state has continuously exercised jurisdiction with the general acceptance of other states.[17]

Mention should also be made of the issue of *port and harbour installations* that extend into the water. Article 11 of LOSC stipulates that harbour installations can be regarded as forming part of the coastline. The works must, however, be attached to the coast.

Article 121(2) of LOSC specifies that *islands* generate the same jurisdictional rights (territorial sea, contiguous zone etc.) as other territory. An 'island' is a 'naturally formed area of land, surrounded by water, which is above water at high tide'.[18] ICJ case law illustrates that there is no rule on the minimum size of an island.[19] The requirement of attachment to the seabed and natural formation means that artificial installations, such as lighthouses or oil platforms, do not constitute 'islands' and do not therefore possess territorial seas or other maritime zones.

An island is different from *a low-tide elevation* that is a naturally formed area of land 'surrounded by and above water at low tide but submerged at high tide'.[20] A low-tide elevation may be used as the baseline for measuring the territorial sea if it is situated at a distance not exceeding the breadth of the territorial sea from the mainland or an island but it does not have a territorial sea if located outside.[21]

Article 121(3) states that a maritime feature is only an 'island' if it can 'sustain human habitation or economic life' of its own.[22] If it cannot, it is a *rock* and rocks do

---

[12] *Fisheries* (n 6) 131. See also LOSC art. 7(5).

[13] See also *Fisheries* (n 6) 131. But see *Maritime Delimitation and Territorial Questions between Qatar and Bahrain* (n 9) 103, para. 212.

[14] Art. 10(2).   [15] Art. 10(4).

[16] *Land, Island and Maritime Frontier Dispute* [1992] ICJ Rep 588, para. 383.

[17] See also *Continental Shelf (Tunisia v Libyan Arab Jamahiriya)*, Judgment [1982] ICJ Rep 18, 74, para. 100.

[18] Art. 121(1).

[19] *Maritime Delimitation and Territorial Questions between Qatar and Bahrain* (n 9) 97, para. 185.

[20] LOSC art. 13(1).

[21] LOSC art. 13(2). On low-tide elevations, see also *Fisheries* (n 6) 128; *Maritime Delimitation and Territorial Questions between Qatar and Bahrain* (n 9) 99, para. 193.

[22] LOSC art. 121(3).

not have EEZs or a continental shelf. According to the ICJ, the definition of an island in LOSC reflects customary international law.[23] The decisive issue is the *ability* of the feature to sustain human habitation or economic life and not whether humans actually have a presence on it.[24] The size of feature is not relevant.[25] Article 121(3) was extensively discussed in the recent arbitral award in the *South China Sea Arbitration* concerning a series of—controversial—Chinese claims in the South China Sea. One of the most important issues in the case involved the legal status of a range of maritime features in the area. The court found that the term 'human habitation' refers to the 'non-transient character of the inhabitation, such that the inhabitants can fairly be said to constitute the natural population of the feature'. It refers to 'a stable community of people for whom the feature constitutes a home and on which they can remain'. So while an indigenous population would suffice, a non-indigenous inhabitation may also suffice if the population truly intends 'to reside in and make their lives on the islands in question'.[26] According to the court, the term 'economic life of their own' refers to a notion of 'economic life' and not 'economic value' and that the economic life is ordinarily linked to the 'life and livelihoods' of the human population inhabiting the maritime feature. The economic life 'must be oriented around the feature itself and not focused solely on the waters or seabed of the surrounding territorial sea'. Importantly, the extraction of natural resources 'for the benefit of a population elsewhere' falls outside the definition.[27] The court also noted that in practice, a maritime feature will ordinarily only possess an economic life of its own if it is also inhabited by a stable human community.[28]

In response to China's build-up on the maritime features in the area, the court noted that the status of a feature takes its departure point as the *natural condition* and not the man-made alterations/installations. So a low-tide elevation will 'remain a low-tide elevation under the Convention, regardless of the scale of the island or installation built atop it':[29] just as 'a rock cannot be transformed into a fully entitled island through land reclamation'.[30] The court considered that the 'status of a feature [should] be ascertained on the basis of its earlier, natural condition, prior to the onset of significant human modification'.[31] The court dealt a major blow to China's territorial ambitions in the area by concluding that none of the maritime features could be considered islands for the purposes of international law.[32]

---

[23] *Territorial and Maritime Dispute (Nicaragua v Colombia)* [2012] ICJ Rep 624, para. 139. For a sceptical view, see Tanaka (n 7) 69.

[24] *The Republic of the Philippines and the People's Republic of China*, Award, PCA Case No. 2013-19, 12 July 2016, paras 482 and 545.

[25] Ibid, para. 482. See also *Territorial and Maritime Dispute (Nicaragua v Colombia)* (n 23) paras 139 and 37. The Norwegian Supreme Court has held, however, that a feature may simply be too large to be considered a mere 'rock', see reference in Tanaka (n 7) 69. See *Public Prosecutor v Haraldson et al.*, Rt. 1996 p. 624. For an overview in English, see Robin Churchill, 'Norway: Supreme Court Judgment on Law of the Sea Issues' (1996) 11 *International Journal of Marine and Coastal Law* 576–580.

[26] *The Republic of the Philippines and the People's Republic of China* (n 24) para. 542.

[27] Ibid, para. 543.   [28] Ibid, para. 544. See also the debate in Tanaka (n 7) 67.

[29] *The Republic of the Philippines and the People's Republic of China* (n 24) para. 305.

[30] Ibid, para. 508.   [31] Ibid. para. 306. See also para. 511.

[32] See the Court's conclusions in ibid, paras 554, 557, 560, 563, 566, 569, 625–626 and 643–648.

8.3.3 **Internal waters and the territorial sea**

Internal waters primarily consist of water on the landward side of a straight baseline from which the territorial sea is measured and water on the landward side of an enclosed bay.[33] In general, a state enjoys full sovereignty over its internal waters but transit in internal waters on the landward side of a straight baseline is governed by the rules on innocent passage (see later in this section).[34] In its internal waters, a coastal state is entitled to regulate all access to its ports and it is only in the event of distress that it is obliged to allow entry to a foreign vessel. A coastal state enjoys full sovereignty over all vessels located in its internal waters, including over ships in its ports. In practice, however, a coastal state tends to exercise its jurisdiction with restraint and with due consideration to the fact that the flag state will often be in a more natural position to exercise jurisdiction.

The *territorial sea* is a belt of the sea that runs adjacent to the coast. The maximum breadth of the territorial sea has been a long-standing issue in international law and it was not until the adoption of the 1982 LOSC that agreement was reached. Article 3 of LOSC sets the maximum breadth to 12 nautical miles when measured from the baseline.[35] The majority of states now claim a territorial sea of 12 miles and the limit appears to be reflected in customary international law. The territorial sea is not limited to the water in the sea but also includes the air space above the sea as well as the seabed and its subsoil. Unlike the contiguous zone and the EEZ (see Sections 8.3.4 and 8.3.5), the territorial sea is an inseparable appurtenance of the land territory and thus an inherent feature of sovereignty over the land.

In general, a coastal state enjoys exclusive territorial sovereignty in its territorial sea and may lawfully exert the same jurisdictional powers in the area as it does on land.[36] According to the right of *innocent passage*, however, foreign vessels may traverse the territorial sea of another state without entering the internal waters or a port facility within the territorial sea.[37] For navigation to be considered 'passage', it must be 'continuous and expedited' and stopping and anchoring must be either an incidental element to ordinary navigation or justified under principles of *force majeure*, distress or in order to render assistance to others in danger or distress. Passage is considered 'innocent' when it is not 'prejudicial to the peace, good order or security of the coastal State'.[38] LOSC lists a number of acts that are deemed to be at variance with innocent passage. These include exercises with weapons, spying, acts of propaganda, the loading or unloading of commodities, currency or persons contrary to the regulations of the coastal state, serious pollution, fishing activities, research activities or interferences with coastal communications.[39] Submarines and other underwater vehicles must navigate on the surface and show their flag.[40] *Foreign warships* may seemingly also rely on a right of innocent passage. [41] The same right is enjoyed by ships that are

---

[33] LOSC art. 8(1). On internal waters, see also V. D. Degan, 'Internal waters' (1986) 17 *Netherlands Yearbook of International Law* 3–44.

[34] See Art. 8(1) of the LOSC.   [35] LOSC art. 3   [36] Art. 17.   [37] Art. 18(1).

[38] Art. 19(1).   [39] Art. 19(2).   [40] Art. 20.

[41] See the discussion in Tanaka (n 7) 89–92.

either *nuclear-powered or which carry dangerous or noxious materials*.[42] While LOSC explicitly specifies that such ships enjoy a right of innocent passage,[43] it also states that a coastal state may designate certain sea lanes for the passage of such vessels.[44]

If a coastal state suspects that passage in its territorial waters is not innocent, it may take the steps necessary to prevent the passage from occurring.[45] Article 27 governs the exercise of criminal jurisdiction on foreign ships and article 27(1) stipulates that such jurisdiction 'should not be exercised on board a foreign ship passing through the territorial sea to arrest any person or to conduct any investigation in connection with any crime committed on board the ship during its passage' unless it concerns the following instances:

(a) the consequences of the crime extend to the coastal State;

(b) the crime is of a kind to disturb the peace of the country or the good order of the territorial sea;

(c) the assistance of the local authorities has been requested by the master of the ship or by a diplomatic agent or consular officer of the flag state; or

(d) such measures are necessary for the suppression of illicit traffic in narcotic drugs or psychotropic substances.

A coastal state is also entitled to exercise measures of criminal jurisdiction on board foreign ships that pass through the territorial sea after leaving the internal waters.[46] When considering if, and in what manner, an arrest should be made, the local authorities must always have 'due regard to the interests of navigation'.[47] LOSC is even stricter in relation to a coastal state's exercise of *civil jurisdiction*. Thus, according to article 28(1), a coastal state 'should not stop or divert a foreign ship passing through the territorial sea for the purpose of exercising civil jurisdiction in relation to a person on board the ship'.

Special rules apply for *archipelagic waters* within an archipelagic state—generally speaking, a group of islands situated in the middle of an ocean that form a geographical, economic and political unit.[48] Examples of archipelagic states include Indonesia, the Philippines and Fiji. Although the water within the baselines of an archipelagic state would prima facie appear to be 'internal' in nature, it is governed by different rules. Thus, LOSC stipulates that navigation in archipelagic waters is generally governed by the right of innocent passage.[49] The archipelagic state may, however, designate sea lanes and air routes that it deems suitable for continuous and expeditious passage through its waters.[50]

The vital importance of *international straits* also calls for a special legal regime.[51] LOSC defines an 'international strait' as a strait used for international navigation between one part of the high seas or an EEZ and part of the high seas or an EEZ.[52]

---

[42] LOSC art. 23. See also Tanaka (n 7) 93–94.   [43] Art. 23.   [44] Art. 22(2).
[45] LOSC art. 25(1).   [46] Art. 27(2)   [47] Art. 27(4).
[48] For a definition, see LOSC art. 46(a).   [49] Art. 52(1).   [50] Art. 53.
[51] For an overview, see Tanaka (n 7) 97–110.   [52] Art. 37.

Well-known international straits include the Malacca Strait (connecting the Pacific with the Indian Ocean), the Strait of Hormuz (linking the Persian Gulf with the Gulf of Oman and Arabian Sea) and the Strait of Gibraltar (connecting the Atlantic Ocean and the Mediterranean). *Historic straits* are exempted from the regulation of international straits in LOSC. A historic strait is one 'in which passage is regulated in whole or in part by long-standing international conventions in force specifically relating to such straits'.[53] Examples include the Great Belt (Storebælt) and Øresund in Denmark that are governed by the 1857 Copenhagen Convention.[54] The *Great Belt* case concerned the construction of a bridge in an international strait. Finland initiated proceedings against Denmark when the latter decided to build a bridge across 'Storebælt' (Great Belt) that would affect access to the North Sea for a certain type of very high Finnish vessels.[55] Denmark and Finland reached a settlement before the Court could hear oral arguments (Denmark paid Finland 90 million Danish kroner) and the Court did not therefore offer its views on the legality under international law of constructing bridges in international straits.[56]

The dramatic decrease of ice in the Arctic region has led to speculation that navigation through the so-called Northwest Passage may soon be possible for commercial shipping. The Passage consists of a number of alternative maritime transit routes that link Europe and the Atlantic Ocean with Asia and the Pacific Ocean above the North American continent. Canada claims that the route would lie within Canadian territorial or even internal waters. The United States and the EU, on the other hand, argue that the Passage must be conceived of and governed as an international strait.[57] Issues about status under international law also arise in relation to the so-called Northeast Passage and passage from the Atlantic Ocean to the Pacific Ocean along the Norwegian and Russian Arctic coasts.[58]

The sovereignty and jurisdiction of coastal states must be exercised with respect to the importance straits play for the well functioning of international communication and trade. Importantly, navigation though an international strait is governed by the right of *transit passage*.[59] Unlike the right of innocent passage through the territorial seas, transit passage cannot be suspended by a coastal state.[60] In addition, it is not only ships that enjoy a right to transit passage; aircraft that overfly the international

---

[53] Art. 35(c).

[54] See Copenhagen Convention, 14 March 1857. See also Denmark's declaration on ratification, Declaration of Denmark dated 16 November 2004 ('It is the position of the Government of the Kingdom of Denmark that the exception from the transit passage regime provided for in article 35 (c) of the Convention applies to the specific regime in the Danish straits (the Great Belt, the Little Belt and the Danish part of the Sound), which has developed on the basis of the Copenhagen Treaty of 1857. The present legal regime of the Danish straits will therefore remain unchanged').

[55] See ICJ, *Passage Through the Great Belt (Finland v Denmark)*, Application Instituting Proceedings, 17 May 1991 and the subsequent Order of 12 September 1992.

[56] See also Tanaka (n 7) 110.

[57] For a discussion, see James Kraska, 'The Law of the Sea Convention and the Northwest Passage' (2007) 22(2) *International Journal of Marine and Coastal Law* 257–282.

[58] See Erik Franckx, 'The Legal Regime of Navigation on the Russian Arctic' (2008–2009) 18 *Journal of Transnational Law and Policy* 327–342.

[59] Art. 38.   [60] Art. 38(1).

strait also possess the right. Ships and aircraft must 'proceed without delay' as well as 'refrain from any threat or use of force'. There is also a requirement to comply with generally accepted international regulations regarding safety procedures.[61] A coastal state may designate sea lanes and prescribe similar schemes if necessary to enhance the safe passage of ships.[62]

8.3.4 **The contiguous zone**

The contiguous zone is a stretch of the sea contiguous to the territorial sea where the coastal state may exercise necessary control to prevent and punish 'infringements of its customs, fiscal, immigration or sanitary laws and regulations within its territory or territorial sea'.[63] The maximum breadth of the zone is 24 nautical miles when measured from the baseline.[64] The purpose of the contiguous zone is to allow a coastal state to extend the reach of its enforcement jurisdiction for a range of specified purposes only. The term 'punish' suggests that a coastal state has the authority to arrest a ship that has committed an offence in the territorial sea but has since left and is now located in the contiguous zone. The term 'prevent', on the other hand, indicates that a coastal state is authorized to impede/stop a ship that is suspected of committing such an offence before it enters its territorial waters.

8.3.5 **The exclusive economic zone (EEZ)**

One of the primary concerns of a coastal state is to claim a privileged position with regard to harvesting the economic resources, primarily fish, in the waters off its shores. Disagreements about fishing rights and legitimate concerns about overfishing have been a recurrent source of animosity between states and vastly different positions have been adopted by states. In the 1970s, for example, some Latin American states claimed a right to exploit the natural resources of the sea for up to 200 nautical miles from their coasts.[65] In the *Fisheries Jurisdiction* case, the UK brought a case against Iceland in relation to the latter's proclamation of a 50-mile exclusive fishing zone.[66] In LOSC, the issue is dealt with by the establishment of an EEZ—a *sui generis* area of the sea adjacent to the coast. According to article 57, the EEZ may reach a maximum breadth of 200 nautical miles from the baseline. In the zone, a coastal state may claim and hold the exclusive right to the economic resources of the sea. Since the adoption of LOSC, most states have replaced their demands for exclusive fishing zones (EFZ) with EEZs. The ICJ has found that the existence of an EEZ is part of customary international law.[67]

Two initial things must be noted about the EEZ. First, according to article 61(1), it consists of not only the water within the area but also the seabed and subsoil as well as

---

[61] Art. 39.   [62] Art. 41(1).   [63] LOSC art. 33(1).   [64] Art. 33(2).

[65] See 1952 Declaration of Santiago and the 1974 Montevideo Declaration on the Law of the Sea. See also the overview in *Maritime Dispute (Peru v Chile)*, Judgment [2014] ICJ Rep 3, para. 19.

[66] *Fisheries Jurisdiction (UK v Iceland)*, Merits, Judgment [1974] ICJ Rep 3.

[67] *Continental Shelf (Libyan Arab Jamahiriya v Malta)* [1985] ICJ Rep 13, para. 34.

the airspace above the water.[68] Secondly, it is an 'economic' zone in the broad sense and therefore covers much more than just fishing. Article 56(1) stipulates that the rights of a coastal state relate to 'exploring and exploiting, conserving and managing the natural resources, whether living or non-living' as well as 'other activities for the economic exploitation and exploration of the zone, such as the production of energy from the water, currents and winds'.[69] A coastal state has the exclusive right to construct and operate offshore wind farms in its EEZ, as Denmark has done.

The rights that a coastal state possesses in the EEZ are exclusive in the sense that other states are barred from undertaking economic activities in the zone unless the coastal state has given its consent.

In general, under article 73 a coastal state may take the necessary measures to ensure compliance with its laws and regulations that conforms with the Convention. In practice, therefore, a coastal state may exercise both legislative and enforcement jurisdiction over foreign vessels in the EEZ. According to article 73(1), for example, a coastal state may board and inspect foreign vessels suspected of unlawful fishing activities and, if necessary, arrest the ship and initiate judicial proceedings. A coastal state's jurisdiction is limited, however, to that required to protect its economic rights. In the *M/V 'Saiga' (No. 2)* case, ITLOS did not find that Guinea could generally extend its customs laws to its EEZ.[70] In the *M/V 'Virginia G'* case, the Tribunal found that the regulation by a coastal state of so-called 'bunkering' (the refuelling of ships) of foreign vessels fishing in the EEZ was included in the measures which a coastal state could take to conserve and manage its living resources.[71]

The exclusive right to exploit and explore the resources of the EEZ includes the right to construct and operate necessary artificial islands or other structures as long as they do not interfere with the use of recognized sea lanes essential to international navigation.[72] A coastal state may also regulate, authorize and conduct marine scientific research in its EEZ[73] as well as protect and preserve the marine environment.[74]

As a main rule, article 58(1) specifies that other states are entitled to enjoy the freedoms of navigation and overflight as well as other related freedoms of the high seas (see Section 8.3.8) as long as they do not interfere with the coastal state's exclusive right to exploit and explore its EEZ. Navigation, however, may be subject to coastal state regulation to protect the marine environment. As long as *military exercises* are conducted with due regard to a coastal state's rights to exploit and explore the marine resources in its EEZ, they do not seem incompatible with the rights of the coastal state.[75]

---

[68] See art. 56(1).   [69] LOSC art. 56(1)(a).

[70] *The M/V 'Saiga' (No. 2) (Saint Vincent and the Grenadines v Guinea)*, Case No. 2, Judgment, 1 July 1999, para. 127.

[71] *The M/V 'Virginia G' (Panama v Guinea-Bissau)*, Judgment, Case No. 19, 14 April 2014, paras 215, 217 and 223.

[72] Arts 56(1)(b) and 60(1) and (7).   [73] Arts 56(1)(b)(ii) and 246(2).   [74] Art. 56(1)(iii).

[75] See the discussion in Tanaka (n 7) 394–397.

8.3.6 **The continental shelf**

In September 1945, US President Truman proclaimed that 'the natural resources of
the subsoil and seabed of the continental shelf beneath the high seas but contiguous
to the coasts of the US' appertained to the United States.[76] At the time, recent technological developments had made it possible to exploit the resources (primarily oil and
subsequently natural gas) contained in the seabed and subsoil below the surface of the
sea. Many states soon followed the US policy and the 1958 Geneva Convention on the
Continental Shelf states that a coastal state exercises sovereign rights over the continental shelf for the 'purposes of exploring it and exploiting its natural resources'.[77]
In the *North Sea Continental Shelf Cases*, the ICJ referred to the latter as a reflection
of the 'emergent rules of customary international law'.[78] Today, the sovereign rights
of a coastal state over the continental shelf can be regarded as part of customary law.
Unlike the EEZ, the continental shelf is an inherent feature of sovereignty and does
not need to be proclaimed by a coastal state.[79]

In practice, the continental shelf primarily concerns the extraction of oil and gas. In
LOSC, the continental shelf is regulated in Part IV. According to article 76(1), the continental shelf is composed of the seabed and subsoil of the submarine areas that extend
beyond the territorial sea throughout the natural prolongation of the land territory to
the outer edge of the continental margin, or to a distance of 200 nautical miles from
the baselines from which the breadth of the territorial sea is measured where the outer
edge of the continental margin does not extend up to that distance. There are, in other
words, two alternative modes of determining the outer limits of the shelf: one based on
geological factors (the edge of the continental margin) and one based on distance (200
nautical miles). The 200-miles limit—that ties the legal regime for governing the shelf
to that governing the EEZ—is reflected in customary international law.[80]

If the outer edge of the continental margin goes beyond 200 miles, the limit of the
shelf may under certain circumstances be set on the basis of a number of fairly complicated geological criteria. Thus, under article 76(4)(a), two modes of setting the limit
of the shelf beyond 200 miles may be relevant. While the first takes its departure point
in the thickness of sedimentary rocks, the second relies on a distance criterion of fixed
points not more than 60 miles from the foot of the continental shelf. Regardless of
the method, however, article 76(5) specifies that the extension of the continental shelf
cannot exceed 350 miles from the baseline or more than 100 miles from a point at
which the depth of the water is 2,500 metres. In practice, it may be difficult to locate
the points of the 2,500-metre isobaths. In this case, it is less easy to apply the rule concerning 100 nautical miles from the 2,500-metre isobaths.

Claims to a continental shelf exceeding 200 miles must be forwarded to a
Commission on the Limits of the Continental Shelf that assesses the claim and issues a
recommendation to the state.[81] The Commission does not offer its view on delimitation

---

[76] Truman Declaration.   [77] See art. 2(1).   [78] *North Sea Continental Shelf* (n 6) para. 63.
[79] Art. 77(3).   [80] *Continental Shelf (Libyan Arab Jamahiriya v Malta)* (n 67) para. 34.
[81] Art. 76(8). See Annex II to the Convention.

of overlapping claims to the shelf. The first state to submit a claim to the Commission was Russia which, in December 2001, made extensive claims to the continental shelf in the Arctic and Pacific Oceans.[82] A number of states have since made overlapping claims to certain area of the continental shelf in the Arctic Ocean. In November 2006, for example, Norway claimed parts of the shelf north of Svalbard and in December 2014, on behalf of the Kingdom of Denmark, the Danish government forwarded its claim to a large part of the continental shelf situated to the north of Greenland.[83]

Article 77(2) specifies that a coastal state's sovereign rights to explore and exploit the natural resources of the continental shelf are exclusive in the sense that if the coastal state does not explore the continental shelf or exploit its natural resources, no one may undertake those activities without the express consent of the coastal state. According to article 77(4), the natural resources in the continental shelf consist of the 'mineral and other non-living resources of the seabed and subsoil together with living organisms belonging to sedentary species'. The latter refers to 'organisms which, at the harvestable stage, either are immobile on or under the seabed or are unable to move except in constant physical contact with the seabed or the subsoil'. While the organisms in question certainly include clams and oysters, there is less agreement about whether crabs and lobsters are also included. With regard to its EEZ, a coastal state also possesses the right to construct artificial islands or other structures that do not obstruct the use of recognized sea lanes essential to international navigation.[84]

A coastal state may exercise both legislative and enforcement jurisdiction over foreign individuals and vessels in its EEZ to ensure respect for its rights on the continental shelf. It also has jurisdiction in relation to marine scientific research. In practice, of course, there are only limited means by which other states can interfere with a coastal state's exploitation of its continental shelf. All states may lay submarine cables and pipelines on the surface of the continental shelf subject to the consent of the relevant coastal state.[85]

8.3.7 **The Area—exploitation of the deep seabed**

The deep seabed beyond the outer limit of where states claim a right to the continental shelf is called the 'Area'.[86] Reaching agreement on the regulation of the Area was one of the most difficult aspects of the negotiations of LOSC and dissatisfaction about the legal regime created was so profound that it threatened to undermine the almost universal support for the Convention.[87] An Implementation Agreement was therefore adopted in 1994 to modify the original regime.

The regulation of the Area is based on an underlying premise articulated in article 136 that the deep seabed and its resources form part of the 'common heritage of

---

[82] See http://www.un.org/depts/los/clcs_new/submissions_files/submission_rus.htm.
[83] Ibid. See submission nos 7 and 76 respectively.   [84] Art. 80.   [85] Art. 79.
[86] Art. 1(1).
[87] For an overview, see Bernard H. Oxman, 'The 1994 Agreement and the Convention' (1994) 88 *American Journal of International Law* 687–696. See also James Harrison, *Making the Law of the Sea: A Study in the Development of International Law* (Cambridge University Press, 2013) 85–99.

mankind'.[88] Thus, no state can claim or exercise sovereignty or sovereign rights over the Area and exploitation must be carried out for the benefit of all.[89] In addition, the Area may only be used for peaceful purposes.[90] Article 133(a) defines 'resources' as 'all solid, liquid or gaseous mineral resources *in situ* in the Area at or beneath the seabed, including polymetallic nodules'.[91] Importantly, marine genetic resources are not covered. When recovered from the Area, the resources are referred to as 'minerals'.

To ensure that exploitation of the Area benefits all of mankind, activities are organized, carried out and controlled by an International Seabed Authority (ISA).[92] No activity can be undertaken without the approval of the ISA. All parties to LOSC are automatically members of the ISA which is based in Jamaica.

Article 153(2) specifies that activities in the Area can take a number of forms. First of all, activities may be undertaken by the ISA itself, acting through its own operational entity—the Enterprise. That entity has, however, yet to be established. Secondly, activities in the Area can be undertaken by state parties or other entities, in association with the ISA. In those cases, an application for exploitation must include two areas, one for the activities of the applicant and one reserved for activities by the ISA, acting through the Enterprise.[93] The third option is for activities to be conducted through joint ventures between the ISA and states or other entities. The obligations and responsibilities of activities in the Area is governed by a number of general principles, including core principles of international environmental law, listed in a 2011 advisory opinion by ITLOS.[94]

8.3.8 The high seas

Under article 86 of LOSC, the high seas are 'all parts of the sea which are not included in the EEZ, in the territorial sea or in the internal waters of a State, or in the archipelagic waters of an archipelagic State'. The high seas are *res communis* and thus beyond the sovereignty and jurisdiction of any state and they are governed by the principle of the freedom of the high seas. All states have an equal right, among other things, to navigation and overflight and, subject to certain stipulations, to lay submarine cables and pipelines as well as to construct artificial islands and other installations and to fish and conduct scientific research.[95] It is reserved for peaceful purposes[96] but military exercises that comply with article 2(4) of the UN Charter are allowed.[97]

Article 92(1) contains the well-established principle of both customary and treaty law that the flag state has exclusive jurisdiction over a vessel on the high seas.[98] The jurisdiction of the flag state includes both legislative and enforcement jurisdiction. It is up to each state to set the conditions for granting a vessel its nationality/flag

---

[88] See also art. 137(1) and UN Res. 2749 (XXV) Declaration of Principles Governing the Sea-Bed and the Ocean Floor, and the Subsoil Thereof, Beyond the Limits of National Jurisdiction (1970).
[89] LOSC art. 140(1).   [90] Art. 141.   [91] Art. 133.   [92] Art. 153(1).
[93] Art. 153(3). See also art. 3 of Annex III.
[94] *Responsibilities and Obligations of States Sponsoring Persons and Entities with Respect to Activities in the Area*, Case No. 17, Advisory Opinion, 1 February 2011.
[95] Art. 87(1).   [96] Art. 88   [97] Art. 301.   [98] See also art. 92(2).

and it is a well-known fact that some states profit from a policy of 'flags of convenience' whereby they permit shipowners with very limited connection to the state to register their ships and their national flags. Article 91(1) requires 'a genuine link' between the state and the ship.[99] In the *M/V 'Virginia G'* case, ITLOS stressed that, once a ship is registered, the flag state must 'exercise effective jurisdiction and control over that ship in order to ensure that it operates in accordance with generally accepted international regulations, procedures and practices'.[100]

Although vessels enjoy widespread freedom from the jurisdiction of foreign states on the high seas, a number of exceptions do exist. Article 110(1) contains *a right to visit* whereby a foreign warship may board a ship on the high seas if there are reasonable grounds for suspecting that:

(a) the ship is engaged in piracy;

(b) the ship is engaged in the slave trade;

(c) the ship is engaged in unauthorized broadcasting and the flag state of the warship has jurisdiction under article 109;

(d) the ship is without nationality; or

(e) though flying a foreign flag or refusing to show its flag, the ship is, in reality, of the same nationality as the warship.

Some conventions contain provisions whereby contracting parties accept that a ship of another contracting party may request authorization from the flag state to board a vessel suspected of engaging in certain prescribed activities, such as illicit trafficking of narcotics or illegal transportation of migrants.[101] If individuals found on 'visited' vessels are forced to return to their home states it may raise issues in relation to the human rights prohibition against the return of individuals to states where there is a risk of ill-treatment.[102]

Piracy has been the object of substantial attention in recent years. As noted in Chapter 5, customary international law grants all states a right to assert universal jurisdiction over the crime of piracy.[103] In LOSC, piracy is governed by articles 100–107 and article 110. Article 101 defines piracy as 'illegal acts of violence or detention, or any act of depredation, committed for private ends by the crew or the passengers of a private ship or a private aircraft, and directed: (i) on the high seas, against another ship or aircraft, or against persons or property on board such ship or aircraft; (ii) against a ship, aircraft, persons or property in a place outside the jurisdiction of

---

[99] See also *The M/V 'Saiga' (No. 2)* (n 70) para. 63.   [100] *The M/V 'Virginia G'* (n 71) para. 113.

[101] See, inter alia, the 1988 Vienna Convention Against Illicit Traffic in Narcotic Drugs and Psychotropic Substances and the 2000 Protocol against the Smuggling of Migrants by Land, Sea and Air, supplementing the 2000 UN Convention against Transnational Organized Crime.

[102] ECtHR, *Hirsi Jaman and Others v Italy*, App. no. 27765/09 (Grand Chamber), 23 February 2012. See also the discussion in Chapter 9.

[103] See Commentary to art. 9 in the Harvard Research in International Law's Draft Convention on Jurisdiction with Respect to Crime, 'Article 9. Universality—Piracy' (1935) 29 *American Journal of International Law* 563–572. See Chapters 5 and 15.

any State'.[104] The definition is therefore limited in a number of important ways. First, the illegal acts of violence must be committed for 'private ends'. Courts in Belgium and the United States have interpreted this requirement to include acts of violence perpetrated by environmental groups, such as Greenpeace and the Sea Shepherd Conservation Society.[105] Secondly, piracy involves two ships, a pirate ship and a victim ship. So-called 'internal hijacking', where the seizure of a ship is perpetrated by members of its own crew or its passengers, is not covered by the definition. Instead, such acts may be covered by the 1988 Rome Convention on the Suppression of Unlawful Acts Against the Safety of Maritime Navigation. The Rome Convention was adopted in the wake of the so-called *Achille Lauro* incident in October 1985 where four members of the Palestinian Liberation Front (PLF) hijacked an Italian-flagged cruise ship in the Mediterranean. The hijackers had boarded the ship disguised as tourists.[106] The third important caveat is the requirement that piracy must be committed either on the high seas or in a place outside the jurisdiction of any state. Acts of piracy committed in an EEZ are also covered by article 101.[107] However, acts of violence committed in the territorial sea or internal waters of a state fall outside the definition of piracy in article 101. Such acts are instead often classified as 'armed robbery' and may be covered by the 2009 International Maritime Organization (IMO) Code of Practice for the Investigation of the Crimes of Piracy and Armed Robbery against Ships.[108]

Article 105 states that 'every State may seize a pirate ship or aircraft, or a ship or aircraft taken by piracy and under the control of pirates, and arrest the persons and seize the property on board'. In addition, the courts of the state which 'carried out the seizure may decide upon the penalties to be imposed, and may also determine the action to be taken with regard to the ships, aircraft or property, subject to the rights of third parties acting in good faith'.

In response to widespread piracy in the Gulf of Aden which began in 2008, the UN Security Council greatly expanded the existing authorities under LOSC to fight piracy.[109] In December 2008, for example, the Council authorized states to use necessary means to fight piracy in the territorial waters of Somalia.[110] Two weeks later, it authorized states to use a counter-piracy force on land in Somalia.[111] The counter-piracy

---

[104] Art. 101 includes certain acts of participation and incitement or facilitating piracy.

[105] See *Castle John v NV Mabeco*, Cour de Cassation, 19 December 1986, 77 ILR 537 (Belgium) and *Institute of Cetacean Research v Sea Shepherd Conservation Society*, 725 F.3d 940 (9th Cir. 2013).

[106] Malvina Halberstam, 'Terrorism on the High Seas: The *Achille Lauro*, Piracy and the IMO Convention on Maritime Safety' (1988) 82(2) *American Journal of International Law* 269–310.

[107] See also Anna Petrig and Robin Geiss, *Piracy and Armed Robbery at Sea: The Legal Framework for Counter-Piracy Operations in Somalia and the Gulf of Aden* (Oxford University Press, 2011) 64.

[108] See the Convention's art. 2(2).

[109] See also the overview in Tullio Treves, 'Piracy, Law of the Sea, and Use of Force: Developments off the Coast of Somalia' (2009) 20 *European Journal of International Law* 399–414. As at August 2016, three international naval task forces are conducting counter-piracy operations in the Gulf of Aden. NATO operates 'Operation Ocean Shield', see http://www.nato.int/cps/en/natohq/topics_48815.htm (accessed 20 June 2016), the EU has 'Operation Atalanta', see http://eunavfor.eu/ (accessed 20 June 2016) and a number of states are engaged in the activities of 'Combined Task Force 151', see https://combinedmaritimeforces.com/ctf-151-counter-piracy/ (accessed 20 June 2016).

[110] SC Res. 1846 (2 December 2008), para. 10.   [111] SC Res. 1851 (16 December 2008), para. 6.

operations in the Gulf of Aden have raised a host of challenges. Participating states have, for example, struggled to find local states willing to prosecute suspected pirates. Agreements have, however, been concluded with states such as Kenya, Mauritius and the Seychelles.[112] Human rights law has also complicated counter-piracy efforts. In *Medvedyev v France*, the European Court of Human Rights (ECtHR) concluded that the transfer of suspected pirates is governed by the prohibition against transfer when there is a risk of ill-treatment in the receiving state.[113]

Mention should also be made of the right of so-called *hot pursuit*. According to article 111 of LOSC, a warship or military aircraft or other governmental ship or aircraft may chase a vessel out into the high seas if it has breached the laws of the state in one of the maritime zones.[114] The pursuit must be 'hot' and continuous. In the *M/V 'Saiga' (No. 2)* case, ITLOS found that the recall of a small patrol boat engaged in the alleged pursuit of a ship constituted a 'clear interruption' with the effect that Guinea could not rely on article 111.[115] A hot pursuit must cease if the vessel pursued enters the territorial sea of another state. The *M/V 'Saiga' (No. 2)* case also stipulated the principle that the use of force 'must be avoided as far as possible, and where force is unavoidable, it must not go beyond what is reasonable and necessary in the circumstances'.[116]

8.3.9 Delimitation of maritime zones

The various maritime zones discussed so far will often overlap with the zones of other states and it is therefore of vital importance that international law stipulates how overlapping maritime zones must be delimited.[117] In practice, of course, a delimitation issue may arise in relation to the delimitation of, respectively, the territorial sea, the contiguous zone, the EEZ and the continental shelf. In most cases, states tend to draw a single boundary for both the EEZ and the continental shelf. LOSC's approach to delimitation differs according to the zones in question.

Overlapping claims to the territorial sea and contiguous zone are governed by article 15 and the so-called 'equidistance—special circumstance rule'. According to this, the territorial sea between two coastal states that are opposite or adjacent to each other is divided by a median line every point of which is the same distance from the nearest

---

[112] For an overview, see Håkan Friman and Jens Lindborg, 'Initiating Criminal Proceedings with Military Force: Some Legal Aspects of Policing Somali Pirates by Navies' in Douglas Guilfoyle, *Modern Piracy, Legal Challenges and Responses* (Edward Elgar Publishing, 2013) 172–200.

[113] ECtHR, *Medvedyev and Others v France*, App. no. 3394/03 (Grand Chamber), Judgment, 29 March 2010.

[114] Art. 111. A violation committed in the contiguous zone must relate to violations of customs, fiscal, immigration or sanitary laws.

[115] *The M/V 'Saiga' (No. 2)* (n 70) para. 148.

[116] Ibid, para. 155. See also *SS 'I'm Alone' (Canada v United States)* (1935) III RIAA 1609–1618 and *The Red Crusader* incident, see *Investigation of certain incidents affecting the British trawler Red Crusader* (1962) XXIX RIAA 521–539.

[117] For a thorough discussion, see Yoshifumi Tanaka, *Predictability and Flexibility in the Law of Maritime Delimitation* (Hart Publishing, 2006).

points on the baselines from which the breadth of the territorial seas of the two states are measured. The exception is where reasons of historic title or other special circumstance requires a different delimitation.[118] What warrants classification as a 'special circumstance' is not mentioned in LOSC and must therefore be clarified by state practice and case law.

Articles 74(1) and 83(1) govern the delimitation of, respectively, overlapping claims to the EEZ and the continental shelf. Here, overlapping claims are dealt with on the basis of an 'equitable solution'.[119] But what this means in practice is not clear and international case law has not been uniform. Initially, the ICJ adopted the position that there was no generally applicable method of delimiting maritime zones and it repeatedly stated that it was focused on the goal—the identification of an equitable delimitation—and not the method used to reach that goal.[120] While the advantage of this 'goal-oriented approach' was that it gave a high degree of flexibility to the judges who were required to find an 'equitable' result, it also suffered from a lack of predictability.[121] The goal-oriented approach was subsequently replaced with a more fixed method of delimiting maritime zones. In the *Jan Mayen* case, the ICJ stated that it is 'in accord with precedents' to initiate delimitation with 'the median line' and then inquire whether 'special circumstances' exist that 'require any adjustment or shifting of that line'.[122] A similar approach has been adopted in subsequent cases.[123] Thus, while this test allows for the consideration of circumstances that may be peculiar to the delimitation in question, it also requires that the delimitation must take its point of departure as the median line and thus it introduces more predictability in delimitation cases. Then, in 2009 in *Maritime Delimitation in the Black Sea*, the ICJ developed the latter approach by introducing a three-stage process to the delimitation of a maritime boundary. According to the Court, the first step is to identify the provisional line of equidistance. The second phase consists of an examination of whether relevant circumstances exist that call for an adjustment of the equidistance line with a view to reaching an equitable result. The third and final stage is a proportionality test carried out on a case-by-case basis to verify whether the delimitation line leads to an inequitable result.[124] The latest test—which is referred to as the 'equidistance/relevant circumstances method'—has since been applied in a number of decisions, including by

---

[118] LOSC art. 15 (territorial sea), TSC art. 24 (contiguous zone). LOSC is silent with regard to delimitations of the contiguous zone.

[119] LOSC arts 74(1) and 83(1).

[120] *Continental Shelf (Tunisia/Libyan Arab Jamahiriya)* (n 17) para. 70. See also *North Sea Continental Shelf* (n 6) paras 101B and 92; *Delimitation of the Maritime Boundary in the Gulf of Maine Area*, Judgment [1984] ICJ Rep 246, para. 112 and *Continental Shelf (Libyan Arab Jamahiriya v Malta)* (n 67) paras 28 and 45.

[121] See also Tanaka (n 7) 207.

[122] *Maritime Delimitation in the Area between Greenland and Jan Mayen*, Judgment [1993] ICJ Rep 38, para. 51.

[123] See *Maritime Delimitation and Territorial Questions between Qatar and Bahrain* (n 10) 40, paras 167 and 230; *Land and Maritime Boundary between Cameroon and Nigeria (Cameroon v Nigeria: Equatorial Guinea intervening)*, Judgment [2002] ICJ Rep 303, paras 288–290.

[124] *Maritime Delimitation in the Black Sea (Romania v Ukraine)*, Judgment [2009] ICJ Rep 61, paras 115–122.

ITLOS in the 2012 *Delimitation in the Bay of Bengal* case[125] and, more recently, by the ICJ in a case from 2014 between Peru and Chile.[126] The three-stage approach ensures that cases can be resolved in an equitable manner while at the same time ensuring clarity about the principles and methods applied.[127]

The question is, of course, what circumstances may require a variance from the line of equidistance? Case law illustrates that the ICJ attributes particular weight to certain *geographical* issues, including the direction of the coastline and the configuration of the coasts of the two states, a proportionality assessment of the amount of marine space allotted to each state compared to the length of their coastlines and the presence of islands. In *North Sea Continental Shelf*, for example, the ICJ found that it was unacceptable for Germany to be allotted a continental shelf considerably different from those of its neighbours merely as a result of its concave coastline.[128] In *Libya v Malta*, the Court disregarded the existence of an uninhabited Maltese island when it drew a provisional median line.[129] It also rejected, however, a claim by Libya that it should be allotted a greater proportion of the continental shelf because it had a greater landmass than Malta.[130] *Economic considerations* are unlikely to be given any weight in the delimitation of maritime zones. The delimitation does not, therefore, take account of the wealth of the respective states or the 'fairness' of the concentration of more resources within the zones in question. As the ICJ noted in *Libya v Malta*, it did not find that it should be 'influenced by the relative economic position of the two States in question'.[131] Marine delimitation is concerned with limiting geography and physical space and not economic fairness or redistribution.

8.4 Conservation of marine life

It is a prime concern of the international law of the sea to conserve the living resources of the sea and oceans.[132] Many communities depend for their livelihood on the exploitation of marine life, primarily fishing, and the risk of depletion of certain forms of marine life is an ongoing concern in many parts of the world. International awareness of the need for conservation rose in the decades after the end of Second World War and some of the early treaties that contain explicit obligations to conserve marine

---

[125] *Dispute Concerning Delimitation of the Maritime Boundary Between Bangladesh and Myanmar in the Bay of Bengal*, Case No. 16, Judgment, 14 March 2012, para. 240.

[126] See, inter alia, *Territorial and Maritime Dispute (Nicaragua v Colombia)* (n 23) paras 190–199 and *Maritime Dispute (Peru v Chile)* (n 65) paras 180–195.

[127] See also Tanaka (n 7) 208–209.

[128] *North Sea Continental Shelf* (n 6) para. 91. On the direction of the coastline, see also *Continental Shelf (Tunisia v Libyan Arab Jamahiriya)* (n 17) para. 120 and *Delimitation of the Maritime Boundary in the Gulf of Maine Area* (n 120) para. 225.

[129] *Continental Shelf (Libyan Arab Jamahiriya v Malta)* (n 67) paras 64 and 71.

[130] Ibid, para. 49.

[131] Ibid, para. 50. See also *Land and Maritime Boundary between Cameroon and Nigeria (Cameroon v Nigeria: Equatorial Guinea intervening)* (n 123) para. 304.

[132] See also the Preamble to LOSC.

life were adopted in the 1950s. An example is the 1958 Convention on Fishing and Conservation of the Living Resources of the High Seas, the adoption of which was motivated by a desire to solve some of the conservation challenges associated with the 'development of modern techniques for the exploitation of the living resources of the Sea'.[133]

The zonal system in LOSC imposes only limited obligations on coastal states in relation to conserving marine life. In its territorial waters, a coastal state exercises sovereignty and is generally free to catch all the fish it wants. A general freedom to fish in the high seas also exists for all states. In an EEZ—where the vast majority of fish are caught—LOSC introduced a special regime that seeks to balance conservation and the proper utilization of the living resources of the zone. Thus, in order to prevent over-fishing, article 61(1) require coastal states to determine the allowable catch of the living resources in their EEZ and ensure that 'the maintenance of the living resources in the exclusive economic zone is not endangered by over-exploitation'.[134] The conservation aims in article 61 must, however, be considered in the light of article 62 that stipulates that coastal states shall also 'promote the objective of optimum utilization of the living resources' in the EEZ. According to that article, a coastal state that does not have the capacity to harvest all of the allowable catch itself, must allow other states access to the surplus. In its practical implementation and the determination of the allowable catch, articles 61 and 62 leave a substantial amount of discretion to the coastal state.[135]

The highly migratory nature of many species of marine life makes the artificial maritime zone system in LOSC a less than optimal tool for the conservation of marine life. When it comes to conservation, therefore, the primary approach is to tailor the regulation around the needs of the individual species of marine life. Article 63(1) of LOSC, for example, obliges states to cooperate in ensuring the conservation and development of *shared and straddling fish stocks*, such as herring and mackerel, that occur within the EEZs of two or more coastal states. Similar obligations exist in relation to *highly migratory species*, such as tuna, marlin, dolphin and shark.[136] In 1995, the UN Agreement on Straddling Stocks and Highly Migratory Species was adopted to enhance the conservation and management of such fish stocks and it sets up minimum standards of conservation and introduces a system for compliance and enforcement on the high seas. LOSC also regulates *anadromous stocks* that spawn in fresh water but otherwise spend the majority of their lives in the sea, such as salmon and sturgeon.[137] Conservation of anadromous stocks is also subject to fairly detailed regional and bilateral regulation, including in the 1992 Convention for the Conservation of Anadromous Stocks in the North Pacific Ocean.

The exploitation of *marine mammals*, such as whales, dolphins, polar bears and seals had been a topic of major attention for decades. Article 65 of LOSC specifies that

---

[133] See the Preamble.   [134] Art. 61(2).   [135] See also Tanaka (n 7) 234–236.
[136] Art. 64(1).   [137] Art. 66.

Part V of the Convention does not prejudice the right of a coastal state or an international organization to regulate the exploitation of marine mammals more strictly than provided for in the Convention. In some cases, conservation of marine mammals is covered by the 1973 Convention on International Trade in Endangered Species of Wild Fauna and Flora that seeks to ensure that international trade in specimens of wild animals, such as some marine mammals, and plants does not threaten their survival. Regionally, numerous relevant conventions exist for the conservation and protection of marine mammals.[138]

The regulation of *whaling* has been a particularly sensitive topic since the advent in the first decades of the 20th century of large factory ships that enabled whaling far from land. Thus, conventions on whaling had already began to be adopted in the 1930s.[139] The key international legal instrument is the 1946 International Convention for the Regulation of Whaling (ICRW) that was adopted in Washington DC and entered into force in November 1948. While the ICRW does not contain any substantive provisions, it sets up an International Whaling Commission tasked with adopting the relevant rules and regulations for whaling in the form of amendments to a schedule that is an integral part of the ICRW.[140] The ICRW applies to whaling in all waters and, in 1982, the Commission adopted a moratorium to suspend all commercial whaling commencing in the 1985–1986 season.[141] The moratorium remains in force but certain exemptions have been made for *aboriginal communities*, such as those in Greenland.[142] Unlike commercial whaling, whaling by indigenous peoples does not seek to maximize catches or profit. It is up to states to provide the Commission with the required information on the needs of their indigenous people in the form of 'Needs Statements'.[143] Despite the moratorium, Norway resumed commercial whaling of minke whales in 1993.[144] Iceland objects to the moratorium and also hunts whales.[145] Both states set their own catch limits but provide relevant information about their catches to the ICRW. The Commission has also established two 'whale sanctuaries', one in the Indian Ocean and the other in the Southern Ocean in the Pacific.

---

[138] See, inter alia, the 1971 Agreement on Sealing and the Conservation of the Seal Stocks in the Northwest Atlantic, the 1972 Convention for the Conservation of Antarctic Seals, the 1973 Agreement on the Preservation of Polar Bears and the 1992 Agreement on the Conservation of Small Cetaceans of the Baltic and North Seas.

[139] See the 1931 Convention for the Regulation of Whaling and the 1937 International Agreement for the Regulating of Whaling.

[140] ICRW art. 5. See the schedule to the International Convention for the Regulation of Whaling, last amended by the Commission at the 65th Meeting, September 2014.

[141] See rule 10(c) of the schedule.   [142] See rule 13.

[143] See also the overview by the International Whaling Commission, 'Aboriginal Subsistence Whaling', https://iwc.int/aboriginal (accessed 20 August 2016).

[144] See Martha Howron, 'International Regulation of Commercial Whaling: The Consequences of Norway's Decision to Hunt the Minke Whale' (1994) 18 *Hastings International and Comparative Law Review* 175–193.

[145] Iceland's official position on whaling is available at http://www.fisheries.is/management/government-policy/whaling/ (accessed 20 August 2016).

Much attention has focused on the legality of whaling for scientific purposes. According to article VIII of the ICRW, regardless of the moratorium, states are allowed to grant permits that authorize whaling for the purposes of scientific research. In *Whaling in the Antarctic*, the ICJ concluded that a special whaling programme instituted by Japan in the Southern Ocean breached the 1982 moratorium because the permits granted did not have an entirely scientific purpose.[146]

8.5 Protection of the marine environment

It was not until the late 1960s and early 1970s that marine protection became a key priority for international society. Up until that time, the law had almost exclusively focused on the exploitation of the sea and not its protection. But marine protection features prominently in LOSC that devotes an entire Part of the Convention— Part XII—to the issue. In many ways, LOSC has been characterized as reflecting a paradigm shift in international law and a shift from a general freedom to pollute to an obligation to prevent pollution.[147] Among other things, article 192 contains a general obligation on all states to 'protect and preserve the marine environment'. In practice, the substantive regulation for the protection of the marine environment focuses on the source of the pollution.[148]

Land-based sources of pollution are the greatest source of marine pollution but due to the obvious tension between limiting pollution and economic and industrial growth, international regulation is weak. The general obligations to prevent pollution, including article 192 mentioned above, are essentially the only substantive obligations of a universal character that apply. However, a number of initiatives have been proposed under the UN Environment Programme (UNEP), including the non-binding 1985 Montreal Guidelines for the Protection of the Marine Environment against Pollution from Land-Based Sources. The—limited—regulation of land-based pollution is supplemented by regional conventions.

Dumping is the deliberate disposal of waste at sea of waste or other matters from vessels, aircraft, platforms or other man-made structures at sea.[149] The regulation of dumping has gone from an approach which generally allowed dumping unless it was explicitly prohibited, to the current approach where dumping is prohibited unless explicitly allowed. The 1972 London Dumping Convention that has since been amended, most importantly in 1996 with the adoption of a London Protocol,

---

[146] *Whaling in the Antarctic (Australia v Japan: New Zealand intervening)*, Judgment [2014] ICJ Rep 226, paras 227–233.

[147] Tanaka (n 7) 276.

[148] The source-based regulation is supplemented by a number of regional treaties adopted to protect the marine environment in certain regions of the world. Examples include the 1976 Convention for the Protection of the Mediterranean Sea against Pollution and the 1992 Convention for the Protection of the Marine Environment of the North-East Atlantic (OSPAR).

[149] London Convention, art. 3(1)(a).

obliges states to prohibit and prevent dumping of certain waste listed in a number of annexes.

Vessels may pollute the marine environment through the release of oil or other harmful substances in the course of normal operations or as a result of an accident. The primary legal instruments are the so-called MARPOL instruments that consist of a 1973 International Convention for the Prevention of Pollution from Ships and a 1978 Protocol thereto.[150] MARPOL seeks to limit the discharge of oil and to assist in the management of an accident at sea and applies to discharges by 'ships' (including submarines or fixed or floating platforms).[151] Substantive regulation is found in a number of annexes. Accidents such as the 1989 *Exxon Valdez* oil spill in Alaska and the 2010 *Deep Water Horizon* oil spill in the Gulf of Mexico illustrate the devastating effects major accidents may have on the marine environment. In response to the *Exxon Valdez* oil spill, the 1990 International Convention on Oil Pollution Preparedness, Response and Cooperation (OPRC) was adopted in the framework of the IMO. As we shall see in Chapter 10, oil spills are also governed by a special regime of liability for environmental damage.

On a final note, mention should be made of the decision in June 2015 by the UN General Assembly to initiate work on the development of an international legally binding instrument on the conservation and sustainable use of marine biodiversity in areas beyond national jurisdiction under LOSC.[152] The decision stemmed from the fact that the general principle of the freedom of the high seas was outdated for the purposes of conservation and regulation of the sustainable use of biodiversity in areas beyond national jurisdictions. As noted earlier, marine genetic resources are not covered by the concept of 'resources' in the Area and LOSC does not specifically refer to biodiversity or sustainability.

8.6 Dispute settlement in the law of the sea

In Part XV, LOSC establishes an elaborate system for the settlement of disputes that combines voluntary and mandatory measures.[153] The voluntary component is reflected in article 280 whereby states agree to settle a dispute between them concerning the interpretation of the Convention by any peaceful means of their own choice. The mandatory element enters the picture if the disputing states cannot settle their disagreement by their own means. Article 286 stipulates that any party to the dispute may bring it before the court or tribunal that has been given jurisdiction under Part XV. Under article 287, a contracting

---

[150] See also the earlier 1954 International Convention for the Prevention of Pollution of the Sea by Oil (OILPOL).

[151] MARPOL, art. 3(1).   [152] GA Res. 69/292 (19 June 2015).

[153] For an overview, see Natalie Klein, *Dispute Settlement in the UN Convention on the Law of the Sea* (Cambridge University Press, 2006).

state is free to choose one or more of four possible options for the settlement of disputes:

- the ITLOS;
- the ICJ;
- an arbitral tribunal constituted in accordance with Annex VII of LOSC;
- a special arbitral tribunal constituted in accordance with Annex VIII of LOSC.

When ratifying LOSC, Denmark, Sweden and Norway all declared that they chose the ICJ for the settlement of disputes, while Finland chose both the ICJ and ITLOS. Iceland did not state any preferences.[154] If the parties to a dispute have accepted the same settlement procedure for a dispute, it can only be submitted according to that procedure, unless the parties agree otherwise.[155] If, however, the parties have not accepted the same settlement procedure, it may only be submitted to arbitration pursuant to Annex VII, unless the parties agree otherwise.[156]

Some of the discretionary powers enjoyed by coastal states are not covered by compulsory dispute settlement, such as setting an allowable catch in an EEZ.[157] In addition, article 298 allows a state to exempt itself from submitting certain categories of dispute to the settlement mechanisms, such as disputes concerning the application of the rules on sea boundary delimitations, historic bays or titles[158] or military activities.[159]

One of the notable features of LOSC was the creation of *ITLOS* as a permanent judicial organ. ITLOS consists of 21 members who serve in their individual capacity. The Tribunal has jurisdiction over any dispute that concerns the interpretation and application of LOSC, as well as any other related international law of the sea agreement that confers jurisdiction on it.[160] The Tribunal has established a Seabed Disputes Chamber that deals with disputes related to activities in the Area. The decisions of the Tribunal in contentious cases are final and must be complied with by the parties to the dispute.[161] The Tribunal may prescribe provisional measures if deemed 'appropriate under the circumstances to preserve the respective rights of the parties to the dispute or to prevent serious harm to the marine environment'.[162] Decisions on provisional measures are binding.[163] The Statute of the Tribunal includes a provision that grants the Tribunal jurisdiction to render advisory opinions.[164] The first contentious case submitted to the Tribunal was the *M/V Saiga* case. By July 2016, a total of 23 contentious cases had been referred to the Tribunal and, in addition, it has issued two advisory opinions.[165]

---

[154] For an overview of statements and declarations, see http://www.un.org/depts/los/convention_agreements/convention_declarations.htm#Finland.

[155] Art. 287(4).   [156] Art. 287(5).   [157] See art. 297(3)(a).   [158] Art. 298(1)(a).

[159] Art. 298(1)(b).   [160] See the ITLOS Statute, arts 21–22.

[161] LOSC art. 296. See also ITLOS Statute, art. 33.   [162] LOSC art 290(1).

[163] LOSC, art. 290(6).   [164] See ITLOS Statute, art. 138.

[165] An overview of contentious cases and advisory proceedings is available at https://www.itlos.org/cases/list-of-cases/case-no-21/.

Summary

The international law of the sea is one of the oldest disciplines of public international law. The most important rules are found in the 1982 LOSC. The primary purpose of the law is to balance the legitimate interests of coastal states with the interests of other states. The practical result is the division of the sea into maritime zones in which coastal and other states hold a variety of rights and obligations. As a main rule, the rights of a costal state decrease relevant to the distance from the shore. Maritime zones can be divided into those spaces that are located *in the national jurisdiction of a coastal state* and those that lie *beyond*. It is a primary concern of the international law of the sea to conserve the living resources of the seas and oceans. To that end, the law relies less on the zonal system and focuses more on individual species of marine life and the particular needs of those species. LOSC has an elaborate system for dispute settlement that combines voluntary and mandatory measures.

Recommended reading

A solid presentation of the law of the sea is Yoshifumi Tanaka, *The International Law of the Sea* (2nd edn, Cambridge University Press, 2015).

See also Donal Rothwell and Tim Stephens, *The International Law of the Sea* (2nd edn, Hart Publishing, 2016); James Harrison, *Making the Law of the Sea: A Study in the Development of International Law* (Cambridge University Press, 2013).

For some of the legal challenges in the Arctic, see Michael Byers, *International Law and the Arctic* (Cambridge University Press, 2013); James Kraska, 'The Law of the Sea Convention and the Northwest Passage' (2007) 22(2) *International Journal of Marine and Coastal Law* 257.

On piracy, see Anna Petrig and Robin Geiss, *Piracy and Armed Robbery at Sea: The Legal Framework for Counter-Piracy Operations in Somalia and the Gulf of Aden* (Oxford University Press, 2011).

Maritime delimitation is dealt with in Yoshifumi Tanaka, *Predictability and Flexibility in the Law of Maritime Delimitation* (Hart Publishing, 2006).

On dispute settlement, see Natalie Klein, *Dispute Settlement in the UN Convention on the Law of the Sea* (Cambridge University Press, 2006).

Questions for discussion

1. Can you come up with some examples of where the interests of a coastal state collide with the interests of other states?

2. Which actors are deemed to have a legitimate interest in the regulation of the seas?

3. What is the difference between internal waters and territorial waters? And to what extent does the regulation of the two zones differ?

4. What is the difference between the right of innocent passage and the right of transit passage?

5. What is the difference between an 'island' and a 'rock'? Does it matter?

6. Which principles govern the delimitation of overlapping continental shelves?

7. Why is the zonal system a less than ideal system for conserving marine life? What approach does international law adopt towards the system?

8. What are some of the challenges of limiting marine pollution?

9

International human rights law

CENTRAL ISSUES

1. This chapter discusses the system of human rights protection that has emerged since the end of the Second World War.

2. It presents the most important sources of international human rights law.

3. The chapter also examines the mechanisms for the enforcement of human rights that have been developed both within the realm of the United Nations and on a regional basis, including the robust European system for the protection of human rights.

4. It discusses the territorial scope of the most important human rights conventions and the applicability of human rights conventions in times of armed conflict and emergencies.

9.1 Introduction

As we have seen throughout this book, international law is at its core a horizontal legal system, the primary purpose of which is to avoid undue friction between sovereign states. In fact, up until the middle of the 20th century, the manner in which sovereign authority was exercised within a state was by and large considered a matter in which other states had no business meddling. With a few exceptions, it was not until after the end of the Second World War that international law began to afford individuals protection from their own state. The reason why human rights law is a field of public international law is not because its substance is inherently international (in fact, it is not), but because states have turned the manner in which they treat individuals under their jurisdiction into a matter of international concern through the adoption of treaties. Human rights law belongs, in other words, in the international law of cooperation.

The idea that an individual possesses certain rights as an individual vis-à-vis his or her own state, has its origins in the era of the Enlightenment in the 18th century and in early Western constitutional thought.[1] In the 19th century, many states adopted national constitutions containing fundamental rights protection. In general, though, the

---

[1] See the English Bill of Rights (1689), the US Declaration of Independence (1776), the French Declaration of the Rights of Man and Citizen (1789).

rights granted were tied to citizenship or a similar nexus to the state, and were often based on theories of 'social contract', and could therefore not be relied on by all human beings. The modern conception of human rights is different because it is based on an understanding—derived from natural law thinking—that human rights are inherent in *all* individuals and therefore of universal application.[2] Contemporary human rights law originates from the establishment of the United Nations in 1945 and the belief that persecutions by the Axis Powers called for the creation of a legal framework that would prevent something similar from ever happening again. Article 1(3) of the UN Charter therefore stipulates that promoting of respect for human rights and fundamental freedoms is one of the primary purposes of the organization.[3] An important development in the creation of the human rights system was the adoption in 1948 of the General Assembly's Universal Declaration of Human Rights (UDHR). The first article in the Declaration states that all 'human beings are born free and equal in dignity and rights. They are endowed with reason and conscience and should act towards one another in a spirit of brotherhood.'[4]

The alleged universal character of human rights has been criticized by 'cultural relativists' for unjustifiably imposing one particular conception of justice on all others.[5] During the Cold War, for example, the communist East defended its dismal human rights record by arguing that the implementation of civil and political rights (see Section 9.3.2) depended on the political ideology of a state and it in turn criticized the capitalist West for not sufficiently respecting economic and social rights (see Section 9.3.3). The East/West debate has since been replaced by a North/South debate between the developed and the less developed world, with the latter arguing that the priority afforded to certain civil and political rights comes at the expense of all states' right to self-determination. Human rights' claim to universalism is also challenged by claims that greater account should be taken of religious dogma, most notably those derived from Islam. In Europe and North America, for example, the large influx of immigrants and refugees has led to complicated exchanges about the extent to which secular societies based on fundamental rights protection must make room for what are often perceived as 'foreign' cultural practices and religious beliefs.[6] The debate about how much an immigrant must give up and how much the receiving state must compromise is often cast in terms of human rights relativism. In practice, the extent to which a human rights convention is a 'fair' compromise between cultural and political differences is irrelevant for the purposes of determining a state's obligations under international law. When a state consents to a human rights convention and becomes a

---

[2] See also preamble to the 1966 ICCPR and ICESCR.   [3] See also art. 53 of the Charter.

[4] GA Res. 217 (III) (10 December 1948). Also of major importance was the 1975 Final Act of the Conference on Security and Co-operation in Europe—also known as the Helsinki Act—that helped to pave the way for the spread of democracy and human rights protection to Eastern Europe after the end of the Cold War, see Conference on Security and Co-operation in Europe Final Act, 1 August 1975.

[5] Jack Donnelly, 'Cultural Relativism and Universal Human Rights' (1984) 6(4) *Human Rights Quarterly* 400–419. For a critique of cultural relativism, see John J. Tilley, 'Cultural Relativism' (2000) 22(2) *Human Rights Quarterly* 501–547.

[6] For a good overview, see the selection of articles and perspectives in Henry J. Steiner, Philip Alston and Ryan Goodman, *International Human Rights in Context* (Oxford University Press, 2007) 616–639.

party thereto, it is legally obliged to carry out its treaty-based obligations. If the state believes that certain elements of the treaty are incompatible with its religious traditions or social and cultural sentiments, it will generally be allowed to make a reservation to the treaty as many states have in fact done.

International human rights law is a huge area of international law and it is impossible to cover all aspects in the present chapter. Here, the primary focus is on the human rights law *system*. We begin in Section 9.2 with the primary sources of human rights law before Section 9.3 discusses the different categories of human rights. Section 9.4 discusses the obligation on states to offer protection to individuals from the acts of other private individuals. Section 9.5 provides an overview of the enforcement mechanisms in the UN and Section 9.6 focuses on the regional protection of human rights. Section 9.7 discusses the territorial scope of human rights treaties and Section 9.8 concerns the application of human rights in times of emergency.

9.2 Sources of human rights law

We have already seen that the modern history of international human rights law begins with the 1948 UDHR. Throughout the years, the UN has been instrumental in drafting a wide range of human rights instruments,[7] including nine core universal human rights treaties open to all states. The most important of these are the 1966 International Covenant on Civil and Political Rights (ICCPR) and the 1966 International Covenant on Economic, Social and Cultural Rights (ICESCR). The ICCPR and the ICESCR are *general conventions* and deal with a wide array of human rights. The UN has also adopted numerous universal conventions addressing *a particular human rights issue*, such as the 1965 International Convention on the Elimination of All Forms of Racial Discrimination (CERD), the 1984 Convention Against Torture and Other Cruel, Inhuman or Degrading Treatment or Punishment (CAT) and the 2006 International Convention for the Protection of All Persons from Enforced Disappearance (ICPPED). Other UN conventions seek to *protect certain categories of individuals deemed vulnerable*. Such conventions include the 1979 Convention on the Elimination of All Forms of Discrimination Against Women (CEDAW) and the 1989 Convention on the Rights of the Child (CRC), the 1990 International Convention on the Protection of the Rights of All Migrant Workers and Members of Their Families (ICRMW) and the 2007 Convention on the Rights of Persons with Disabilities (CRPD). Additional universal treaties with a human rights scope worth noting are the 1951 Convention Relating to the Status of Refugees and the 1961 Convention on the Reduction of Statelessness.

There is also a range of important *regional* human rights conventions. The first of these was the 1950 European Convention on Human Rights (ECHR) adopted by the Council of Europe. In fact, as we shall see later, human rights protection in Europe is highly developed with strong enforcement. Other regional conventions include

---

[7] For an overview, see http://www.ohchr.org/EN/ProfessionalInterest/Pages/UniversalHumanRights Instruments.aspx.

the 1969 American Convention on Human Rights and the 1981 African Charter on Human and Peoples' Rights. In 2004, the Arab League adopted an Arab Charter on Human Rights that replaced an earlier charter that never entered into force.

Fundamental human rights are also protected under *customary international law* and thus binding on all states regardless of their treaty obligations. This is particular the case for most civil and political rights. Some of the rights may also be protected as norms of a peremptory/*jus cogens* nature. As discussed in Chapter 2, these rights include the prohibition against torture, slavery, genocide and various forms of gross racial discrimination.

9.3 The categories of human rights

9.3.1 Introduction

Individual human rights can meaningfully be divided into categories, or classes, that reflect the nature of the rights and the evolution of international human rights law. The categories are civil and political rights (Section 9.3.2), economic and social rights (Section 9.3.3) and certain collective rights (Section 9.3.4). Since civil and political rights play a more dominant rule in international law, priority is given here to their treatment. It must be noted, however, that it is now generally considered that the rights are interrelated as well as interdependent.[8]

9.3.2 Civil and political rights

The oldest category of rights is those of a *civil and political nature*. These rights—at times referred to as 'first generation' human rights—constitute the backbone of the general human rights treaties, including the ICCPR and the ECHR. They include the prohibition against torture and slavery, the right to life, liberty, fair trial, equality before the law, freedom of speech, religious freedoms as well as certain political participatory rights. Most of these rights are 'negative' in the sense that they primarily seek to offer protection from the excesses of the state. They are concerned, in other words, with freedom *from* government. In practice, though, effective enjoyment of civil and political rights often requires at least a minimum degree of positive action on the part of the state, such as the creation of an effective police force and a well-functioning judicial system.

Civil and political rights are derived from a set of core principles and values that inform their articulation and practical application. Some rights are tied to more than one of these principles. One such principle or value is *human dignity*. The preamble to the ICCPR states, for example, that it is derived from the inherent dignity of the human person. Some civil and political rights are directly linked to respect for human dignity, the clearest example being the right to life and the prohibition against torture

---

[8] See also the 1993 Vienna Declaration and Programme of Action, 25 June 1993.

and cruel, inhuman or degrading treatment or punishment. Other examples include the abolition of the death penalty and the prohibition against enforced disappearances. Rights derived from human dignity are generally absolute in the sense that they do not allow limitations or balancing.[9] Another core value is *freedom* which can be translated into both intellectual and physical freedom. Notions of *intellectual* freedom are visible in those rights that relate to freedom of expression, freedom of thought, freedom of conscience, freedom of religion, freedom of association and freedom of peaceful assembly. Since the practical exercise of intellectual freedoms may collide with the interests of other individuals and/or with wider societal goals, they can generally be limited if required to fulfil a legitimate purpose and the limiting measure is deemed proportionate. In practice, this limitation often takes the form of a balancing act where the value is held up against a competing value or consideration.[10] Respect for *physical freedom* is reflected in the right to liberty and the accompanying prohibition against arbitrary detention as well as the freedom of movement. Equality and *non-discrimination* are yet other powerful values in international human rights law. Differential treatment based solely on the basis of traits and attributes that cannot be altered is hard to reconcile with basic notions of justice and the equal status of all individuals. Non-discrimination is reflected in the overall obligation on all states to respect and ensure the enjoyment of rights without distinction on the basis of race, sex, language, religion, political opinion or national or social origin.[11] In practice, of course, not all these traits are inalienable. Importantly, the principle of non-discrimination does not prohibit a state from taking account of a particular ground (race, sex, language etc.) when it is a legitimate consideration to the issue at hand. Principles of *justice and fairness* are core human rights values in their own right. They are most clearly reflected in the legal principles of proper administration of justice in the legal system. Most notably, the principle of justice is translated into a right to a fair trial—also known as 'due process'—and in the prohibition against retroactive criminality (*nullum crimen sine lege*). The last set of principles or values worth noting are those concerning *political participation*. The right of citizens to participate in the political processes of their societies has become a fundamental principle in international human rights protection, in particular in Europe. In practice, political participation is reflected in the intellectual freedoms noted earlier as well as in more direct rights of access to public service, to participate in general elections and to run for political office.

9.3.3 Economic and social rights

The second category of rights concerns *economic and social issues* and, on the universal level, these rights—at times referred to as 'second generation' human rights—are

---

[9] The right to life, however, does accept deprivation of life that results from lawful acts of war. ICCPR art 6 only prohibits the 'arbitrary' deprivation of life. See also ECHR art. 2(2).

[10] See, inter alia, ICCPR arts 18(3), 19(3), 21, 22(2). See also ECHR arts 9(2), 10(2), 11(2).

[11] See ICCPR art. 2(1). See also ECHR art. 14.

primarily found in the ICESCR. In Europe, they are listed in the European Social Charter. The rights include a right to work, adequate working conditions including fair wages, a right to social security, an adequate living standard, physical and mental health and a right to education. As the examples illustrate, the rights differ from civil and political rights not only due to their character and the values they seek to promote but also because of the role the state must play in order to fulfil those rights. In practice, enjoyment of economic and social rights such as work, social security and education, requires a substantial element of state action and initiative. For this reason, the rights are also referred to as 'positive' rights, in the sense that their fulfilment requires not freedom from government but rather action *by* it. Economic and social rights are generally fairly abstract and thus leave wide discretion for the states. Judicial enforcement of social and economic rights is also much weaker than enforcement of civil and political rights.

9.3.4 **Collective rights**

Some human rights instruments focus on the protection of various *groups of individuals*, most often those groups deemed to be particularly vulnerable and thus in need of special attention. The *1948 Genocide Convention*, for example, obliges states to prevent and punish acts intended to destroy, in whole or in part, 'a national, ethnical, racial or religious group as such'.[12] The notion of 'group rights' is also central to *the right to self-determination* according to which all 'peoples' have a right to freely determine their political status and pursue their economic, social and cultural development.[13] As we also saw in Chapter 4, the right to self-determination is listed in article 1 in the two 1966 UN Covenants. International human rights law also grants protection to various *minorities*, such as ethnic or religious minorities. According to article 27 of the ICCPR, for example, individuals belonging to ethnic, religious or linguistic minorities 'shall not be denied the right, in community with the other members of their group, to enjoy their own culture, to profess and practise their own religion, or to use their own language'.[14] In Europe, minority protection was enhanced with the adoption of the 1994 European Framework Convention for the Protection of National Minorities. *Indigenous peoples* enjoy a particular form of human rights protection.[15] In 1989, the International Labour Organization (ILO) updated an existing 1957 Convention on Indigenous and Tribal Peoples in Independent Countries.[16] Indigenous rights have also been brought up in a number of cases before the Inter-American Court of Human Rights.[17]

---

[12] See art. 2.   [13] See also the overview in Chapter 4.

[14] See too GA Res. 47/135 Declaration on the Rights of Persons Belonging to National or Ethnic, Religious or Linguistic Minorities (8 December 1992).

[15] See generally, S. James Anaya, *Indigenous Peoples in International Law* (2nd edn, Oxford University Press, 2004).

[16] See also the 2007 Declaration on the Rights of Indigenous Peoples.

[17] See, inter alia, *The Mayagna (Sumo) Awas Tingni Community v Nicaragua*, Judgment of 31 August 2001, Inter-AmCtHR, Series C, No. 79 (2001).

Claims have additionally been made for the existence of other more intangible 'third generation' rights, such as a right to development, a right to peace and a right to the environment.[18] In 1986, the UN General Assembly adopted a Declaration on the Right to Development according to which such a right 'is an inalienable human right by virtue of which every human person and all peoples are entitled to participate in, contribute to, and enjoy economic, social, cultural and political development in which all human rights and fundamental freedoms can be fully realized'.[19] It remains unclear, however, how the content of a (vague) right to development differs from that already subsumed under the well-established right to self-determination, let alone how it can be applied in practice. In fact, the existence of these 'alternative' third generation rights probably remain mere political aspirations. To that end, it must also be noted that the exact content of the 'rights' is difficult to identify and that their vagueness makes any practical application almost impossible.

9.4 Human rights and responsibility for private acts

As a main rule, international human rights law is only binding on states.[20] When determining if an act is a 'state act', reference must be made to the general principles of state responsibility and attribution in international law that we visited in Chapter 7. It follows therefrom that a state cannot avoid its responsibilities under international human rights law by delegating state functions to private organs or individuals.[21]

The conclusion that only states can violate international human rights law does not mean that a state's responsibility cannot be triggered by the acts of private actors, most notably private individuals. Especially in relation to the enjoyment of civil and political rights, a state may be obliged to offer positive protection from private acts. The European Court of Human Rights (ECtHR) has concluded, for example, that the prohibition against torture or inhuman or degrading treatment or punishment requires positive measures on the part of a state to ensure that individuals are not subjected to prohibited treatment at the hands of private individuals. In practice, the obligation— at times also referred to as a 'horizontal' obligation—must 'at least, provide effective protection in particular of children and other vulnerable persons and should include reasonable steps to prevent ill-treatment of which the authorities had or ought to have had knowledge'.[22] In *Begheluri and Others v Georgia*, the ECtHR stressed the existence of a positive obligation to offer protection in relation to religiously motivated violence perpetrated by private individuals.[23]

---

[18] See the overview in Steiner et al. (n 6) 1433–1462.   [19] GA Res. 41/28 (1986), art. 1

[20] But see General Recommendation No. 30 on women in conflict prevention, conflict and post-conflict situations (18 October 2013), UN Doc. CEDAW/C/GC/30, paras 13–18.

[21] *Costello-Roberts v UK*, App. no. 13134/87, 25 March 1993, para. 27. See also *O'Keeffe v Ireland*, App. no. 35810/09, 28 January 2014, para. 150.

[22] *O'Keeffe v Ireland* (n 21) para. 144. See *also X and Y v The Netherlands*, App. no. 8978/80, 26 March 1985, paras 23–27.

[23] *Begheluri and Others v Georgia*, App. no. 28490/02,7 January 2015, paras 160, 164.

9.5 Enforcement of human rights in the United Nations

9.5.1 Introduction

Over the years, the UN has developed an elaborated system for monitoring and enforcing compliance with human rights law. In practice, there are two parallel systems; one based on the UN Charter and one based on the universal human rights treaties. We begin with the charter-based system in Section 9.5.2 and then turn to the treaty-based system in Section 9.5.3.

9.5.2 Charter-based human rights mechanisms

The *Human Rights Commission* was created in 1946 by the Economic and Social Council (ECOSOC) to enhance respect and set standards for the human rights conduct of the members of the UN. Beginning in the 1960s, the Commission had developed a number of Special Procedures to facilitate the study and discussion of human rights issues and country-specific compliance. Among other things, the Commission created ad hoc working groups of experts and a series of Special Rapporteurs on thematic topics. The first thematic procedure created was the Working Group on Enforced or Involuntary Disappearances which was created in 1980. The Working Group was followed by the creation of a Special Rapporteur on extra-judicial, summary and arbitrary executions (1982) and one on torture and ill-treatment (1985). But the Commission was criticized for being too politicized and intentionally ignoring obvious situations of gross human rights violations.[24] In 2006, it was therefore replaced by the *Human Rights Council* (HRC) with a mandate to promote and protect all human rights around the world. The HRC was created as a subsidiary organ under the General Assembly[25] and has 47 members divided regionally and elected by a majority of the Assembly. With the Council came a new mechanism—the Universal Periodic Review—whereby the human rights compliance of *all* states is examined by the Council.[26] The HRC has retained the system of Special Procedures and by July 2016, 41 thematic and 14 country-specific mandates had been created. The Working Group on Arbitrary Detention is particularly interesting because it has the competence to make appeals in cases of alleged arbitrary attention. In December 2015, for example, it adopted a—controversial—finding that the year-long presence at the embassy of Ecuador in London of Julian Assange, the founder of WikiLeaks, constituted arbitrary detention by the governments of Sweden and the UK.[27]

---

[24] See, inter alia, Report of the Secretary-General's High-Level Panel on Threats, Challenges and Change, *A More Secure World: Our Shared Responsibility* (2 December 2004), UN Doc. A/59/565, para. 283. For an overview, see also Paul Gordon Lauran, 'To Preserve and Build on Its Achievements and to Redress Its Shortcomings: The Journey from the Commission on Human Rights to the Human Rights Council' (2007) 29(2) *Human Rights Quarterly* 307–345.

[25] GA Res. 60/151 (2006).   [26] Res. 5/1 Institution Building (18 June 2007).

[27] Working Group on Arbitrary Detention, Opinion 54/2015, 4 December 2015.

The creation of the HRC has unfortunately not brought an end to excessive politicization. Thus, in its first year, the departing Secretary-General had already noted how the Council had 'clearly not justified all the hopes' placed in it and also stressed the importance of avoiding a politicization of the system of Special Procedures.[28]

In 1993, the General Assembly created the position of *High Commissioner for Human Rights* to promote the enjoyment and protection of all human rights and coordinate and facilitate, among other things, advisory services and technical assistance in the field of human rights.[29]

9.5.3 **Treaty-based enforcement mechanisms**

The second system in the UN for the protection and promotion of human rights is the collection of committees that have been created to monitor implementation and compliance with the nine specific universal human rights treaties mentioned earlier. The committees are composed of between 10 and 25 experts who serve in their independent capacity for terms of, typically, four years. Importantly, the experts are chosen due to their expertise in the given subject matter and they need not be trained lawyers. With a few exceptions, the functions and competences of the committees are broadly similar.[30]

Arguably, the most notable of the committees is the *Human Rights Committee* (CCPR) that monitors the implementation of the ICCPR. The CCPR comments on *periodic reports* submitted by states on the national measures of relevance to their obligations under the ICCPR.[31] In practice, the reports are to be submitted every three to six years depending on the human rights situation in the state in question. At a hearing before the Committee, a state may be asked to respond to a previously notified 'list of issues' of particular interest. The treatment of the periodic reports concludes with the Committee's adoption of 'concluding observations' primarily containing a list of concerns about compliance with the Convention and recommendations for improvement. Since the early 1980s, the CCPR has also adopted *General Comments* on the interpretation and application of the ICCPR. The Comments are not binding on the states. The CCPR may also hear complaints brought by one state party against another regarding the latter's non-fulfilment of its obligations under the ICCPR.[32] So far, however, this procedure has not yet been used. Of greater practical importance is the procedure for *individual complaints* under which parties to an optional protocol to the Convention accept that the CCPR may consider complaints ('communications') from individuals who claim to be victims of a violation of the ICCPR.[33] In July 2016, 115 states were parties to the optional protocol, including the majority of European states. In cases of irreparable harm, the Committee may request a state to adopt interim

---

[28] 'Secretary-General urges human rights activists to "fill leadership vacuum", hold world leaders to account' (8 December 2006), UN Doc. SG/SM/10788-HR/4909-OBV/601.

[29] GA Res. 48/141 (20 December 1993).

[30] For a complete overview of the committees, see http://www.ohchr.org/EN/HRBodies/Pages/TreatyBodies.aspx.

[31] See ICCPR art. 40.   [32] ICCPR arts 41–42.   [33] See Optional Protocol 1 to the ICCPR.

measures.[34] Like the General Comments, the Committee's conclusions in individual cases are not binding on the states. This, however, does not mean that its findings are simply brushed aside by the state found in breach of its obligations.[35]

The *Committee Against Torture* (CAT) also merits special attention. The Committee monitors implementation and compliance with the 1984 Convention Against Torture and, like the CCPR, it receives periodic reports from the state parties[36] and has a procedure for both interstate and individual complaints if the relevant state has accepted the competence of the Committee.[37] The Committee's conclusions are similarly not binding. A 2002 optional protocol to the Convention established a Subcommittee on Prevention (SPT) and a system of regular visits by independent international and national bodies to detention facilities in order to prevent treatment contrary to the Convention.[38]

9.6 Regional systems for the protection of human rights

9.6.1 Introduction

The human rights system in the UN system is supplemented by regional human rights protection. The protection differs substantially from region to region, stretching from the robust system of human rights protection in Europe to the fairly toothless systems in the Middle East and Asia. The following overview is limited to the human rights system in Europe (Section 9.6.2) and—to a lesser extent—the system created in the Americas (Section 9.6.3) and Africa (Section 9.6.4).

9.6.2 Human rights protection in Europe

In 1949, the Council of Europe was founded to strengthen intergovernmental and inter-parliamentary cooperation in a ravaged post-Second World War Europe. The Council is composed of, among other things, a Committee of Ministers with a seat for the foreign ministers of the member states and a Parliamentary Assembly consisting of delegations from the national parliaments of the state parties.[39] The Council's greatest achievement was its adoption in 1950 of the *European Convention on Human Rights (ECHR)* that remains the cornerstone of human rights protection in Europe. Accession to the ECHR is now a precondition for membership of the Council of Europe. The ECHR entered into force in 1953 and today has 47 parties. It covers primarily civil and political rights, including the right to life, the prohibition of torture

---

[34] HRC, 'General Comment No 33' (2008), UN Doc. CCPR/C/GC/33, para. 19.

[35] See also *Ahmadou Sadio Diallo (Republic of Guinea v Democratic Republic of the Congo)*, Merits, Judgment [2010] ICJ Rep 639, para. 66.

[36] Art. 19.   [37] Arts 21 and 22.

[38] Subcommittee on Prevention of Torture and other Cruel, Inhuman or Degrading Treatment or Punishment.

[39] See Statute of the Council of Europe, 5 May 1949.

and slavery, the right to liberty and security of person, the right to a fair trial and a public hearing, the prohibition against retroactive criminal legislation, the right to respect for private and family life, freedom of thought, conscience and religion, freedom of expression, freedom of assembly and association, the right to marry, the right to an effective remedy and a prohibition on discrimination (articles 2–14). Additional rights are found in some of the 16 additional protocols, including the right to property, freedom of movement and the abolition of the death penalty.

The European Court of Human Rights (ECtHR) enforces compliance with the ECHR and it deals with both interstate complaints and individual complaints. States are generally reluctant to bring legal cases against each other and *interstate* cases are therefore relatively rare.[40] Recently, however, a series of cases has been brought against Russia and, in 2014, the Court found that Russia had violated its obligations under the ECHR in a policy of arresting, detaining and expelling Georgian nationals.[41] The case was initiated by Georgia and, in 2008, it initiated another case against Russia, this time over alleged human rights violations committed during the August 2008 armed conflict in Georgia.[42] In March 2014, Ukraine lodged an interstate application against Russia in relation to the latter's intervention in Crimea[43] and Ukraine has since launched an additional case against Russia concerning Russian activities in Eastern Ukraine.[44]

The key to the success of the ECHR is the procedure for *individual complaints* whereby the ECtHR is able to receive applications from any person, non-governmental organization or group of individuals claiming to be victims of a violation of the Convention.[45] The number of individual complaints received by the Court is massive and over the years the Court has adopted various initiatives to deal effectively with its ever increasing caseload. With the adoption of Protocol 14, the Court succeeded in streamlining the process substantially and since then it has been able to bring the number of pending cases down from a staggering 161,000 in September 2011 to a 'mere' 70,000 by the end of 2014.[46]

The Court can only deal with an application if the applicant has *exhausted all domestic remedies* and the complaint was launched within six months of the date of the final decision or act that is the subject of the complaint.[47] In addition, in nine out of ten instances, the Court declares an application inadmissible as it is *manifestly illfounded*. If, however, the Court finds that the Convention has been violated, it will conclude accordingly and consider *satisfaction*.[48] In most cases, satisfaction will consist of monetary compensation but other measures may also be relevant. The Court's

---

[40] See *Ireland v UK*, App. no. 5310/71, 18 January 1978; *Denmark v Turkey*, App. no. 34382/97, 5 April 2000; *Cyprus v Turkey*, App. no. 25781/94, 10 May 2001.

[41] *Georgia v Russia (I)*, App. no. 13255/07, 3 July 2014

[42] *Georgia v Russia (II)*, App. no. 38263/08. A third case brought by Georgia against Russia in November 2009 was discontinued when Georgia stated that it wished to discontinue the case.

[43] Press Release, 'Interim measure granted in inter-State case brought by Ukraine against Russia', ECHR 073 (2014), 13 March 2014.

[44] *Ukraine v Russia (IV)*, App. no. 42410/15.   [45] ECHR art. 34.

[46] See European Court of Human Rights, Annual Report 2014.   [47] Art. 35.

[48] ECHR art. 41.

judgments and decisions are final and binding on the respondent states.[49] The states are free to determine how they will comply with a judgment but the Committee of Ministers in the Council of Europe monitors the proper implementation of the Court's judgments.[50]

A few words must be said about the *interpretation* of the ECHR. The ECtHR has repeatedly stated that the Convention has a 'special character' and must be interpreted and applied in order to make its safeguards practical and effective.[51] Its interpretation is 'dynamic' and the Convention is a 'living instrument' whose provisions must be interpreted in the light of the current social and political climate rather than in accordance with the sentiments at the time the Convention was adopted.[52] In *Tyrer v UK*, for example, the Court stated that it could not avoid being 'influenced by the developments and commonly accepted standards in the penal policy of the member States of the Council of Europe in this field'.[53] And in *Stafford v UK*, the Court noted that a failure to maintain a dynamic approach to interpretation would risk rendering it a bar to reform or improvement.[54] It must also be noted, however, that the Court often grants a state a certain *margin of appreciation* and thus a substantial degree of deference in particularly sensitive matters in which there is no common European position.[55] In *Handyside v UK*, for example, the Court found that national authorities, due to their 'direct and continuous contact with the vital forces of their countries', may in principle be in a 'better position than the international judge to give an opinion' on the exact content of the requirements of morals.[56] Among other things, the Court has so far not found that the right to marriage obliges state parties to provide the right to same-sex couples.[57] The margin of appreciation has also been relied on in relation to sensitive issues concerning religion[58] and blasphemy.[59]

In addition, the Council of Europe has adopted other important human rights instruments, including the 1994 European Framework Convention for the Protection of National Minorities mentioned earlier. Reference must also be made of the 1961 European Social Charter, later replaced by a revised Charter in 1996, that includes economic and social rights, such as entitlements associated with adequate and affordable housing, accessible health care, free education and employment and working conditions. Its implementation is monitored by a European Committee of Social Rights.

---

[49] See, respectively, arts 44 and 46(1).   [50] Art. 46(2).

[51] *Soering v UK*, App. no. 14038/88, 7 July 1989, para. 89. See also the discussion of treaty interpretation in Chapter 3.

[52] See, among others, *Tyrer v UK*, App. no. 5856/72, 25 April 1978, para. 31 and *Loizidou v Turkey*, App. no. 15318/89, 23 March 1995, para. 71.

[53] *Tyrer v UK* (n 52) para. 31.

[54] *Stafford v UK*, App. no. 46295/99, 28 May 2002, paras 68–69. See also *Christine Goodwin v UK*, App. no. 28957/95, 11 July 2002, para. 93.

[55] *Handyside v UK*, App. no. 5493/72, 7 December 1976, para. 48; *Wingrove v UK*, App. no. 17419/90, 25 November 1996, para. 58; *Leyla Sahin v Turkey*, App. no. 44774/98, 10 November 2005, para. 109. For a thorough examination, see, inter alia, Jonas Christoffersen, *Fair Balance, Proportionality, Subsidiarity and Primarity in the European Convention on Human Rights* (Brill Nijhoff, 2009).

[56] *Handyside v UK* (n 55) para. 48.

[57] *Schalk and Kopf v Austria*, App. no. 30141/04, 22 November 2010, paras 57–58 and 62.

[58] *Wingrove v UK* (n 55) para. 58.   [59] *Leyla Sahin v Turkey* (n 55) para. 109.

In 1995, a mechanism for collective complaints was established in an additional protocol to the Charter.[60] Also of relevance is the 1987 European Convention for the Prevention of Torture and Inhuman and Degrading Treatment or Punishment. The Convention creates a Committee for the Prevention of Torture (CPT) that has a fact-finding and reporting mandate.[61]

The treaties of the EU also offer protection of human rights and fundamental freedoms. In December 2000, the EU adopted a Charter of Fundamental Rights of the European Union addressed both to the EU institutions as well as individual member states.[62] When compared to the ECHR, the EU Charter contains more rights, including numerous rights of an economic and social nature. While it was initially without binding effect, that changed following the entry into force of the Treaty of Lisbon in December 2009.[63] The Lisbon Treaty also paved the way for the accession of the EU to the ECHR.[64] The two-tier system of protection provided by the EU and the ECHR raises a number of questions about the relationship between the two systems. Importantly, the ECtHR maintains a prioritized position when it comes to the protection of human rights in Europe. The Court balances respect for the autonomy of the EU with its role as the guardian of the ECHR through a general doctrine of 'equivalent protection' whereby it presumes that a state has not departed from the requirements of the Convention when it implements legal obligations that flow from its membership of another organization that provides for equivalent protection of fundamental rights.[65] 'Equivalent' means 'comparable' and not 'identical'.[66] In *Bosphorus*, the Grand Chamber of the ECtHR found that the protection of fundamental rights by EU law in general, and at the time of the case, could be considered 'equivalent' to those of the Convention system and that there was therefore a presumption that the state (Ireland) had not departed from the Convention when it implemented its EU obligations.[67] The Court also stated, however, that the presumption can be rebutted if the protection of Convention rights is 'manifestly deficient'.[68] The Court thereby placed itself on a higher footing than the Court of Justice for the European Union (CJEU) in the hierarchy of fundamental rights issues.[69]

---

[60] Additional Protocol to the European Social Charter Providing for a System of Collective Complaints, 9 November 1995.

[61] Other Council of Europe conventions include a 1977 European Convention on the Legal Status of Migrant Workers, a 2000 European Convention on the Exercise of Children's Rights, a 2007 Convention on the Protection of Children against Sexual Exploitation and Sexual Abuse, a 2008 Convention on Action against Trafficking in Human Beings and a 2011 Convention on preventing and combating violence against women and domestic violence.

[62] Charter of Fundamental Rights of the European Union (18 December 2000), 2000/C 364/01. But see also the scepticism from the CJEU in *Opinion 2/13*, 18 December 2014, paras 158 and 200.

[63] See Treaty of the European Union, art. 6(1).

[64] Ibid, art. 6(2). However, in a December 2014 opinion, the CJEU found that an agreement on the accession of the EU to the ECtHR was incompatible with the TEU, see Opinion 2/13 of 18 December 2014.

[65] *M & Co. v Germany*, App. no. 13258/87, Admissibility, 9 February 1990, 145 and *Bosphorus Hava Yollari Turizan v Ireland*, App. no. 45036/98 (Grand Chamber), Judgment, 30 June 2005, para. 155.

[66] Ibid.   [67] Ibid, para. 165.   [68] Ibid, para. 156.

[69] See also the discussion in Cathryn Costello, 'The *Bosphorus* Ruling of the European Court of Human Rights: Fundamental Rights and Blurred Boundaries in Europe' (2006) 6(1) *Human Rights Law Review* 103–104.

It must be noted that the CJEU has on numerous occasions held that 'fundamental rights form an integral part of the general principles of law' it protects and that it draws particular inspiration from the ECHR.[70] It has stated that respect for fundamental human rights is a 'condition of the legality' of EU acts and it has also begun to refer directly to ECHR standards in its decisions.[71] In practice, of course, the two-tier human rights system will require a certain level of coordination and there is a risk that inconsistency in the protection of fundamental rights will develop in the case law of the CJEU and the ECtHR.[72]

9.6.3 Human rights protection in the Americas

The primary human rights instrument in the Americas is the American Convention on Human Rights adopted by the Organization of American States (OAS) in 1969 and which entered into force in 1978. The Convention, which has 25 member states, builds on the 1948 American Declaration of the Rights and Duties of Man and lists both civil and political rights as well as economic, social and cultural rights. The Convention also created the Inter-American Commission of Human Rights and the Inter-American Court of Human Rights.[73] The *Commission* promotes respect for human rights and deals with both interstate and individual complaints.[74] The Inter-American *Court* of Human Rights hears cases referred to it by the Commission.[75] Up until now, however, the Court has not received many contentious cases for consideration.[76] The Court may also issue advisory opinions.[77] The OAS has additionally adopted a 1985 Convention to Prevent and Punish Torture, an 1998 Additional Protocol on Economic, Social and Cultural Rights, a 1990 Protocol on the Abolition of the Death Penalty, a 1994 Convention on Forced Disappearances and, more recently, a 2013 Convention Against Racism, Racial Discrimination and related forms of Intolerance.

9.6.4 Human rights protection in Africa

Regional human rights protection in *Africa* centres around the 1981 Banjul Charter on Human and Peoples' Rights adopted by the Organisation of African Unity (OAU). All 55 members of the African Union (AU) are parties to the Charter that contains

---

[70] See, among others, Case C-11/70 *Internationale Handelsgesellschaft*, 17 December 1970, para. 4 and Case C-36/02 *Omega Spielhallen- und Automatenaufstellungs-GmbH v Oberbürgermeisterin der Bundesstadt Bonn*, 14 October 2004, para. 33.

[71] See, inter alia, Case C-117/01 *KB v National Health Service and the Secretary of State for Health* [2004] ECR I-541 and C-112/00 *Schmidberger Transporte und Planzuge v Austria* [2003] ECR I-5659. See also *Bosphorus Hava Yollari Turizan* (n 65) para. 159 and Costello (n 69) 114.

[72] Frederic van den Berghe, 'The EU and Issues of Human Rights Protection: Same Solutions to More Acute Problems' (2010) 16(2) *European Law Review* 112–157.

[73] For an assessment of the Inter-American experience, see James L. Cavallaro and Stephanie Erin Brewer, 'Reevaluating Regional Human Rights Litigation in the Twenty-First Century: The Case of the Inter-American Court' (2008) 102(4) *American Journal of International Law* 768–827.

[74] Arts 44–45.   [75] Art. 61.

[76] For an overview, see Inter-American Court of Justice, Annual Report 2014.   [77] Art. 64.

both civil and political rights, economic, social and cultural rights as well as 'collective' rights, including the right of all peoples to self-determination, to freely dispose of their wealth and natural resources, the right to national and international peace and security and the right to a generally satisfactory environment.[78] The Charter established an African Commission on Human and Peoples' Rights that promotes and ensures the protection of the rights in the Charter and receives complaints from both states[79] and 'other parties', including individuals.[80] If the Commission finds that one of the communications relates to 'a series of serious or massive' violations of the rights contained in the Charter, it will notify the Assembly of Heads of State and Government which may then ask the Commission to further study the issue and submit a factual report that includes both findings and recommendations.[81]

9.7 The territorial scope of human rights treaties

The territorial reach of a human rights treaty is one of the most debated topics in international human rights law.[82] A treaty will have an 'extraterritorial' effect when a protected individual is not physically present on the territory of the state when the violation of the individual's rights occurs. Importantly, 'extraterritoriality' must not be conflated with the principle of *'non-refoulement'* where a convention prohibits the extradition or transfer of an individual *located on the territory of the state* to another state where the individual risks being treated in a manner that violates that convention. An explicit *non-refoulement* provision is found in article 3 of the UN Convention Against Torture.[83] As noted in Chapter 5, the concept of 'jurisdiction' in human rights law is a *sui generis* concept that is unrelated to the different forms of jurisdiction found elsewhere in international law.[84]

Some treaties contain jurisdictional provisions that govern the geographical scope of the treaty. According to article 2(1) of the *ICCPR*, a state party must respect and ensure the rights of the Convention to 'all individuals within its territory and subject to its jurisdiction'. The United States has consistently argued that the Convention

---

[78] Banjul Charter on Human and Peoples' Rights, arts 20–24. For background, see U. O. Umozurike, 'The African Charter on Human and Peoples' Rights' (1983) 77(4) *American Journal of International Law* 902–912.

[79] Art. 47   [80] Arts 55–56.   [81] Art. 58(1) and (2).

[82] Marko Milanovic, *Extraterritorial Application of Human Rights Treaties* (Oxford University Press, 2011).

[83] In relation to the ICCPR and *non-refoulement*, see Human Rights Committee, 'General Comment No. 20' (10 March 1992), UN Doc. HRI/GEN/1/Rev.7, para. 9. In relation to the ECHR, see *Soering v UK* (n 51) para. 88. See also *Cruz Varas and Others v Sweden*, App. no. 15576/89, 20 March 1991, para. 70 and *Vilvarajah and Others v UK*, App. nos 13163/87 etc., 30 October 1991, para. 107. *Non-refoulement* will become an example of extraterritorial application of a treaty where an individual transferred to another state is physically located outside the territory of the state party, as may be the case in situations where soldiers on military operations abroad hand over detainees to the authorities of another state.

[84] See, however, the erroneous remarks on this aspect in *Banković and Others v Belgium and Others*, App. no. 52207/99, 12 December 2001, paras 59–61 and *Issa v Turkey*, App. no. 31821/96, 16 November 2004, para. 67.

does not apply outside sovereign US territory and it has therefore also refused to grant protection under the ICCPR to individuals detained at detention facilities outside the United States, including in Guantanamo Bay, Cuba.[85] In *The Wall*, however, the ICJ found that jurisdiction under the ICCPR 'may sometimes be exercised outside the national territory'.[86] Among other things, the Court noted that the drafters of the ICCPR 'surely' did not intend to 'allow States to escape from their obligations when they exercise jurisdiction outside their national territory'.[87] According to the Human Rights Committee, the ICCPR applies as soon as a state has an individual in its physical custody abroad 'regardless of the circumstances in which such power or effective control was obtained'.[88] Following the revelations by Edward Snowden of extensive surveillance practices by, inter alia, the US National Security Agency, the Committee has expressed concern at the 'surveillance of communications in the interests of protecting national security, conducted by the National Security Agency (NSA) both within and outside the United States ... and their adverse impact on the right to privacy'.[89]

Article 1 of the *ECHR* specifies that state parties shall secure the rights and freedoms of the Convention to 'everyone within their jurisdiction'. Unfortunately, however, it has been somewhat difficult to ascertain when 'jurisdiction' exists.[90] For now (at least), the leading case is the Grand Chamber's judgment in 2011 in *Al-Skeini v UK* that arose from the killing of a number of Iraqi nationals by British forces during the US/UK occupation of Iraq in 2003–20004. The Court listed a number of instances where extraterritorial acts fall within the concept of 'jurisdiction' in article 1.[91] The first relates to acts by diplomatic consular agents who exert authority and control over others.[92] The second is where a state 'through the consent, invitation or acquiescence of the Government of that territory' 'exercises all or some of the public powers normally to be exercised by that Government ... as long as the acts in question are attributable to it rather than to the territorial State'. [93] Thirdly, a state will exercise 'jurisdiction' in relation to an individual who is taken into the custody of state agents abroad. What is

---

[85] See Human Rights Committee, 'Consideration of reports submitted by States parties under article 40 of the Covenant', Fourth periodic report, United States of America (22 May 2012), UN Doc. CCPR/C/USA/4, para. 505.

[86] *Legal Consequences of the Construction of a Wall in the Occupied Palestinian Territory*, Advisory Opinion [2004] ICJ Rep 136, paras 109–111.

[87] Ibid, para. 119. *Armed Activities on the Territory of the Congo (New Application: 2002) (Democratic Republic of the Congo v Rwanda)*, Jurisdiction and Admissibility [2006] ICJ Rep 6, paras 178–180, 216 and 345.

[88] Human Rights Committee, 'General Comment 31' (2004), UN Doc. CCPR/C/21/Rev.1/Add.13, para. 10. See also *Lopez Burgos v Uruguay*, Communication No. 52/1979, 29 July 1981, para. 12.3.

[89] Human Rights Committee, 'Concluding observations on the fourth periodic report of the United States of America' (23 April 2014), UN Doc. CCPR/C/USA/CO/4, para. 22. See also Ilina Georgieva, 'The Right to Privacy under Fire—Foreign Surveillance under the NSA and the GCHQ and Its Compatibility with Art. 17 ICCPR and Art. 8 ECHR' (2015) 31 *Utrecht Journal of International and European Law* 104.

[90] Compare, inter alia, the following judgments and decisions: *Loizidou*, App. no. 15318/89, Judgment, Preliminary Objections, 23 February 1995, para. 62; *Banković* (n 84) paras 67–81, *Issa* (n 84) paras 71, 74–75; *Öcalan v Turkey*, App. no. 64221/99, 12 March 2003, para. 93, *Pad and Others v Turkey*, App. no. 60167/00, 28 June 2007, paras 53–54; and *Medvedyev and Others v France*, App. no. 3394/03, 10 July 2008, paras 64–67.

[91] *Al-Skeini and Others v UK*, App. no. 55721/07, 7 July 2011, paras 131–132.

[92] Ibid, para. 134.   [93] Ibid, para. 135.

decisive in such cases is 'the exercise of physical power and control over the person in question'.[94] The fourth instance is when a state exercises 'effective control of an area' outside its own national territory as a consequence of military action.[95] The emphasis here is primarily to 'the strength of the State's military presence in the area'.[96] In *Jaloud v the Netherlands*, the Court did not find that the status of 'occupying power' under the Hague Regulations in the law of armed conflict was '*per se* determinative'.[97] In *Al-Skeini*, the Court concluded that a number of Iraqis killed by British soldiers on patrol were within British 'jurisdiction' and the decisive factor seems to be that the UK (together with the United States) exercised 'some of the public powers normally to be exercised by a sovereign government' after the removal of the Baath regime and before the accession of the interim Iraqi government.[98] On the face of it, the *Al-Skeini* judgment implies that a state is *not* bound by its obligations under the ECHR if it uses deadly force (e.g. through the use of a remotely piloted drone) against an individual who is neither within the physical control of the state nor located on a territory where the state has effective control or at least exercises 'public powers'. Since this is hard to reconcile with the 'universality' of human rights, some argue that a state should be bound by the Convention in respect of *all* individuals whose lives it can affect no matter where the individuals are located.[99] A different position holds that certain core human rights, such as the right to life, are protected in customary international law and that states are therefore always obliged to protect those rights no matter where its agents operate.[100] At the time of writing, however, there is little case law or actual state practice to support such views.

9.8 Human rights in times of public emergency

The ICJ has on numerous occasions stated that the protection offered by the ICCPR 'does not cease in times of war'.[101] In practice, though, this does not mean that the

[94] Ibid, para. 136.   [95] Ibid, para. 138.   [96] Ibid, para. 139.

[97] *Jaloud v the Netherlands*, App. no. 47708/08, 20 November 2014, para. 142.

[98] Ibid, para. 149. See also Marko Milanonic, '*Al-Skeini* and *Al-Jedda* in Strasbourg' (2012) 23(1) *European Journal of International Law* 121–139.

[99] See also *Al-Skeini*, Concurring Opinion of Judge Bonello, paras 11–16; Milanovic, *Extraterritorial Application of Human Rights Treaties* (n 82) 209. See also John Cerone, 'Jurisdiction and Power: The Intersection of Human Rights Law & The Law of Non-International Armed Conflict in an Extraterritorial Context' (2007) 40 *Israel Law Review* 396–452 and 446–449.

[100] David Kretzmer, 'Targeted Killing of Suspected Terrorists: Extra-Judicial Executions or Legitimate Means of Defence?' (2005) 16 *European Journal of International Law* 184–185.

[101] *Legality of the Threat or Use of Nuclear Weapons*, Advisory Opinion [1996] ICJ Rep 226, para. 25. See also *The Wall* (n 86) para. 105 and *Armed Activities* (n 87) para. 216. See also Human Rights Committee, 'General Comment No. 31 of the General Legal Obligation Imposed on States Parties to the Covenant' (26 May 2004) UN Doc. CCPR/C/21/Rev.1/Add.13, para. 11. For practice from the Inter-American Commission on Human Rights, see *Coard et al. v United States*, Report No. 109/99, Case No. 10.951, 29 September 1999, para. 39. But see also the Israeli position in *The Wall* (n 86) para. 102. For the US view, see United Nations Commission on Human Rights, 'Explanation of Vote of the United States of America to resolution on the Protection of the Human Rights of Civilians in Armed Conflict', 20 April 2005.

norms contained in the applicable human rights treaties will apply to their fullest degree. First, as we shall return to in more detail in Chapter 14, the test of what constitutes a violation of human rights law in times of armed conflict will be influenced by the content of the law of armed conflict that is the relevant *lex specialis*.[102] Secondly, a state may be entitled to suspend the application of parts of a human rights convention in times of emergency, including in the event of war.[103] A valid derogation is conditioned on the existence of a public emergency of *a certain gravity* and both the ICCPR and the ECHR require that 'the life of the nation' is under threat.[104] Practice from the ECtHR refers to a threat to 'the organized life of the community of which the State is composed'.[105] In addition, the emergency must be 'actual or imminent'.[106] The Court has found that the situation that previously existed in Northern Ireland,[107] the threat to Turkish society from Kurdish terrorism[108] and the fear of terrorist attacks from al Qaida in the UK qualified for the suspension of certain provisions of the Convention.[109] In June 2015, Ukraine suspended a range of its obligations 'in respect of those areas in the Donetsk and Luhansk regions where Ukrainian authorities have been conducting an anti-terrorist operation in view of the actions of armed groups there'.[110] And in November 2015, France derogated from the Convention after the declaration of a state of emergency in France after the 13 November terrorist attacks in Paris.[111] The extent to which participation in military operations abroad may warrant derogation is not clear.[112] Measures that derogate must be *strictly required* by the situation. Although the ECtHR has recognized that 'a wide margin of appreciation should be left to the national authorities',[113] in *Aksoy v Turkey* it found that detention without judicial intervention for 14 days was necessary to fight terrorism.[114] In *A and Others*,

---

[102] See also ICJ, *Nuclear Weapons* (n 101) para. 25 and ECtHR, *Hassan v UK*, App. no. 29750/09, Judgment, 16 September 2014, paras 102–104.

[103] See ICCPR art. 4 (1) and ECHR art. 15(1). See also art. 27 of the American Convention on Human Rights. But not all rights can be suspended, however. For the ICCPR, see art. 4(2) and HRC, 'General Comment 29, States of Emergency (article 4)' (2001), UN Doc. CCPR/C/21/Rev.1/Add.11, paras 13–16. For the ECHR, see art. 15(2) and art. 3 of Protocol 6 and art. 2 of Protocol 13.

[104] See also Siracusa Principles on the Limitation and Derogation of Provisions in the International Covenant on Civil and Political Rights (1985), UN Doc. E/CN.4/1985/4, para. 39.

[105] *Lawless v Ireland*, App. no. 332/57, 1 July 1961, para. 28.

[106] *Denmark, Norway, Sweden and the Netherlands v Greece*, App. Nos 3321/67, 3322/67, 3323/67 and 3344/67, 5 November 1969, para. 113.

[107] *Ireland v UK* (n 40) para. 205.

[108] See, inter alia, *Aksoy v Turkey*, App. no. 21987/93, 18 December 1996, para. 68.

[109] *A and Others v UK*, App. no. 3455/05, 19 February 2009, para. 177. The UK was the only state in the Council of Europe that derogated from its obligations under the ECHR after the 9/11 attacks, see Declaration contained in a Note Verbale from the Permanent Representation of the United Kingdom, dated 18 December 2001, registered by the Secretariat General on 18 December 2001. The derogation was revoked on 14 May 2005.

[110] See http://www.coe.int/en/web/conventions/full-list/-/conventions/treaty/005/declarations?p_auth= N5hF4XrW.

[111] Ibid.

[112] On this issue, see the House of Lords, *R (on the application of Al-Jedda) (FC) (Appellant) v Secretary of State for Defence (Respondent*, [2007] UKHL 58, [38].

[113] *Aksoy* (n 108) para. 68. See also *Ireland v UK* (n 40) para. 207 and *A and Others v UK* (n 109) para. 180.

[114] *Aksoy*, § 78.

the Court agreed with an earlier judgment by the UK House of Lords that had found that British legislation authorizing indefinite detention of a suspected terrorist of non-British nationality was disproportionate and therefore in violation of article 15 of the ECHR because the law did not allow for the detention of British nationals who posed a similar threat.[115] A decision to derogate from a human rights convention does not alter a state's obligations under other parts of international law, such as under customary international law. In addition, a decision to derogate must be communicated and justified to the other state parties to that convention.[116]

Summary

International human rights law derives from a basic notion that human rights are inherent to *all* human beings. The modern human rights law system was created after the end of the Second World War with the establishment of the UN. The most important human rights instruments are those adopted under the auspices of the UN and a number of regional conventions, most notably the ECHR. Individual human rights are traditionally divided into categories or classes that reflect the nature of the rights and the evolution of international human rights law. The arguably most important of the rights are those of a civil and political character. There are two systems for monitoring and enforcing compliance with human rights law in the UN; one based on the UN Charter and the other on universal human rights treaties. At the regional level, human rights protection is particularly strong in Europe where the ECHR is a cornerstone of human rights protection. The geographical scope of human rights conventions is not necessarily limited to the territory of the state. The application of human rights does not cease in times of public emergency or armed conflict but the determination of what constitutes a violation of human rights may be influenced by standards from the law of armed conflict. A state may also be allowed to temporarily suspend the application of parts of a human rights convention in the case of a public emergency.

Recommended reading

The literature on human rights is immense. A solid, comprehensive work on the law and politics of human rights is Henry J. Steiner, Philip Alston and Ryan Goodman, *International Human Rights in Context* (Oxford University Press, 2007).

---

[115] *A and Others v UK* (n 109) para. 190. For the House of Lords decision, see the individual judgments of the law lords in *A and others v Secretary of State for the Home Department* [2004] UKHL 56, see esp. [126] and [132].

[116] ICCPR art 4(3) and ECHR art. 15(3). But see also ECtHR, *Hassan v UK* (n 102) paras 101–103 where the Court concluded that it was not the practice of the state parties to derogate from their obligations under art. 5 of the Convention when they detained individuals under the authority of the laws of war in international armed conflicts and the lack of a British derogation should therefore not prevent the Court from being influenced by international humanitarian law when interpreting and applying art. 5. For criticism, see the minority's partly dissenting opinion, para. 9.

For a comprehensive examination of the UN Covenant on Civil and Political Rights, see Manfred Novak, *UN Covenant on Civil and Political Rights, CCPR Commentary* (N. P. Engel Publishers, 1993) and Sarah Joseph and Melissa Castan, *The International Covenant on Civil and Political Rights: Cases, Materials, and Commentary* (3rd edn, Oxford University Press, 2013).

For a solid discussion of the ECHR, see Bernadette Rainey, Elizabeth Wicks and Clare Ovey, *Jacobs, White & Ovey: The European Convention on Human Rights* (6th edn, Oxford University Press, 2014).

For a discussion of human rights protection in the UN, see Paul Gordon Lauran, 'To Preserve and Build on Its Achievements and to Redress Its Shortcomings: The Journey from the Commission on Human Rights to the Human Rights Council' (2007) 29(2) *Human Rights Quarterly* 307.

On more recent human rights protection in the EU, see Frederic van den Berghe, 'The EU and Issues of Human Rights Protection: Same Solutions to More Acute Problems' (2010) 16(2) *European Law Review* 112.

The seminal work on the extraterritorial effect of the ECHR is Marko Milanovic, *Extraterritorial Application of Human Rights Treaties* (Oxford University Press, 2011).

The margin of appreciation and proportionality in the ECHR is thoroughly discussed in Jonas Christoffersen, *Fair Balance, Proportionality, Subsidiarity and Primarity in the European Convention on Human Rights* (Brill Nijhoff, 2009).

Questions for discussion

1. What is the basis of the cultural relativist critique of human rights law?

2. The chapter notes that the human rights debate before the Human Rights Council is (still) highly politicized. Can you think of some examples?

3. What are some of the common features of the various monitoring organs that have been established with a view to monitoring compliance with specific UN human rights conventions?

4. The interpretational style of the ECtHR has been criticized for, among other things, disregarding state consent/intention. Why do you think that has been the case?

5. Case law from the ECtHR illustrates that a state party to the ECHR is not always bound by its obligations under the Convention when it acts abroad. Why could that be problematic when considered from the perspective of the alleged universal nature of human rights law?

6. What are the conditions for lawful derogation from a human rights convention?

10
International environmental law

CENTRAL ISSUES

1. This chapter discusses the most important parts of international environmental law and its main legal sources.

2. It presents the fundamental principles of international environmental law, including those that seek to prevent damage to the environment and those that seek to ensure a balanced approach to environmental protection.

3. The chapter provides an overview of the most important parts of the substantial regulation in international environmental law, including the legal regime for the protection of the atmosphere, the conservation of nature and the regulation of hazardous substances.

4. The chapter also discusses a number of features related to implementation and enforcement that are particular to international environmental law.

10.1 Introduction

International environmental law emerged as a separate field of international law in the late 1960s and early 1970s as awareness of the need for international regulation to address environmental problems gradually arose. While existing international law already regulated certain environmental issues, that regulation was primarily focused on protecting the environment as an economic resource[1]—such as a shared watercourse[2] or in order to alleviate the immediate economic costs of pollution[3]—and not on the protection of the environment *as such*.[4] International environmental law is

---

[1] See, inter alia, *Award between the United States and the United Kingdom relating to the rights of jurisdiction of United States in the Bering's sea and the preservation of fur seals* (1893) XXVIII RIAA 263–276. See also the 1946 International Convention for the Regulation of Whaling.

[2] See *Lake Lanoux Arbitration (Spain v France)* (1957) XII RIAA 281f.

[3] See *Trail Smelter Arbitration (United States v Canada)* (1938 and 1941) III RIAA 1905. See the 1954 International Convention for the Prevention of Pollution of the Sea by Oil.

[4] See Philippe Sands and Jacqueline Peel, *Principles of International Environmental Law* (3rd edn, Cambridge University Press, 2012) 22–49. See also Pierre-Marie Dupuy and Jorge E. Viñuales, *International Environmental Law* (Cambridge University Press, 2015) 8–12.

an area of international law where states have decided to cooperate with each other in order to fulfil certain goals of common interest and for the most part its rules and principles belong in the category of the international law of cooperation. It covers those parts of international law—whether public or private law—that relate to the environment and there is therefore often an overlap with other fields of international law, such as the law of the sea, international economic law and human rights law. It is not a separate and independent legal discipline and regulation is generally very piecemeal and sectoral. In addition, there is no international institution with overall competence on all matters of concern to the environment.

There is no authoritative definition of 'the environment'. In *Nuclear Weapons*, the International Court of Justice (ICJ) referred to the environment as 'the living space, the quality of life and the very health of human beings, including generations un-born'.[5] For present purposes, it suffices to note that there is an operational dimension to the term 'environment' that springs from the legal instruments generally referred to as falling within 'international environmental law'. Here, then, the 'environment' primarily consists of a range of physical components (air, water and land), as well as biological (species, habitats, ecosystems and diversity) and various cultural components.[6]

We begin in Section 10.2 with a brief overview of some of the major conferences and events that have served as important catalysts for the development of the law. Section 10.3 then discusses the most relevant legal sources in this field of law and Section 10.4 provides an overview of the main principles of international environmental law. Section 10.5 introduces the most important elements of the substantive regulation. Section 10.6 discusses implementation and enforcement.

10.2 From Stockholm to Rio and back to Rio

The development of international environmental law has in many ways been cata-pulted by major conferences. The first was the *1972 Stockholm Conference on the Human Environment* that adopted a 'Declaration on the Human Environment' with 26 principles and an 'Action plan for the Human Environment'. It also paved the way for the UN Environment Programme (UNEP) that promotes international cooperation on environmental matters and has been instrumental in the development of legal instruments.[7] The Stockholm Conference also helped to create momentum for the establishment of many national environmental agencies and ministries and the conclusion of a range of environmental law treaties.

The second major event was the *1992 Rio Conference on Environmental and Development*—also known as the 'Earth Summit'.[8] The organizing principle of the

---

[5] *Legality of the Threat or Use of Nuclear Weapons*, Opinion [1996] ICJ Rep 226, para. 29. See also *Award in the Arbitration regarding the Iron Rhine ('Ijzeren Rijn') Railway between the Kingdom of Belgium and the Kingdom of the Netherlands*, Decision of 24 May 2005 (2005) XXVII RIAA 35–125, para. 58.

[6] See Dupuy and Viñuales (n 4) 27.   [7] GA Res. 2997 (XXVII) (15 December 1972).

[8] See Dupuy and Viñuales (n 4) 16.

Summit—often heralded as a 'foundational moment' in international environmental law—was the emerging concept of 'sustainable development'. Like its Stockholm predecessor, the Rio Summit adopted a seminal declaration—the Rio 'Declaration on Environment and Development'. The declaration contains a range of principles on sustainable development that illustrate the extent to which environmental protection and economic development had become increasingly linked in the years since Stockholm. The extent to which developing states should be allowed to exploit their natural resources without limitations imposed by international society remains an ongoing tension in international environmental law.[9] A number of the principles in the Rio Declaration are the building blocks on which the more substantial regulation is built. Examples include the principle of prevention (Principle 2), inter-generational equity (Principle 3), the principle of cooperation (Principles 5, 7, 9, 27), respect for the special needs of the least developed states (Principle 6), precaution (Principle 15) and Environmental Impact Assessments (Principle 17). The Rio Summit also led to the adoption of a plan of action—'Agenda 21'—and to a number of important conventions, including a framework convention on climate change and a convention on biological diversity. These treaties are highly complex instruments that integrate a host of issues that had up until then been dealt with as separate issues.

The ten-year anniversary of the Rio Conference was marked in 2002 with a World Summit on Sustainable Development in Johannesburg, South Africa. Though the results of the Summit were fairly modest, it illustrated the increasing importance of a variety of partnerships, including with the private sector. In September 2000, the General Assembly had adopted a Millennium Declaration with eight measurable goals—the Millennium Development Goals (MDGs)—to be reached before 2015. The goals included environmental sustainability (Goal 7) and developing a global partnership for development (Goal 8).

The most recent major conference was the 2012 (second) Rio Summit that sought to secure a renewed commitment for sustainable development and to address new and emerging challenges.[10] The conference adopted the document 'The Future We Want' that led to the replacement of the MDGs with 17 Sustainable Development Goals (SDGs) that will set out the global development agenda from 2015 to 2030.[11] Among the goals are ending poverty in all forms (Goal 1), taking urgent action to end climate change and its impacts (Goal 13), conserving and sustainably using the oceans, sea and marine resources for sustainable development (Goal 14), protecting, restoring and promoting sustainable use of terrestrial ecosystems, sustainable management of forests, combating desertification, halting and reversing land degradation and halting biodiversity loss (Goal 15) and strengthening global partnerships (Goal 17).

---

[9] See also Nico Schrijver, *Sovereignty over Natural Resources: Balancing Rights and Duties* (Cambridge University Press, 1997).

[10] See also 'The Future We Want' (11 September 2012), UN Doc. A/Res/66/288.

[11] GA Res. 70/1, *Transforming our world: the 2030 Agenda for Sustainable Development* (25 September 2015).

10.3 Sources of international environmental law

International environmental law is primarily made up of treaties. In part, this is due to the recent 'birth' of the law and the detailed character of much of the substantive regulation. In order to take account of changes to the environment, shifting scientific assessments as well as political prioritization of the environment, states make frequent use of framework conventions. The primary purpose of such conventions is not to exhaustively regulate a topic but to establish an organizational entity with the mandate to adopt the substantive regulation. A well-known example is the 1992 UN Framework Convention on Climate Change (UNFCCC) that—as we shall see later—only contains a few substantive provisions but establishes a Conference of the Parties as the 'supreme body' of the Convention. Some environmental law treaties adopt a so-called 'list technique' whereby the treaty-based obligations are tied to periodically updated lists in protocols or annexes. An example is the 1972 World Heritage Convention and the regularly updated World Heritage List of cultural and natural sites of outstanding universal interest. An additional feature is the occasional differentiation in the substantial obligations imposed on the parties. For example, the 1992 UNFCCC is explicitly based on the notion that developed countries 'should take the lead in combating climate change and the adverse effects thereof'.[12]

Customary international law only plays a limited role in international environmental law but as we will see later, a number of customary legal principles do exist. The most well established are the so-called 'no harm' principle—also known as the principle of due diligence— and the obligation to consult and notify in the event of possible transboundary harm and the obligation to conduct a prior transboundary environmental impact assessment (EIA).

International courts have made important contributions to the development of international environmental law. Noticeable examples include the seminal award of the Permanent Court of Arbitration (PCA) in the *Trail Smelter* case[13] and, from the ICJ, the *Gabčíkovo-Nagymaros Project* case and the *Pulp Mills* case.[14] Since environmental law is increasingly being applied and interpreted by specialized international courts, such as the European Court of Human Rights (ECtHR), the International Tribunal for the Law of the Sea (ITLOS) and the World Trade Organizations' Dispute Settlement Body (DSB), decisions from these organs become of greater relevance.[15]

There is an abundance of non-binding 'soft law' instruments in international environmental law and some of the most cited instruments, including the 1972 Stockholm

---

[12] Art. 3(1). See also Annex B to the 1997 Kyoto Protocol.   [13] *Trail Smelter* (n 3).

[14] *Gabčíkovo-Nagymaros Project (Hungary v Slovakia)*, Judgment [1997] ICJ Rep 7; *Pulp Mills on the River Uruguay (Argentina v Uruguay)*, Provisional Measures, Order of 13 July 2006 [2006] ICJ Rep 113.

[15] See, inter alia, ECtHR, *López Ostra v Spain*, App. no. 16798/90, Judgment, 9 December 1994. From ITLOS, see *Responsibilities and Obligations of States Sponsoring Persons and Entities with Respect to Activities in the Area*, Advisory Opinion, 1 February 2011, ITLOS Rep 2011, 10.

Declaration and the 1992 Rio Declaration, are for the most part of a non-binding character. The 2009 Copenhagen Accord on climate change is a case in point.[16] As discussed in Chapter 2, these instruments may assist in the formation of customary law. A possible example includes the principle of prevention listed in both the Stockholm and Rio Declarations.[17]

10.4 Basic principles of international environmental law

10.4.1 Introduction

In this section we shall examine some of the core principles/approaches that govern and guide the application of international environmental law.[18] The principles are of general application and apply to all actors and in respect of all activities. They are derived from a combination of state practice, treaties, soft law instruments and decisions from international courts and their legal status varies. Some merely constitute aspirations of a soft law character[19] whose primary role is to guide the operation and implementation of more concrete and substantive obligations.[20]

The principles can be divided into two groups, each seeking to fulfil a more overarching goal.[21] The first group of principles seeks *to prevent damage to the environment* while the second seeks to *ensure that environmental protection is balanced and—when necessary—distributed*. We begin with the principles of prevention in Section 10.4.2 before we turn to the balancing principles in Section 10.4.3.

10.4.2 Principles that seek to prevent environmental damage

The first principle is linked to the sovereign right of all states to their natural resources. Principle 21 of the 1972 Stockholm Declaration stipulates that 'States have … the sovereign right to exploit their own resources pursuant to their own environmental policies'[22] but also that 'the responsibility to ensure that activities within their jurisdiction or control do not cause damage to the environment of other States or of areas beyond the limits of national jurisdiction.' The obligation not to cause damage to other states is known as the *'no harm' principle*. In the seminal *Trail Smelter* case, where smoke from a smelting company located in Canada caused damage to crops and forests in the United States, an arbitrational court stated that:

---

[16] Copenhagen Accord (18 December 2009) in UNFCCC, Report of the Conference of the Parties on Its Fifteenth Session (hereinafter COP Report and session number), Addendum (30 March 2010), UN Doc. FCCC/CP/2009/11/Add.1, 5. See also Daniel Bodansky, 'The Copenhagen Climate Change Conference: A Postmortem' (2010) 104(2) *American Journal of International Law* 230–240.

[17] See, respectively, Principle nos 21 and 2 and *Nuclear Weapons* (n 5) para. 29, *Gabčíkovo-Nagymaros Project* (n 14) para. 53, *Pulp Mills* (n 14) para. 72.

[18] An overview is available in Sands and Peel (n 4) 187–237.   [19] *Iron Rhine* (n 5) para. 58.

[20] See also Sands and Peel (n 4) 188–190.

[21] For this approach, see Dupuy and Viñuales (n 4) 51–87.

[22] See also GA Res. 1803 on Permanent Sovereignty over Natural Resources (14 December 1962).

> no State has the right to use or permit the use of its territory in such a manner as to cause injury by fumes in or to the territory of another or the properties or persons therein, when the case is of serious consequence and the injury is established by clear and convincing evidence.[23]

The ICJ has since confirmed that the principle reflects customary international law.[24] Importantly, though, it only applies to a risk of significant or serious harm.[25] While the no harm principle was initially solely relied on in the context of transboundary harm, the ICJ has indicated the existence of a more overarching *principle of prevention* and a corresponding duty not to cause damage to areas *beyond the territorial confines of states*.[26] In *Nuclear Weapons*, the Court found that:

> the existence of the general obligation of States to ensure that activities within their jurisdiction and control respect the environment of other States or of areas beyond national control is now part of the corpus of international law relating to the environment.[27]

This points to the existence of a (vague and ill-defined) obligation under international law not to cause harm to the environment per se.

In the *Pulp Mills* case, concerning a dispute between Argentina and Uruguay in relation to the construction of pulp mills on a stretch of the River Uruguay which separates the two states, the ICJ stated that the customary principle of prevention originates in notions of *due diligence* and a state's obligation to 'use all the means at its disposal in order to avoid activities which take place in its territory, or in any area under its jurisdiction, causing significant damage to the environment of another State'.[28] Due diligence is not an obligation of result but of conduct and concrete means required to fulfil the due diligence obligation will vary according to the circumstances.[29] Relevant factors include the timing of the potential damage, the type of activity and the capacities of the state. So activities that entail a more serious risk, such as nuclear energy, require a higher degree of diligence. In addition, measures that may be considered 'sufficiently diligent at a certain moment may become not diligent enough in light, for instance, of new scientific or technological knowledge'.[30]

---

[23]   *Trail Smelter* (n 3) 1965.

[24]   See *Corfu Channel (UK v Albania)*, Judgment of 9 April 1949 [1949] ICJ Rep 4, 22; *Pulp Mills on the River Uruguay (Argentina v Uruguay)*, Judgment [2010] ICJ Rep 14, para. 101.

[25]   *Pulp Mills* (n 24) para. 101. See also the International Law Commission's 2001 Draft Articles on Prevention of Transboundary Harm from Hazardous Activities, with commentaries, *Yearbook of the International Law Commission*, 2001, vol. II, Part Two, see commentary to art. 2, p. 152, para. 6 and commentary to art. 3, p. 153, para. 5.

[26]   See also Principle 21 of the 1972 Stockholm Declaration.

[27]   *Nuclear Weapons* (n 5) para. 29. See also *Gabčíkovo-Nagymaros Project* (n 14) para. 140 and *Pulp Mills* (n 24) paras 101, 185 and 193.

[28]   *Pulp Mills* (n 24) para. 101.

[29]   Ibid, paras 186–187. To that end, it is worth noting that with the exception of damage caused by space objects, see art. 2 of the 1972 Convention on International Liability for Damage Caused by Space Objects, international law does not operate with strict liability (liability without fault) for states.

[30]   *Responsibilities and Obligations of States* (n 15) para. 117; *Pulp Mills* (n 24) para. 197. See also ILC Draft Articles (n 25) see commentary to art. 3, p. 154, paras 11, 17–18.

The ICJ and ITLOS have stated that a state must undertake an *environmental impact assessment* (EIA) before it initiates an activity if there is a risk of significant adverse impact in a transboundary context.[31] The obligation seems to reflect customary international law. EIAs are explicitly governed by the 1991 Convention on Environmental Impact Assessment in a Transboundary Context (also known as the ESPOO Convention).[32] If the EIA indicates that a planned activity poses a risk of significant transboundary harm, the state must notify potentially affected states and consult on remedies to prevent significant harm or minimize the risk.[33] The latter illustrates that cooperation on implementing and applying measures to protect the environment is also considered to be an important guiding principle in international environmental law.[34]

The so-called *precautionary approach* stipulates that a lack of scientific certainty about the negative effects of an activity must not prevent states from taking preventive measures. Notions of precaution are found in many treaties in international environmental law, including in the 1985 Vienna Convention for the Protection of the Ozone Layer[35] and the 1992 UNFCCC.[36] In *Tatar v Romania*, the ECtHR found that Romania has breached the principle of precaution by allowing a company to continue its industrial operations after a preliminary impact assessment had highlighted the risks entailed by the activity for the environment and human health.[37] ITLOS has stated that the precautionary approach is 'an integral part of the due diligence obligation'[38] and that the incorporation of the approach into a growing number of treaties has 'initiated a trend towards making this approach part of customary international law'.[39] Currently, however, this would appear to be too optimistic.[40] The approach is fairly imprecise and hardly suitable to serve as anything other than an interpretational aid.[41]

10.4.3 Principles that seek to ensure a balanced approach to environment protection

The second group of principles are concerned with a 'fair' and sensible balance between environmental protection and a host of other considerations. The first is the so-called '*polluter-pays*' principle whereby a state should ensure that it is the actor responsible for pollution that bears both the more immediate and the longer terms costs thereof.[42] While the principle is hardly reflective of customary international law,

---

[31] *Pulp Mills* (n 24) paras 204–205 and *Responsibilities and Obligations of States* (n 15) para. 145. See also Principle 17 of the Rio Declaration and art. 7 in the ILC Draft Articles (n 25).

[32] See, inter alia, art. 2(3).   [33] See arts 8–9 in the ILC's Draft Articles (n 25).

[34] See also art. 4 in the ILC Draft Articles (n 25) and Principle 24 of the Stockholm Declaration and Principle 7 in the Rio Declaration.

[35] See the Preamble.   [36] Art. 3(3). See also Principle 15 of the Rio Declaration.

[37] *Tatar v Romania*, App. no. 67021/01.

[38] *Responsibilities and Obligations of States* (n 15) para. 131.   [39] Ibid, para. 135.

[40] See the debate in Dupuy and Viñuales (n 4) 61–64.   [41] See also *Pulp Mills* (n 24) para. 165.

[42] See the 1972 OECD Council Recommendation on Guiding Principles Concerning the International Economic Aspects of Environmental Policies. See also art. 16 of the 1992 Rio Declaration and see the overview in Sands and Peel (n 4) 228–233.

it features as an important guiding principle in a wide range of conventions and legal instruments, including in EU law.[43]

The principle of *'common but differentiated responsibilities'* (CBDR) is derived from more overarching principles of equity and seeks to take account of the special needs of developing states and the fact that developed states generally hold greater responsibility for existing environmental damage and are better equipped to deal with the consequences than developing states.[44] There is, in other words, both an element of *contribution* or responsibility for the creation of an environmental problem as well as an element of *ability* to offer a remedy inherent in the principle. CBDR is reflected in a number of important conventions, including, as already mentioned, the 1992 UNFCCC. Thus, although all state parties to the UNFCCC are deemed to hold responsibilities, the burden is primarily laid on the developed countries.[45] In the 1987 Montreal Protocol to the 1985 Vienna Convention on the Protection of the Ozone Layer, CBDR led to delayed compliance with particular requirements by some developing states.[46] And in the (infamous) 1997 Kyoto Protocol to the UNFCCC, CBDR was translated into a system whereby omission targets only applied to developed states on the basis of historical contributions and capabilities.[47] In practice, CBDR is a major impediment to reaching agreement on important environmental issues, most notably climate change.

The principle *of inter-generational equity* seeks to ensure a sensible balance between the needs of the present and future generations. The need to preserve the environment for future generations is noted in, inter alia, the 1946 International Whaling Convention.[48] Article 3 of the Rio Declaration states that the 'right to development must be fulfilled so as to meet developmental and environmental needs of present and future generation'.[49] The principle is closely tied to the concept of *sustainable development* that was coined in the 1987 Brundtland Report.[50] It has been referred to as a 'comprehensive and integrated approach to economic, social and political processes, which aims at the sustainable use of natural resources of the Earth and the protection of the environment ...'[51] The ICJ referred to sustainable development in the *Gabčíkovo-Nagymaros Project* case.[52] Although the principle is hard to define in any precise manner, it generally encompasses (at least) four elements.[53] Apart from the principle of inter-generational equity mentioned above, it covers 'sustainable' exploitation of natural resources that may entail setting limits on exploitation, a balanced

---

[43] See, inter alia, art. 191 of the EU Treaty as amended by the Treaty of Lisbon.

[44] The principle is reflected in art. 7 of the Rio Declaration. For an overview, see Sands and Peel (n 4) 233–236 and Philippe Cullet, 'Common but Differentiated Responsibilities' in Malgosia Fitzmaurice et al. (eds), *Research Handbook on International Environmental Law* (Edward Elgar Publishing, 2010) 161–180.

[45] UNFCCC art. 3(1).   [46] See art. 5(1).   [47] See the Kyoto Protocol's annexes.

[48] Preamble.

[49] See also *Gabčíkovo-Nagymaros Project* (n 14) para. 140 and *Nuclear Weapons* (n 5) para. 29.

[50] Report of the World Commission on Environment and Development, 'Our Common Future', 10 March 1987.

[51] International Law Association, 2002 New Delhi Declaration on the Principles of International Law Related to Sustainable Development, see the Preamble.

[52] *Gabčíkovo-Nagymaros Project* (n 14) para. 140.   [53] Sands and Peel (n 4) 206–217.

and 'sustainable' use of resources where states take account of the needs of other states and, finally, a need to ensure the integration of environmental considerations in economic and other forms of development plans.[54]

The *principle of participation* imposes on all states a duty to ensure that various groups and individuals affected by environmental matters are heard and are able to participate in important environmental projects and processes.[55] Among other things, the requirement of so-called 'prior informed consent' obliges a state to consult with and seek the informed consent of indigenous peoples before the displacement or relocation of those peoples.[56] The 1998 Aarhus Convention on Access to Information, Public Participation in Decision-Making and Access to Justice in Environmental Matters contains a number of important rights for the public, such as rights to receive environmental information held by public authorities, to participate in environmental decision-making and to challenge decisions that have been taken without regard to the other two rights. The ECtHR has found that the authorities of a state must ensure public access to the conclusions of investigations and studies on the consequences of environmental incidents.[57]

10.5 Substantive regulation

10.5.1 Introduction

International environmental law covers a wide array of both public and private law topics and the substantive regulation is enormous. We begin our overview of the most important parts of the law with the legal efforts to protect the atmosphere (Section 10.5.2). We then examine the conservation of nature (Section 10.5.3) and the regulation of hazardous substances (Section 10.5.4).

10.5.2 Protection of the atmosphere

The protection of the air and overall atmosphere is one of the most important areas in international environmental law and it is certainly one of the topics to which most public attention is devoted. In practice, the regulation can be divided into three legal regimes.

Transboundary air pollution caused by industrialization has been a concern among states for a substantial period of time, in particularly in North America and Europe. In fact, the seminal *Trail Smelter* case arose from a dispute about air pollution back in the 1930s. However, it was not until the 1970s that international awareness of the dangers to health and the environmental associated with emissions of various toxic

---

[54] *Iron Rhine* (n 5) para. 59. See also Principle 4 in the 1992 Rio Declaration.

[55] See Principle 10 in the 1992 Rio Declaration.

[56] GA Res. 61/295 Declaration on the Rights of Indigenous Peoples (13 September 2007), see art. 10. See also art. 8(j) of the Convention on Biodiversity.

[57] *Tatar v Romania* (n 37) para. 69.

substances into the air led to the first legally binding international measures. In 1979, the Convention on Long-Range Transboundary Air Pollution (LRTAP) was adopted in order to limit and 'as far as possible, gradually reduce and prevent air pollution including long-range transboundary air pollution'.[58] LRTAP is a framework convention and the substantive obligations required to fulfil the objective of limiting air pollution are found in eight protocols. Over time, the regulatory scheme in the protocols has become fairly complex.[59] LRTAP creates an institutional structure consisting of an executive body, a secretariat and a scientific body.

Efforts to combat *ozone depletion* have resulted in one of the most successful outcomes in international environmental law.[60] At an attitude of around 25 km, the planet is surrounded by a thin layer of ozone that absorbs the vast majority of the ultraviolet radiation from the sun. Depletion of ozone is thought to have an adverse effect on environmental and human health and, in the 1980s, scientists began to link a gradual weakening of, and in some areas a 'hole' in, the ozone layer caused by the emission of a range of substances used in industrial activities and products. The 1985 framework Vienna Convention on the Protection of the Ozone Layer was adopted to protect the 'layer of atmospheric ozone above the planetary boundary line'.[61] The Convention was built around a precautionary approach[62] and the institutional structure tasked with adopting the relevant substantive obligations was a Conference of the Parties (COP).[63] The 1987 Montreal Protocol introduced a sophisticated system of obligations, including provisions on trade in controlled substances and a flexible system for the transfer of production capacities. This system influenced the system created for limiting damaging emissions in the efforts to combat climate change. The Montreal Protocol's approach to non-compliance would also later become a general characteristic of international environmental law. Instead of punishing non-compliance, the Protocol took the approach of offer to non-complying states both technical and economic assistance in order to improve performance.

Reaching international agreement on how to combat *climate change* has turned out to be one of the most pressing—and difficult—political issues of the 21st century. Scientific evidence indicates that an increase in certain greenhouse gases in the atmosphere (seemingly due to human activity) is directly related to the so-called 'greenhouse effect' and a change in the global climate.[64] The increase in temperature is linked to an already visible decrease in the area of sea ice and snow cover in arctic regions[65] as well as a potential rise in sea levels and more extreme weather events, such as heat waves, heavy precipitation and storms.[66] Concerns about climate change emerged in the late 1980s and resulted in the adoption in 1992 of the *UNFCCC* at the 1992 Rio Conference. Today, the Convention has an impressive 197 parties. The primary purpose of the Convention is to stabilize 'greenhouse gas concentrations

---

[58] LRTAP art. 2.   [59] For an overview, see Sands and Peel (n 4) 246–257.

[60] See the overview in Dupuy and Viñuales (n 4) 131–141 and Sands and Peel (n 4) 262–274.

[61] Art. 1(1).   [62] See also the Preamble to the Convention   [63] Art. 6.

[64] See, inter alia, Intergovernmental Panel on Climate Change, *Climate Change 2013: The Physical Science Basis, Summary for Policymakers*, see sections B.1. and D.3.

[65] Ibid, section B.3.   [66] Ibid, section B.1.

in the atmosphere at a level that would prevent dangerous anthropogenic interference with the climate system' and overall agreement has gradually settled on the ambition of holding the increase in global average temperature to below 2° Celsius from pre-industrial levels.[67] The UNFCCC only contains limited substantive provisions and instead establishes a COP to adopt the substantive measures required.[68] The Convention is guided by the principle of CBDR, a precautionary approach, the promotion of sustainable development and overall cooperation.[69] The 1997 *Kyoto Protocol* was based on the premise that the developed world should take the lead in combating the adverse effects of climate change and the developed world agreed to commit to explicit targets and timetables for reducing their greenhouse emissions.[70] However, major states with some of the highest emission levels, such as China, India and Brazil, were under no substantive obligations. The Protocol also introduced mechanisms for purchasing or acquiring credits that represented greenhouse gas reductions in other states (AAUs and CDMs).[71] By the time the Protocol entered into force in 2005, it was already clear that it was insufficient to keep greenhouse emissions in check and the ambition then turned towards reaching a comprehensive climate agreement at the 2009 COP 15 in Copenhagen, Denmark.[72] But the negotiations in Copenhagen failed and the 'Copenhagen Accords' did not contain any binding reduction targets. At COP 21 in December 2015 in Paris, France, the *Paris Agreement* was adopted to keep the increase in 'the global average temperature to well below 2°C above pre-industrial levels and to pursue efforts to limit the temperature increase to 1.5°C above pre-industrial levels'. It also seeks to enhance states' abilities to 'adapt to the adverse impacts of climate change and foster climate resilience' and to make 'finance flows consistent with a pathway towards low greenhouse gas emissions and climate-resilient development'.[73] The Agreement allows each state to determine for itself what contribution it should make—so-called 'nationally determined contributions' (NDCs)—to fulfil the purposes of the Agreement,[74] but the voluntary contributions must represent a progression over time.[75] There is no enforcement mechanism for non-compliance. To enter into force, the Paris Agreement must have 55 parties that represent 55 per cent of global greenhouse gas emissions. By July 2016, the three states with the biggest 'CO_2 footprint' (the United States, China and India), had all committed to joining the Agreement,[76] but only 18 states had ratified it and Norway was the only developed state to become a party to the Agreement.[77]

---

[67] Decision 1/CP.16, Cancun Agreement: Outcome of the Work of the Ad Hoc Working Group on Long-Term Cooperative Action under the Convention, see section I.4.

[68] See art. 7.   [69] See arts 2–4.   [70] Art. 3(1).

[71] For an overview, see Sands and Peel (n 4) 287–292.

[72] The agreement is available in Report of the Conference of the Parties on its fifteenth session, held in Copenhagen from 7 to 19 December 2009 (30 March 2010), UN Doc. FCCC/CP/2009/11/Add.1.

[73] See art. 2(1).   [74] Art. 4(2).   [75] Arts 3 and 4(3).

[76] In a 9 February 2016 order, the US Supreme Court halted part of the government's implementation program—the so-called Clean Power Plan—until it could rule on its constitutionality, see *Chamber of Commerce, et al. v EPA, et al.*, order in pending case, docket no. 15A787.

[77] See the updated list at https://treaties.un.org/pages/ViewDetails.aspx?src=TREATY&mtdsg_no=XXVII-7-d&chapter=27&lang=en.

10.5.3 **Conservation of nature**

Antarctica is governed by a system of international instruments known as the Antarctic Treaty System (ATS), that seek to ensure that Antarctica is used solely for peaceful purposes with due regard to the interests of all humankind.[78] The 1959 Antarctic Treaty specifies that no state can make claims of territorial sovereignty over Antarctica as long as the treaty is in force[79] and that military activities are prohibited.[80] The same holds for the disposal of radioactive waste.[81] The Treaty is supplemented with a range of protocols, including a 1991 Madrid Protocol that preserve all of Antarctica as a natural reserve 'devoted to peace and science'.[82] All activities relating to Antarctic mineral resources, except for scientific research, are prohibited.[83]

The 1972 Convention Concerning the Protection of the World Cultural and Natural Heritage—also known as the '*World Heritage Convention*' (WHC)—seeks to promote international cooperation to protect heritage of outstanding universal value.[84] It is administered by a World Heritage Committee that keeps a World Heritage List of both cultural and natural sites or properties of outstanding universal value. By June 2016, the list had 1,031 sites of which 197 were natural properties.[85] Criteria for what qualifies as 'outstanding universal value' are set up in Operational Guidelines regularly updated by the World Heritage Committee.[86] The state on whose territory a natural heritage site is located must ensure the 'identification, protection, conservation, presentation and transmission to future generations' of the heritage site.[87] It retains full sovereignty over the site but recognizes that it constitutes a part of world heritage for 'whose protection it is the duty of the international community as a whole to co-operate'.[88] It also accepts not to 'take any deliberate measures which might damage directly or indirectly' the natural heritage located on the territory of another state.[89] It is up to the states themselves to nominate potential sites for listing by the World Heritage Committee.[90] If a site is under threat, it will be referred by the Committee to a List of World Heritage in Danger.

The 1971 Convention on Wetlands of International Importance especially as Waterfowl Habitat—also known as the Ramsar Convention—provides a legal framework for the conservation and wise use, including 'sustainable' use, of wetlands and their resources. Wetlands are generally considered among the most diverse ecosystems

---

[78] See the Preamble to the 1959 Antarctic Treaty. For a full overview, see Francesco Francioni and Tullio Scovazzi (eds), *International Law for Antarctica* (Martinus Nijhoff, 1996).

[79] Art. IV.   [80] Antarctic Treaty art. I.

[81] Art. V. See also art. 27(1) of the IAEA Joint Convention on the Safety of Spent Fuel and Radioactive Waste Management.

[82] See Protocol, art. 2.   [83] Protocol, art. 7.

[84] See also Francesco Francioni (ed.), *The 1972 World Heritage Convention: A Commentary* (Oxford University Press, 2008).

[85] Thirty-two properties were listed as fulfilling both cultural and natural criteria. The updated list is available at http://whc.unesco.org/en/list/.

[86] For the most recent 2012 guidelines, see United Nations Educational, Scientific and Cultural Organisation Intergovernmental Committee for the Protection of the World Cultural and Natural Heritage, *Operational Guidelines for the Implementation of the World Heritage Convention*, (8 July 2015) WHC.15/01.

[87] Art. 4.   [88] Art. 6(1).   [89] Art. 6(3).   [90] See art. 11(1)–(3).

and they are under threat in many regions of the world. The Convention bears certain similarities to the WHC and the most important feature of the protection is the listing of sites that must be protected under national law.[91] By July 2016, it had designated 2,241 sites maintained by a Secretariat.[92] Of these, some are also listed under the WHC. It is the state itself that designates suitable wetlands within its territory for listing,[93] and the selection should consider the 'international significance in terms of ecology, botany, zoology, limnology or hydrology'.[94] The territorial state retains exclusive sovereign rights to the territory where the listed wetland is situated.[95] But, once listed, the territorial state must conserve and ensure 'wise' use of the wetlands by 'formulate and implement their planning' accordingly.[96] If it fails to do so, the site may be listed on another list of sites—the Montreux Record—that require priority attention.[97]

The threat posed by *desertification* and the ensuing loss of productivity of arid land led to the adoption of the 1994 UN Convention to Combat Desertification in those Countries Experiencing Serious Drought and/or Desertification, Particularly in Africa.[98] The Convention primarily obliges the parties to adopt national action programmes with longer term strategies with international assistance. It is a framework convention whose broad obligations are implemented through reliance on a set of annexes that form an integral part of the Convention. Since the problems associated with desertification are particularly acute in Africa, priority is given to that region.[99]

The 1992 Convention on Biological Diversity (CBD) was adopted at the 1992 Rio Summit as the first international convention to protect the diversity of the species and spaces in the environment and their complex interaction. It affirms that the conservation of *biological diversity* is a 'common concern to humankind'.[100] It seeks to conserve biological diversity, 'a sustainable use of its components and a fair and equitable sharing of the benefits arising out of the utilization of genetic resources'.[101] Importantly, the CBD is not merely focused on conservation but seeks to balance it with sustainable use of the biological resources. The CBD leaves much of the responsibility on the states and their practical implementation of the aims of the Convention. Implementation is scrutinized pursuant to reporting to the COP. A key provision is article 6 that obliges states to develop—in accordance with their conditions and capabilities—'national strategies, plans or programmes for the conservation and sustainable use of biological diversity' and to integrate 'as far as possible and as appropriate, the conservation and sustainable use of biological diversity into relevant sectoral or cross-sectoral plans, programmes and policies'.

It has been a core priority of the CBD to control the risks associated with genetically modified organisms (GMOs) resulting from modern biotechnology.[102] To that

---

[91] See art. 2.   [92] Art. 8(2).   [93] Art. 2(1).

[94] Art. 2(2).   [95] Art. 2(3).   [96] Art. 3(1).

[97] See the updated list at http://ramsar.rgis.ch/cda/en/ramsar-documents-montreux-montreux-record/main/ramsar/1-31-118%5E20972_4000_0__.

[98] The Convention defines desertification as: 'land degradation in arid, semi-arid and dry sub-humid areas resulting from various factors, including climatic variations and human activities', see art. 1(a).

[99] See also art. 7.   [100] Preamble.   [101] Art. 1.

[102] See, inter alia, arts 8(g) and 19(3) of the CBD.

end, much progress was made with the 2000 Cartagena Protocol on Biosafety that focuses on the transboundary movement of Living Modified Organisms (LMOs) that may have an adverse effect on diversity and health. The Protocol essentially adopts an advanced information agreement procedure that seeks to ensure that importing states receive the information about the LMOs required to make an informed decision.

Another important area is access to genetic resources—an issue that has been fraught with contention.[103] Due to technological advances, the potential use—and rights—of modified seeds have grown in importance and agreement on benefit sharing and access has been hard to reach. Progress was made, however, with the 2010 Nagoya Protocol on Access to Genetic Resources and the Fair and Equitable Sharing of Benefits Arising from their Utilization. Among other things, the Protocol facilitates interstate access to genetic resources for environmentally sound uses and improves benefit sharing through the adoption of more predictable conditions for access.

10.5.4 The regulation of hazardous substances

Environmentally sound management of dangerous and hazardous substances is another important part of international environmental law. The potentially catastrophic international consequences of nuclear accidents have made the *nuclear energy* sector an obvious target for elaborate international regulation.[104] The International Atomic Energy Agency (IAEA) was created in 1957 to promote peaceful development and use of nuclear energy and prevent its military use. One of the main tasks of the IAEA is to assist states in balancing the many benefits of sound civilian exploitation of nuclear technology and the health and environmental hazards. The IAEA makes recommendations and designs programmes for the safe development and use of nuclear technology and nuclear materials and has been instrumental in the adoption of a number of relevant conventions. The 1986 Chernobyl disaster led to the adoption of the 1986 Convention on Early Notification of a Nuclear Accident or Radiological Emergency and the Convention on Assistance in the Case of a Nuclear Accident or Radiological Emergency. In 1994, the Convention on Nuclear Safety was adopted to give effect to some of the IAEA's standards on nuclear safety, waste management and fuel disposal and reprocessing. While the Convention affirmed that 'responsibility for nuclear safety rests with the State having jurisdiction over a nuclear installation',[105] it obliges states to, inter alia, 'take appropriate steps' to ensure that safety is given due priority,[106] that radiation is 'as low as reasonably achievable'[107] and that adequate emergency plans are developed.[108] The terms used are vague, however, and enforcement is weak and merely based on periodic reviews of report on implementation measures taken.[109] In 1997, IAEA members adopted the Joint Convention on

---

[103] See Dupuy and Viñuales (n 4) 192–196.

[104] For an overview, see Patricia Birnie et al., *International Law and the Environment* (Oxford University Press, 2009) ch. 9. The secondary rules on responsibility and liability for nuclear damage have been a particular point of focus, see ibid, 516–534.

[105] Preamble.   [106] Art. 6.   [107] Art. 15.   [108] Art. 16.   [109] Art. 20.

the Safety of Spent Fuel and Radioactive Waste Management to improve the management and disposal of nuclear waste. A noticeable feature of the Convention is the reference to the principle of inter-generational equity and the aim to 'avoid imposing undue burdens on future generations'.[110] On a regional level, the 1957 *Euratom Treaty* sets up European standards for nuclear energy.[111] In response to the 11 March 2011 accident at the Fukushima nuclear power plant in Japan, the IAEA adopted an Action Plan on Nuclear Safety and, in 2015, the parties to the Convention on Nuclear Safety adopted the Vienna Declaration on Nuclear Safety with the aim of strengthening relevant nuclear procedures.[112]

The regulation of the *military use of nuclear energy* has generally followed a separate track from the one just described, with the law reflecting the paramount national security concerns and power politics associated with the advent and potential use of nuclear weapons. In the *Nuclear Weapons* opinion, the ICJ did note, however, that 'the use of nuclear weapons could constitute a catastrophe for the environment'.[113] The legality of *testing nuclear explosions* has been a cause of decades-long contention. The practical effect of the 1963 Nuclear Test Ban Treaty is that test explosions must be conducted outside Antarctica, underground and cause no pollution. However, not all 'nuclear relevant states' are parties to the treaty and its status under customary international law is unclear. In the *Nuclear Tests* case, the ICJ refrained from ruling on whether or not atmospheric tests carried out by France were in violation of customary international law.[114] A number of regional agreements prohibit the testing of nuclear weapons in regions of Latin America, the South Pacific, South-East Asia and Africa.[115] Like environmental damage caused by oil, nuclear damage is governed by a special liability regime. We shall return to this subject in Section 10.6.

Many of the chemicals in industrial processes pose substantial risks to the environment and public health, and as scientific understanding of the detrimental effects of various chemicals has increased, so has international regulation.[116] For the most part, however, regulation remains fairly fragmented and different treaties regulate different stages/phases of the management of the substance. In 2001, the Stockholm Convention on Persistent Organic Pollutants was adopted on the basis of Agenda 21 which developed from the 1992 Rio Summit with a view to restricting and, in many

---

[110] Arts 4(iv) and 11(iv).   [111] See Birnie et al. (n 104) 505–507.

[112] Vienna Declaration on Nuclear Safety on principles for the implementation of the objective of the Convention on Nuclear Safety to prevent accidents and mitigate radiological consequences (9 February 2015), CNS/DC/2015/2/Rev.1.

[113] *Nuclear Weapons* (n 5) para. 29. The legality of using nuclear weapons is discussed in Chapter 14. Efforts by the IAEA to prevent military use of nuclear energy were enhanced substantially with the adoption in 1968 of the Nuclear Non-Proliferation Treaty (NPT) that obliges state parties to accept certain non-proliferation safeguards by bilateral agreement with the IAEA and to permit periodic verification inspections.

[114] The Court held instead that France had made a unilateral commitment to refrain from conducting such tests, see *Nuclear Tests Case (New Zealand v France)* [1974] ICJ Rep 457, paras 51–53 and *Nuclear Test Case (Australia v France)* [1974] ICJ Rep 253, paras 49–51.

[115] See the discussion Birnie et al. (n 104) 509–510.

[116] See also Dupuy and Viñuales (n 4) 202–204.

cases, eliminating the most harmful *chemical substances*.[117] It obliges state parties to eliminate or severely restrict the production and use of a set of persistent organic pollutants (POP) and to take a range of measures to prevent or control the release of certain POPs that are created as an unintentional by-product of certain activities. The Convention is based on a precautionary approach[118] as well as on principles of CBDR.[119] It adopts a 'list technique' and establishes three annexes that are governed by different obligations.

The Basel Convention on the Control of Transboundary Movements of Hazardous Wastes and Their Disposal is a framework convention that was adopted to limit the transfer of hazardous waste from developed states to developing states for disposal—'toxic transfers'.[120] The Convention seeks to reduce the generation of hazardous waste, ensure environmentally sound disposal of the waste as close to the source of the generation as possible, prohibit the export of hazardous waste to certain states and to ensure that the export of hazardous waste in all other situations is carried out in an environmentally sound manner. The definition of what constitutes 'hazardous waste' is tied to a list contained in an annex to the Convention.[121] Another annex lists waste that is presumed to be non-hazardous and therefore not subject to the regulation of the Convention.[122] Both export and import of hazardous waste to and from non-parties to the Convention is prohibited.[123] Parties are allowed to enter into other agreements on the transboundary movement of hazardous waste with both parties and non-parties as long as such agreements are no less 'environmentally sound', in particular with regard to the 'interests of developing countries'.[124] Transport and trade in hazardous substances is also regulated by the Rotterdam Convention on Prior Informed Consent Procedure for Certain Hazardous Chemicals and Pesticides. It too grew out of Agenda 21, a product of the 1992 Rio Summit, and it seeks to ensure that importing states—usually developing states—understand the risks associated with the import of a harmful substance and are in a position to make an informed decision about whether or not to allow it.[125] It sets up a system for the compulsory exchange of relevant information and relies on lists found in a number of annexes.

Unlike the fragmented approach to the handling and management of hazardous substances in the Stockholm, Basel and Rotterdam Conventions, the 2013 Minamata Convention on Mercury adopts an integrated approach to the regulation of hazardous substances.[126] The purpose of the Convention is to protect human health and the

---

[117] For an overview, see Peter L. Lallas, 'The Stockholm Convention on Persistent Organic Pollutants' (2001) 95 *American Journal of International Law* 692–708.

[118] See the Preamble and art. 1. See also arts 8(7)(a) and 8(9).   [119] See the Preamble.

[120] A comprehensive overview is available in Katharina Kummer, *International Management of Hazardous Wastes: The Basel Convention and Related Legal Rules* (Oxford University Press, 1999).

[121] Annex VIII.   [122] Annex IV.   [123] Art. 4(5).

[124] Art. 11(1). For a list of such agreements, see www.basel.int.

[125] See Katharina Kummer, 'Prior Informed Consent for Chemicals in International Trade: The 1998 Rotterdam Convention' (1999) 8(3) *Review of European Community and International Environmental Law* 323–330.

[126] For an overview, see Jessica Templeton and Pia Kohler, 'Implementation and Compliance under the Minamata Convention on Mercury' (2014) 23(2) *Review of European, Comparative & International Environmental Law* 211–220.

environment from the emission and release of mercury and mercury compounds and it regulates the entire life cycle of mercury and thus contains obligations in relation to, respectively, the extraction, use, trade, storage and disposal of mercury.

10.6 Implementation and enforcement

A few points are worth noting in relation to implementation and enforcement of international environmental law. The first point is that the *traditional approaches to state responsibility and reparation for damage* in international law are often ill-suited to environmental damage. In part, this is due to the difficulties of drawing a causal link between an act (or omission) and the environmental damage that may or may not be the result thereof. A further complication is the fact that environmental damage is often the result of progressive acts or omissions by a plurality of states that may have contributed to the damage in an unequal manner. Climate change may be the best example of this. Then there is the question of appropriate compensation, in particular in relation to environmental damage that may be irreversible. What is, for example, the right way to compensate for the extinction of an endangered species or an otherwise negative effect on biological diversity? While the law is still grappling with such issues, a number of approaches and remedies are becoming increasingly relevant. One example is the concept of *erga omnes* obligations discussed in Chapter 2 whereby a state need not always be 'injured' by a violation of an international obligation by another state to be entitled to invoke the responsibility of that state. Another example is the establishment of special funds for collective compensation for environmental damage where the source of the damage is unidentified. In relation to damage to the environment per se, a 1997 Declaration on Responsibility and Liability under International Law for Environmental Damage adopted by the Institut de Droit International stipulates that environmental regimes 'should provide for the reparation of damage to the environment as such separately from or in addition to the reparation of damage relating to death, personal injury or loss of property or economic value'[127] and that the 'fact that environmental damage is irreparable or unquantifiable shall not result in exemption from compensation'.[128]

The traditional approaches to state responsibility and compensation may also be less than optimal when breaches of environmental obligations are not due to ill-will on the part of the responsible state but rather to a lack of technical or financial ability to prevent violations of the law. This, of course, is particularly the case for developing states with scarce resources. Rather than resorting to the more traditional means of enforcing violations of international law, non-compliance with international environmental standards by poorer states is therefore often met with various forms of financial and technical assistance intended to give the non-complying state the ability

---

[127] Institut de Droit International, *Declaration on Responsibility and Liability under International Law for Environmental Damage* (Strasbourg, 1997), art. 23.
[128] Ibid, art. 25.

to create the infrastructure required for effectively implementing its environmental obligations.[129]

The second point to note about implementation and enforcement of international environmental law concerns *the mechanisms for judicial adjudication of disputes*. An international environmental law court has not (yet) been created[130] and the existing courts that specialize in environmental law disputes have so far been of limited significance. The ICJ's 1993 Chamber for Environmental Matters never heard any cases and is no longer convened.[131] In 1997, ITLOS created a Chamber for Marine Environmental Disputes tasked with dealing with disputes relating to the protection and preservation of the marine environment but it has yet to hear a case. The PCA has, however, been involved in a number of disputes involving environmental matters[132] and in 2001 it adopted a set of Optional Rules for Arbitration of Disputes Relating to Natural Resources and/or the Environment. The rules have, however, only been relied upon in a few cases.

In practice, therefore, international environmental law disputes are for the most part dealt with before courts that either have general jurisdiction—such as the ICJ—or courts that specialize in other branches of international law, such as ITLOS,[133] the ECtHR[134] and the World Trade Organization's' DSB. In such cases, however, environmental law considerations may sometimes 'compete' with potentially conflicting legal norms of particular interest to the court in question.

The final point to note about implementation and enforcement of international environmental law is the importance played by special *liability regimes for the economic operator* (whether public or private) responsible for environmental damage. Such regimes are particular relevant in the area of nuclear energy and oil pollution and to an increasing extent also in relation to the movement of some hazardous waste. In general, the regimes establish strict liability for the operator (in most cases without fault), the requirement of insurance, the establishment of a multi-layered system of compensation and a prohibition on discrimination in relation to access to compensation.[135]

Summary

International environmental law covers those parts of international law that relate to the environment. It is not a separate and independent legal discipline and the regulation is generally extremely piecemeal and sectoral. The development of the law has been catapulted by major events and conferences, the most notable being the 1972

---

[129] An overview is available in Dupuy and Viñuales (n 4) 272–284.

[130] For arguments in favour of such a court, see Amedeo Postiglione, 'A More Efficient International Law on the Environment and Setting Up an International Court for the Environment within the United Nations' (1990) 20 *Environmental Law* 321–328.

[131] http://www.icj-cij.org/court/index.php?p1=1&p2=4 (accessed 1 April 2016).

[132] See https://pca-cpa.org/en/services/arbitration-services/environmental-dispute-resolution/.

[133] *Responsibilities and Obligations of States* (n 15).   [134] See e.g. *López Ostra* (n 15).

[135] Dupuy and Viñuales (n 4) 259–264.

Stockholm Conference on the Human Environment and the 1992 Rio Conference on Environmental and Development. International environmental law is guided by a range of principles that are focused on preventing damage to the environment and ensuring that environmental protection is balanced and—where necessary—distributed among states. The substantive regulation covers a wide array of topics such as efforts to protect the atmosphere, the conservation of nature, and the regulation of hazardous substances.

Recommended reading

Solid introductions to international environmental law includes Philippe Sands and Jacqueline Peel, *Principles of International Environmental Law* (3rd edn, Cambridge University Press, 2012); Pierre-Marie Dupuy and Jorge E. Viñuales, *International Environmental Law* (Cambridge University Press, 2015) and Patricia Birnie et al., *International Law and the Environment* (Oxford University Press, 2009).

For an overview of the tension between environmental protection and development, see Nico Schrijver, *Sovereignty over Natural Resources: Balancing Rights and Duties* (Cambridge University Press, 1997).

On CBDR, see Philippe Cullet, 'Common but Differentiated Responsibilities' in Malgosia Fitzmaurice et al. (eds), *Research Handbook on International Environmental Law* (Edward Elgar Publishing, 2010) 161–180.

On contemporary nuclear energy, see Patrick Reyners, 'A New World Governance for Nuclear Safety after Fukushima?' (2013) 4(1) *International Journal of Nuclear Law* 63.

On the Stockholm Convention on POPs, see Peter L. Lallas, 'The Stockholm Convention on Persistent Organic Pollutants' (2001) 95 *American Journal of International Law* 692.

For the Basel Convention, see Katharina Kummer, *International Management of Hazardous Wastes: The Basel Convention and Related Legal Rules* (Oxford University Press, 1999).

On PIC, see the same author in 'Prior Informed Consent for Chemicals in International Trade: The 1998 Rotterdam Convention' (1999) 8(3) *Review of European Community and International Environmental Law* 323.

An introduction to the Minamata Convention is available in Jessica Templeton and Pia Kohler, 'Implementation and Compliance under the Minamata Convention on Mercury' (2014) 23(2) *Review of European, Comparative & International Environmental Law* 211.

On world heritage, see Francesco Francioni (ed.), *The 1972 World Heritage Convention: A Commentary* (Oxford University Press, 2008).

Questions for discussion

1. Why does international environmental law generally form part of the international law of cooperation? Can you think of some principles of international environmental law that could be said to be part of the international law of coexistence?

2. Can you think of some concrete examples of where environmental law overlaps with other fields of public international law?

3. Why is there often a tension between environmental protection and economic development? Can you think of some examples of where this tension is visible?

4. The chapter notes that some of the basic principles of international environmental law are merely guiding principles. Does this mean that they are not legally binding?

5. Can you provide some examples of the techniques used in the treaty-based regulation of international environmental law?

6. Why are the traditional principles on state responsibility and compensation sometimes ill-suited for enforcing international environmental law?

11

International economic law

CENTRAL ISSUES

1. This chapter discusses international economic law with a particular focus on the Bretton Woods institutions.

2. It introduces the World Trade Organization and the most important principles governing international trade, including those contained in the General Agreement on Tariffs and Trade.

3. The chapter also presents international monetary law with a particular emphasis on the role and the activities of the International Monetary Fund.

4. The chapter also discusses the international regulation of international investments and the most important principles thereof, including those that govern expropriation of foreign property.

11.1 Introduction

International economic law covers a vast range of rules and principles on economic conduct and relations between states, international organizations and private actors, both individuals and corporations. While certain aspects of it are covered elsewhere in this book,[1] the present chapter deals with the most fundamental areas of the law: the international law of trade, international monetary law and international investment law.

International law generally leaves it up to states to regulate their own economic affairs. As the International Court of Justice (ICJ) stated in *Nicaragua*, every 'State possesses a fundamental right to choose and implement its own political, economic and social system'.[2] In addition, states are not required to have economic relations with other states. To quote the ICJ again: 'A State is not bound to continue particular trade

---

[1] The issue of extraterritorial application of economic legislation, such as antitrust laws, is discussed in Chapter 5. Aspects of state immunity are covered in Chapter 6. See also the overview of international environmental law in Chapter 10.

[2] *Military and Paramilitary Activities in and against Nicaragua (Nicaragua v United States)*, Merits, Judgment, [1986] ICJ Rep 14, para. 258.

relations longer than it sees fit to do so, in the absence of a treaty commitment or other specific legal obligations.'[3] In practice, though, the vast majority of states have limited their freedom in economic affairs by becoming parties to a range of treaties.

The modern international economic system originates in the 1944 Bretton Woods conference in New Hampshire, the United States, where participating states sought to plant the seeds for a liberal international economic order with free-flowing economic transactions and equal market access. Much of the inspiration came from the latter part of the 19th century when liberal domestic legislation, bilateral trade agreements and treaties on friendship, commerce and navigation had helped international trade to flourish. The positive trends had been reversed by the outbreak of the First World War and the widespread protectionism that followed in the interwar period.

The Bretton Woods conference created the three most important international organizations for the regulation of trade and monetary policy: the International Monetary Fund (IMF), the International Bank for Reconstruction and Development (the 'World Bank') and the General Agreement on Tariffs and Trade (GATT). While the GATT was created to liberalize world trade by reducing tariffs and other barriers to trade, the IMF ensures exchange stability and provides loans to states with economic difficulties. To supplement the IMF, the World Bank provides loans to developing countries. The GATT was meant to be an interim agreement but, as attempts to establish an elaborate international trade organization failed,[4] it ended up being the 'organizational' structure for international trade agreements for nearly half a century. It was not until January 1995 that a new organization—the World Trade Organization (WTO)—replaced the GATT system.[5]

The Bretton Woods institutions are not the only players in the governance of global economic matters. On a regional level, they are supplemented by important actors, such as the EU. Historically, the Organisation for Economic Co-operation and Development (OECD) has also served as an important forum for economic cooperation between industrialized Western states.[6] In 1964, the General Assembly created the United Nations Conference on Trade and Development (UNCTAD), and in 1966 a United Nations Commission on International Trade Law (UNCITRAL) was established. A range of specialized agencies are also involved in economic-related activities. The International Labour Organization (ILO), for example, sets international labour standards and, among other things, seeks to counteract 'social dumping'. Mention should also be made of the Food and Agriculture Organization (FAO), the World Health Organization (WHO), the International Fund for Agricultural Development (IFAD), the International Maritime Organization (IMO) and the International Civil Aviation Organization (ICAO). Important informal networks include the Group of Twenty (G20) consisting of the 19 major world economies and

---

[3] Ibid, para. 275.   [4] See the Havana Charter for an International Trade Organization.
[5] For an overview, see Andreas F. Lowenfeld, *International Economic Law* (2nd edn, Oxford University Press, 2008) 25–28.
[6] Convention on the Organisation for Economic Co-operation and Development, 14 December 1960.

the EU.[7] It emerged from the G7 that encompassed the six most important industrialized Western states and Japan.[8]

We begin in Section 11.2 with a brief introduction to the capitalist theory that constitutes the foundation for the international economic system. Section 11.3 discusses the international regulation of trade and the GATT and WTO. Section 11.4 focuses on international monetary law, most notably the IMF, and Section 11.5 discusses the core principles of international investment law.

11.2 The capitalist basis of the Bretton Woods system

The economic system created at Bretton Woods derives from theories of market capitalism as developed by, among others, Adam Smith (1723–1790). Of particular importance was the theory of *comparative advantage* advanced by economists like John Stuart Mill (1803–1873) and in particular David Ricardo (1772–1823).[9] In essence, the theory holds that the advantages of international trade and liberalization outweigh the disadvantages even when the needs of the poorest states are taken into account. To understand the theory, it is important to distinguish it from absolute advantage that refers to an ability to produce more or better products or services than someone else. Comparative advantage refers to the ability to produce products and services at a lower opportunity cost and not necessarily at a greater volume. To illustrate, consider the case of an architect and a secretary. The architect is both better at producing architectural services and at administering and organizing. The architect therefore has an absolute advantage when it comes to both producing architectural services and secretarial work. However, both the architect and the secretary benefit from their exchange because of their comparative advantages and disadvantages. It is here that the role of opportunity costs enters the picture. Imagine that the architect produces the equivalent of €100 per hour in architectural services and €50 per hour in secretarial tasks. The secretary can produce the equivalent of €0 in architectural services and €40 in secretarial duties per hour. To produce €40 in secretarial tasks, the architect will lose €100 because he or she has to abandon one hour of architectural production. So the opportunity cost of secretarial work is high and the architect is better off producing one hour's worth of architectural services and employing a secretary to do all the administration and organizing. The secretary is much better off administrating and organizing for the architect because his or her opportunity costs are very low. This, of course, is where the comparative advantage is found.

---

[7] The states are Argentina, Brazil, Canada, China, France, Germany, India, Indonesia, Italy, Japan, Mexico, Russia, Saudi Arabia, Spain, South Africa, South Korea, Turkey, the UK and the United States.

[8] Canada, France, Germany, Italy, Japan, the UK and the United States. In 1997, the G7 became the G8 when Russia joined.

[9] Adam Smith, *An Inquiry Into the Nature and Causes of Wealth of Nations* (1776); David Ricardo, *Principles of Political Economy and Taxation* (1817); John Stuart Mill, *The Principles of Political Economy: With Some of Their Applications to Social Philosophy* (1848).

David Ricardo applied the theory of comparative advantage to international trade and showed how two states (England and Portugal) were both better off by specializing and trading according to their comparative advantages in wine (Portugal) and cloth (England). Nowadays, the theory of comparative advantages explains why iPhones are assembled in China and not in the United States where they are invented and designed. China's comparative advantage with the United States is cheap labour and the fact that workers in China can assemble iPhones at a much lower opportunity cost. The comparative advantages of the United States, on the other hand, are in costly specialized labour in the sense that US workers invent and design sophisticated products at lower opportunity costs.

The capitalistic origin of the international economic system has made it the object of much criticism, and during the Cold War most of the communist states remained outside the Bretton Woods institutions. In the 1960s and 1970s, developing states made persistent calls for the creation of what they perceived to be a more fair and equitable 'New International Economic Order'.[10] Today, opposition mainly comes from the so-called Global Justice Movement which argues that more attention should be paid to non-economic considerations, such as the reduction of global poverty and protection of the environment.[11]

11.3 The WTO and international trade

11.3.1 Introduction

The 1994 Agreement Establishing the World Trade Organization created the WTO as the principal international trade organization with a global reach. By July 2016, it had 164 members, including the EU. The principal organ of the WTO is the Ministerial Conference where all members are represented.[12] Other important organs include three Special Councils in specific sectors (trade in goods, trade in services and trade-related aspects of intellectual property rights)[13] and a Secretariat headed by a Director-General.[14] Since September 2013, the post has been occupied by Roberto Azevédo (Brazil).

In general terms, the evolution of international trade law within the GATT and WTO revolves around a series of *rounds of multilateral trade negotiations*.[15] While the first such round focused on reducing tariffs on goods, attention was gradually also turned to non-tariff measures affecting trade, such as dumping and state subsidies.

---

[10] See, inter alia, GA Res. 1803 (XVII) Permanent Sovereignty over Natural Resources (14 December 1962) and GA Res. 3281 (XXIX) Charter of Economic Rights and Duties of States (12 December 1974). See also Robert W. Cox, 'Ideologies and the New International Economic Order: Reflections on some Recent Literature' (1979) 33(2) *International Organization* 257–302.

[11] Donatella Della Porta et al., *Global Justice Movement: Cross-National and Transnational Perspectives* (Routledge, 2007). See also Marc Doucet, *Global Justice and Democracy: The Anti-Globalisation Movement* (Routledge, 2010).

[12] WTO Agreement art. IV:1.   [13] Ibid, art. IV:5.   [14] Ibid, art. VI:1.

[15] For an overview, see Lowenfeld (n 5) 48–71.

The breakthrough came at the highly successful Uruguay Round (1986–1993) where agreement on a host of contentious issues, such as trade in services and intellectual property as well as a new mechanism for the settlement of disputes, was reached. It was also at the Uruguay Round that the GATT system was replaced by the WTO. The ninth—and so far latest—round of negotiations was initiated in Doha in 2001, but by July 2016 it looked unlikely to be concluded in the foreseeable future. The major hurdle is the requirement that WTO agreements must be approved by all member states. The increase in the number of states when compared to the first rounds of trade negotiations and the emergence of a number of powerful regional actors has made the attainment of unanimity on controversial areas of international trade policy seemingly impossible. The deadlock has led to calls to abandon consensus-based decision-making[16] and some major actors have turned their attention to bilateral and regional negotiations. In February 2016, for example, 12 Pacific Rim states adopted the *Trans-Pacific Partnership Agreement* (TPPA). In addition, the EU and the United States are presently negotiating an ambitious *Transatlantic Trade and Investment Partnership* (TTIP).[17]

We start our overview of the WTO with its core principles (Section 11.3.2) and then turn our focus to the most important aspects of its regulation (Section 11.3.3). Brief mention is then made of the dispute settlement mechanism (Section 11.3.4) and of the primary forms of regional trade cooperation (Section 11.3.5).

11.3.2 The principles of regulation in the WTO

The overall purpose of the WTO is to further the liberalization of international trade and economic transactions through to the reduction and elimination of tariffs and other barriers to trade. In practice, the various WTO agreements are governed by a number of core principles. The most fundamental principle in international trade law is the principle of *non-discrimination* that seeks to ensure that foreign goods and services compete with domestic goods and services on the same conditions ('a level playing field'). The non-discrimination principle is reflected in two obligations often found in the agreements. The first is an obligation of so-called *most-favoured-nation (MFN) treatment*. An MFN clause allows a party to a trade agreement treaty and its nationals to benefit from an advantage that is granted to another (third) state and its nationals pursuant to another agreement concluded between one of the parties to the first treaty and the third state. For example, a MFN clause in a trade agreement between state A and state B gives state A and its nationals the same advantages granted to state C in a treaty concluded between state C and state B. The benefits of a MFN clause require identity in the subject matter of the clause and the advantage granted to the

---

[16] See, inter alia, Dr Emily Jones, 'Which Way Forward for the WTO? The Plurilaterals Debate', Background Note, *The Global Economic Governance Program* (14 February 2014), available at http://www.globaleconomicgovernance.org/background-note-which-way-forward-wto-plurilaterals-debate-2014.

[17] See more at http://ec.europa.eu/trade/policy/in-focus/ttip/. See also Simon Lester and Inu Barbee, 'The Challenge of Cooperation: Regulatory Trade Barriers in the Transatlantic Trade and Investment Partnership' (2013) 16 *Journal of International Economic Law* 847–867.

third state.[18] The non-discrimination principle is also reflected in an obligation of *national treatment*. Here, an importing state is obliged to treat imported goods or services no less favourably than it treats like national products. The obligation requires, in other words, that state B does not subject goods or services imported from state A to less favourable conditions in relation to, for example, requirements of internal sale, transportation, distribution, use etc., than those governing goods or services from state B itself.

The trade relationship between the developed and the developing world is an issue of continuing contention and allegations of unjust treatment of poorer states are not hard to come by. However, there are principles in international trade law that seek to take account of the *special needs of developing states*. The Preamble to the WTO Agreement recognizes 'the need for positive efforts designed to ensure that developing countries, and especially the least developed among them, secure a share in the growth in international trade commensurate with the needs of their economic development'.[19] In practice, developing states benefit from a host of preferential treatments, including *preferential tariffs* and *exemptions from general obligations*. As we shall see later, developing states have, for example, benefited from preferential treatment in relation to the protection of intellectual property and patents. International trade law also seeks to take account of the special needs of developing states via the facilitation of *transfer of technological know-how and processes*.[20]

11.3.3 Substantive regulation in the WTO

11.3.3.1 Introduction

The 1994 WTO Agreement is a short document with a mere 16 articles that establish the WTO. Through its annexes, however, the 1994 Agreement incorporates all the agreements of the Uruguay Round of negotiations that form an integral part of the Agreement, binding on all members.[21] The following overview provides a brief overview of the three most important WTO agreements: the General Agreement on Tariffs and Trade (GATT) (Section 11.3.3.2), the General Agreement on Trade in Services (GATS) (Section 11.3.3.3) and the Agreement on Trade-Related Aspects of Intellectual Property Rights (TRIPS) (Section 11.3.3.4).

11.3.3.2 The 1994 General Agreement on Tariffs and Trade

The GATT's primary purpose is to contribute to the liberalization of trade by substantially reducing tariffs and other barriers to trade and eliminating 'discriminatory

---

[18] See also arts 9–10 of the International Law Commission's 1978 Draft Articles on Most-Favoured-Nation Clauses.

[19] See also *Differential and More Favourable Treatment: Reciprocity and Fuller Participation of Developing Countries*, Decision of 28 November 1979 (L/4903).

[20] As noted in Chapter 10, the transfer of technology from the developed to the developing states also plays an important role in conventions on environmental protection, such as in the UN Convention on Biological Diversity (CBD).

[21] WTO Agreement art. II:2.

treatment in international commerce'.[22] To that end, it is supplemented by a number of agreements on specific topics, such as agriculture, the application of sanitary and phytosanitary measures, technical barriers to trade, anti-dumping, subsidies and safeguards.[23] Two initial points are worth noting. First, the GATT does not prohibit tariffs on imported goods as such. Article II merely obliges states to commit to certain 'tariff ceilings' on imported goods as well as to only decrease—and not increase— the tariffs in the future. Secondly, the GATT seeks to ensure that tariffs are the *only* restrictions on trade employed by states and quantitative restrictions, such as quotas, are generally prohibited.[24]

As a legal instrument, the GATT is based on the principle of non-discrimination and the principle of most-favoured-nation (MFN). Thus, article 1(1) of the 1994 GATT specifies:

> With respect to customs duties and charges of any kind imposed on or in connection with importation or exportation or imposed on the international transfer of payments for imports or exports, and with respect to the method of levying such duties and charges, and with respect to all rules and formalities in connection with importation and export- ation, and with respect to all matters referred to in paragraphs 2 and 4 of Article III, any advantage, favour, privilege or immunity granted by any contracting party to any product originating in or destined for any other country shall be accorded immediately and un- conditionally to the like product originating in or destined for the territories of all other contracting parties.

The principles of national treatment also form an integral part of the GATT. This is reflected in article III. For example, according to the first part of article III:4:

> The products of the territory of any contracting party imported into the territory of any other contracting party shall be accorded treatment no less favourable than that accorded to like products of national origin in respect of all laws, regulations and requirements affecting their internal sale, offering for sale, purchase, transportation, distribution or use.[25]

Article III:2 prohibits discriminatory 'internal taxes or other internal charges of any kind in excess of those applied, directly or indirectly, to like domestic products'. In practice, of course, it may be difficult to determine if an imported and a domestic products are 'like'.[26] As noted previously, the purpose of the requirements of national

---

[22] GATT Preamble.   [23] See Annex 1A to the WTO Agreement.

[24] See GATT art. XI(1). Exceptions may be applied to certain imports of agricultural or fisheries prod- ucts, see art. XI(2)(c). See also art. XII(1) relating to restrictions due to safeguards concerning external financial positions and balance of payments.

[25] See also art. III:1.

[26] See, inter alia, WTO, *Philippines: Taxes on Distilled Spirits—Report of the Appellate Body*, WT/DS396/ AB/R; WT/DS403/AB/R, 21 December 2011, see para. 125, and WTO, *European Communities: Measures Affecting Asbestos and Asbestos-Containing Products—Report of the Appellate Body*, WT/DS135/AB/R, para. 99. See also the discussion in Matthias Herdegen, *Principles of International Economic Law* (Oxford University Press, 2013) 198–203 and 214–218.

treatment is to eliminate all forms of protectionist regulations and practices and secure equal market access for imported and domestic products.[27]

Certain *exceptions* to the MFN and national treatment principles exist. For one
thing, as we shall return to later, the MFN principle does not apply to customs unions
and free-trade areas, such as the EU.[28] Exceptions also exist for developing states.[29]
Article XX stipulates that a state may be entitled to adopt measures that deviate from
its obligations under the GATT if they fulfil certain aims, such as the protection of
public morals or human, animal or plant life or health, if they are adopted to ensure
compliance with laws that protect patents, trademarks and copyrights, or if they are
essential to the acquisition or distribution of products in general or local short supply.
Trade restricting measures must not constitute a means of arbitrary or unjustifiable
discrimination between states where the same conditions prevail or constitute a disguised restriction on international trade.[30] In addition, article XXI authorizes states
to make certain security-related exceptions to their GATT obligations and under article XIX a state may take 'emergency action on imports of particular products' if 'as a
result of unforeseen developments ... any product is being imported into the territory
of that contracting party in such increased quantities and under such conditions as
to cause or threaten serious injury to domestic producers in that territory of like or
directly competitive products'.[31] Agreement on the application and implementation of
safeguard measures was reached at the Uruguay Round of negotiations.[32]

11.3.3.3 The General Agreement on Trade in Services

Until the Uruguay Round of negotiations, the GATT regime only dealt with goods
and not the increasingly important area of trade in services. This changed with the
adoption of the General Agreement on Trade in Services (GATS). The Agreement covers all forms of measures affecting trade in services and all sectors, with the exclusion
of services 'supplied in the exercise of governmental authority'.[33] Like the GATT, the
GATS incorporates the MFN principle,[34] but it also goes further by prohibiting certain non-discriminatory but restrictive measures.[35] The obligation of national treatment, on the other hand, only applies when a state has made special commitments in
a certain sector.[36] A key feature of the Agreement is the prohibition of quantitative
restrictions.[37] Like the GATT, the GATS lists a number of general and security-related
exceptions to the obligations of the Agreement, including references to the protection
of public morals or the maintenance of public order, the protection of human, animal
or plant life or health, the protection of the privacy of individuals etc.[38] All restrictions
must be 'necessary'. In the *US Gambling* case, the United Stated was found to be in
violation of the GATS for prohibiting gambling and betting services on the US market

---

[27] WTO, *Japan—Taxes on Alcoholic Beverages—AB-1996-2—Report of the Appellate Body*, WT/DS8/AB/R;
WT/DS10/AB/R; WT/DS11/AB/R, 4 October 1996, paras 16–18.
[28] See GATT art. XXIV.   [29] Ibid, Part IV (Trade and Development).
[30] See also Herdegen (n 26) 203–211.   [31] Art. XIX:1(a).
[32] See Agreement on Safeguards.   [33] GATS art. I:3(b).   [34] Art. II:1.   [35] Art. VI.
[36] See Part III, art. XVII.   [37] Art. XVI:2
[38] Art. XIV(a), (b) and (c)(ii). See also art. XIV*bis*.

from actors outside the United States because it had not demonstrated that the prohibition was necessary in order to protect public morals and maintain public order when it simultaneously permitted remote betting on horse racing.[39]

Special rules apply for telecommunication services and financial services.[40] With regard to the former, an annex stipulates that service suppliers must be 'accorded access to and use of public telecommunications transport networks and services on reasonable and nondiscriminatory terms and conditions'.[41]

11.3.3.4 The Agreement on Trade-Related Aspects of Intellectual Property Rights

The Agreement on Trade-Related Aspects of Intellectual Property Rights (TRIPS) introduces substantial protection of patents, trademarks and other forms of intellectual property rights. The Agreement generally provides for both national treatment and MFN treatment.[42] It covers trademarks,[43] geographical indications,[44] industrial designs,[45] layout designs[46] and undisclosed information.[47] TRIPS specifies that patents must be available in all fields of technology and only limited exceptions can be made.[48] The relationship between intellectual property rights for expensive pharmaceuticals and the provision of vital health care in developing states with limited financial resources has turned out to be a matter of contention.[49] Although the issue is not yet resolved, a few points are worth noting. First, the least developed states have been exempted for a certain period of time from some of the obligations under TRIPS.[50] Secondly, TRIPS may allow a state to issue compulsory licences when required.[51] Recently, controversy has also emerged in relation to patents for inventions in biotechnology, such as DNA.[52] The transfer of technology is a key component of TRIPS and it explicitly specifies that developed states shall 'provide incentives to enterprises and institutions in their territories for the purpose of promoting and encouraging technology transfer to least-developed country Members in order to enable them to create a sound and viable technological base'.[53]

In its practical application, TRIPS is supplemented by a range of other international treaties for the protection of intellectual property, including the 1883 Paris Convention for the Protection of Industrial Property, the 1886 Berne Convention for the Protection of Literary and Artistic Works and the 1952 Universal Copyright Convention.

---

[39] WTO, *United States: Measures Affecting the Cross-Border Supply of Gambling and Betting Services—Report of the Appellate Body*, WT/DS285/AB/R, 7 April 2005, para. 369.

[40] See Annex on Financial Services.   [41] See art. 5(a) of Annex on Telecommunications.

[42] See TRIPS arts 3 and 4.   [43] Arts 15–21.   [44] Arts 22–24.   [45] Arts 25–26.

[46] Arts 35–38.   [47] Art. 39.

[48] Art. 27. Accepted exceptions are covered in art. 27(2) and (3).

[49] See also Declaration on the TRIPS Agreement and public health, WT/MIN(01)/DEC/2, 20 November 2001. For a discussion, see Madhavi Sunder, 'IP3' (2006) 59(2) *Stanford Law Review* 257–332.

[50] TRIPS art. 66(1) exempted the least-developed states from the relevant obligations of the Agreement for a period of ten years. See also Declaration on the TRIPS Agreement and public health (n 49). On 11 June 2013, the Council for Trade-Related Aspects of Intellectual Property Rights extended the transitions period until 1 July 2012, see *Decision of the Council for TRIPS of 11 June 2013*, Doc. IP/C/64.

[51] Art. 31.   [52] See the overview in Herdegen (n 26) 239–241.   [53] Art. 66(2).

11.3.4 **Dispute settlement in the WTO**

Another major achievement of the Uruguay Round of negotiations was the improvement of the existing procedure for dispute settlement with the establishment of a permanent Dispute Settlement Body (DSB).[54] In general, the new dispute settlement system applies to all WTO agreement. The DSB refers disputes to a Panel that make a binding decision through the adoption of a report and supervises proper implementation.[55] The Panels are composed of 'well-qualified governmental and/or non-governmental individuals'[56] selected in order to ensure the 'independence of the members, a sufficiently diverse background and a wide spectrum of experience'.[57] An Appellate Body reviews the Panel reports.[58] The procedure at the DSB is governed by fairly tight time limits in order to ensure both prompt dispute settlement and subsequent implementation.[59] If a measure by a member is found to breach a WTO obligation, it must withdraw the measure in question[60] and compliance must be achieved in a reasonable period of time.[61] If a state does not comply with the decision of the DSB, the DSB may authorize the complaining state to take certain proportionate countermeasures in cases of non-compliance.[62] The countermeasures should preferably be of a symmetrical nature but they can also be applied to other areas under the agreement that has been violated. In the *Beef Hormones* case, for example, the European Community (EC) was found to be in violation of its obligations under the WTO's SPS Agreement for imposing a ban on the sale or importation of meat and meat products from farm animals to which a number of specified hormones had been administered.[63] When the EC failed to comply with the decision, the DSB authorized the United States and Canada to implement certain countermeasures.[64] Although the EC later revised its regulations, the United States and Canada maintained that it had still not complied with the decision and upheld their countermeasures.[65] In 2013, the DSB also authorized Antigua and Barbuda to proceed with countermeasures in response to the lack of compliance by the United States in the *US Gambling* case.[66]

---

[54] See also WTO Agreement art. IV:3. The Understanding on Rules and Procedures Governing the Settlement of Disputes (DSU) constitutes Annex 2 to the WTO Agreement.

[55] DSU art. 2.1. See also arts 6, 11 and 21.　　　[56] Art. 8(1).　　　[57] Art. 8(2).　　　[58] Art. 17.

[59] See art. 20.　　　[60] Art. 3(7).　　　[61] Art. 21.

[62] Art. 22. In practice, states tend to comply, see Bruce Wilson, 'Compliance by WTO Members with Adverse WTO Dispute Settlement Rulings: The Record To Date' (2007) 10(2) *Journal of International Economic Law* 397–403.

[63] WTO, *European Communities—EC Measures Concerning Meat and Meat Products (Hormones)— Report of the Appellate Body*, WT/DS26/AB/R; WT/DS48/AB/R, 16 January 1998, para. 208.

[64] See WTO, *Decision by the Arbitrators, European Communities—Measures Concerning Meat and Meat Products (Hormones)*, WT/DS26/ARB, 12 July 1999, para. 84.

[65] WTO, *United States: Continued Suspension of Obligations of the EC—Hormones Dispute—Report of the Appellate Body*, WT/DS320/AB/R, 16 October 2008. For a discussion of the case, see Suzanne Bermann, 'EC-Hormones and the Case for an Express WTO Postretaliation Procedure' (2007) 107 *Columbia Law Review* 131–168. The prolonged dispute was brought to a close in May 2009 with an agreement that provided for a phased reduction of US sanctions and a gradual increase in the EU tariff quota for high-quality, hormone-free beef.

[66] See WTO, *Authorization to Retaliate Granted, United States: Measures Affecting the Cross-Border Supply of Gambling and Betting Services*, WT/DS285/AB/R, 28 January 2013.

11.3.5 **Regional economic cooperation**

The WTO encourages the regional integration of economic markets as a means of gradually eliminating barriers to international trade and investment,[67] and the GATT explicitly exempts the application of the MFN principle from customs unions and free-trade areas.[68] By far the most advanced form of regional economic integration is found in *the EU*. The EU was founded on a customs union without internal customs duties on imports and exports and a common external customs tariff.[69] The Single European Act created an internal market with free movement of goods, persons, services and capital to be established by 31 December 1992. Within that market, quantitative restrictions on both the import and export of goods as well as all 'measures having equivalent effect' are prohibited unless justified on the basis of an explicitly mentioned interest and applied in a non-discriminatory and proportionate manner.[70] Similar restrictions apply to services.[71] Over the years, the EU has developed common rules on competition and in the very politically sensitive area of agricultural policy and, as we will see in Section 11.4.5, in 1999 a single common currency—the euro— was introduced.

The *North American Free Trade Agreement* (NAFTA) was adopted in 1992 to establish a free trade area between the United States, Canada and Mexico. Among other things, NAFTA seeks to eliminate internal barriers to trade and facilitate the cross-border movement of goods and services, to promote conditions of fair competition and to increase investments in the member states.[72] In South America, *Mercado Común del Sur* (MERCOSUR) was created in 1991 by Argentina, Brazil, Paraguay and Uruguay to promote trade and the free movement of goods, people and currency.[73] Over time, it has developed into a tentative customs union. In 1996, Bolivia, Colombia, Ecuador and Peru created the *Andean Community of Nations* (CAN) on the basis of the 1969 Cartagena Agreement on Sub-Regional Integration (the Andean Pact). Although the Cartagena Agreement abolishes internal tariffs, CAN is not yet a proper customs union. In May 2008, the constitutive treaty of the *Union of South American Nations* (UNASUR) was signed in Brasilia with the aim of integrating the policies of MERCOSUR and CAN.[74] In Africa, the *Economic Community of West African States* (ECOWAS) was formed in 1975 as an ambitious customs union involving 15 West African states. In Asia, the most significant regional organization for the purposes of economic cooperation is the *Association of Southeast Asian Nations* (ASEAN).

---

[67] GATT art. XXIV:4. See also arts V and V*bis* of the GATS Agreement.

[68] See GATT art. XXIV.

[69] Treaty on the Functioning of the European Union (TFEU), art. 28(1).

[70] Ibid, art. 26(2). See also arts 34–36 and the seminal ECJ *Cassis de Dijon* case: Case 120/78 *Rewe-Zentral AG v Federal Monopoly Administration for Spirits* [1979] ECR 649.

[71] See TFEU arts 56–62. The free movement of workers is covered by arts 45–48, the right of establishment by arts 49–55 and capital and payments by arts 63–66.

[72] NAFTA art. 102.

[73] See also the 1994 Protocol of Ouro Preto. Venezuela joined in July 2012 and efforts to incorporate Bolivia were initiated in July 2015.

[74] Aside from the members of MERCOSUR and CAN, initial membership of UNASUR included Chile, Guyana and Suriname.

11.4 International monetary law

11.4.1 Introduction–the IMF

The *International Monetary Fund (IMF)* was established in order to introduce a monetary legal regime—overseen by an international organization of global reach—that would prevent a repetition of the interwar policies of competitive and manipulative devaluation of currencies.[75] In the 1920s and 1930s, when economies started to contract and unemployment began to increase, individual states resorted to a variety of measures, including devaluation, trade restrictions and subsidies, with a disastrous effect on the global economy and monetary stability. The primary purposes of the IMF are to promote international monetary cooperation, promote exchange stability and to make resources available to members with balance of payment difficulties. Today, it has 189 member states. The daily operations of the IMF are conducted by an *Executive Board* composed of 25 directors appointed by member states or groups of states. The Board is led by a *Managing Director* who serves in an independent capacity. The Managing Director has always been a European and, since July 2011, the position has been held by Christine Lagarde (France). The *Board of Governors* consists of one governor appointed by each member state who meet at least once a year.

The money in the IMF comes from the member states on the basis of a system of quotas. In practice, each member is assigned a quota based on its relative share of the world economy. The quota determines the state's maximum contribution to the financial resources of the Fund. The biggest quotas are held by the United States (16.5 per cent), China (6.1 per cent), Germany (5.3 per cent) and the UK and France (both hold 4.05 per cent). When joining the IMF, a state generally pays up to a quarter of its quota with widely accepted currencies (US dollars, euros, yen or pound sterling) and the remaining quota in its own currency. The quotas are revised at least every five years and in 2010 the IMF's members decided to double the Fund's resources as of January 2016.[76] The total value of the quotas is now around $650 billion. The Fund has additional pledges or committed resources of around the same amount and also has one of the largest gold reserves in the world. By March 2016, the Fund had committed $120 billion under existing lending arrangements. The biggest borrowers were Portugal, Greece, Ukraine and Ireland.[77] Since voting on both the Executive Board and the Board of Governors is based on the quota system, the most powerful states in the IMF are those which hold the largest quotas.

In this section, we will focus on the IMF's approach to exchange rate policy (Section 11.4.2) and lending arrangements, including the controversial issue of conditionality (Section 11.4.3). Brief attention will also be turned to the World Bank (Section 11.4.4) and the monetary system in the EU (Section 11.4.5).

---

[75] See Articles of Agreement of the International Monetary Fund, art. 1.

[76] See the Fourteenth General Review of Quotas.

[77] The International Monetary Fund, 'The IMF at a Glance: Factsheet' (23 March 2016), available at http://www.imf.org/external/np/exr/facts/glance.htm.

11.4.2 **Exchange rate policies**

In its original form, the 1944 IMF Agreement created a regime of fixed exchange rates by which each member state was obliged to set the value of its currency in relation to gold or the US dollar (that was tied to gold) and maintain that value.[78] The system lasted until 1971 when the United States abandoned the Gold Standard and exchange rates began to float freely.[79] However, states are still under obligations in relation to their exchange arrangements. Thus, under article IV(1) of the 1976 Amended Articles of Agreement, states shall:

(i) endeavor to direct its economic and financial policies toward the objective of fostering orderly economic growth with reasonable price stability, with due regard to its circumstances;

(ii) seek to promote stability by fostering orderly underlying economic and financial conditions and a monetary system that does not tend to produce erratic disruptions;

(iii) avoid manipulating exchange rates or the international monetary system in order to prevent effective balance of payments adjustment or to gain an unfair competitive advantage over other members; and

(iv) follow exchange policies compatible with the undertakings under this Section.

Of the obligations listed, requirement (iii)—to desist from exchange rate manipulation in order to gain an unfair competitive advantage—is the most specific. For many years, Western states, and in particular the United States, have accused China of violating the provision by intentionally keeping its currency, the yuan, at a low value in order to reap trade benefits.[80]

The IMF oversee compliance with article IV and states are obliged to provide the Fund with the necessary information. While the IMF conducts regular consultations with the member states and issues country reports,[81] it does not have any means of enforcing violations of article IV. In 2007, the Executive Board adopted a decision that provides additional guidance on the obligations of the member states and the surveillance regime.[82] The extent of the Fund's surveillance of the domestic affairs of its members has been a matter of contention. While article IV(3) stipulates that the IMF 'shall respect the domestic social and political policies of members' and shall 'pay due regard to the circumstances of members', the exact line between justified and unjustified surveillance is hard to distinguish.[83] In general terms, basic monetary and fiscal policies are appropriate objects of

---

[78] See art. IV of the original Articles of Agreement.

[79] Under the Amended Articles of the IMF Agreement, states can arrange their exchange rates as they choose. Some states, including a number of European states such as Denmark, decided to link their currencies to each other.

[80] See, inter alia, Wei Gu, 'Is Yuan Undervalued or Overvalued?', *Wall Street Journal* (11 August 2015), available at http://www.wsj.com/articles/yuan-devaluation-enters-debate-on-whether-currency-is-undervalued-1439307298.

[81] See art. IV(3).

[82] Bilateral Surveillance over Members' Policies Executive Board Decision, 15 June 2007.

[83] See the overview and discussion in Lowenfeld (n 5) 639–643. See also Herdegen (n 26) 443–444.

inquiry and comment by the IMF while detailed policy choices are for the state itself to make.[84]

11.4.3 Lending arrangements and the issue of 'conditionality'

One of the core functions of the IMF is to provide loans to states with acute balance of payment problems. In fact, to many states the IMF serves as a 'lender of last resort'.[85] Drawing funds is governed by article V of the Amended Articles of the IMF. Under section 3 of that article, a state is entitled to funds under the following conditions:

(i)   the member's use of the general resources of the Fund would be in accordance with the provisions of this Agreement and the policies adopted under them;

(ii) the member represents that it has a need to make the purchase because of its balance of payments or its reserve position or developments in its reserves;

(iii) the proposed purchase would be a reserve tranche purchase, or would not cause the Fund's holdings of the purchasing member's currency to exceed two hundred percent of its quota;

(iv) the Fund has not previously declared … that the member desiring to purchase is ineligible to use the general resources of the Fund.

Conditions (i) refers to the highly politicized principle of so-called 'conditionality' where issuing a loan to a member state is subject to conditions set by the IMF. Unlike some of the other conditions,[86] conditionality cannot be waived. In fact, article V(3)(c) explicitly states that the IMF shall examine if a request for a loan 'would be consistent with the provisions of this Agreement and the policies adopted under them'.

In practice, the IMF issues loans on the basis of a 'letter of intent' to the Executive Board that has been prepared by the lending state after consultation with the IMF. The purpose of the letter is to commit the lending state to adopt certain economic and financial policies and concrete programmes for addressing its underlying economic problems. The content of a letter of intent is not legally binding but is instead tied to the IMF's political commitment to continue lending money to the state. Since its creation, the lending policies and practices of the IMF have evolved substantially as the Fund has sought to learn from its experience. The economic crises in states in South-East Asia and in Russia in the mid to late 1990s, as well as the collapse of the economy in Argentina in the early 2000s, posed major challenges to the Fund's approach to conditionality.[87]

More recently, it has been the economic crisis in Greece that has tested the IMF and other international creditors. In October 2009, as the global economic crisis was still unfolding, Greece announced that its public deficit was higher than previously stated.[88] As a result, Greece was unable to borrow money on the financial markets and

---

[84] Lowenfeld (n 5) 640.   [85] Herdegen (n 26) 450.   [86] See art. V(4).

[87] For a historical account, see Lowenfeld (n 5) 667–733.

[88] In 2008, the deficit was around 10 per cent and in 2009 the deficit was estimated to be roughly 15 per cent. An overview of Greek deficits is available at http://www.tradingeconomics.com/greece/government-budget.

quickly drifted towards bankruptcy. To assist Greece, a 'troika' consisting of the IMF, the European Central Bank (ECB) and the EU Commission provided Greece with the first of two 'bailout' programmes totalling €220 billion. True to the principle of conditionality, the bailouts were conditioned on tough austerity measures, including cuts in public spending, tax increases, as well as measures aimed at improving Greece's overall and more long-term economic conditions. On 30 June 2015, however, Greece became the first developed state to default on a payment to the IMF. At that time, its debt was estimated to be in the vicinity of an astounding €240 billion.[89]

The troika's approach and the general politics of 'austerity' have been heavily criticized for being counter-productive in getting the Greek economy back on track and for forcing the Greek government to impose overly severe conditions on the Greek population. Like Argentinean politicians in the early 2000, many Greek politicians protested against what they perceived to be the international financial institutions' unwarranted interference in the domestic affairs of their state. Defenders of austerity stress that institutions such as the IMF are not charitable organizations and that the money Greece received was provided by other states, including developing states, which expect to have their money returned. Defenders also argue that a number of the austerity measures should have been adopted many years earlier by the state itself, and they question why it required outside 'intervention' from institutions such as the IMF before the Greek government began to collect taxes in a modern and organized manner and to reform a pension system that allowed employees in the public sector to retire on taxpayer-funded pensions in their late 50s.

By mid-2016, the Greek economy was still in recession and unemployment remained at around 25 per cent.[90]

11.4.4 **The World Bank—and debt assistance to the poorest states**

The *International Bank for Reconstruction and Development*—also known as the World Bank was created alongside the IMF to reduce poverty by providing loans to developing countries for the purpose of reconstruction and development.[91] While it was the original intention that the IMF would render short- and medium-term aid to states with payment difficulties and the World Bank would provide longer-term assistance, this division of functions has become somewhat blurred in recent decades. Like the IMF, the World Bank has a board of 25 Executive Directors and an independent staff headed by a President. The latter has always been an American. The voting system is also similar to that used by the IMF in the sense that voting is allocated on the basis of shares. The five largest pools of shares belong to the United States, Japan, Germany, France and China. In recent years, processes have been initiated to

---

[89] Reuters, 'How Much Greece Owes to International Creditors' (28 June 2015), available at http://www.reuters.com/article/us-eurozone-greece-debt-factbox-idUSKCN0P80XW20150628 (accessed 30 July 2016).

[90] European Commission, 'Greece—Economic Outlook' (3 May 2016), http://ec.europa.eu/economy_finance/eu/countries/greece_en.htm (accessed 30 July 2016).

[91] See IBRD Articles of Agreement, art. 1.

increase the representation of developing states. In contrast to the IMF, the Bank does not receive its resources from the governments of states but primarily via the capital markets of industrial states.

The World Bank has adopted a number of initiatives and programmes aimed at assisting the poorest states in the world. In 1960, for example, the International Development Association (IDA) was created as a subsidiary of the World Bank to provide loans on very generous terms to the weakest and poorest of the developing states. In 1996, the IMF and the World Bank initiated a Heavily Indebted Poor Countries Initiative that provides extensive debt relief for poor countries that fulfil certain conditions.

The World Bank is not the only institutions to focus on providing financial assistance to poor countries. In 2005, for instance, the Group of Eight (G8) adopted a Multilateral Debt Relief Initiative. Mention should also be made of the so-called 'Paris Club'[92] and the 'London Club'.[93] While the former is composed of creditor states, the latter consists of commercial banks. Both 'clubs' negotiate sovereign debt restructuring for highly indebted countries.

11.4.5 The monetary system in the EU

Any discussion of the basic aspects of the international monetary system must include a brief overview of the monetary system in the EU. From the 1979 until 1992, members of the European Community (with the exception of the UK), were parties to the European Monetary System (EMS) and an Exchange Rate Mechanism (ERM) that ensured all currencies were fixed in relation to each other.[94] The system created reasonable stability in exchange rates and was a means to create greater convergence in the economics of the participating states. The EMS paved the way for the creation in the 1992 Treaty of Maastricht of a European Monetary Union (EMU) with a common currency and a single European Central Bank (ECB). In 1999, the euro was introduced in 11 of the EU member states.[95] The UK, Denmark and Sweden, however, decided to remain outside the EMU. The introduction of the euro in Greece was delayed until 2001 because its public deficit and debt did not fulfil the criteria for joining the EMU. The EU member states that did not join the EMU and the common currency became (optional) parties to an updated version of the ERM.[96]

After joining the common currency, states are no longer able to change their interest rates, devalue their currency or control the supply of money; all of which are now controlled by the ECB. So, in contrast to other states, an EU state with the euro cannot respond to an economic crisis by, for example, printing more money. Importantly, however, the EMU is based on exclusive individual liability in the sense that each

---

[92] See Lowenfeld (n 5) 756–760.   [93] Ibid and Herdegen (n 26) 465.
[94] See the overview in Lowenfeld (n 5) 772–781.
[95] See TFEU art. 128. For an overview, see Lowenfeld (n 5) 781–787.
[96] See Resolution of the European Council on the establishment of an exchange-rate mechanism in the third stage of economic and monetary union, Amsterdam, 16 June 1997.

member is responsible for its own financial commitments. The principle is also known as the 'no-bail out principle'.[97] To prevent the participating states from diverting too far from each other in their economic policies, they are bound by certain conditions relating to fiscal discipline and the avoidance of excessive public debt.[98] The 1998 Stability and Growth Pact (SGP) authorizes the imposition of sanctions on a state that exceeds certain limits relating to public deficit and debt.[99] In 2005, the requirements were relaxed.[100] As the debt crisis in states like Greece illustrate, however, the construction of a monetary union without centralized economic governance and with great disparity in economic growth and fiscal discipline between the members is far from flawless.

11.5 International investment law

11.5.1 Introduction

Foreign investments are a vital element in achieving sustainable economic growth and overall improvements in social conditions. As a general rule, states are free to decide whether they want to accept foreign investment in their territories, and they are also free to set their own conditions for admitting foreign investment. Once an investment has been permitted and established, however, international law provides protection to the investor. As the ICJ stated in *Barcelona Traction*, when 'a State admits into its territory foreign investments or foreign nationals, whether natural or juristic persons, it is bound to extend to them the protection of the law and assumes obligations concerning the treatment to be afforded them'.[101] In reality, the purpose of international investment law is to balance the sovereign rights of the host state to govern its own economic affairs with the legitimate rights of foreign investors. For political and ideological reasons, this balancing act has been an issue of ongoing contention and the regulation has not always been clear. The following discussion is limited to the question of expropriation of foreign investments (Section 11.5.2), treaties on investment protection (Section 11.5.3) and dispute settlement (Section 11.5.4).

11.5.2 Expropriation and protection of foreign investors under customary international law

Expropriation of foreign property is one of the few areas in international economic law that is governed by both treaties and customary law principles.[102] As a legal

---

[97] TFEU art. 125.   [98] Art. 126(1).

[99] See European Council Regulation Nos 1466/97 and 1467/97 and Resolution of the European Council on the Stability and Growth Pact, 17 June 1997. See also ECJ, Case C-27/04 *Commission of the European Union v Council of the European Union* [2004] ECR I-6649, paras 80–81 and 97.

[100] European Council Regulation No. 1055/2005 amending Regulation 1466/97, and European Council Regulation No. 1056/2005 amending Regulation 1467/97, 27 June 2005.

[101] *Barcelona Traction, Light and Power Co., Ltd*, Judgment [1970] ICJ Rep 3, para. 33.

[102] See also the discussion in Lowenfeld (n 5) 469–494. For a—generous—enumeration of customary law principles applicable to foreign investments, see Surya P. Subedi, 'International Investment Law' in

term, 'expropriation' generally refers to the taking by the state of private property for public purposes. The term 'nationalization' is used when the state takes control over entire sectors, such as the banking sector or oil sector, by statute or decree. The term 'property' includes alienable rights with a market value, such as title to real and movable property, intellectual property rights, claims to payment and stocks. While goodwill is included, it does not cover more volatile expectations.[103] As a legal concept, expropriation also covers instances where the property in question is subject to such severe legal restrictions that its economic benefits is essentially destroyed—*de facto* or *indirect* expropriation.[104] Expropriation is termed *creeping* when it consists of the gradual imposition of measures that destroy the economic benefit of the property. What is decisive is the *effect* of the governmental measures imposed on the property and the motives of the government are immaterial. Expropriation does not, therefore, require the state to obtain control of the property. General regulatory action, such as the introduction of new and tougher legislation in a certain sector, may in principle suffice. The relationship between environmental regulation and expropriation is controversial, however, and case law is not uniform.[105] The threshold is high, though, and expropriation requires that the investor is no longer in 'control of its business operation, or that the value of the business has been virtually annihilated'.[106]

Customary international law grants foreign investors a certain *minimum standard of protection*.[107] The actual content of the standard is not clear, though. A classic articulation is found in the 1926 *Neer* case where an arbitral tribunal stated that the standard protected against authorities that behaved 'in an outrageous way, in bad faith, in wilful neglect of their duties, or in a pronounced degree of improper action'.[108] In *Mondev International v United States*, the International Centre for Settlement of Investment Disputes (ICSID, on which see Section 11.5.4) noted that the minimum

---

Malcolm D. Evans (ed.), *International Law* (4th edn, Oxford University Press, 2014) 740–741. See also Lowenfeld (n 5) 586. Expropriation of property owned by the state's own nationals is governed by the national laws of the state; in practice, constitutional law. Expropriation may also be covered by provisions in human rights law conventions. In the European Convention on Human Rights, expropriation is governed by art. 1 of the First Protocol according to which expropriation must be 'in the public interest' and subject to due compensation. In practice, the European Court of Human Rights applies a principle of proportionality, see ECtHR, *James and Others v UK*, App. no. 8793/79, 21 February 1986. See also *Jahn and Others v Germany*, App. no. 46720/99, 22 January 2004.

[103] Herdegen (n 26) 360.

[104] *Starrett Housing Corp. v Islamic Republic of Iran* (1987 III) 16 Iran–USCTR 112, 154.

[105] Lowenfeld (n 5) 559–564. See e.g. ICSID, *Técnicas Medioambientales Tecmed SA v United Mexican States*, Case No. ARB (AF)/00/2, 29 May 2003, para. 116 and *S.D. Myers, Inc. v Government of Canada*, Partial Award, 13 November 2000, paras 281–286.

[106] ICSID, *Sempera Energy International v Argentine Republic*, Case No. ARB/02/16, para. 285.

[107] It should be noted, however, that some Latin American states applied the so-called 'Calvo Doctrine' according to which foreign investors were not entitled to any greater protection than that offered to the nationals of the home state.

[108] *L. F. H. Neer and Pauline Neer (USA) v United Mexican States* (1926) IV RIAA 60–66, para. 5.

standard today cannot 'be limited to the content of customary international law as recognized in arbitral decisions in the 1920s'.[109]

Customary international law allows a state to expropriate foreign property subject to certain conditions. The expropriation must serve public—and not private—purposes and it must be non-discriminatory. Therefore, once accepted, the foreign investments must benefit from the same protection against expropriation as investments made by nationals of the host state. In addition, expropriation is subject to compensation. The most politicized issue relates to the standard of compensation.[110] In essence, while Western states have generally stressed rigorous protection for investors and *full* compensation for expropriation,[111] developing states and communist states have been shown to have lowered their standards of compensation. Non-Western resistance to full compensation was particularly noticeable in the 1960s and 1970s in the calls for a 'New International Economic Order'. For example, the 1962 Resolution 1803 on Permanent Sovereignty over Natural Resources calls not for 'full' but merely 'appropriate' compensations in the event of nationalization and expropriation.[112] The same—ambivalent—wording was inserted in the 1974 Charter of Economic Rights and Duties of States.[113] In recent decades, however, states are generally in agreement that expropriation triggers full compensation. In part, this is due to the collapse of communism after the end of the Cold War and the realization in the developing world that uncertainty about compensation has a negative impact on a state's ability to attract much needed foreign investment. As we shall see in the next section, just and full compensation is also the general standard adopted in the large number of bilateral investment treaties concluded over the years. International jurisprudence is by and large supportive of the standard of full compensation. In the *Factory at Chorzów* case, for example, the Permanent Court of International Justice (PCIJ) had in 1928 already stated that reparation for unlawful compensation 'must, as far as possible, wipe out all the consequences of the illegal act and re-establish the situation which would have existed if that act had not been committed'.[114] The rich jurisprudence of the Iran–US Claims Tribunal relating to Iran's expropriation of US assets after the 1979 revolution also supports full compensation.[115]

---

[109] ICSID, *Mondev International Ltd v United States*, Case No. ARB(AF)/99, 11 October 2002, para. 123. See also the debate in Herdegen (n 26) 395–403.

[110] For an overview, see Lowenfeld (n 5) 469–494.

[111] See e.g. the so-called 'Hull Formula' named after Cordell Hull, US Secretary of State and the overview in Lowenfeld (n 5) 475–481.

[112] GA Res. 1803 (XVII) Permanent Sovereignty over Natural Resources (14 December 1962) and GA Res. 3281 (XXIX), para. 4.

[113] Charter of Economic Rights and Duties of States, 12 December 1974, para. 2(2)(c).

[114] *Factory at Chorzów*, 1928, PCIJ, Series A, No. 17, 47. See also *Norwegian Shipowners' Claims (Norway v United States)* (1922) I RIAA 307, 338.

[115] See, inter alia, *American International Group, Inc. v Islamic Republic of Iran* (1983 III) 4 Iran–USCTR 96, see 105ff and *Sola Tiles Inc. v Islamic Republic of Iran* (1987 I) 14 Iran–USCTR 223, 234ff. For an overview, see Lowenfeld (n 5) 541–554. For a thorough account, see George H. Aldrich, *The Jurisprudence of the Iran-United States Claims Tribunal* (Oxford University Press, 1996).

In practice, full compensation refers to the *market value of the asset* in question. In *Starrett Housing Corp. v Islamic Republic of Iran*, the Iran–US Claims Tribunal determined that the concept of market value should be determined on the basis of the price a 'willing buyer would pay to a willing seller in circumstances in which each had good information, each desired to maximize his financial gain, and neither was under duress or threat'.[116]

11.5.3 Treaties on investment protection

A *bilateral investment treaty* (BIT) is concluded between two states in order to introduce clear safeguards and guarantees under international law to foreign investors. As such, a BIT complements the level of protection offered to the foreign investment by the national laws of the host state. Germany was the first state to conclude BITs with developing states but the practice quickly spread and, by July 2016, UNCTAD had registered 2,954 such treaties.[117] While the content of individual BITs differs, they generally follow a fairly standardized format and structure. In practice, the treaties seek to offer as many incentives as possible to foreign investors and these are reflected in the level of protection. The concept of an 'investment' is generally defined as broadly as possible in order to attract all possible forms of foreign investment.

The standard BIT contains the following elements. First, BITs generally offer '*fair and equitable treatment*' as well as '*full protection and security*'. In practice, this is translated not only into protection from discrimination with regard to access to courts and administrative bodies and for taxes and other regulations but also into a certain international standard of protection even in the absence of discrimination. 'Security' refers primarily to physical protection from attacks by not just the government but also various non-state actors, such as rebel groups.[118] In practice, it is a due diligence obligation. Secondly, BITs regulate *expropriation*, including *de facto* expropriation. In general, expropriation is permitted as long as it is carried out for public purposes, is non-discriminatory, accords with principles of due process and is accompanied by payment of compensation, usually of a 'prompt, adequate and effective' nature. The latter refers to full compensation according to the market value of the property, the effect of which should be to put the investor in a position similar to that which would have existed had the expropriation or breach not taken place. Thirdly, as we will see in Section 11.5.4, BITs generally also make provisions for dispute settlement in the event of a dispute between the investor and the host state. In cases where the treaty provides for arbitration pursuant to ICSID, it serves as consent to the exercise of jurisdiction by ICSID.

Many investment treaties also contain provisions on extraordinary circumstances, including severe economic crises. Protection of foreign investments in times

---

[116] *Starrett Housing Corporation* (n 104) 201. See also Lowenfeld (n 5) 550–552.

[117] See the overview at http://investmentpolicyhub.unctad.org/IIA (accessed 30 July 2016).

[118] ICSID, *Asian Agricultural Products Ltd v Republic of Sri Lanka*, Case No. ARB/87/3, 27 June 1990.

of economic crises became a contentious issue in connection with Argentina's economic collapse in 2000–2003.[119] After Argentina had defaulted on its foreign debt and adopted a range of controversial 'emergency' financial measures (including abandoning a policy where the local peso was tied one-to-one with the US dollar and also freezing US dollar deposits), many foreign investors brought cases against Argentina before ICSID alleging violation of the BITs and the principle of fair and equitable treatment. Argentina, for its part, defended some of its policies on the ground of the existent financial emergency that left it with no other choice.

ICSID tribunals did not agree on whether Argentina could invoke necessity as a ground for precluding the wrongfulness of the acts, either on the basis of customary international law or pursuant to provisions in the BITs. In *LG&E v Argentine Republic*, the tribunal found in favour of Argentina,[120] but other tribunals reached opposite results. The latter found that Argentina had not proved that it did not have other options and that it contributed to the situation that gave rise to the state of necessity.[121]

ICSID case law illustrates that investments secured through corruption are not protected.[122] Protection may also be absent in other instances where an investment does not conform with the laws of the host state. This, however, will probably depend on the particular circumstances of the case, including the gravity of the infringement.[123]

Although BITs have been the primary instrument for the regulation and protection of foreign investments, a number of *regional investment treaties* have also been concluded. Within the EU, investments between member states are protected by the freedom of establishment and the free movement of capital as well as by the fundamental rights protection in EU law. Since all member states of the EU are also parties to the European Convention on Human Rights, investment additionally benefits from protection under the Convention. The 1952 Protocol to the Convention protects the right to property and stipulates that every 'natural or legal person is entitled to the peaceful enjoyment of his possessions'.[124] Here, expropriation must be 'in the public interest' and duly compensated.[125] Foreign investors benefit from extensive enforcement mechanisms, such as the Court of Justice for the European Union and

---

[119] See the overview in Lowenfeld (n 5) 577–583. See also Alberto Alvarez-Jiménez, 'Foreign Investment Protection and Regulatory Failures as States' Contribution to the State of Necessity under Customary International Law' (2010) 27(2) *Journal of International Arbitration* 141–177.

[120] ICSID, *LG&E Energy Corp., LG&E Capital Corp., and LG&E International, Inc. v Argentine Republic*, Case No. ARB/02/1, 25 July 2007, para. 238. For support in the literature, see Lowenfeld (n 5) 581–582.

[121] See ICSID, *CMS Gas Transmissions Co. v Argentine Republic*, Case No. ARB/01/8, 12 May 2005, paras 354–355. See also ICSID, *Sempera Energy International v Argentine Republic*, Case No. ARB/02/16, paras 351–354. In the latter case, the Tribunal found that the conditions for necessity in the BIT were identical to those found in customary international law, see para. 388. For an overview, see also Herdegen (n 26) 467–472. It bears noting that the investors generally also claimed that their investments had been expropriated. This was, however, rejected by all tribunals.

[122] ICSID, *World Duty Free Co. Ltd v Republic of Kenya*, Case No. ARB/00/7, 4 October 2006, para. 157.

[123] ICSID, *Fraport AG Frankfurt Airport Services Worldwide v Republic of the Philippines*, Case No. ARB/03/25, 16 August 2007, para. 402. See also *Tokios Tokeles v Ukraine*, Case No. ARB/02/18, Decision on Jurisdiction, 29 April 2004, para. 182.

[124] Art. 1.   [125] ECtHR, *James and Others* (n 102) See also *Jahn and Others* (n 102).

the European Court of Human Rights. The EU is also expected to play an increasing role in relation to international investments with non-EU states. The Treaty of Lisbon stipulates that the EU holds exclusive competence to conclude agreements on foreign investment.[126] The practical effects of the 'transfer' of competence on matters of international investments to the EU are currently not clear.

NAFTA also covers investment protection and has its own investment dispute mechanism. Mention should be made too of the 1994 Energy Charter Treaty (ECT) that seeks to enhance energy cooperation and promote energy security by operating open and competitive energy markets. It has 54 members, including the EU and Euratom. The ECT primarily offers protection to foreign investment on the basis of the principles of national treatment and MFN status.

In recent years, dissatisfaction with the existing investment regime has spread and a growing number of states have criticized the system for a lack of respect for concerns associated with development and sustainable development. As a result, some states have decided to disengage with the investment regime while others have made adjustments in order to address specific concerns.[127] Notably, calls have been made for more systematic reforms that will comprehensively address the system's alleged challenges.[128]

11.5.4 **Settlement of investment disputes**

There are a number of avenues for arbitration in investment disputes and the BITs generally provide a number of options. The primary international dispute settlement organ in investment disputes is the *International Centre for Settlement of Investment Disputes* (ICSID) based in Washington DC. It was created pursuant to the 1965 Convention on the Settlement of Investment Disputes between States and Nationals of Other States. ICSID is competent to hear a case if the state party to the dispute and the home state of the investor are contracting parties and the parties to the dispute have consented to submit the dispute to ICSID.[129] Jurisdiction covers 'any legal dispute' arising directly out of an investment dispute.[130] The decisions ('awards') are binding on the parties and generally not subject to an appeal procedure.[131] They are also directly enforceable. The arguably most important ICSID decision to date was *Abaclat v Argentine Republic* where the arbitral tribunal found that it had jurisdiction to deal with claims by around 60,000 Italian nationals in a case brought against Argentina after its financial collapse and debt restructuring.[132] Alternatives to ICSID include arbitration under a legal regime created under the auspices of the UN Commission on International Trade Law (UNCITRAL). Dispute settlement is also available under the ECT.[133]

---

[126] TFEU art. 207(1).
[127] See also UNCTAD, 'Reform of the IIA Regime: Four Paths of Action and a Way Forward', June 2014, 4–5.
[128] Ibid.   [129] ICSID art. 25(1).   [130] Art. 25(1).   [131] Art. 53.
[132] ICSID, *Abaclat and Others v Argentine Republic*, Case No ARB/07/5, Award 2011.
[133] See ECT arts 26–27.

Summary

International economic law covers a vast range of rules and principles on economic conduct and relations between states, international organizations and private actors, both individuals and corporations. The most important areas are those that relate to international trade, international monetary law and international investment law. The primary institutions governing the global economic system are the WTO and the IMF. The purpose of the WTO is to further the liberalization of international trade and economic transactions through the reduction and elimination of tariffs and other barriers to trade. Its trade agreements are governed by a number of core principles, including the principle of non-discrimination. The IMF promotes international monetary cooperation and exchange stability and makes resources available to members with balance of payment difficulties. IMF loans are subject to certain conditions. Foreign investments—including the expropriation of foreign property—are governed by a number basic principles derived from both customary international law and treaty law. The purpose of the law is to find a balance between the sovereign rights of the host state to govern its own economic affairs with the legitimate rights of foreign investors. A host state may expropriate foreign property if it serves public purposes, is non-discriminatory and is subject to full compensation.

Recommended reading

For an excellent presentation of international economic law, see Andreas F. Lowenfeld, *International Economic Law* (2nd edn, Oxford University Press, 2008) and Matthias Herdegen, *Principles of International Economic Law* (Oxford University Press, 2013).

An introduction to investment law is also available in Surya P. Subedi, 'International Investment Law' in Malcolm D. Evans (ed.), *International Law* (4th edn, Oxford University Press, 2014) 727.

Politics play a major role in international economic law. See, inter alia, the contributions in Tomer Broude et al., *The Politics of International Economic Law* (Cambridge University Press, 2011).

For a discussion of the New International Economic Order, see Robert W. Cox, 'Ideologies and the New International Economic Order: Reflections on Some Recent Literature' (1979) 33(2) *International Organization* 257.

On the politics of economic law and the Global Justice Movement, see Marc Doucet, *Global Justice and Democracy: The Anti-Globalisation Movement* (Routledge, 2010).

For a thorough account of the jurisprudence of the Iran–US Claims Tribunal, see George H. Aldrich, *The Jurisprudence of the Iran-United States Claims Tribunal* (Oxford University Press, 1996).

A discussion of economic crises and necessity is available in Alberto Alvarez-Jiménez, 'Foreign Investment Protection and Regulatory Failures as States' Contribution to the State of Necessity under Customary International Law' (2010) 27(2) *Journal of International Arbitration* 141.

Questions for discussion

1. Can you think of some concrete examples where international economic law overlaps with other fields of public international law? What role do the Bretton Woods institutions play in the international economic system?

2. The international economic system is frequently the object of criticism. Can you give some examples?

3. What is the difference between the MFN principle and the principle of national treatment? Why is it necessary for the GATT to exempt the application of the MFN principle in the EU?

4. Why is the IMF vital to the maintenance of a stable international economic order?

5. In what way does the monetary system in the EU differ from the system created under the IMF?

6. Under what conditions does international law allow a host state to expropriate foreign property?

12

The peaceful settlement of disputes

CENTRAL ISSUES

1. This chapter examines the most important methods for the peaceful settlement of disputes in international society.

2. It introduces a number of non-adjudicatory settlement mechanisms and provides a brief overview of the role played by the UN.

3. The chapter also discusses the adjudicatory means of settling disputes, including international arbitration.

4. It discusses the competences and powers of the International Court of Justice and analyses issues of access to the Court and the Court's jurisdiction in contentious cases. It also discusses the power of the Court to issue provisional measures, the effects of the Court's decisions and the relationship between the Court and the UN Security Council. In addition, the chapter discusses the Court's competence to issue advisory opinions.

12.1 Introduction

At its core, the purpose of international law is to provide the answers required to separate the powers of sovereign states and, to that end, help to avoid undue friction between states. The maintenance of international peace and stability through the peaceful settlement of disputes therefore occupies a central place in international law. In order to further the chances of maintaining peace and stability, the international system must be able to point adversaries to viable options that will assist them in de-escalating and hopefully resolving destabilizing disputes.

At the outset it is important to note that international law does not actually *oblige* states to settle their disputes and it is a well-known fact that disagreements between states may linger and simmer for years. States disagree with each other all the time and fairly persistent disagreements continue to exist on a number of important issues, such as drawing territorial boundaries or maritime zones. Denmark and Canada have, for example, agreed to disagree about entitlement to Hans Ø—an uninhabited piece of land situated in the middle of the Kennedy Canal in Nares Strait between Canada and Greenland.[1] What international law *does* require is that states find peaceful solutions to the disputes they do try to resolve. Article 2(3) of the UN Charter stipulates that members must resolve their disputes by 'peaceful means' so that 'international peace and security, and justice are not endangered'. Article 2(3) is closely tied to the prohibition on the threat or use of force contained in article 2(4) that we shall examine in more detail in Chapter 13.[2] The Charter also mandates that states seek a peaceful resolution to a dispute that is likely to endanger international peace and security.[3]

This chapter lists and discusses some of the more relevant methods for peaceful dispute settlement. To that end, there is merit in a conceptual distinction between those means of settlement that are of an adjudicatory nature and those that seek to solve disputes through other means. Not surprisingly, it is towards international legal adjudication, and in particular the role of the International Court of Justice (ICJ), that the majority of the attention in this chapter is aimed. We begin in Section 12.2 with a brief overview of diplomatic dispute settlement and some general remarks about the role played by the UN in this regard. Section 12.3 concerns international arbitration and Section 12.4 deals with the competences and powers of the ICJ. Section 12.5 provides an overview of a number of permanent international courts that have special jurisdiction.

12.2 Non-adjudicatory means of settling international disputes

There are many political and diplomatic ways to solve international disputes. Since states remain in control of the resolution process, diplomatic means are by far the most preferred by states. The most common means of resolving a dispute is for the parties to directly *negotiate* a suitable solution. States negotiate with each other all the time and there are no established procedures or firm practices for when and how negotiations must be conducted. In some areas, states commit themselves legally to initiate negotiations if a dispute arises. Members of the UN, for example, must 'seek a resolution by negotiation ... or other peaceful means of their own choice' if they are parties to a dispute the continuance of which may endanger international peace and security.[4] The term *'good offices'* is used when a third party—usually an entity that is deemed neutral and trustworthy by the parties—offers to facilitate and support potential efforts to enter into direct negotiations. A noteworthy example was Iceland's facilitation of the crucial 1986 Reykjavik Summit on US and Soviet arms reduction. 'Good offices' evolve into *mediation* when the third party assumes a more direct role in the negotiations and begins to suggest terms for potential settlement or offers solutions for compromise. In practice, of course, the line separating the two functions is a thin one. In many cases, the introduction of a powerful and/or trusted state into

---

[1] The Kingdom of Denmark includes the island of Greenland and the Faroe Islands.
[2] See also the 1982 Manila Declaration on the Peaceful Settlement of International Disputes, GA Res. 37/10 (15 November 1982).
[3] UN Charter art. 33.   [4] Ibid.

difficult negotiations will facilitate a dispute settlement process. This is particularly the case when the third party is also interested in peaceful settlement of the dispute. A well-known example is the role played by the United States in the efforts—often frustrated—to find a peaceful solution to the dispute between Israel and the Palestinians in the Middle East. In practice, mediation is highly relevant to successful conflict resolution and it was, for instance, the tough and firm intervention of the United States that led to the conclusion of the 1995 Dayton Agreement that brought an end to the civil war in Bosnia. As a mode of settling disputes, mediation is not governed by any specific rules or principles and the mediator is generally free to approach the negotiations as he or she prefers. But successful mediation usually requires the mediator to play an active role and seek to identify the underlying interests of the parties to the dispute. In many cases, it requires both common and separate—often confidential—meetings with the parties. The solutions offered by a mediator are not binding.

When parties are in disagreement about the factual circumstances surrounding a dispute, they may appoint an impartial *commission of inquiry* tasked with ascertaining the relevant facts. In 1961, for example, a commission of inquiry was established by the UK and Denmark in relation to the so-called 'Red Crusader incident' that involved the arrest by a Danish frigate of a British vessel for illegal fishing in the waters off the Faroe Islands.[5] A commission of inquiry may also be established by an international organization or a supervisory organ in order to determine if a state has breached a relevant treaty obligation and additional steps may be warranted. The UN Human Rights Council, for example, often sets up commissions tasked with investigating potential human rights violations in individual states. In August 2011, for instance, the Council established an Independent International Commission of Inquiry on the Syrian Arab Republic to investigate alleged violations of international human rights since March 2011 in Syria.[6]

The term *conciliation* refers to the production of a report with non-legally binding recommendations by a third party trusted by the parties on the proper settlement of a dispute. The report of the conciliatory body will present all the relevant aspects of the dispute. The purpose of the report is not to determine who is wrong or right but merely to offer a tentative solution to the dispute. An example of successful conciliation was the 1981 conciliation between Iceland and Norway on the boundaries of the continental shelf between Iceland and Jan Mayen (Norway). The commission adopted a report with a set of recommendations that was accepted by both parties as the foundation for the subsequent negotiations that eventually led to an agreement.[7] As a potential form of dispute settlement, conciliation is increasing in importance and a number of conventions, in particular in international environmental law, explicitly list conciliation as a potential form of settlement. Examples include the 1992

---

[5] *Investigation of Certain Incidents affecting the British Trawler Red Crusader*, see (1962) XXIX RIAA 521.

[6] HRC Res. S-17/1 (22 August 2011). For some of the finding of the Commission, see '"They came to destroy": ISIS Crimes Against the Yazidis' (16 June 2016), http://www.ohchr.org/EN/NewsEvents/Pages/DisplayNews.aspx?NewsID=20113&LangID=E (accessed 20 August 2016).

[7] *Conciliation Commission on the Continental Shelf area between Iceland and Jan Mayen: Report and recommendations to the governments of Iceland and Norway*, Decision of June 1981 (1981) XXVII RIAA 1.

UN Convention on Biological Diversity[8] and the 1998 Rotterdam Convention on the Prior Informed Consent Procedure for Certain Hazardous Chemicals and Pesticides in International Trade.[9] Mention should also be made of the 1980 conciliatory rules of the UN Commission on International Trade Law (UNCITRAL) for the purpose of settling disputes on international commercial relations[10] and the adoption by the Permanent Court of Arbitration (PCA) of its own Optional Conciliation Rules and Optional Rules for Conciliation of Disputes Relating to Natural Resources and/ or the Environment. Both sets of rules are based on the UNCITRAL Conciliation Rules.[11] Conciliation is also offered in the framework of the International Centre for Settlement of Investment Disputes (ICSID).

The different means of dispute settlement are particularly well developed within the *UN*. Apart from the possibility of adjudicatory settlement by the ICJ which we shall return to later, the most important dispute mechanisms involve the Security Council, the Secretary-General and the General Assembly all of which have roles to play in the efforts to settle disputes peacefully. The *Security Council* has primary responsibility for the maintenance of international peace and security and, to that end, possesses wide-ranging powers. As we will see in Chapter 13, the Council even has the authority under Chapter VII of the UN Charter to take enforcement measures if they are required 'to maintain or restore international peace and se-curity'.[12] Chapter IV of the Charter deals with the powers of the Council in relation to the pacific and therefore non-coercive settlement of disputes the continuance of which are 'likely to endanger the maintenance of international peace and se-curity'. According to article 33, the parties to such a dispute shall first seek a so-lution by means of their own choice (negotiation, mediation, arbitration etc.) but the Council may also 'call upon the parties to settle their disputes by such means'. Article 34 stipulates that the Council may investigate any dispute or situation 'which might lead to international friction or give rise to a dispute' and under art-icle 36 the Council may, at any stage, 'recommend appropriate procedures or meth-ods of adjustment', taking into consideration that legal disputes should generally be referred by the parties to the ICJ. Articles 37 and 38 specify that the parties shall refer the dispute to the Security Council if they fail to settle it themselves and that the Council may then make recommendations with a view to reaching a pacific settlement. In Resolution 242 in November 1967, for example, the Council made an infamous recommendation after the Six Day War on the settlement of the Israeli/ Palestinian dispute that included the withdrawal of Israeli armed forces from the occupied territories as well as acknowledgement of the sovereignty of all states in the area and their right to live in peace with secure and recognized boundaries free from threats or acts of force.[13] The recommendations made by the Council in accordance with Chapter VI are just that—recommendations—and they are there-fore not legally binding on the parties. If the Security Council determines that an

---

[8] See Annex II, Part 2.   [9] See Annex VI, B.   [10] GA Res. 35/52 (4 December 1980).
[11] See more at https://pca-cpa.org/en/services/mediation-conciliation/ (accessed 20 August 2016).
[12] Art. 42.   [13] SC Res. 242 (22 November 1967).

ongoing dispute constitutes a threat to the peace, it may adopt additional measures provided for in Chapter VII of the Charter and, unlike the recommendations under Chapter VI, decisions adopted under Chapter VII may be binding on the parties. We shall return to Chapter VII in Chapter 13 in the treatment of the regulation of the use of force.

The *UN General Assembly* also fulfils an important role in finding peaceful solutions to disputes. Since all members of the UN are represented in the Assembly, it offers a crucial institutional setting for all sorts of debates, negotiations and interstate dialogue. In addition, the Assembly may discuss and make recommendations on any issue within the scope of the UN Charter and article 14 explicitly stipulates that it may 'recommend measures for the peaceful adjustment of any situation ... which it deems likely impair the general welfare or friendly relations among nations'.[14] Two things must be noted in regard to the powers of the General Assembly, though. First, the Assembly is subordinate to the Security Council in the sense that it may not make any recommendation with regard to a 'dispute or situation' while the Security Council is 'exercising ... the functions assigned to it' in the Charter.[15] Secondly, unlike the Security Council, the Assembly does not have the authority to issue binding decisions or resolutions and states are therefore under no legal obligation to comply with its decisions and recommendations.

The *Secretary-General of the UN* plays an increasing role in the peaceful settlement of disputes. Among other things, the Secretary-General often offers his 'good offices' as a method of trying to pave the way for the negotiation of peaceful solutions to ongoing disputes.[16] According to article 99, the Secretary-General may bring any matter to the attention of the Security Council which 'in his opinion may threaten the maintenance of international peace and security'.

12.3 Arbitration

International arbitration is an adjudicatory method for resolving a dispute that has a long history in international law. In fact, it was the experiences and practices of arbitration that led to the creation of the Permanent Court of International Justice (PCIJ) in 1921. The modern history of international arbitration is generally traced back to the 1794 Jay Treaty between Britain and the United States and the establishment of mixed commissions for resolving, inter alia, a number of issues that arose in relation to the American War of Independence (1775–1783).[17] Another historical

---

[14] See also *Certain Expenses of the United Nations*, Advisory Opinion, 20 July 1962, 16.

[15] Art. 12(1).

[16] Thomas M. Franck, *Fairness in International Law and Institutions* (Oxford University Press, 1995) 173–217.

[17] Treaty of Amity, Commerce and Navigation between Great Britain and the United States, 19 November 1794. For a historical overview, see Cornelis G. Roelofsen, 'International Arbitration and Courts' in Bardo Fassbender and Anne Peters (eds), *The Oxford Handbook of the History of International Law* (Oxford University Press, 2012) 151–168.

example of a successful arbitration is the *Alabama* arbitration when a commission was created in order to resolve a range of US claims against Britain stemming from the American Civil War (1861–1865) as well as border issues with the newly created state of Canada.[18] In 1899, the first Hague Peace Conference adopted the Hague Convention for the Pacific Settlement of International Disputes that created the PCA, a still existing mechanism for the settlement of disputes between states, international organizations and private parties. The PCA has a secretariat and maintains a roster of potential judges who may be appointed by the parties to a dispute. It has rendered assistance to numerous important arbitral bodies, including two important arbitral bodies created in 2000 by Eritrea and Ethiopia after the conclusion of the armed conflict between the states.[19] International arbitration is not limited to disputes between states, however, and the term 'mixed arbitration' refers to the settlement of disputes between states on the one side and individuals or corporations on the other. A notable example of a mixed arbitration was the establishment of an Iran–US Claims Tribunal primarily tasked with issues relating to the nationalization of US property and assets after the 1979 revolution in Iran.

Adjudicatory dispute settlement is always based on the consent of the disputing parties and international arbitration is no exception. A number of conventions include provisions that stipulate that disputes about the interpretation of the convention may be solved by arbitration. An example is the 1982 UN Law of the Sea Convention (LOSC).[20] In practice, many disputes under the LOSC end up before arbitration. A recent very noteworthy example was the complicated maritime dispute between the Philippines and China concerning the latter's activities and controversial sovereign claims in the South China Sea. In a lengthy award, in July 2016 an arbitrational court ruled in favour of the Philippines.[21] Unfortunately, China has refused to accept the award.[22] When compared with the procedure before the ICJ (see Section 12.4), arbitration is generally a much more flexible and speedy method of adjudicatory dispute settlement. The parties to the arbitration have substantial influence over the judicial process, including the composition of the tribunal and the number and identity of the arbitrators. The parties may decide on the applicable legal sources and procedural rules and, if they so request, they may determine that the proceedings should be conducted confidentiality. The latter obviously makes arbitration a desirable dispute mechanism in politically sensitive disputes. It must also be noted, however, that arbitral proceedings may be quite costly for the parties. It addition, arbitration lacks the consistent practice offered by a permanent court, such as the ICJ. The judgments/final decisions—termed 'awards'—are final and will be binding on the parties to the dispute.

---

[18] Treaty of Washington, 8 May 1871.

[19] Agreement on Cessation of Hostilities between the Government of the Federal Democratic Republic of Ethiopia and the Government of the State of Eritrea, 18 June 2000.

[20] See UNCLOS art. 287(1) and Annex VII.

[21] *The Republic of the Philippines and the People's Republic of China*, Award, PCA Case No 2013-19, 12 July 2016.

[22] Jane Perlez, 'Tribunal Rejects Beijing's Claims in South China Sea', *New York Times* (12 July 2016).

12.4 The International Court of Justice

12.4.1 Introduction

The ICJ is the only court in international law that has a *general* jurisdiction to deal with interstate disputes, and as we see throughout this book, the Court has made notable contributions to the development of international law. The Court was established in 1945 as a principal organ of the UN and its Statute is attached to the UN Charter. All members of the UN are automatically parties to the ICJ Statute. The ICJ replaced the PCIJ that had been established in 1921 pursuant to article 14 of the 1919 Covenant of the League of Nations as the first permanent international tribunal with general jurisdiction. Between 1922 and 1940, the PCIJ dealt with 29 contentious interstate cases and rendered a total of 27 advisory opinions.[23]

The ICJ is based in The Hague in the Netherlands and is composed of 15 judges elected by the Security Council and the General Assembly for terms of nine years. The judges elect its President and Vice-President who sit for three-year terms.[24] In practice, most of the ICJ judges are men and it was not until the appointment of Rosalyn Higgins in 1995 that a female judge was introduced to the Court. The five permanent members of the Security Council each appoint a judge and the remainder (ten judges) are chosen with regard to a reasonable geographical distribution between geographical and political groups within the UN. The judges must be 'persons of high moral character, who possess the qualifications required in their respective countries for appointment to the highest judicial offices' as well as being representative of 'the main forms of civilization and of the principal legal systems of the world'.[25] The judges are independent and in principle elected without consideration of their nationality.[26] If, however, one of the parties to a dispute before the Court does not have a judge of its nationality on the Court, it may appoint an ad hoc judge who will sit on the bench in the case in question.[27] While the disputes that are brought to the Court are generally heard by all 15 regular members of the Court (and potentially one or two specially appointed ad hoc judges), the Court has since 1982 made use of an authority contained in article 26 of the Statute to form chambers of three or more judges for dealing with particular categories of case if the parties so request. In total, six such ad hoc chambers have been created, the first being a chamber of five judges in the *Gulf of Maine* case that concerned the delimitation of a maritime boundary between Canada and the United States.[28] At the time of writing, however, there are no active ad hoc chambers. In 1993, the Court created a Chamber for Environmental Matters but since no state ever sought to utilize it, the Court decided in 2006 to stop appointing judges to its bench.[29]

---

[23] For a thorough discussion of the PCIJ, see Ole Spiermann, *International Legal Argument in the Permanent Court of International Justice* (Cambridge University Press, 2005). All cases and opinions are available via the homepage of the ICJ, see http://www.icj-cij.org/pcij/?p1=9.

[24] Art. 21.   [25] See arts 2 and 9 respectively.   [26] Art. 2.   [27] Art. 31(2).

[28] *Delimitation of the Maritime Boundary in the Gulf of Maine Area*, Judgment [1984] ICJ Rep 246.

[29] http://www.icj-cij.org/court/index.php?p1=1&p2=4 (accessed 1 April 2016).

The purpose of the ICJ is to 'decide in accordance with international law such disputes as are submitted to it' and it is competent to deal with both contentious cases and issue advisory opinions on request by organs of the UN. Its judgments are binding on the parties and not subject to appeal. Decisions are made by majority vote and the judges may attach individual views/positions in the form of either a 'Separate' or 'Dissenting' Opinion to the decision. The legal sources available to the Court were discussed in Chapter 2.

The remainder of the chapter is devoted to a presentation of the competences of the ICJ. We begin with access to the Court in contentious cases (Section 12.4.2) and then discuss the role of consent to the jurisdiction of the Court (Section 12.4.3). We then examine the Court's competence to issue provisional measures (Section 12.4.4) and the legal effect of the Court's decisions (Section 12.4.5). Attention then briefly turns to the relationship between the Court and the Security Council (Section 12.4.6) before the final section provides an overview of the Court's competence to issue advisory opinions (Section 12.4.7).

12.4.2 Access to the Court in contentious cases

Article 34 of the ICJ Statute specifies that only states can be parties to a contentious case before the Court.[30] The issue of access to the Court is dealt with in article 35. For that reason, it is important to note that the question of access to the Court and that of the Court's jurisdiction over a particular dispute are two separate issues.[31] *Access* deals with the question of who may bring or be brought before the Court while *jurisdiction* concerns whether the Court has the power to settle a dispute that is brought before it (by parties with access). So although the Court will only have jurisdiction over a case if the parties to it have access to the Court, jurisdiction does not follow automatically from access. As we shall see in Section 12.4.3, for the Court to have jurisdiction over a dispute the parties involved must have given their consent. Logically, the question of access must be resolved prior to the issue of jurisdiction.

Article 35(1) specifies that the Court is open to the state parties to the Statute. Since the Statute is an integral part of the UN Charter to which the vast majority of states are party, article 35(1) therefore serves as the primary method for obtaining access to the Court. The almost universal membership of the UN makes it of limited relevance that article 93(2) provides that a state may become a party to the ICJ Statute without joining the UN. Article 35(2) is concerned with access to the Court for *other states* and stipulates that there are two ways non-state parties may gain access. First, the Security Council may provide a non-party state with access to the Court[32] and, although this option is no longer of any practical relevance, it was relied on in the *Corfu Channel* case in which Albania was not a member of the UN or a party to the ICJ Statute.[33]

---

[30] Art. 34(1).

[31] See also *Legality of Use of Force (Serbia and Montenegro v Belgium)*, Preliminary Objections, Judgment [2004] ICJ Rep 279, para. 36.

[32] See also SC Res. 9 (15 October 1946).

[33] *Corfu Channel (UK v Albania)*, Judgment on Preliminary Objection [1948] ICJ Rep 15.

Secondly, a non-party state may gain access to the Court on the basis of 'special provisions contained in treaties in force'. As we shall return to below, the ICJ has stated that this option only refers to treaties already in force when the Statute was adopted in October 1945.[34]

Although access is rarely a contentious issue, it was debated in relation to the disintegration of Yugoslavia in the 1990s. In the 2004 *Legality of Use of Force* case, the Court found that the former Federal Republic of Yugoslavia (FRY) could not bring a case against a number of NATO states for their use of force against Yugoslavian in the course of the 1999 'humanitarian intervention' because it did not have access to the Court when it filed the application in April 1999. The Court found that the FRY could not obtain access from article 35(1) because it was not considered a UN member state (and on that basis a party to the ICJ Statute) in the period from 1992 until 2000.[35] And it could not gain access pursuant to article 35(2) and the existence of a 'special provision' in a treaty because this only covered treaties already in force when the Statute entered into force on 24 October 1945.[36] The relevant treaty was the 1948 Genocide Convention[37] which did not enter into force until 12 January 1951.

The Court's conclusions in the *Legality of Use of Force* were, however, hard to reconcile with its earlier decisions concerning the disintegration and civil war in the FRY. In a 1996 decision in the *Genocide* case, the Court had found that the Genocide Convention could serve as the basis for jurisdiction in a case brought by Bosnia and Herzegovina against the FRY in relation to, among other things, the 1995 Srebrenica massacres.[38] When the Court was later confronted with its inconsistent practice in the *Genocide* case, it applied the principle of *rex judicata*— where a matter already resolved by a court cannot be raised again—and concluded that it was bound by its 1996 decision.[39] In 2008, the Court's practice concerning

---

[34] See also the discussion in Andreas Zimmermann, 'Article 35' in Andreas Zimmerman et al. (eds), *The Statute of the International Court of Justice: A Commentary* (2nd edn, Oxford University Press, 2012) 625–628.

[35] *Legality of Use of Force* (n 31) paras 79 and 91. The Court based its conclusion on the fact that Yugoslavia began to break up in the early 1990s and that both the Security Council and the General Assembly had found that the FRY/Serbia and Montenegro could not automatically continue the membership of the former Yugoslavian state that had ceased to exist, see paras 58–64. See SC Res. 757 (30 May 1992), SC Res. 777 (19 September 1992) and GA Res. 47/1 (22 September 1992). For a discussion, see Chester Brown, 'Access to International justice in the *Legality of Use of Force* Cases' (2005) 64(2) *Cambridge Law Journal* 267–271.

[36] *Legality of Use of Force* (n 31) paras 113–114. For a critique of the majority decisions, see Joint Declaration of Vice-President Ranjeva, Judges Guillaume, Higgins, Kooijmans, Al-Khasawneh, Buergenthal and Elaraby.

[37] See art. IX of the Convention on the Prevention and Punishment of the Crime of Genocide, 9 December 1948.

[38] *Application of the Convention on the Prevention and Punishment of the Crime of Genocide*, Preliminary Objections, Judgment [1996] ICJ Rep 595. See also *Application for Revision of the Judgment of 11 July 1996 on the Case concerning Application of the Convention on the Prevention and Punishment of the Crime of Genocide (Bosnia and Herzegovina v Yugoslavia), Preliminary Objections (Yugoslavia v Bosnia and Herzegovina)*, Judgment [2003] ICJ Rep 7.

[39] *Application of the Convention on the Prevention and Punishment of the Crime of Genocide (Bosnia and Herzegovina v Serbia and Montenegro)*, Judgment [2007] ICJ Rep 43, para. 140.

the FRY became even more confusing when it concluded that it had jurisdiction in a case brought by Croatia against the FRY even though the application was filed in July 1999.[40] This seemed to contradict the conclusion in the *Legality of Use of Force* case where the Court had found that the FRY should be considered a non-party state and therefore unable to bring a case before the Court pursuant to article 35(1) until 1 November 2000. The Court defended its zig-zag course by noting that it had earlier shown a certain degree of 'realism and flexibility' in its interpretations of the formal provisions of the Statute.[41] The Court's less than impressive practice in relation to the FRY had obvious implications for the latter: while it was denied the opportunity to bring other states before the ICJ, those states could bring the FRY before the ICJ.

12.4.3 Consent to jurisdiction in contentious cases

12.4.3.1 Introduction

Early thoughts about granting the Court universal compulsory jurisdiction quickly proved to be unrealistic and the Court's jurisdiction is therefore conditioned on the *consent* of the parties to a dispute.[42] Thus, even though the parties may have access to the Court, it can only deal with a dispute if the parties involved have consented to the jurisdiction of the Court in the specific case or in a category of disputes of which the existing case is part.

12.4.3.2 Third states

The consensual nature of jurisdiction means that the Court will decline to exercise its jurisdiction in a dispute between two consenting states if it finds that the rights and obligations of a non-consenting third state form the subject matter of the dispute. The seminal case is the *Monetary Gold Removed from Rome in 1943* case in which the Court concluded that it could not decide a dispute between Italy and the UK in the absence of consent from Albania because the Court would have to determine if Albania had committed an international wrong against Italy and, on that basis, was obliged to pay compensation.[43] In the *East Timor* case, the Court also declined to exercise its

---

[40] *Application of the Convention on the Prevention and Punishment of the Crime of Genocide (Croatia v Serbia)*, Preliminary Objections, Judgment [2008] ICJ Rep 412.

[41] See paras 81–82 and the references to the judgments by the PCIJ in *Mavrommatis Palestine Concessions*, Judgment No. 2, 1924, PCIJ, Series A, No. 2, 34 and *Certain German Interests in Polish Upper Silesia*, Jurisdiction, Judgment No. 6, 1925, PCIJ, Series A, No. 6, 14. For a critique, see Yehuda Z. Blum, 'Consistently Inconsistent: The International Court of Justice and the Former Yugoslavia (*Croatia v Serbia*)' (2009) 103(2) *American Journal of International Law* 264–271. See also the overview and discussion in Fernando Lusa Bordin, 'Continuation of Membership in the United Nations Revisited: Lessons from Fifteen Years of Inconsistency in the Jurisprudence of the ICJ' (2001) 10 *Law and Practice of International Courts and Tribunals* 315–350.

[42] For a brief overview, see Stanimir A. Alexanderov, 'The Compulsory Jurisdiction of the International Court of Justice: How Compulsory Is It?' (2006) 5(1) *Chinese Journal of International Law* 29–38.

[43] *Case of the Monetary Gold Removed from Rome in 1943*, Preliminary Question, Judgment of 15 June 1954 [1954] ICJ Rep 19, 32.

jurisdiction in a case brought against Australia by Portugal because it would not be possible for the Court to decide on the Portuguese claims without having to rule, as a prerequisite, on the legality of Indonesia's actions. Indonesia had not given its consent to the Court's jurisdiction.[44] The Court will, however, only decline to exercise jurisdiction if the interest of the third party is central to the case, and there are many examples where it deals with disputes that could reasonably be said to have at least some effect on a non-consenting third state. In the *Frontier Dispute* case, for example, a chamber of the Court did not find that it should refrain from delimiting the frontier between Mali and Burkina Faso even though the delimitation was of interest to Niger that was not a party to the proceedings. The Court noted that its decisions are only binding on the parties to the dispute (see Section 12.4.5) and that Niger's rights could be considered at a later stage.[45]

Article 62 of the Statute stipulates that a state with a legal interest in a case to which it is not a party may request permission to intervene. Case law from the Court illustrates that the intervening state need not have a jurisdictional link to the case nor is the right to intervene conditioned on the acceptance of the parties to the dispute.[46]

12.4.3.3 The expression of consent

Article 36 of the ICJ Statute specifies that consent to the Court's jurisdiction may be expressed in a number of ways, including by: (1) an explicit agreement on jurisdiction; (2) a treaty; or (3) a declaration under an optional clause.[47] The first option—consent by explicit agreement—is also referred to as a *compromis* and relates to those instances where the parties to a dispute make an express agreement to submit it to the Court. Such voluntary referrals by the parties generally raise few jurisdictional problems. Consent by treaty is the second option and will be found to exist when states are party to a treaty that contains a special provision stipulating that all future disputes in relation to the application or interpretation of the treaty can be brought before the Court by either of the parties. Consent is therefore given *in advance* of the dispute. For a state that is not a party to the ICJ, a special provision can therefore serve as both a basis for access to the Court (under article 35(2)) and as a basis for jurisdiction. As we saw in the previous section, the 1948 Genocide Convention contains such a provision as does the 1984 Convention against Torture. Article 30(1) of the latter stipulates:

> Any dispute between two or more States Parties concerning the interpretation or application of this Convention which cannot be settled through negotiation shall, at the request

---

[44] *East Timor (Portugal v Australia)*, Judgment [1995] ICJ Rep 90, para. 35.

[45] *Frontier Dispute*, Judgment [1986] ICJ Rep 554, paras 46–50. See also *Certain Phosphate Lands in Nauru (Nauru v Australia)* [1992] ICJ Rep 240, para. 55. See also *Continental Shelf (Libyan Arab Jamahiriya v Malta)*, Judgment [1985] ICJ Rep 13, para. 21.

[46] *Land, Island and Maritime Frontier Dispute (El Salvador v Honduras)*, Application to Intervene, Judgment [1990] ICJ Rep 92, para. 100. See also *Land and Maritime Boundary between Cameroon and Nigeria (Cameroon v Nigeria: Equatorial Guinea intervening)*, Judgment [2002] ICJ Rep 303, para. 15.

[47] See also *Corfu Channel* (n 33) 27.

of one of them, be submitted to arbitration. If within six months from the date of the request for arbitration the Parties are unable to agree on the organization of the arbitration, any one of those Parties may refer the dispute to the International Court of Justice by request in conformity with the Statute of the Court.[48]

Advance consent may also be found in a treaty that serves to refer disputes to the Court. In the *Great Belt* case, for example, Finland initiated proceedings against Denmark partly on the basis of Danish acceptance of a 1958 Optional Protocol of Signature concerning the Compulsory Settlement of Disputes adopted in the field of the law of the sea.[49]

The third option is found in article 36(2) whereby a state may declare that it accepts the jurisdiction of the Court in relation to international legal disputes that may arise in the future with another state 'accepting the same obligation'. This is the so-called 'optional clause' system that enables states that are willing to accept the compulsory jurisdiction of the Court to do so. The practical operation of the optional clause system is complicated by the fact that many states have made reservations to their declarations under article 36.[50] In reality, therefore, the system consists of a detailed patchwork of various bilateral obligations.

The doctrine of *forum prorogatum* refers to the rare case where a state that has not consented to the jurisdiction of the Court at the time an application is filed against it but subsequently accepts the Court's jurisdiction. The Court has stressed that the state must show 'an unequivocal indication' of a wish to accept the Court's jurisdiction in a 'voluntary and indisputable' manner.[51] The mere fact that a state has participated in the proceedings of a case and has not refused to appear before the Court or to make submissions, cannot be interpreted as consent to the Court's jurisdiction over the merits.[52]

If the state against which the case is brought—the respondent state—disputes the fact that it has consented to the jurisdiction of the Court, it will raise the jurisdictional issue as a preliminary matter that must be dealt with by the Court before dealing with the merits of the dispute. Article 36(6) of the Statute stipulates that the Court has the final say in the event of a dispute about its jurisdiction. It has, in other words, the jurisdiction to rule on its own jurisdiction—also known as *compétence de la compétence* or *Kompetenz-Kompetenz*—and the decision by the Court is binding on the parties.

---

[48] See also *Questions relating to the Obligation to Prosecute or Extradite (Belgium v Senegal)*, Judgment [2002] ICJ Rep 422, para. 63. See also *LaGrand (Germany v United States)*, Provisional Measures, Order of 3 March 1999 [1999] ICJ Rep 9 and *Avena and Other Mexican Nationals (Mexico v United States)*, Provisional Measures, Order of 5 February 2003 [2003] ICJ Rep 77.

[49] See ICJ, *Passage Through the Great Belt (Finland v Denmark)*, Application Instituting Proceedings, 17 May 1991, paras 9–10.

[50] Art. 36(3).

[51] *Armed Activities on the Territory of the Congo (New Application: 2002) (Democratic Republic of the Congo v Rwanda)*, Jurisdiction and Admissibility, Judgment [2006] ICJ Rep 6, para. 21. See also *Corfu Channel* (n 33) 27.

[52] *Armed Activities* (n 51) para. 22.

12.4.4 The power of the ICJ to indicate provisional measures

Article 41 of the ICJ Statute stipulates that the Court has the 'power to indicate, if it considers that circumstances so require, any provisional measures which ought to be taken to preserve the respective rights of either party'. The purpose of such provisional or interim measures is to call a temporary halt to conduct that would make the final outcome of the case futile. It is, in other words, tied to notions of effective decision-making. The purpose of provisional measures is to 'preserve the respective rights of the parties pending the decision of the Court'.[53]

The Court's jurisprudence on provisional measures illustrates that its power to issue such measures is subject to a number of conditions. First of all, it must appear that the Court has jurisdiction in relation to the merits of the case. Importantly, though, the Court does not have to 'satisfy itself in a definitive manner' that it has jurisdiction and a prima facie determination is sufficient.[54] In the *Fisheries Jurisdiction Case (Germany v Iceland)*, the Court stated that it should not act under article 41 if the 'absence of jurisdiction on the merits is manifest'.[55]

The second requirement for issuing provisional measures is that the rights asserted by the requesting party 'are at least plausible'.[56] There must also be a link between the rights which form the substance of the merits of the case and the provisional measures sought.[57] The third requirement is an urgent need for action. There must be 'a real and imminent risk that irreparable prejudice will be caused to the rights in the dispute before the Court gives its final decision'.[58]

Issuing provisional measures has so far been an exceptional step for the Court. In the *Great Belt* case, the Court did not grant a request for provisional measures because

---

[53] *Anglo-Iranian Oil Co. Case*, Order of 5 July 1951 [1951] ICJ Rep 89, 93; *Fisheries Jurisdiction (Federal Republic of Germany v Iceland)*, Interim Protection, Order of 17 August 1972 [1972] ICJ Rep 30, para. 22, and *Questions relating to the Seizure and Detention of Certain Documents and Data (Timor-Leste v Australia)*, Provisional Measures, Order of 3 March 2014 [2014] ICJ Rep 147, para. 22.

[54] See, inter alia, *Questions relating to the Seizure and Detention of Certain Documents and Data* (n 53) para. 18; *Certain Activities Carried Out by Nicaragua in the Border Area (Costa Rica v Nicaragua)*, Provisional Measures, Order of 8 March 2011 [2011] ICJ Rep 6, para. 49. *Questions relating to the Obligation to Prosecute or Extradite (Belgium v Senegal)*, Provisional Measures, Order of 28 May 2009 [2009] ICJ Rep 139, para. 40.

[55] *Fisheries Jurisdiction (Federal Republic of Germany v Iceland)* (n 53) para. 16.

[56] *Questions relating to the Seizure and Detention of Certain Documents and Data (Timor-Leste v Australia)* (n 53) para. 22; *Construction of a Road in Costa Rica along the San Juan River (Nicaragua v Costa Rica); Certain Activities Carried Out by Nicaragua in the Border Area (Costa Rica v Nicaragua)*, Provisional Measures, Order of 13 December 2013 [2013] ICJ Rep 398, para. 15. See also *Certain Activities Carried Out by Nicaragua in the Border Area (Costa Rica v Nicaragua)*, Provisional Measures, Order of 8 March 2011 (n 54) para. 53; *Questions relating to the Obligation to Prosecute or Extradite (Belgium v Senegal)*, Provisional Measures, Order of 28 May 2009 (n 54) para. 57; *Pulp Mills on the River Uruguay (Argentina v Uruguay)*, Provisional Measures, Order of 13 July 2006 [2006] ICJ Rep 113, para. 57.

[57] *Questions relating to the Seizure and Detention of Certain Documents and Data (Timor-Leste v Australia)* (n 53) para. 23. *Certain Activities Carried Out by Nicaragua in the Border Area (Costa Rica v Nicaragua)*, Provisional Measures, Order of 13 December 2013 (n 56) para. 54.

[58] *Fisheries Jurisdiction (Federal Republic of Germany v Iceland)* (n 53) para. 22. See also *Questions relating to the Seizure and Detention of Certain Documents and Data (Timor-Leste v Australia)* (n 53) para. 32. *Certain Activities Carried Out by Nicaragua in the Border Area (Costa Rica v Nicaragua)*, Provisional Measures, Order of 13 December 2013 (n 56) para. 64.

the case would be settled by the time the construction of the bridge proved to be a hindrance to the passage of the Great Belt.[59] And in *Questions Relating to the Obligation to Prosecute or Extradite*, the Court did not find that it was necessary to ask Senegal to keep an individual wanted for extradition under control and surveillance because Senegal had on numerous occasions assured the Court that it would not allow the individual to leave the territory before the Court had given its final decision.[60] The Court has, however, granted requests for provisional measures in cases involving the potential infringement of basic human rights. In both the *LaGrand* and *Avena* cases, for example, the ICJ asked the United States to adopt precautionary measures in order to ensure that non-American nationals on death row were not executed before the Court was given the opportunity to determine if their rights under the Vienna Convention on Consular Rights had been violated.[61] With regard to the provisional measures to be adopted, article 75 of the Rules of the Court stipulates that the Court is not bound by the measures requested by the party to the dispute. This has also been noted by the Court in its case law.[62]

It has been the topic of much debate whether an order for provisional measures under article 41 is legally binding on the parties. The Court answered the question in the affirmative in the *LaGrand* case where it noted that the object and purpose of the Statute of the Court is to enable the ICJ to fulfil its function as an organ that settles international disputes by binding decisions, and that article 41 is meant to prevent the Court from being hampered in exercising that function.[63] The Court has upheld the binding effect of its provisional measures in subsequent cases.[64]

12.4.5 The effects of the Court's decisions

Article 60 of the ICJ Statute expresses the fundamental rule that a judgment by the Court is 'final and without appeal'. As we saw earlier, the same principle applies to the Court's decisions on jurisdiction and provisional measures. The Court's judgments

---

[59] See *Passage through the Great Belt (Finland v Denmark)*, Provisional Measures, Order of 29 July 1991 [1991] ICJ Rep 12, para. 27.

[60] *Questions relating to the Obligation to Prosecute or Extradite (Belgium v Senegal)*, Provisional Measures, Order of 28 May 2009 (n 54) paras 72–73. See also *Pulp Mills on the River Uruguay (Argentina v Uruguay)*, Provisional Measures, Order of 13 July 2006 [2006] ICJ Rep 113, paras 73–77 and *Pulp Mills on the River Uruguay (Argentina v Uruguay)*, Provisional Measures, Order of 23 January 2007 [2007] ICJ Rep 3, para. 50.

[61] *LaGrand*, Provisional Measures, Order of 3 March 1999 (n 48) para. 28 and *Avena*, Provisional Measures, Order of 5 February 2003 (n 48) para. 55.

[62] See, inter alia, *Certain Activities Carried Out by Nicaragua in the Border Area (Costa Rica v Nicaragua)*, Provisional Measures, Order of 8 March 2011 (n 54) para. 76 and *Request for Interpretation of the Judgment of 15 June 1962 in the Case concerning the Temple of Preah Vihear (Cambodia v Thailand)*, Provisional Measures, Order of 18 July 2011 [2011] ICJ Rep 537, para. 58.

[63] *LaGrand (Germany v United States)*, Judgment [2001] ICJ Rep 466, para. 102.

[64] See, inter alia, *Request for Interpretation of the Judgment of 31 March 2004 in the Case concerning Avena and Other Mexican Nationals (Mexico v United States)*, Provisional Measures, Order of 16 July 2008 [2008] ICJ Rep 311; *Request for Interpretation of the Judgment of 15 June 1962 in the Case concerning the Temple of Preah Vihear (Cambodia v Thailand)*, Provisional Measures, Order of 18 July 2011 [2011] ICJ Rep 537, para. 67; *Questions relating to the Seizure and Detention of Certain Documents and Data (Timor-Leste v Australia)* (n 53) para. 53.

are only binding on the parties to the dispute and cannot oblige third parties. Article 60 also provides that disputes about 'the meaning and scope of the judgment' will be settled by the Court on the request of one of the parties. Although it is not usual for parties to disagree on the meaning of the Court's judgments, requests for clarifications are not unheard of. In 2008, for example, Mexico requested the ICJ to interpret certain aspects of its 2004 judgment in the *Avena* case and to clarify the extent of the US obligations.[65] Article 61 provides for the possibility of a review of a judgment if the application for such a revision is based on the 'discovery of some fact of such a nature as to be a decisive factor' that was previously unknown to the Court.

According to article 94 of the UN Charter, members of the UN are obliged to comply with the decisions of the Court and, if a party does not comply, the other party may bring the matter before the UN Security Council which may, 'if it deems necessary, make recommendations or decide upon measures to be taken to give effect to the judgment'. Though this aspect of article 94(2) is seldom relied on, the Security Council did become involved after the ICJ's 2007 judgment in the *Genocide* case.[66]

12.4.6   The relationship between the Court and the Security Council

Since the UN Charter grants both the ICJ and the Security Council a role in efforts to resolve disputes peacefully, it is not rare for the two organs to become involved in the same dispute. Unlike the General Assembly, however, the Court is not subordinate to the Council and has consistently found that it is not bound to dismiss a case merely because the dispute is also being considered by the Council.[67] To that end, it is worth noting that the role and powers of the Court are different from those of the Council. While the Council (like the Assembly) has political functions, the Court only exercises functions of a judicial nature.[68] The functions of the two organs do not thus overlap but are complementary. In the *Lockerbie* case, Libya instituted proceedings against the UK and the United States and argued that a request by those states—subsequently endorsed by a binding resolution by the Security Council[69]—that Libya surrender to trial two nationals suspected of bombing a civilian airliner in December 1998 violated Libya's rights under the 1971 Convention for the Suppression of Unlawful Acts against the Safety of Civil Aviation. Libya also

---

[65] *Request for Interpretation of the Judgment of 31 March 2004 in the Case concerning Avena and Other Mexican Nationals (Mexico v United States)*, Judgment [2009] ICJ Rep 3. See also *Request for Interpretation of the Judgment of 15 June 1962 in the Case concerning the Temple of Preah Vihear (Cambodia v Thailand)*, Judgment [2013] ICJ Rep 281 and *Application for Revision and Interpretation of the Judgment of 24 February 1982 in the Case concerning the Continental Shelf (Tunisia v Libyan Arab Jamahiriya)*, Judgment [1985] ICJ Rep 192.

[66] S/PV.5675, pp. 3–17, S/PV.5697, p. 19.

[67] See, inter alia, *United States Diplomatic and Consular Staff in Tehran (United States v Iran)* [1980] ICJ Rep 3, para. 40 and *United States Diplomatic and Consular Staff in Tehran*, Judgment [1980] ICJ Rep 3, para. 37.

[68] See also the discussion in Vera Gowlland-Debbas, 'The Relationship between the International Court of Justice and the Security Council in the Light of the Lockerbie Case' (1994) 88(4) *American Journal of International Law* 643–677.

[69] SC Res. 748 (31 March 1992).

requested the Court to order provisional measures that would prevent the UK and the United States from taking any action that would coerce Libya into surrendering the two nationals.[70] Although the Court dismissed the applications for provisional measures, it did *not* do so because the Security Council had become involved and demanded the surrender of the individuals under its powers under Chapter VII of the Charter and the Court was therefore under an obligation to defer to the Council. Instead, the Court's decision derived from the fact that under article 103 of the UN Charter Libya's obligations under the Charter prevailed over obligations under other international agreements and, since the Council had ordered Libya to surrender its nationals, its obligation to comply with that order trumped its rights under the 1971 Convention.[71]

12.4.7 **Advisory opinions**

Apart from dealing with contentious cases, article 65(1) of the ICJ Statute provides that the Court may give an advisory opinion on 'any legal question' at the request of a body authorized to make such a request. According to article 96 of the UN Charter, the General Assembly and the Security Council may make requests for advisory opinions. The same goes for other organs and specialized agencies if so authorized by the General Assembly. In *Legality of the Use by a State of Nuclear Weapons in Armed Conflict*, the Court declined to issue an advisory opinion because the subject of the request did not fall within the 'scope of activities' of the requesting organ—the World Health Organization.[72] It subsequently found that the General Assembly was entitled to ask for a more or less similar request.[73] The purpose of an advisory opinion is not to settle a particular dispute but instead to assist the requesting organ in *its* efforts to deal with an issue. Opinions are not binding but since they express the view of the ICJ on a particular issue, they provide important contributions to identifying the status of international law.

Over the years, the Court has been asked for its legal opinion on a number of highly politically sensitive issues, including the situation in Namibia[74] and, in more recent times, the legality of the use of nuclear weapons,[75] the legality of Israel's construction of a wall in the occupied Palestinian territories[76] and the legality of Kosovo's declaration of independence.[77] While the Court does possess

---

[70] *Case Concerning Questions of Interpretation and Application of the 1971 Montreal Convention arising from the Aerial Incident at Lockerbie*, Request for the Indication of Provisional Measures, Order of 14 April 1992.

[71] Ibid, paras 42–43.

[72] *Legality of the Use by a State of Nuclear Weapons in Armed Conflict* [1996] ICJ Rep 61, paras 25–26.

[73] *Legality of the Use by a State of Nuclear Weapons* [1996] ICJ Rep 226.

[74] *Legal Consequences for States of the Continued Presence of South Africa in Namibia (South West Africa) notwithstanding Security Council Resolution 276 (1970)* [1971] ICJ Rep 16.

[75] *Legality of the Use by a State of Nuclear Weapons* (n 73).

[76] *Legal Consequences of the Construction of a Wall in Occupied Palestinian Territory* [2004] ICJ Rep 136.

[77] *Accordance with International Law of the Unilateral Declaration of Independence in respect of Kosovo*, Advisory Opinion of 22 July 2010 [2010] ICJ Rep 403.

a discretionary power to decline to give an advisory opinion, it has so far been unwilling to decline jurisdiction due to the political character of the situation.[78] The Court has expressly stated that the fact that a legal question also has political aspects 'does not deprive it of its character as a "legal question" and to "deprive the Court of a competence expressly conferred on it by its Statute".'[79] In practice, of course, it will often be situations where 'political considerations are prominent' that may be particularly useful for obtaining an advisory opinion.[80] The motives for requesting an opinion are irrelevant[81] and the Court has noted that a request for an advisory opinion should, in principle, 'not be refused'.[82] The decisive issue is whether the questions asked are legal questions in the sense that they are 'framed in terms of law and raises problems of international law'.[83] As it stated in the *Legality of the Use of Nuclear Weapons*, the Court 'may give an advisory opinion on any legal question, abstract or otherwise'.[84]

There is no requirement of consent from a state whose actions may be the object of the Court's attention. In *The Wall*, Israel argued that the Court should decline to exercise its jurisdiction because the request in practice related to a contentious matter between Israel and Palestine and that Israel had not consented to the Court's exercise of jurisdiction.[85] In refusing Israel's argument, the Court noted that its opinions are merely of an advisory nature, and thus without any binding force, and that its opinions are given not to states but to the requesting organ.[86] It also noted that the subject matter of the request (the legality of Israel's wall) could not be regarded 'as only a bilateral matter between Israel and Palestine' but was also 'deemed to be directly of concern to the United Nations' due to the powers and responsibilities of the UN in questions relating to international peace and security.[87]

With regard to the procedure before the Court, article 68 of the ICJ Statute provides that 'the exercise of its advisory functions ... shall be guided by the provisions ... which apply in contentious cases to the extent to which it recognized them to be applicable'. In applying article 68, the Court has been reluctant to grant states with a special interest the right to appoint a judge ad hoc.

---

[78] For PCIJ practice, see *Status of Eastern Carelia*, Advisory Opinion, 1923, PCIJ, Series B, No. 5.

[79] *Application for Review of Judgment No. 158 of the United Nations Administrative Tribunal*, Advisory Opinion [1973] ICJ Rep 172, para. 14. See also *Legality of the Use by a State of Nuclear Weapons* (n 73) para. 13, *The Wall* (n 76) para. 41 and *Accordance with the International Law of the Unilateral Declaration of Independence in respect of Kosovo*, Advisory Opinion of 22 July 2010 (n 77), para. 27.

[80] *Interpretation of the Agreement of 25 March 1951 between the WHO and Egypt* [1980] ICJ Rep 87, para. 33. See also *Legality of the Use of Nuclear Weapons* (n 73) para. 13.

[81] *Legality of the Use of Nuclear Weapons* (n 73) para. 13. See also *The Wall* (n 76) para. 41.

[82] *Interpretation of Peace Treaties with Bulgaria, Hungary and Romania, First Phase*, Advisory Opinion [1950] ICJ Rep 71. *Certain Expenses of the United Nations*, Advisory Opinion [1962] ICJ Rep 155. See also *Legality of the Use of Nuclear Weapons* (n 73) para. 14.

[83] *Western Sahara*, Advisory Opinion [1975] ICJ Rep 18, para. 15. See also *The Wall* (n 76) para. 37.

[84] *Legality of the Use of Nuclear Weapons* (n 73) para. 15.   [85] *The Wall* (n 76) para. 46.

[86] Ibid, para. 47.   [87] Ibid, para. 59.

12.5 International courts and tribunals with a specialized mandate

One of the most important developments in international in the last couple of decades has been the creation of a number of specialized international courts and tribunals that are competent to adjudicate legal disputes in a specific area of international law. A particularly important example is that of the *International Tribunal for the Law of the Sea* (ITLOS) that we visited in Chapter 8. As noted there, ITLOS was set up as a permanent judicial organ by the 1982 UN Convention for the Law of the Sea (LOSC) and it is competent to deal with contentious disputes as well as to issue advisory opinions. ITLOS has created a Seabed Disputes Chamber for disputes concerning activities in the deep seabed—the 'Area'. Decisions by ITLOS in contentious cases are final and binding on the parties and the tribunal may order provisional measures if required to preserve the rights of the parties or to prevent serious environmental harm.

Permanent adjudicatory dispute settlement mechanisms have also been established in international economic law. We saw in Chapter 11 that the Uruguay Round of trade negotiations paved the way for the creation of the *Dispute Settlement Body* (DSB).[88] Among other things, the DSB refers disputes to a Panel that makes binding decisions by report and supervises their proper implementation. There is also a procedure for review of reports by an Appellate Body. One of the noticeable features about the DSB is the emphasis on a speedy process and implementation of the decisions, if necessary pursuant to proportionate countermeasures in cases of non-compliance. A permanent mechanism for adjudicatory dispute settlement has also been created in international investment law with the establishment of ICSID. ICSID was also discussed in Chapter 11 and we saw there that it issues binding awards in certain disputes arising out of international investments.

In international criminal law, an important development was the introduction by the 1998 Rome Statute of a permanent *International Criminal Court* (ICC) based in The Hague in the Netherlands. As we shall see in more detail in Chapter 15, the ICC is meant to supplement national prosecutions of international crime and the Court is competent to criminally prosecute the most serious offences under international law. Among the notable features of the Court is the competence of the prosecutor to initiate investigations of potential international crime on his or her own initiative.

The area of international law in which most specialized and permanent adjudicatory bodies have been created is international human rights law. As Chapter 9 discusses at length, the UN has created a highly elaborate system for resolving disputes about the interpretation and application of human rights, including a range of Special Procedures and committees. In practice, of course, the many bodies primarily deal with 'disputes' that involve complaints by individuals against their own states but treatment of disputes between states is also possible. Human rights dispute settlement

---

[88] See also WTO Agreement art. IV:3. The Understanding on rules and procedures governing the settlement of disputes (DSU) constitutes Annex 2 to the WTO Agreement.

is also available at a regional level, in particular in Europe where the European Court of Human Rights plays a pivotal rule.

Finally, mention must also be made of the dispute settlement system in the EU and in particular of the Court of Justice of the European Union (CJEU) in Luxembourg.

Summary

The international system contains a range of methods by which states can resolve their disputes in a peaceful manner. While some mechanisms are of a diplomatic and non-adjudicatory nature, there are also a number of adjudicatory methods of dispute settlement available. Diplomatic methods include negotiation, mediation and conciliation. The most important adjudicatory means of settling disputes are arbitration and reliance on a number of permanent international courts and tribunals. The most important of the latter is the ICJ which is the only international court with general jurisdiction to deal with interstate disputes. The ICJ deals with contentious cases and has the competence to issue advisory opinions. The jurisdiction of the Court in contentious cases is based on consent from the state parties involved. A number of more specialized international courts and tribunals also exist.

Recommended reading

For peace settlement of disputes in general, see John Merrills, 'The Means of Dispute Settlement' in Malcolm D. Evans (ed.), *International Law* (4th edn, Oxford University Press, 2014).

On the UN and peaceful dispute settlement, see Thomas M. Franck, *Fairness in International Law and Institutions* (Oxford University Press, 1995).

For peacekeeping, see Christine Gray, *International Law and the Use of Force* (3rd edn, Oxford University Press, 2008) chs 7–9, and the United Nations, *The Blue Helmets: A Review of United Nations Peacekeeping* (3rd edn, United Nations, 1997).

For the history of international arbitration, see Cornelis G. Roelofsen, 'International Arbitration and Courts' in Bardo Fassbender and Anne Peters (eds), *The Oxford Handbook of the History of International Law* (Oxford University Press, 2012) 151.

The most thorough discussion of the PCIJ is Ole Spiermann, *International Legal Argument in the Permanent Court of International Justice* (Cambridge University Press, 2005).

For the ICJ, see Andreas Zimmermann et al. (eds), *The Statute of the International Court of Justice: A Commentary* (2nd edn, Oxford University Press, 2012).

A more concise overview is available in Hugh Thirlway, 'The International Court of Justice' in Malcolm D. Evans (ed.), *International Law* (4th edn, Oxford University Press, 2014).

Questions for discussion

1. Why is arbitration often a more tempting choice than the ICJ for states that seek to settle their disputes in a peaceful manner?

2. What are the conditions that must be fulfilled before a state can successfully bring proceedings against another state before the ICJ?

3. The text notes that a state is entitled to make reservations to a declaration under article 36(2). Is that problematic with regard to making states utilize the ICJ?

4. What is the interpretative value of an advisory opinion issued by the ICJ?

13

The international regulation of the use of force

CENTRAL ISSUES

1. This chapter discusses the regulation of when and for what purpose a state may use force against another state—*jus ad bellum*.

2. The chapter provdes an overview of the legal framework in the 1945 UN Charter and to that end analyses the content of the prohibition on the use of force in article 2(4), discusses the competences of the UN Security Council and examines the right to self-defence.

3. The Security Council is entrusted with primary responsibility for the maintenance of international peace and security and under Chapter VII of the Charter, the Council may authorize the use of force if required to maintain and/or restore the peace.

4. Article 51 of the Charter allows a state to defend itself in the case of armed attack.

13.1 Introduction

The initiation of war has always been one of the most debated—and politicized—topics of international relations and public international law. The answers to the questions of when, for what reasons and how a member of a community may forcefully submit another to its will is of paramount importance for the maintenance of peaceful relations between the members. Hence, the international rules and principles governing force constitute a vital component of the international law of coexistence.

International law distinguishes between those rules that regulate *when* and *for what purpose* a state may use force against another state—termed *jus ad bellum*—and those that regulate how *military hostilities must be conducted—jus in bello.*[1] While the first primarily relates to the initial political decision of a state to use force in another state, the latter is concerned with the manner in which that political decision is

---

[1] Christopher Greenwood, 'The Relationship Between *Ius ad Bellum* and *Ius in Bello*' (1983) 9 *Review of International Studies* 221–234.

implemented. To illustrate, the legality under international law of the 2003 decision of the US-led coalition to invade Iraq is a matter for *jus ad bellum*. But once the invasion commenced and hostilities were initiated, the focus turned to the requirements for the proper conduct of military operations under *jus in bello*. In practical terms, therefore, the legal regimes potentially implicate different actors of a state. They are independent of one another and must be so applied.

In this chapter, we discuss *jus ad bellum* while Chapter 14 focuses on *jus in bello*. Here, we begin in Section 13.2 with the framework in the UN Charter and the prohibition on the use of force in article 2(4). In Section 13.3, we turn to the Security Council and in Section 13.4 we examine the unilateral use of force. In Section 13.5, we discuss two examples of particularly contentious uses of force.

13.2 The UN Charter and the prohibition on the use of force

13.2.1 Introduction

It was not until the very end of the 19th century that legal attempts were made to curtail the freedom of states to use force against other states. Initially, the endeavour took the form of *procedural* limitations, such as the requirement in article 2 of the 1899 Convention for the Pacific Settlement of International Disputes to 'have recourse, as far as circumstances allow', to peaceful settlements of disputes before 'an appeal to arms'. Under the 1919 post-First World War Covenant of the League of Nations, member states agreed to submit a dispute 'likely to lead to a rupture' to either arbitration, judicial settlement or inquiry by the League's Council and agreed that resort to war had to wait 'until three months after the award by the arbitrators or the judicial decision, or the report by the Council'.[2] The first effort to limit the *substantive* right of states to resort to war was the adoption in Paris in 1928 of the *General Treaty for Renunciation of War as an Instrument of National Policy*—also known as the Kellogg–Briand Pact—in which the parties renounced war as an instrument of dispute settlement.[3]

Like so many aspects of international law, the Second World War was a turning point. As mentioned in Chapter 1, the 1945 UN Charter created the UN with the primary purpose of upholding international peace and security and avoiding yet another major conflict. The Charter entered into force on 24 October 1945. At its core, the UN is about securing stability, preventing the use of unilateral force and thereby 'save succeeding generations from the scourge of war'.[4] All other considerations remain secondary. While the Charter goes to great lengths to limit the *unilateral* use of force, it is not an inherently pacifistic document. Indeed, in 1945 states were all too aware

---

[2] Covenant of the League of Nations (1919), art. 12.
[3] General Treaty for the Renunciation of War as an Instrument of National Policy (1928), art. 2.
[4] Preamble to the UN Charter (1945).

that, at times, to win the peace one had to be prepared to fight the war. Rather than outlawing the use of force as a means of dispute settlement, the Charter simply *collectivizes* it. It establishes a system whereby the international community, acting through the Security Council, can take the measures required to keep or restore international peace and security. The 1945 vision was that, from then on, save in the case of self-defence in response to an armed attack, force should be used only in the common interests of the international community.

13.2.2 **The prohibition on the use of force**

The starting point is the prohibition on the use of force contained in article 2(4) of the UN Charter that stipulates that all members of the UN:

> shall refrain in their international relations from the threat or use of force against the territorial integrity or political independence of any state, or in any other manner inconsistent with the Purposes of the United Nations.

The concept of '*force*' has been debated ever since the adoption of the Charter in 1945, but the prevailing view is that it is limited to *armed* measures.[5] So while various forms of non-armed means of coercion, such as economic and political measures, may constitute breaches of sovereignty or infringe a principle of non-intervention, they will not constitute 'force'. The General Assembly's 1970 Declaration on Friendly Relations[6] and its 1987 Declaration on the Non-Use of Force[7] support the conclusion that article 2(4) only covers the use of armed force. A 2013 manual on cyber warfare found that a computer network operation could constitute 'force' if its 'scale and effects are comparable to non-cyber operations rising to the level of a use of force'.[8]

Some have argued that the wording 'against the territorial integrity and political independence … or any other manner inconsistent with the Purposes of the United Nations' implies that only use of force directed at territorial integrity and political independence is covered by the prohibition.[9] Most, however, reject such a reading of the article, and the better view is that the prohibition covers *all* use of force.[10] This interpretation is also supported by the *travaux préparatoires* of the Charter that testifies

---

[5] Bruno Simma (ed.), *The Charter of the United Nations: A Commentary* (Oxford University Press, 2012) 208–209.

[6] GA Res. 2625 (XXV) Declaration on Principles of International Law concerning Friendly Relations and Co-operation among States in accordance with the Charter of the United Nations (24 October 1970).

[7] GA Res. 42/22 Declaration on the Enhancement of the Effectiveness of the Principles of Refraining from the Threat or Use of Force in International Relations (18 November 1987).

[8] Michael N. Schmitt (ed.), *The Tallinn Manual on the International Law applicable to Cyber Warfare* (Cambridge University Press, 2013) rule 11.

[9] See e.g. Derek W. Bowett, *Self-Defence in International Law* (Frederik A. Praeger, 1958) 152; see also *Legality of Use of Force (Serbia and Montenegro v Belgium)*, Oral Proceedings, Public sitting, 10 May 1999, 12.

[10] Yoram Dinstein, *War, Aggression and Self-Defence* (5th edn, Cambridge University Press, 2011) 90; Ian Brownlie, *International Law and the Use of Force by States* (Oxford University Press, 1963) 265–268; Thomas Franck, *Recourse to Force: State Action Against Threats and Armed Attacks* (Cambridge University Press, 2002) 12; see also *Corfu Channel (UK v Albania)*, Merits [1949] ICJ Rep 4, 35. But see Rosalyn Higgins, *Problems & Process: International Law and How We Use It* (Oxford University Press, 1994) 245–246.

to the efforts of the drafters to limit, to the extent possible, the use of non-Security Council sanctioned force.[11]

In *Nicaragua*, the ICJ stated that the use of force is regulated in both the UN Charter and in customary international law[12] and that the content of the two sources of law are not identical in all relevant aspects.[13] In practice, however, it is hard to imagine the existence of a substantial material difference between the content of the prohibition on the use of force in the Charter and in customary international law.[14] It would seem, in other words, that the principles on the use of force in the Charter, including the ban on the use of force, correspond to those found in customary international law.

It is important to note that the use of force on the basis of consent (invitation) from a host state is not prescribed by article 2(4). As we saw in Chapter 7, valid consent is a circumstance that precludes the wrongfulness of an act otherwise in violation of an international obligation.[15] There are many uncontroversial instances when the use of international force is justified on the basis of consent from the host state, the most obvious example being peacekeeping operations. Other examples include NATO's military presence in Afghanistan from December 2001 onwards and the existing international military campaign against the so-called 'Islamic State' (ISIL) in Iraq.[16] As noted in Chapter 7, it is less certain whether consent can always be relied on as a justification for using force in an ongoing civil war as is presently the case in Syria.[17]

13.3 The Security Council and the maintenance of international peace and security

13.3.1 Introduction

As already noted, the UN Charter gives the Security Council primary responsibility for the maintenance of international peace and security, and use of force authorized by the Council does not violate the prohibition on the use of force in article 2(4). Only 15 states have a seat on the Council and the five most powerful states in the 1945 world, China, France, the Soviet Union (today Russia), the UK and the United States are permanent members.[18] All decisions of a non-procedural nature

---

[11] See the overview in Simma (n 5) 216–217.

[12] *Military and Paramilitary Activities in and against Nicaragua (Nicaragua v United States)*, Merits [1986] ICJ Rep 14, para. 174.

[13] Ibid, para. 181.

[14] Ibid. See also *Legal Consequences of the Construction of a Wall in the Occupied Palestinian Territory*, Advisory Opinion [2004] ICJ Rep 136, para. 87, and GA Res. 2625 (n 6).

[15] Draft Articles on State Responsibility, Report of the International Law Commission, 53rd Session, (2001), art. 20.

[16] *Letter dated 25 June 2014 from the Permanent Representative of Iraq to the United Nations addressed to the Secretary-General* (25 June 2014), UN Doc. S/2014/440. Of course, ISIL is not a 'state' for the purposes of international law.

[17] See also Chapter 7, Section 7.4.2.   [18] UN Charter art. 23.

are made by an affirmative vote of nine members including the concurring votes of the permanent members.[19] In practice, therefore, any of the five permanent members can block significant initiatives by the Council. This, of course, can hardly be said to be 'democratic' and numerous suggestions for reform of the Council have been advanced. It is important to note, however, that the whole idea of establishing the Security Council was based on the belief that not all states are of equal importance. The five permanent members not only have a right of veto due to the fact they won the Second World War but also because of a belief that the efforts to maintain international peace and security are best served by ascertaining that the five states agree on resort to the use of force.

The Charter gives the Security Council wide-ranging powers. As we saw in the previous chapter, the Council can adopt non-coercive and non-binding measures under Chapter VI of the Charter to settle disputes that may lead to a situation where international peace and security are threatened. If, however, the Security Council determines that an ongoing dispute constitutes a threat to the peace, Chapter VII of the Charter authorizes it to adopt binding measures that can include *coercive* measures. Article 25 stipulates that member states agree to carry out the decisions of the Council and under article 103 obligations undertaken under the Charter—including those stemming from Security Council resolutions—prevail over other international obligations.

We start by examining the Council's determination of a threat to the peace in article 39 (Section 13.3.2) and then briefly look at provisional measures (Section 13.3.3). We then discuss the non-forcible measures available to the Council (Section 13.3.4) before examining the Council's competence to authorize the use of forcible measures to uphold international peace and security (Section 13.3.5). Attention is then turned to the limits to the Council's authority (Section 13.3.6), interpretation of the Council's resolutions (Section 13.3.7) and regional organizations (Section 13.3.8).

13.3.2 **Determinations under Article 39**

Article 39 of the Charter specifies that the Security Council shall initially determine the existence of 'any threat to the peace, breach of the peace, or act of aggression'. The Council enjoys considerable discretion and the concept of a 'threat to the peace' has evolved substantially. In the last few decades, the Council has found that everything from internal conflicts, humanitarian crises, violations of democratic principles, acts of terrorism, piracy and arms control issues may fall within the concept of a threat to the peace under article 39. In 2014, it even found that the Ebola outbreak in Africa fell within article 39.[20] In practice, as long as a matter can be reasonably tied to international peace and security, the Council possesses the authority to find that its powers under Chapter VII are triggered.[21]

---

[19] Ibid, art. 27.   [20] SC Res. 2177 (18 September 2014).
[21] ICTY, *Tadić (Jurisdiction)*, Appeals Chamber Judgment (2 October 1995), paras 28–29.

13.3.3 **Provisional measures under Article 40**

Article 40 authorizes the Security Council to call on the parties to a dispute to comply with such provisional measures it may deem necessary to 'prevent an aggravation of the situation'. The Council may, for example, call for a ceasefire and/or for the withdrawal of troops from foreign territory. The measures in question must, however, be temporary in nature and leave the legal positions of the parties to the dispute unaffected. Practice illustrates that, although the wording of article 40 ('may ... call upon') indicates that provisional measures are only recommendations, the measures may be binding.[22]

13.3.4 **Non-forcible measures under Article 41**

Articles 41 and 42 provide the Council with the authority they need to resolve a matter in order that international peace and security is maintained. Under article 41, the Security Council may take 'measures not involving the use of force and it may make binding calls upon' the members of the United Nations to 'apply such measures'. Such non-coercive measures may include 'complete or partial interruption of economic relations and of rail, sea, air, postal, telegraphic, radio, and other means of communications, and the severance of diplomatic relations'. The list is not exhaustive. The Council often responds to an ongoing crisis by imposing economic sanctions on the parties, such as an arms embargo. The most comprehensive sanctions regime was imposed on Iraq after its invasion of Kuwait in August 1990 and its subsequent refusal to cooperate fully with the UN weapons inspectors.[23] The sanctions led to a widespread humanitarian crisis in the country and paved the way for more targeted—or 'smart'—sanctions that focused on those individuals or institutions determined to be the primary cause of the threat to the peace.[24] For example, when the Security Council in 2006 imposed sanctions, such as an arms embargo, on Iran for its failure to cooperate with the International Atomic Energy Agency (IAEA), it also targeted individuals and entities in Iran involved with the nuclear programme.[25] And when sanctions were also imposed on North Korea in 2006 for its nuclear programme, the list of sanctions included restrictions on the import of certain luxury goods aimed at targeting the elite policymakers.[26]

The Security Council has generally become more creative in how it applies its powers under article 41. As we shall see in Chapter 15, the Council has, for example, relied on article 41 for establishing international tribunals to prosecute international criminals, and for referring situations to the International Criminal Court (ICC).

---

[22] Simma (n 5) 1303. See e.g. SC Res. 660 (2 August 1990).

[23] See, among others, SC Res. 661 (6 August 1990), SC Res. 665 (25 August 1990), SC Res. 687 (3 April 1991).

[24] See also GA Res. 51/242 (26 September 1997), Annex II. See also Matthew Craven, 'Humanitarianism and the Quest for Smarter Sanctions' (2002) 13 *European Journal of International Law* 43–50.

[25] See, among others, SC Res. 1737 (23 December 2006) and SC Res. 1929 (9 June 2010).

[26] SC Res. 1718 (14 October 2006). See e.g. SC Res. 2083 (22 January 2013).

It has also used article 41 to restrict trade in certain goods, such as so-called 'conflict diamonds' from African conflict zones,[27] and by adopting 'legislative' resolutions where it imposes general and more abstract obligations on states. In such resolutions, the Council does not focus on a particular country or entity but instead on a 'phenomenon' or a range of activities it deems inherently threatening to international peace. In Resolution 1373, for example, the Council responded to the terrorist attacks on the United States on 9/11 by imposing a range of terrorism-related obligations and by establishing a Counter-Terrorism Committee to monitor the implementation of the resolution.[28] In Resolution 1540, the Council imposed a number of general obligations on all states to keep weapons of mass destruction and their means of delivery out of the hands of non-state actors.[29] More recently, in September 2014, the Council adopted Resolution 2178 that obliged states to adopt a number of measures to prevent 'foreign terrorist fighters' travelling to areas of armed conflict.[30]

13.3.5 Enforcement under Article 42

When non-coercive measures are insufficient to uphold or restore international peace and security, article 42 gives the Security Council the authority to go even further and mandate 'such action by air, sea, or land forces as may be necessary'. Hence, if required, the Council can authorize the initiation of military operations. While the original idea was that the UN members would put forces at the disposal of the Security Council which could then rely on such 'UN forces', this never materialized and the Council instead relies on 'coalitions of the willing' or, as we shall in Section 13.3.8, on regional organizations.

During the stalemate of the Cold War, the broad authority to use coercive measures lay mostly dormant,[31] and it was not until after the end of the Cold War that the Security Council began, to some degree, to live up to its responsibilities. In 1990, the Council responded to Iraq's August 1990 invasion of Kuwait by authorizing member states to use 'all necessary means' to secure an Iraqi withdrawal and to restore international peace and security in the region.[32] Although the subsequent US-led First Gulf War liberated Kuwait and created optimism for the dawning of a New World Order centred on a revitalized Security Council, it is fair to say that the following decades turned out to be fairly disappointing. The post-Cold War period has, however, seen an unprecedented level of activity in the Security Council with regard to enforcement under Chapter VII. Since the end of the First Gulf War, the Council has authorized the use of force in, among other places, Yugoslavia,[33] Somalia,[34] Haiti,[35] East Timor,[36] the Ivory Coast[37] and Libya.[38] It has also relied on article 42

---

[27] SC Res. 1306 (5 July 2000), SC Res. 1343 (7 March 2001).
[28] SC Res. 1373 (28 September 2001).   [29] SC Res. 1540 (28 April 2004).
[30] SC Res. 2178 (24 September 2014).   [31] But see SC Res. 83 (27 June 1950).
[32] SC Res. 678 (29 November 1990) referred to the earlier Res. 660 (2 August 1990).
[33] SC Res. 836 (4 June 1993).   [34] SC Res. 794 (3 December 1992).
[35] SC Res. 940 (31 July 1994).   [36] SC Res. 1264 (15 September 1999).
[37] SC Res. 1464 (4 February 2003) and SC Res. 1528 (27 February 2004).
[38] SC Res. 1973 (17 March 2011).

to establish large multinational 'security' forces that have been deployed in the aftermath of the international interventions in Kosovo in 1999,[39] in Afghanistan in 2001[40] and in Iraq in 2003.[41] In 2014, the Council expanded the mandate for the large contingent of UN forces deployed to the Democratic Republic of Congo to include 'targeted offensive operations' against armed groups with a view to neutralizing and disarming them.[42]

One of the results of the Cold War paralysis of the Security Council was the emergence of peacekeeping operations.[43] The General Assembly took the early lead with the establishment in 1956–1967 of a major peacekeeping force (UNEF, the UN Emergency Force) in Egypt.[44] UNEF was created pursuant to a 1950 resolution on 'Uniting for Peace' in which the General Assembly declared its willingness to make 'appropriate recommendations … for collective measures including … the use of armed force' when the Security Council was unable to exercise its primary responsibility for the maintenance of international peace and security.[45] In the *Certain Expenses* case, the International Court of Justice (ICJ) confirmed that the Assembly can establish peacekeeping operations on the basis of the consent of the state or states concerned, but that only the Security Council may order *coercive* action.[46] Peacekeeping operations were initially based on the consent of the host state and the peacekeepers were considered impartial, lightly armed and only authorized to use force in self-defence.[47] They were mostly deployed to interstate disputes and their tasks were often limited to monitoring ceasefires and contested borders.[48]

After the end of the Cold War, the Security Council assumed control over UN peacekeeping and began to deploy forces to places where there was simply no peace to keep. The character of UN operations evolved substantially and peacekeeping forces were gradually dragged into the fighting.[49] The most notable examples were the UN missions in Yugoslavia (UNPROFOR) and Somalia (UNOSOM) in the early 1990s.[50] For a time, the experiences in the 1990s in Yugoslavia and Somalia led to a loss of appetite for major peacekeeping operations and subsequent UN missions were much less ambitious. Since the turn of the century, however, there has been a massive increase in UN peacekeeping operations and, in August 2016, the UN Department for Peacekeeping Operations (DPKO) were running 16 missions. The four largest were

---

[39] SC Res. 1244 (10 June 1999).

[40] SC Res. 1386 (6 December 2001). See also SC Res. 1510 (13 October 2003).

[41] SC Res. 1511 (16 October 2003).   [42] SC Res. 2147 (28 March 2014).

[43] Elements of enforcement action were, however, visible in the peacekeeping operation in the Congo, see also Simma (n 5) 1333.

[44] SC Res. 998 (4 November 1956) and SC Res. 1000 (5 November 1956).

[45] GA Res. 377 (V) (3 November 1950).

[46] *Certain Expenses of the United Nations*, Advisory Opinion of 20 July 1962 [1962] ICJ Rep 151, 163–165.

[47] For an overview, see the United Nations, *The Blue Helmets: A Review of United Nations Peacekeeping* (3rd edn, United Nations, 1997).

[48] But see also SC Res. 161 (21 February 1961).

[49] On post-Cold War peacekeeping, see Christine Gray, *International Law and the Use of Force* (3rd edn, Oxford University Press, 2008) 272–281.

[50] Ibid, 281–292.

all in Africa: Congo (MONUSCO), Darfur (UNAMID), South Sudan (UNMISS) and Mali (MINUSMA).[51]

The UN has undertaken a series of reviews and evaluations of its peacekeeping policies and numerous suggestions for reform have been put forward.[52] A 2015 report from a High-Level Panel on Peace Operations concluded that there is (still) 'a widening gap between what is being asked of the United Nations peace operations today and what they can deliver' and that a number of new approaches were called for.[53]

Although enforcement measures under article 42 do not depend on consent from the home state, it is not uncommon for the latter to nevertheless give its consent. The decision by the Security Council to adopt a resolution under Chapter VII despite the existence of consent, may be motivated by a number of factors. First of all, the adoption of a resolution ensures that a UN-mandated operation can continue even if the host state decides to withdraw its consent.[54] Secondly, the Council may need to refer to Chapter VII to create binding obligations on the member states.

13.3.6 Limits on the Security Council's authority

The authority of the Security Council is not unlimited. As already noted, formally, the Council can only deal with threats to international peace and security. We also saw in Chapter 2 that the Council cannot oblige states to disregard norms of a *jus cogens*/peremptory character. In response to the criticism by, most notably, the Court of Justice for the European Union (CJEU) of the Council's sanctions and listing regime, and its seeming lack of concern for due process guarantees, the Council has modified its procedures for delisting individuals.[55] It has also stated that the implementation of sanctions must respect human rights law, refugee law and international humanitarian law,[56] and in 2009 it created the Office of the Ombudsperson to serve as an independent and impartial entity for reviewing the cases of individuals on the sanctions list.[57]

---

[51] For an updated overview, see http://www.un.org/en/peacekeeping/operations/current.shtml.

[52] See, inter alia, 'An Agenda for Peace', Report of the Secretary-General pursuant to the statement adopted by the Summit Meeting of the Security Council on 31 January 1992 (17 June 1992), UN Doc. A/47/277-S/24111 and the follow-up, 'An Agenda for Peace: Supplement' (3 January 1995), UN Doc. A/50/60-S/1995/1; *Report of the Panel on United Nations Peace Operations* ('Brahimi report') (21 August 2000), UN Doc. A/55/305-S/2000/809; and the Report of the High-Level Independent Panel on Peace Operations on uniting our strengths for peace: politics, partnership and people (17 June 2015), UN Doc. A/70/95-S/2015/446, 9.

[53] See Report of the High-Level Independent Panel on Peace Operations on uniting our strengths for peace: politics, partnership and people (n 52).

[54] Simma (n 5) 1344.

[55] SC Res. 1730 (19 December 2006), SC Res. 1822 (30 June 2008), SC Res. 1904 (17 December 2009), SC Res. 1989 (17 June 2011).

[56] SC Res. 1456 (20 January 2003).   [57] SC Res. 1904 (17 December 2009).

13.3.7 **Interpretation of Security Council resolutions**

There are few authoritative sources on the interpretation of Security Council resolutions.[58] Although the principles for treaty interpretation in the Vienna Convention on the Law of Treaties is a good place to start, it should be noted that the Council's resolutions and treaties differ in a number of ways. For one thing, the procedure for drafting resolutions is different from that governing the drafting of treaties. In addition, the words and terms contained in a resolution often reflect hard-won political compromises and the end result may be that certain terms are intentionally left vague and open-ended. As with interpretation of a treaty, however, interpretation of a Security Council resolution should take its point of departure as the ordinary meaning of the text of the resolution and the terms used. Interpretation should also take account of the context of the resolution, such as prior Council resolutions on the matter, statements by the representatives of the states in the Council, reports by the Secretary-General etc., as well as the object and purpose of the resolution and of the Charter as a whole.

At times, it may be difficult to determine if a Council resolution is intended to be binding. In *Namibia*, the ICJ stated that the determination often requires careful analysis of the language used.[59] In practice, the interpretation will usually be assisted by the terms used by the Council. Thus, it tends to rely on terms like 'decide' and 'demand' or specify that it is 'acting under Chapter VII' when it intends its resolutions to be binding. When it wants to supplement a binding decision with an authorization for the use of force, it usually authorizes the use of 'all necessary means'. In non-binding resolutions, it often relies on the terms 'call upon', 'recommend' or 'appeal'. Importantly, some resolutions contains both binding and non-binding provisions. An example was Resolution 1373 adopted in response to the 9/11 attacks on the United States. Thus, while both section 1 and 2 of the operative part of the resolution contain obligations that the Council 'decided' that states 'shall' fulfil, the obligations found in section 3 were of a kind that states were merely 'called upon' to respect.[60]

A number of states have tried to justify their forceful operations on *implied authority* from the Security Council.[61] The most noteworthy—and controversial—example was the US and British reliance on implied authority as the basis for the March 2003 invasion of Iraq.[62] At the time of the invasion, Iraq had been under Security Council-imposed sanctions for more than a decade for its failure to cooperate with UN weapons inspectors. The inspectors were pulled out of Iraq in 1998 due to lack of Iraqi cooperation. On 8 November 2002, the Council adopted Resolution 1441 that recalled previous resolutions with regard to Iraq, including the 1990 resolution that had authorized the use of all necessary means to liberate Kuwait and restore international peace and security in

---

[58] See the limited contributions in *Legal Consequences for States of the Continued Presence of South Africa in Namibia (South West Africa)* [1971] ICJ Rep 53 and *Prosecutor v Tadić*, Appeals Chamber Judgment, IT-94-1-A (15 July 1999), paras 293–304.

[59] *Namibia* (n 58) para. 114.   [60] SC Res. 1373 (28 September 2001).

[61] For an overview, see Gray (n 49) 348–369.

[62] For a recent and comprehensive analysis of the events of the invasion, see the final 2016 report of the UK public inquiry led by Sir John Chilcot—also known as the 'Chilcot Report'—available at http://www.iraqinquiry.org.uk/ (accessed 15 September 2016).

the area, and gave Iraq 'a final opportunity' to comply with its disarmament obliga-tions. It also sent the inspectors back to Iraq and obliged the Iraqis to fully cooperate and provide a complete declaration of its weapons programmes. Resolution 1441 did not, however, contain any express authorization for the use of (renewed) force against Iraq if the latter did not comply with the renewed inspection regime. It merely noted that the 'Council has repeatedly warned Iraq that it will face serious consequences as a result of its continued violations of its obligations'. The United States and the UK subsequently interpreted the feedback from the weapons inspectors as evidence that Iraq had not cooperated and argued that a new resolution with an *express* authoriza-tion for invading Iraq was not necessary.[63] The three other permanent members of the Security Council—France, China and Russia—disagreed.[64] The reliance on implied authority is controversial to say the least because it seems to be more consistent with the purposes of the Charter to conclude that a resolution should give a clear—rather than implicit—indication if it is to be interpreted as authorizing the use of force.[65]

After the Iraq controversy, the Council has gone to great lengths to make it very clear what it authorizes and what it does not.[66] This, however, has not prevented new controversies from arising. In March 2011, the Security Council responded to the civil war in Libya and the brutality of the Gaddafi regime by authorizing the establishment and enforcement of a no-fly zone over Libya and the use of 'all necessary measures' to 'protect civilians and civilian populated areas under threat of attack'.[67] When NATO relied on the authorization to conduct a lengthy bombing campaign that eventually led to the collapse of Gaddafi's regime, a number of states—including Russia and China—accused NATO of going far beyond the mandate and using it as a pretext for regime change in Libya.[68]

13.3.8 Regional organizations

Article 53 of the Charter stipulates that the Security Council may utilize 'regional arrangements or agencies for enforcement action under its authority'. For example, instead of authorizing member states to enforce its resolutions adopted under Chapter VII in their individual capacity, the Council may request states to do so under the

---

[63] See *Letter dated 20 March 2003 from the Permanent Representative of the United States of America to the United Nations Addressed to the President of the Security Council* (21 March 2003), UN Doc. S/2003/351 and *Letter dated 20 March 2003 from the Permanent Representative of the United Kingdom of Great Britain and Northern Ireland to the United Nations addressed to the President of the Security Council* (21 March 2003), UN Doc. S/2003/350. For a more elaborate British justification, see 'Iraq: legal basis for the use of force', UK Foreign and Commonwealth Office, 17 March 2003. For the Australian justification, see UN Doc. S/2003/352 (21 March 2003). In February and March 2003, the United States and the UK tried in vain to secure the adoption of a resolution that would legitimize the use of force against Iraq, see Sean D. Murphy, 'Contemporary Practice of the United States relating to International Law' (2003) 97 *American Journal of International Law* 419, 424.

[64] Murphy (n 63).   [65] Simma (n 5) 1342.

[66] SC Res. 1718 (14 October 2006) and SC Res. 1696 (31 July 2006).

[67] SC Res. 1973 (17 March 2011).

[68] Geir Ulfstein and Hege Føsund Chistiansen, 'The Legality of the NATO Bombing in Libya' (2013) 62 *International and Comparative Law Quarterly* 159–171.

framework of a regional organization.[69] Like states, regional enforcement is contingent on Council authorization. In practice, regional organizations have become increasingly important to the Council and article 53 has been relied on in many instances and by numerous regional organizations. As mentioned in Section 13.3.5, the African Union has begun to play a very active role in Council-mandated missions in Africa. But also NATO (the former Federal Republic of Yugoslavia, Kosovo, Afghanistan, Iraq, counter-piracy off the Horn of Africa and Libya) and the Economic Community of West African States (ECOWAS) (Liberia and the Ivory Coast) have been willing contributors.

13.4 The unilateral use of force by states

13.4.1 The right to self-defence

13.4.1.1 Introduction

The use of force in self-defence constitutes an exception to the prohibition on the use of force in article 2(4). Under article 51 of the Charter:

> Nothing in the present Charter shall impair the inherent right of individual or collective self-defence if an armed attack occurs against a Member of the United Nations, until the Security Council has taken measures necessary to maintain international peace and security. Measures taken by Members in the exercise of this right of self-defence shall be immediately reported to the Security Council and shall not in any way affect the authority and responsibility of the Security Council under the present Charter to take at any time such action as it deems necessary in order to maintain or restore international peace and security.

The scope of the right is one of the most contested areas of international law.[70] One of the matters of contention is the reference to the 'inherent' right to self-defence. In *Nicaragua*, the ICJ stated that the term testifies to the existence of a right to self-defence under customary international law that exists alongside article 51.[71] In particular, US scholars argue that the authority to resort to self-defence under customary law is wider than that under article 51.[72] Others are rightfully sceptical and hold that the material difference between the two 'rights' are very limited.[73] There is little indication that the pre-1945 customary right to self-defence differed in any significant extent from the content of the right adopted under article 51.[74] It is also difficult to see how a potentially more expansive right to self-defence under customary international law could have survived the adoption of the Charter in 1945. Furthermore, in neither of

---

[69] See e.g. UNSCR 816 (31 March 1993).

[70] Jorg Kammerhofer, 'Uncertainties of the Law on Self-Defence in the United Nations Charter' (2004) 35 *Netherlands Yearbook of International Law* 143.

[71] *Nicaragua* (n 12) paras 193 and 176.

[72] See e.g. Bowett (n 9) 185–186 and John Yoo, 'Using Force' (2004) 71 *University of Chicago Law Review* 729, 738–739. See also ICJ, *Nicaragua* (n 12) Dissenting Opinion of Judge Schwebel, para. 173.

[73] Simma (n 5) 1403–1404, Dinstein (n 10) 196–198.   [74] Brownlie (n 10) 271–274.

the cases where the ICJ has dealt with the right to self-defence has it assumed that the content of the right to self-defence under article 51 should be anything but a manifestation of *the* right to self-defence.[75]

In this section, we shall discuss the concept of an 'armed attack' (Section 13.4.1.2), the question of when self-defence can be initiated (Section 13.4.1.3), the dual requirements of necessity and proportionality (Section 13.4.1.4), collective self-defence (Section 13.4.1.5), the relationship between the Security Council and the exercise of self-defence (Section 13.4.1.6) and the link between collective security and self-defence (Section 13.4.1.7).

13.4.1.2 The notion of an 'armed attack'

The right to self-defence is triggered by an 'armed attack'. An attack *must be of a certain intensity* to trigger a right to self-defence and not all uses of force prescribed by article 2(4) qualify. In *Nicaragua*, the ICJ distinguished between the 'the most grave forms of the use of force' and 'other less grave forms'.[76] Since the Charter generally insists that unilateral use of force should be kept to a minimum, this is hardly surprising. In *Nicaragua*, the ICJ also noted that the 'provision of weapons or logistical or other support' to rebels[77] as well as 'a mere frontier incident' fall outside the ambit of article 51.[78] The latter conclusion was reiterated by the Eritrea Ethiopia Claims Commission.[79] In *Nuclear Weapons*, the ICJ stated that the rules on the use of force in the Charter do not refer to any 'specific weapons', but 'apply to any use of force, regardless of the weapons employed'.[80] In *Oil Platforms*, the ICJ noted that the 'mining of a single military vessel might be sufficient' to trigger a right to self-defence.[81] Thus, only acts producing or likely to produce very serious consequences, such as territorial invasions, human fatalities or massive destruction of property, will suffice to constitute an armed attack that triggers a right to self-defence.[82] If an attack perpetrated through cyberspace causes such consequences in a direct and foreseeable manner, it may also constitute an armed attack.[83]

As noted in Chapter 4, on 18 March 2014, Russia annexed the Crimean peninsula in Ukraine after a Russian intervention and a local referendum in which an overwhelming majority had voted to leave Ukraine. The Russian intervention consisted of the use of armed force by members of the Russian armed forces based in the city of Sevastopol pursuant to a treaty between Russia and Ukraine and the introduction of Russian servicemen (the infamous 'little green men') operating alongside local pro-Russian militias.[84] The Russian acts constituted an armed attack on Ukraine that triggered

---

[75] *The Wall* (n 14) paras 87 and 109. See also ICJ, *Armed Activities on the Territory of the Congo (Democratic Republic of the Congo v Uganda)*, Judgment [2005] ICJ Rep 168, paras 118, 128, 130–131, 140–149.

[76] *Nicaragua* (n 12) para. 191. See also *Oil Platforms (Islamic Republic of Iran v United States)*, Judgment [2003] ICJ Rep 161, para. 191. GA Res. 3314 (14 December 1974), para. 2. Dinstein (n 10) 207–208.

[77] *Nicaragua* (n 12) para. 195. See also para. 230.   [78] Ibid, para. 195.

[79] Eritrea Ethiopia Claims Commission, Partial Award, *Jus ad Bellum*, Ethiopia's Claims 1–8, para. 11.

[80] *Legality of the Threat or Use of Nuclear Weapons*, Advisory Opinion [1996] ICJ Rep 226, paras 38–39.

[81] ICJ, *Oil Platforms* (n 76) para. 72.   [82] See also the definition in Dinstein (n 10) 208.

[83] See also Schmitt (n 8) rule 13(3).

[84] See the overview in Veronika Bilkova, 'The Use of Force by the Russian Federation inn Crimea' (2015) 75 *ZaöRV* 31–37.

a Ukrainian right to self-defence under article 51 of the UN Charter.[85] As noted in Chapter 4, the General Assembly responded to the Russian intervention by reaffirming that state territory shall not be the object of acquisition by force and that attempts to disrupt the territorial integrity of a state are incompatible with the purposes and principles of the Charter.[86] It also underscored the fact that the local referendum had no validity and 'cannot form the basis for any alteration of the status' of the area.[87]

Some argue that a series of small-scale attacks not individually sufficiently grave to constitute an armed attack may be weighed cumulatively. Israel, in particular, has been a strong advocate of such an *accumulation of events* doctrine, and in the run up to its 2006 military operation against Hezbollah in southern Lebanon, the Israeli government stressed that a Hezbollah operation killing three and leading to the abduction of two Israeli soldiers should not be considered in isolation but rather as one incident in an ongoing campaign by Hezbollah.[88] The ICJ has made a number of remarks that *could* be interpreted as an implicit endorsement of the doctrine,[89] and though it remains controversial in some circles, international legal opinion in the last decades may have shifted to such an extent that the doctrine seems to enjoy a fair amount of support in legal doctrine.[90]

It has been much debated whether private actors can conduct armed attacks that trigger a right to self-defence, in particular after the terrorist attacks on 9/11 perpetrated by the al Qaida network in Afghanistan. Traditionally, it was controversial to argue for the existence of a right to self-defence against private actors[91] and the prevailing interpretation of the right to self-defence seems to have been that the territorial state *itself* needed to have committed an armed attack before it could be the target of legitimate self-defence aimed at the perpetrators of the attack.[92] But the UN Security Council responded to the attacks by 'recognizing' a right to self-defence and this recognition was not conditioned on establishing state attribution.[93] Indeed, to the majority of scholars, the international response to 9/11 shows that under certain conditions there is indeed a right to self-defence against non-state actors for terrorist attacks.[94] Thus, as discussed in Chapter 7, although the attacks on 9/11 did not result in a lowering of the standard of attribution for acts of private individuals, it seemingly paved the way for an 'unable or unwilling' doctrine whereby a state may be entitled to

---

[85] Ibid, 36.

[86] See the Preamble of GA Res. 68/262 (27 March 2014), UN Doc. A/68/L.39 and Add.1.

[87] Ibid, para. 5.

[88] Yael Ronen, 'Israel, Hizbollah, and the Second Lebanon War' (2006) 9 *Yearbook of International Humanitarian Law* 362, 372.

[89] See *Nicaragua* (n 12) para. 231. See also *Oil Platforms* (n 76) para. 64.

[90] Tom Ruys, *'Armed Attack' and Article 51 of the UN Charter: Evolutions in Customary Law and Practice* (Cambridge University Press, 2010) 169–174. See also Simma (n 5) 1409; Dinstein (n 10) 206–207.

[91] *The Wall* (n 14) Separate Opinion of Judge Kooijmans, para. 35.

[92] See Kammerhofer (n 70) 186. But see Bowett (n 9) 55–56.

[93] SC Res. 1368 (12 September 2001) and SC Res. 1373 (28 September 2001).

[94] Gray (n 49) 199; Dinstein (n 10) 227–230; Franck (n 10) 54. But see Eric P. J. Myjer and Nigel D. White, 'The Twin Towers Attack: An Unlimited Right to Self-Defence?' (2002) 7 *Journal of Conflict and Security Law* 5.

resort to measures of self-defence against a private actor, such as a terrorist organization, located in another state if the host state does not have the ability or willingness to stop the private actor's activities.[95] It must be noted, however, that this—potential—development has yet to be reflected in case law from the ICJ. On the contrary, the Court has so far been sceptical of the existence of a right to self-defence against private actors. In both *The Wall* and *Armed Activities*, the majority of the judges relied on a traditional interpretation of the right to self-defence that excluded such a right.[96]

If the level of gravity is sufficient, an attack on objects or individuals located on the territory of a state or on a state's military installations and/or military personnel may constitute an armed attack on the state.[97] In *Teheran Hostages*, the ICJ also indicated that the same holds true for attacks on a state's diplomatic missions and/or diplomatic representatives abroad.[98] It is less clear, however, if attacks on a state's civilian objects or individual citizens abroad, such as tourists, qualify. While a traditional view holds that this is not the case,[99] there is no universal agreement and in particular the United States and Israel have argued that attacks on the citizens of a state abroad *may* be an armed attack on the home state, at least where the individuals are targeted because of their nationality.[100] In 1979, Israel relied on the right to self-defence as justification for a special operation in Entebbe, Uganda, that evacuated Israeli citizens held hostage in a French civilian airliner. The international reaction to the Israeli operation was mixed.[101]

13.4.1.3 The initiation of self-defence

According to article 51, the right to self-defence is triggered when an armed attack 'occurs'. Hence, while a state that fears a potential attack from another state may make its own military preparations in anticipation of the attack and bring the matter to the attention of the Security Council, it may not resort to any measures of self-defence until the attack actually takes place. Despite the clear wording of the article, however, there appears to be overall agreement that a state may be entitled to resort to *anticipatory self-defence* against an expected assault when the threat is *imminent*.[102] This view was expressed by a 2004 High-Level Panel on Threats, Challenges and Change established by the UN Secretary-General.[103] Two things must be stressed, however.

---

[95] See also the overview in Anders Henriksen, '*Jus ad Bellum* and American Targeted Use of Force to Fight Terrorism Around the World' (2014) 1 *Journal of Conflict and Security Law* 1–40. See also *Letter dated 23 September 2014 from the Permanent Representative of the United States of America to the United Nations addressed to the Secretary-General* (23 September 2016), UN Doc. S/2014/695.

[96] *The Wall* (n 14) para. 139; *Armed Activities* (n 75) paras 146ff. The Court's reasoning drew strong dissenting opinions from some of the judges, see e.g. *The Wall* (n 14) Separate Opinion of Judge Kooijmans, para. 35, Separate Opinion of Judge Higgins, para. 33, Declaration by Judge Buergenthal, para. 6. See also *Armed Activities* (n 75) Separate Opinion of Judge Kooijmans, para. 29; *Armed Activities* (n 75) Separate Opinion of Judge Simma, para. 8.

[97] See also the Definition of Aggression, art. 3(c).

[98] *United States Diplomatic and Consular Staff in Tehran*, Judgment [1980] ICJ Rep 3, para. 57.

[99] See also Simma (n 5) 1413.   [100] Bowett (n 9) 91–94 and Dinstein (n 10) 217–219 and 255.

[101] Franck (n 10) 84. See also Gray (n 49) 202.

[102] See also Simma (n 5) 1324; Dinstein (n 10) 201–206.

[103] Report of the Secretary-General's High-Level Panel on Threats, Challenges and Change, *A More Secure World: Our Shared Responsibility* (2 December 2004), UN Doc. A/59/565, 188.

First, a right to anticipatory self-defence must be strictly interpreted and only relied on in exceptional circumstances. The earlier a state is allowed to defend itself against potential threats, the harder it is to maintain international peace and stability. Secondly, anticipatory self-defence must be distinguished from pre-emptive or preventive self-defence. Unlike the former, the latter is not exercised in response to an imminent threat of attack but instead to remove a potential threat of attack or to eliminate the possibility of a future attack by another state. Pre-emptive/preventive self-defence clearly violates article 51.

On several occasions, Israel has resorted to what can only be termed preventive—and therefore unlawful—self-defence. In 1981, Israel conducted an airstrike on an alleged Iraqi nuclear reactor that the Israeli government feared would be used to develop nuclear weapons for use against Israel. The airstrike was heavily criticized by the Security Council as a clear violation of international law.[104] In September 2007, Israel again bombed a suspected nuclear facility, this time in Syria, and in May 2013 it conducted the third in a series of airstrikes that year against targets in Syria allegedly tied to the shipment of sophisticated missiles from Iran to Hezbollah in Lebanon.[105] One of the ways in which the United States responded to the terrorist attacks on 9/11 was to proclaim the emergence of a new *pre-emptive* or *preventive* self-defence doctrine according to which the United States would act against emerging 'threats before they are fully formed'.[106] Under this so-called 'Bush doctrine', the emergence of a new set of threats creates a need to 'adapt the concept of imminent threat to the capabilities and objectives of today's adversaries'.[107] Outside the United States, however, attempts to rewrite the temporal dimension of article 51 have struggled to find support[108] and even the UK, the closest ally of the United States in the international fight against terrorism, has objected.[109]

13.4.1.4 Necessity and proportionality

To be lawful, self-defence must be necessary and proportionate.[110] The requirement of *necessity* means that a state must ascertain if other, more peaceful, means of redress are available before resorting to the use of force in self-defence. In the words of the US Secretary of State, Daniel Webster, in the famous *Caroline Case*, the state alleging a right to use self-defence is under an obligation to 'show a necessity of self-defence, instant, overwhelming, leaving no choice of means, and no moment for deliberation'.[111]

---

[104] SC Res. 487 (19 June 1981).

[105] Anne Barnard, Michael R. Gordon and Jodi Rudoren, 'Israel Targeted Iranian Missiles in Syria Attack', *New York Times* (4 May 2013).

[106] Covering letter of National Security Strategy of the United States (September 2002).

[107] National Security Strategy of the United States (September 2002), 15.

[108] For US scholarly support for a more 'flexible' approach to the temporal requirements in art. 51, see Yoo (n 72) 751; Abraham D. Sofaer, 'On the Necessity of Pre-Emption' (2003) 14 *European Journal of International Law* 209, 220. For legal criticism see, among others, Gray (n 49) 221.

[109] See the statement of the UK Attorney General, Lord Goldsmith, on 21 April 2004.

[110] *Nicaragua* (n 12) para. 14; *Nuclear Weapons* (n 80) para. 41; *Oil Platforms* (n 76) paras 76–77; *Armed Activities* (n 75) para. 147.

[111] The citation is quoted from R. Y. Jennings, 'The *Caroline* and *McLeod* Cases' (1938) 32 *American Journal of International Law* 82, 89.

In short, self-defence is use of force as a last resort. In addition, the response to an armed attack should be undertaken either while the attack is still in progress or at least not too long thereafter. This requirement of 'immediacy' must, however, be interpreted with a certain degree of flexibility. It may take some time for a victim state to determine the perpetrator of an armed attack, it may need some time for preparation before launching a response and it must also be allowed some time to explore whether a peaceful resolution to the situation is possible. Furthermore, as noted earlier, self-defence against a private actor, such as a terrorist organization, located in another state appears to be conditioned on the inability or unwillingness of the authorities in the host state to stop the private actor's activities.[112] So *before* resorting to the use of force against a private actor in another state, the victim state ought to request the host state to intervene and stop the actor's activities.[113]

The principle of *proportionality* requires the victim state to strike a fair balance between the armed attack and the measures taken to stop it. Under the *Caroline* formula, it is for the victim state to show that it 'did nothing unreasonable or excessive; since the act, justified by the necessity of self-defence, must be limited by that necessity, and kept clearly within it'.[114] Proportionality does not mean, however, that the victim state can never resort to more force than that used in the armed attack[115] nor does it necessarily preclude a state from responding to an armed attack by exercising its right to self-defence in more than one state.[116] To properly assess the proportionality of use of force, it is first necessary to identify the legitimate aim of the use of force and then to determine if the amount of force is either necessary or excessive in order to achieve that aim. In practice, proportionality assessments of instances of alleged self-defence are notoriously difficult to make.[117] In part, this is due to a lack of consensus in the international community on the underlying purpose of the right to self-defence.[118] A traditional understanding holds that the aim of the right to self-defence is limited to offering a state under attack the legal justification to use force to halt and repel the attack for the time necessary for the UN Security Council to have the opportunity to take control of the situation and offer the victim state the protection needed. Accordingly, if there is a need for additional force beyond that deemed necessary to halt and repel the armed attack, such force must be authorized by the Security Council.

It is particularly difficult to assess the proportionality of self-defence against international terrorism.[119] Usually, the act of self-defence occurs *after* the terrorist attack has taken place and it is therefore open to criticism for a number of reasons.

---

[112] Ashley S. Deeks, '"Unwilling or Unable": Toward a Normative Framework for Extraterritorial Self-Defense' (2012) 52 *Virginia Journal of International Law* 484, 487f. See also Dinstein (n 10) 272; Ruys (n 90) 505.

[113] Dinstein (n 10) 275; Ruys (n 90) 506.   [114] Jennings (n 111) 89.

[115] See also Ruys (n 90) 111ff.

[116] Noam Lubell, *Extraterritorial Use of Force Against Non-State Actors* (Oxford University Press, 2010) 66–68.

[117] Simma (n 5) 1426.   [118] Kammerhofer (n 70) 194. See also Ruys (n 90) 111–116.

[119] Henriksen, '*Jus ad Bellum* and American Targeted Use of Force to Fight Terrorism Around the World' (n 95).

First, since the response comes after the attack it appears punitive rather than aimed at preventing a threat against the state. Hence, it may resemble an armed reprisal that is unlawful under international law.[120] Secondly, the armed response may appear to be unlawful pre-emptive or even preventive use of force applied in order to protect against future attacks. Thirdly, the response may appear disproportionate if it is employed against a fairly small-scale terrorist attack. Also in this regard, however, the attitude seems to have changed somewhat following the attacks on 9/11. The overwhelming international support for the US claim that it was entitled to rely on a right to self-defence in response to the terrorist attacks, illustrates that the international community may be willing to accept a delayed response in the exercise of necessary and proportionate self-defence against specific terrorist attacks.

13.4.1.5 Collective self-defence

Article 51 not only permits individual but also collective self-defence and, depending on the circumstances, a state may therefore be entitled to use force in the defence of another state that has been the victim of an armed attack. It is not necessary for the assisting state to also have been attacked or that the exercise of such collective self-defence is triggered by a treaty-based obligation, such as Article 5 of the NATO Treaty. The assistance must, however, be given with the consent of the state under attack. According to the ICJ, resort to collective self-defence under customary international law requires the attacked state to declare itself under attack and make a request for assistance.[121] A recent example of the exercise of collective self-defence is the use of force against ISIL in Syria by a number of states. As already noted, in June 2014 the Iraqi government gave its consent to the use of force by other states in Iraq against ISIL. In September 2014, the Iraqi government also notified the UN Secretary-General that it had asked the United States to lead an international effort to defend Iraq by using force against ISIL in Syria pursuant to the exercise of collective Iraqi self-defence.[122]

13.4.1.6 The relationship between the Security Council and the exercise of self-defence

According to article 51, the right to self-defence can only be exercised 'until the Security Council has taken measures necessary to maintain international peace and security'. Hence, collective security and the wish to centralize the use of force overrides the exercise of unilateral measures in self-defence and even the right to self-defence is subject to the powers of the Security Council. In order to enable the Council to fulfil its role, article 51 requires member states to report any measures taken in self-defence to the Council. Although a lack of reporting may not rule out that the non-reporting state

---

[120] See also GA Res. 2625 (XXV) (24 October 1970); *Nuclear Weapons* (n 80) para. 46.

[121] *Nicaragua* (n 12) para. 199.

[122] *Letter dated 23 September 2014 from the Permanent Representative of the United States of America to the United Nations addressed to the Secretary-General* (23 September 2016), UN Doc. S/2014/695.

acted in legitimate self-defence, the ICJ has noted that it may indicate that the state is not itself satisfied that it is acting in lawful self-defence.[123]

13.4.1.7 Collective security and self-defence

On a few occasions, the Security Council has responded to an armed attack on a member state by authorizing the use of force under Chapter VII. As mentioned earlier, in reaction to Iraq's 1990 invasion of Kuwait, for example, the Council authorized the member states to use of all necessary measures to liberate Kuwait. If the state under attack requests assistance from other states (see Section 13.4.1.5), two separate authorities for the use of force will then exist: one based on collective self-defence and one based on an authorization from the Security Council. The drafting and the terms adopted in the authorization from the Council generally determine if the material content of the two authorities differs. In response to the 9/11 terrorist attacks, the Security Council responded by 'recognizing' the right to self-defence and it thereby indicated an intention to authorize the use of force against those responsible for the attacks if the United States so requested. In the end, though, the United States chose to rely on its right to self-defence in its efforts to fight terrorism, and it subsequently launched *Operation Enduring Freedom* on the basis of article 51 and not resolutions adopted by the Security Council.

13.5 Contentious use of force

13.5.1 The use of force to rescue nationals abroad

One source of legal controversy relates to the legality of the use of force to rescue nationals in another state without the consent of that state. Is it lawful, in other words, for a state to do what the Israelis did in Entebbe in 1974 when Israeli special forces conducted an operation to secure the release of its own citizens being held hostage?

Since the only unilateral Charter-based exception to the prohibition on the use of force is the right to self-defence, a rescue operation would seemingly have to be justified as a legitimate exercise of self-defence in response to an armed attack. This, of course, requires that attacks on the citizens of a state quality as attacks on the state itself and, as we saw earlier, this is unclear. Nevertheless, a rescue operation must comply with the dual requirements of necessity and proportionality and it therefore requires not only the existence of a genuine threat to the safety of the individuals in question but also the lack of willingness or ability of the host state to secure the safety of those individuals. To be considered proportionate, the operation should not pursue goals other than the evacuation of the nationals.[124]

---

[123] *Nicaragua* (n 12) para. 200. See also Eritrea Ethiopia Claims Commission, Partial Award, *Jus ad Bellum*, Ethiopia's Claims 1–8, para. 11.

[124] Dinstein (n 10) 255–256.

Another option is to base a rescue operation not on the right to self-defence in art. 51 but on customary international law. To some, sufficient state practice and *opinio juris* do exist to support such a conclusion.[125] The criteria for the legality of a rescue operation are apparently similar to those under an alleged authority in the right to self-defence. Hence, to be lawful, a genuine threat to the safety of the nationals must exist, the host state must be unwilling or unable to offer the protection needed, the operation cannot pursue other goals and the use of force must be proportionate.[126] At present, there is no universal agreement on the legality of rescue operations and state practice reveals some pragmatism in the reaction of states to specific rescue operations.[127]

Russia has tried to defend the legality of its use of force and subsequent annexation of Crimea on the alleged need to defend Russian citizens from genuine threat. However, not only have the Russians never proved the existence of such a threat but its actions also went far beyond what could reasonably be considered proportionate in order to protect its citizens.[128]

13.5.2 **Humanitarian intervention**

A particular contentious issue in international law concerns the legality of non-Council-sanctioned international force to stop massive human rights violations perpetrated against a civilian population, also referred to as 'humanitarian interventions'. The legality of such interventions was debated in 2013 in connection with the civil war in Syria where a number of Western states, including the United States, asserted in broad terms that the use of force against the Syrian government for its alleged policy of using chemical weapons against its own population did not necessarily need to be sanctioned by the Security Council to be compatible with international law.[129]

It is hard not to sympathize with the underlying humanitarian impulses that may drive the proponents of a right to humanitarian intervention, and there is little doubt that the protection of human rights today features as one of the main purposes of the UN. It is, nevertheless, still very difficult to see how such interventions can be lawful unless authorized by the Security Council. First of all, to reiterate, under the Charter, only force used in self-defence is lawful in the absence of an authorization from the Security Council. As noted earlier, the use of force for humanitarian purposes is also covered by the prohibition on the use of force in article 2(4). Secondly, neither state practice nor *opinio juris* seem to support the claim that a non-UN-mandated right to humanitarian intervention has arisen in customary international law.[130] Those who argue in favour of the existence of a right to unilateral humanitarian intervention frequently rely on NATO's 1999 intervention in Kosovo, but a closer look reveals that the intervention in Kosovo only provides limited support. While it is correct

---

[125] Simma (n 5) 226–228. See also Higgins (n 10) 245–248.
[126] Simma (n 5) 228. See also Franck (n 10) 96.
[127] Gray (n 49) 159–160. See also Franck (n 10) 76–96.   [128] See also Bilkova (n 84) 46–47.
[129] See the overview in Anders Henriksen and March Schack, 'The Crisis in Iraq and Humanitarian Intervention' (2014) 1 *Journal on the Use of Force and International Law* 122–147.
[130] Simma (n 5) 224–226.

that the UK did put forward the argument that the intervention could be based on an emerging notion of humanitarian intervention,[131] other NATO states were more reluctant and within NATO there was 'fundamental division' about the legal basis for the operation. In the end, the operation was primarily justified on moral rather than legal grounds. By August 2016, only three states (the UK, Belgium and Denmark) have *explicitly* argued for the existence of a *right* to humanitarian intervention.[132] Proponents of a customary right to humanitarian intervention also tend to over-look the fact that major non-Western states, such as Russia, China and India, con-sidered the intervention in Kosovo a clear violation of the Charter and international law.[133] Furthermore, both the G77[134] and the Non-Aligned Movement have clearly stated their opposition to humanitarian intervention without authorization from the Security Council.[135] This was also reflected in the international reactions to the 2013 US and British threats of intervention in Syria without authorization from the Security Council.[136]

In the last decade, politicians and commentators have increasingly begun to refer to the doctrine of so-called 'Responsibility to Protect' (R2P) as an important element in their justification for the alleged lawfulness of unilateral humanitarian intervention. R2P has become the latest buzzword in international relations, and in some states the doctrine has even found its way into important foreign policy docu-ments. The doctrine was invented in the early 2000s in response to the debates in the 1990s about the legality of humanitarian intervention and the momentous moral failures of the international community in Rwanda and Bosnia, and it later found its way into UN documents, including the 2005 World Summit Outcome Document. It is built on the notion that sovereignty comes with an obligation to protect civilian populations from atrocities and that all states—both territorial states as well as all states in the international community—have a responsibility to prevent atrocities. Whatever merits R2P may have as an emerging common framework for prevent-ing mass atrocity crimes, it does not justify the use of force for humanitarian pur-poses without the support of the Security Council.[137] Although it is correct that the

---

[131] Gray (n 49) 50.

[132] For the UK position, see Prime Minister's Office, 'Chemical Weapon Use by Syrian Regime—UK Government Legal Position' (29 August 2013). See also the UK's position in relation to Kosovo in UN Doc. S/PV.3988 (24 March 1999). The Danish position can be found in UPN, Alm.del. Bilag 298, 30 August 2013. As mentioned earlier, Belgium argued for the legality of a right to humanitarian intervention in *Legality of Use of Force (Serbia and Montenegro v Belgium)* (n 9).

[133] UN Doc. S/PV.3988 (24 March 1999), 2, 12 and 15, and UN Doc. S/PV.3989 (26 March 1999), 3, 4, 9 and 16.

[134] Group of 77 South Summit, 'Declaration of the South Summit', Havana, Cuba, 10–14 April, para. 54.

[135] Non-Aligned Movement, 'Comments of the Non-Aligned Movement on the Observations and Recommendations Contained in the Report of the High-Level Panel on Threats, Challenges and Change' (n 103) para. 14.

[136] See the overview in Henriksen and Schack (n 129).

[137] Henriksen and Schack (n 129) 132–133. But see Jennifer Welsh and Maria Banda, 'International Law and the Responsibility to Protect: Clarifying or Expanding States' Responsibilities?' (2010) 2 *Global Responsibility to Protect* 213, 230. See also Public International Law and Policy Group (PILPG), 'Humanitarian Intervention in Syria: The Legal Basis' (July 2012).

doctrine holds that the international community also has a responsibility to help to protect populations from atrocities and that 'we are prepared to take collective action' if peaceful means are inadequate, the 2005 Outcome Document explicitly refers to the existing framework in the Charter and clearly states that coercive meas- ures shall be taken 'through the Security Council, in accordance with the Charter, including Chapter VII'.[138]

Summary

The answers to the questions of when, for what reason and how a member of a com- munity may forcefully submit another to its will is of paramount importance for the maintenance of peaceful relations among the members. *Jus ad bellum* regulates when a state is entitled to resort to the use of force against another state. The relevant rules are found in both the 1945 UN Charter as well as in customary international law. In practice, however, the content of the rules and principles in question are identical. The 1945 ambition to create a framework for collective security is the key to understanding the legal framework of the Charter. One of the main provisions of the Charter is art- icle 2(4) that bans the member states from using force in their international relations. Under the Charter, only two exceptions to the prohibition in article 2(4) exist. The first exception is the competence of the UN Security Council to authorize the use of force. The second is the inherent right of all states to defend themselves against an armed attack. Since the primary purposes of the UN is to limit the use of unilateral force and collectivize the use of force that may be required to maintain international peace and security, it is hard to see how unilateral use of force not sanctioned by the Council can be lawful under international law.

Recommended reading

Classic works on the use of force include Ian Brownlie, *International Law and the Use of Force by States* (Oxford University Press, 1963) and D. W. Bowett, *Self-Defence in International Law* (Frederik A. Praeger, 1958).

More recently see, Yoram Dinstein, *War, Aggression and Self-Defence* (5th edn, Cambridge University Press, 2011); Thomas Franck, *Recourse to Force: State Action Against Threats and Armed Attacks* (Cambridge University Press, 2002); and Christine Gray, *International Law and the Use of Force* (3rd edn, Oxford University Press, 2008).

Bruno Simma's edited version of *The Charter of the United Nations: A Commentary* (Oxford University Press, 2012), contains an impressive and meticulous discussion of the UN Charter.

Other useful works include Tom Ruys, '*Armed Attack' and Article 51 of the UN Charter: Evolutions in Customary Law and Practice* (Cambridge University Press, 2010).

---

[138] UN Doc. A/Res/60/1 (24 October 2005), para. 139. See also the Secretary-General's statements in 2009 in UN Doc. A/63/677, para. 3.

Questions for discussion

1. How does the tension between, on the one hand, considerations of order and stability and, on the other, overall notions of justice manifest itself in the international regulation of the use of force?

2. The UN Security Council has primary responsibility for the maintenance of international peace and security and has therefore been vested with certain powers. Are there any limits to what the Council can authorize?

3. What legal authority does a regional organization, such as NATO, possess with regard to the use of force?

4. Why is the notion of 'implied authority' of the use of force in Security Council resolutions controversial?

5. According to the text, the so-called 'accumulation of events' doctrine is controversial. Why is that the case?

6. In what regard has the threat from terrorism led to uncertainty about the applicability of the right to self-defence under article 51?

7. How could one argue for the legality of humanitarian intervention in the absence of an authorization from the UN Security Council?

14

The law of armed conflict

CENTRAL ISSUES

1. This chapter examines the international regulation of the conduct of military operations (*jus in bello*).

2. It introduces the relevant sources of law and discusses the application of the law of armed conflict in the different forms of armed conflict.

3. The chapter also provides an overview of the issue of battlefield status and presents the distinction between combatants and civilians. It also discusses the basic principles on the conduct of hostilities, including the principle of distinction and the prohibition against causing unnecessary suffering to combatants.

4. It discusses the situation that concerns the regulation of non-international armed conflict and examines the interplay between the application of the law of armed conflict and international human rights law in times of armed conflict.

14.1 Introduction

This chapter examines those parts of international law that regulate *how military operations must be conducted—jus in bello*. The identification of norms for proper conduct in times of war has been a topic of interest for thousands of years and some of the most important works in international law have been devoted to the regulation of war.[1] It is, naturally, a field of international law that is of vital importance for the maintenance of peaceful and well-organized relations among states and it constitutes an inherent part of the international law of coexistence. *Jus in bello* is also referred to as the 'law of armed conflict' or 'international humanitarian law' and in the following these terms will be used interchangeably. The term 'war' has rarely been used since the 1945 adoption of the UN Charter.

At the outset it is important to reiterate that *jus ad bellum* and the laws of armed conflict are conceptually distinct and must be applied independently. In practice, *all*

---

[1] Christopher Greenwood, 'Historical Development and Legal Basis' in Dieter Fleck, *The Handbook of International Humanitarian Law* (2nd edn, Oxford University Press, 2008) 15–20.

parties to an armed conflict must comply with the law of armed conflict no matter which party is considered to be the aggressor who may have violated its obligations under *jus ad bellum* and who is the victim of such aggression.[2]

The law of armed conflict is an inherently pragmatic discipline that accepts the unfortunate reality that war is a recurring feature of human existence. Rather than striving for the complete outlawing of war, it merely seeks to offer sensible and balanced solutions taking account of both military necessity and humanitarian sentiments. It presents delicate compromises that limit human suffering to the greatest extent possible without negating the right of the warring parties to pursue their military objectives.

The chapter begins in Section 14.2 with an overview of the most important legal sources before Section 14.3 discusses when humanitarian law applies. Section 14.4 examines the issue of battlefield status and the distinction between combatants and civilians and Section 14.5 provides an overview of some of the most basic principles governing the conduct of hostilities. Section 14.6 deals with the issue of regulation of non-international armed conflict before Section 14.7 explores the relationship between international humanitarian law and human rights law in times of armed conflict.

14.2 The sources of international humanitarian law

The law of armed conflict has developed incrementally in response to often bitter experience of past conflicts and the invention of new means and methods of warfare. As states have continued to develop new modes and forms of killing and maiming other human beings in war, so has the need for revision of and addition to the relevant legal framework by which it is governed.[3] The 'modern' history of international humanitarian law is generally said to start with the introduction in the American Civil War (1861–1865) of a manual on existing rules and principles for the conduct of war developed by a German–American professor, Francis Lieber—the 'Lieber Code'.[4] Also, in 1863 the Swiss national Henry Dunant founded the *International Committee of the Red Cross* (ICRC) in Geneva that has since played a vital role in the development of international humanitarian law.

Historically, the treaty-based regulation of the law of armed conflict has been divided into 'Geneva law' and 'Hague law'' The first category refers to the many conventions adopted in Geneva, Switzerland, that generally seek to protect vulnerable groups and victims of armed conflict. The most important of these are the four 1949 Geneva Conventions that have 196 parties and are the most ratified treaties in the world. The Conventions cover, respectively the Condition of the Wounded and Sick

---

[2] See also the preamble to the 1977 Additional Protocol Concerning the Protection of Victims of International Armed Conflict.

[3] For a debate about contemporary armed conflicts and some of the challenges they pose, see, inter alia, Steven Haines, 'The Nature of War and the Character of Contemporary Armed Conflict' in Elizabeth Wilmshurst (ed.), *International Law and the Classification of Conflicts* (Oxford University Press, 2012) 9–31.

[4] Gary Solis, *The Law of Armed Conflict* (Cambridge University Press, 2010) 39–46.

in Armed Forces in the Field (I), the Condition of Wounded, Sick and Shipwrecked Members of Armed Forces at Sea (II), the Treatment of Prisoners of War (III) and the Protection of Civilian Persons in Time of War (IV). As we shall see in Section 14.3.3, one of the 1949 Conventions' most significant contributions was the inclusion of a Common article 3 with a range of minimum standards of protection for victims of non-international armed conflict. 'Hague law', on the other hand, primarily regulates the means and methods of warfare and consists of a series of conventions adopted at the Hague Peace Conferences in 1899 and 1907. A few of these remain important. Hague Convention IV and the annex thereto, for example, is of vital importance to the regulation of belligerent occupation. In 1977, a number of significant Additional Protocols to the four Geneva Conventions were adopted. The most of important of these were the Additional Protocol Relatinging to the Protection of Victims of International Armed Conflicts (API) and the Additional Protocol Relating to the Protection of Victims of Non-International Armed Conflicts (APII). Since these Protocols cover both protection of individuals and lawful means and methods of warfare, they brought an end to the clear conceptual distinction between 'Geneva' and 'Hague' law.[5] Other important conventions include the 1925 Geneva Protocol on Gas Warfare, the 1954 Convention for the Protection of Cultural Property in the Event of Armed Conflict, the 1972 Convention on Biological Weapons, the 1980 Weapons Convention, the 1993 Chemical Weapons Conventions and the 1997 Ottawa Land Mines Convention on anti-personnel mines.

Some older conventions contain so-called 'general participation' clauses—*clausula si omnes*—whereby the convention only applies if *all* belligerents in a conflict are parties to the convention.[6] Although such a clause is based on the prima facie sensible assumption that all parties to an armed conflict should be bound by the same sets of rules and obligations, it may preclude the application of a convention in a conflict that involves a group of states simply because one of the parties is not a party to the convention. More recent conventions, therefore, stipulate that contracting parties are bound by the conventions in their *mutual relations* even if one of the parties to the conflict is not a party to the convention.[7] While this does not make the convention applicable in an armed conflict between two states unless both states are party to the convention, it ensures that the convention applies at least between the contracting parties in a multistate conflict.

The basic principles in the major treaties in the laws of armed conflict generally reflect customary international law binding on all states.[8] This is certainly the case with regard to the central provisions of the 1907 Hague Convention IV,[9] the 1949 Geneva

---

[5] See also *Legality of the Threat or Use of Nuclear Weapons*, Advisory Opinion [1996] ICJ Rep 226, para. 75.

[6] See, inter alia, art. 2 of the 1907 Hague Convention IV.   [7] See Common art. 2.

[8] For an overview of relevant customary international law, see Jean-Marie Henckaerts and Louise Doswald-Beck, *Customary International Humanitarian Law*, Vol. I (Cambridge University Press, 2005).

[9] See, inter alia, *Legal Consequences of the Construction of a Wall in the Occupied Palestinian Territory*, Advisory Opinion [2004] ICJ Rep 136, para. 89. See also HCJ 769/02 *Public Committee Against Torture v Government*, 14 December 2006, para. 20.

Conventions[10] and the listed weapons conventions with the exception of the 1997 Ottawa Convention.[11] The Additional Protocols contain a number of provisions that were so controversial that a number of important states, including the United States, Israel, India and Pakistan,[12] decided not to ratify them. The provisions in question are therefore not binding under customary international law. In a number of cases, the International Court of Justice (ICJ) has referred to the fundamental rules of the laws of war as constituting a 'minimum yardstick' that reflects 'elementary considerations of humanity'.[13] In *The Wall*, the Court found that these rules are of an *erga omnes* character.[14]

14.3 The application of international humanitarian law

14.3.1 Introduction

International law used to distinguish very clearly between a 'state of peace' and a 'state of war' and the relations between two or more states were perceived to be governed by either of the two. In addition, the determination of when war actually broke out was also governed by formal criteria, most notably by issuing a formal declaration of war. In the 21st century, however, the line separating war and peace is rarely so easily discernible and the application of the laws of armed conflict does not dependent on the subjective intentions of the parties and a declaration of war. In fact, since the adoption of the 1945 UN Charter, declarations of war are rare.

The laws of armed conflict apply in times of armed conflict but neither of the conventions define 'armed conflict'. The most widely cited definition is found in the seminal *Tadić* case where the International Criminal Tribunal for the former Yugoslavia (ICTY) stated that an armed conflict exists 'whenever there is a resort to armed force between States or protracted armed violence between governmental authorities and organized armed groups or between such groups within a State'.[15] The '*Tadić* definition' reflects the treaty-based differentiation between 'international armed conflict' involving the armed forces of two or more states and 'non-international armed conflict' that involves fighting between either a state and a private organized armed group or between two or more such groups.

---

[10] See *Nuclear Weapons* (n 5) para. 79.   [11] Henckaerts and Doswald-Beck (n 8) 282.

[12] See the overview in Yves Sandoz, Christophe Swinarski and Bruno Zimmermann (eds), *Commentary on the Additional Protocols of 8 June 1977 to the Geneva Conventions of 12 August 1949* (ICRC/Martinus Nijhoff, 1987) 39–56. The US position is available in *Letter of Transmittal from president Ronald Reagan, Protocol II Additional to the 1949 Geneva Conventions, and Relating to the Protection of Victims of Noninternational Armed Conflict* (1987) 81 *American Journal of International Law* 910.

[13] *Military and Paramilitary Activities in and against Nicaragua (Nicaragua v United States)*, Merits [1986] ICJ Rep 14, para. 218. See also *Nuclear Weapons* (n 5) para. 79.

[14] *The Wall* (n 9) para. 157.

[15] ICTY, *Prosecutor v Tadić*, Appeals Chamber, Decision on the Defence Motion for Interlocutory Appeal on Jurisdiction, ICTY-91-1 (2 October 1995), para. 70.

In the following we begin by examining 'international armed conflict' (Section 14.3.2), before we discuss 'non-international armed conflict' (Section 14.3.3). We will then discuss the issue of 'transnational armed conflict' (Section 14.3.4) and changes to conflict status (Section 14.3.5).

14.3.2 International armed conflict

Common article 2 of the Geneva Conventions stipulated that the Conventions apply in 'all cases of declared war or of any other armed conflict which may arise between two or more of the High Contracting Parties, even if the state of war is not recognized by one of them'. The Conventions thereby cover 'classic' interstate armed conflicts where two or more states fight each other and it is towards the regulation of such conflicts that the majority of the law of armed conflict is aimed. An international armed conflict arises in relation to 'any difference arising between two States and leading to the intervention of members of the armed forces' and it would seem to make 'no difference how long the conflict lasts, how much slaughter takes place, or how numerous are the participating forces'.[16] It is immaterial whether the involved states recognize the existence of an armed conflict. The determination is *factual* and not technical/formal.[17] It is also immaterial whether one of the parties involved is not formally recognized as a 'state'. As long as two or more parties can be said to satisfy the conditions for statehood that we visited in Chapter 4, the armed conflict will be considered 'international'.[18] Under API, an 'international armed conflict' includes certain armed conflicts involving a state and a non-state actor. Thus, according to article 1(4) of API, armed conflict in which 'peoples are fighting against colonial domination and alien occupation and against racist régimes in the exercise of their right of self-determination' are also deemed to be of an international character. The Protocol has yet to be applied to such a conflict. The Geneva Conventions also cover situations of *belligerent occupation*, whether total or partial, 'even if the said occupation meets with no armed resistance'. Territory is 'occupied' when it is actually placed under the authority of the hostile army.[19] The occupation extends only to the territory where such authority has been established and can be exercised.[20] Thus, 'effective control' seems to be an indispensable condition of belligerent occupation.[21] Examples of belligerent occupation include the 2003–2004 US-led occupation of Iraq following the fall of the Saddam Hussein regime and the situation in Crimea after the March 2014 annexation by Russia. In *The Wall*, the ICJ found that Israel is an occupying power in the Palestinian territories 'situated between the Green Line and the former eastern boundary of Palestine under

---

[16] Jean S. Pictet, *Commentary to the III Geneva Convention Relative to the Treatment of Prisoners of War* (ICRC, 1960) 23. See also Yoram Dinstein, including his *The Conduct of Hostilities under the Law of International Armed Conflict* (2nd edn, Cambridge University Press, 2010) 28–29.

[17] *The Wall* (n 9) para. 95. See also Pictet (n 16) 23.   [18] Dinstein (n 16) 29.

[19] See art. 42 of the 1907 Hague Regulations.

[20] For an overview, see Yoram Dinstein, *The International Law of Belligerent Occupation* (Cambridge University Press, 2009) 42–45.

[21] Ibid, 43.

the Mandate', including in East Jerusalem.[22] With the exception of East Jerusalem, this is recognized by Israel.[23] Whether Israel can also be considered an occupying power in Gaza after its 2005 disengagement is more uncertain.[24]

Historically, international armed conflicts came to an end with the conclusion of a peace treaty—or at least an express declaration—but, like declarations of war, peace treaties are now rare. In practice, hostilities may be terminated either on a temporary or a permanent basis and the conflict cannot generally be considered to have ended unless there is evidence that neither of the parties *intend* to resume the hostilities.[25] At times, an intention to permanently suspend hostilities may be inferred from the overall circumstances. For example, although the 2011 international armed conflict between a number of Western states and Gaddafi's Libya did not end with the conclusion of a formal peace treaty, it is generally assumed that the conflict was brought to an end with the fall of Gaddafi and the general conclusion of the aerial bombing campaign.[26] Importantly, certain obligations arise as soon as active hostilities have ended regardless of the existence of a formal peace treaty. For example, the Third Geneva Convention on Prisoners of War stipulates that prisoners of war 'shall be released and repatriated without delay after the cessation of active hostilities'.[27] It is also worth noting that an occupying power remains bound by its obligations 'for the duration of the occupation'.[28]

14.3.3 **Non-international armed conflict**

The laws of armed conflict also cover armed conflicts not involving two or more states—also known as 'non-international armed conflict'. It was not until 1949 that international law expanded the scope of its regulation to include conflicts between a state and a private actor or between two or more private actors on the territory of a state. Common article 3 of the four Geneva Conventions contains a number of minimum guarantees that must be applied by all parties in 'the case of armed conflict not of an international character occurring in the territory of one of the High Contracting Parties'. Common article 3 conflict has traditionally been referred to as 'internal' armed conflict or 'civil war'.[29]

A non-international armed conflict must be distinguished from 'acts of banditry or unorganized and short-lived insurrections' that are generally considered to fall outside Common article 3.[30] Two conditions must be fulfilled before violence qualifies

---

[22] *The Wall* (n 9) para. 78.   [23] *Public Committee Against Torture* (n 9) paras 19–20.

[24] A discussion is available in Iain Scobbie, 'Gaza' in Wilmshurst (n 3) 280–316.

[25] Dinstein (n 16) 48–49. But see Greenwood (n 1) 72.

[26] A discussion of the war in Libya is available in Louise Arimatsu and Mohbuda Choudhury, 'The Legal Classification of the Armed Conflicts in Syria, Yemen and Libya', Chatham House, March 2014, 34–41.

[27] See also Eritrea Ethiopia Claims Commission, *Partial Award, Prisoners of War, Eritrea's claim 17 between The State of Eritrea and The Federal Democratic Republic of Ethiopia*, 1 July 2003, para. 163.

[28] GC IV art. 6.

[29] See also art. 8(2)(f) of the Rome Statute of the International Criminal Court.

[30] Jean S. Pictet, *Commentary to the IV Geneva Convention Relative to the Protection of Civilian Persons in Time of War* (ICRC, 1958) 36. See also *Tadić*, Trial Judgment, para. 562 and *Prosecutor v Akayesu*, Judgment, ICTR-96-4-T (2 September 1998), para. 619.

as non-international armed conflict. First, *the level of violence must surpass a certain minimum threshold*. As noted in the ICRC commentaries, 'the conflicts referred to in Article 3 are armed conflicts, with armed forces on either side engaged on hostilities—conflicts, in short, which are in many respects similar to an international war, but take place within the confines of a single country'.[31] The second condition relates to the requirement that both parties to the non-international armed conflict must be *militarily organized*. In practice, of course, the forces of a state party are always considered to be sufficiently organized and the requirement is thus only relevant for private actors. Although it is not required that a private actor must be organized in a manner similar to that of the armed forces of a state,[32] the ICRC specifies that it must have a 'military-like formation' that includes 'a certain level of organization and command structure'.[33] The requirement of military organization may be difficult to fulfil. In relation to the outbreak of the civil war in Syria, for example, it took a substantial amount of time before the opposition could be said to be sufficiently militarily organized.[34]

The category of non-international armed conflict was expanded with the adoption of the 1977 Additional Protocol II to the Geneva Conventions. In practice, however, APII has only been applied in a limited number of armed conflicts. It only applies to armed conflicts between a state and an organized armed group under responsible command that is capable of exercising 'such control over a part of its territory as to enable them to carry out sustained and concerted military operations and to implement this Protocol'.[35] The APII seems, however, to have become applicable during the 2011 armed conflict in Libya when the popular 'Arab Spring' uprisings rapidly developed into armed hostilities between pro-government forces and armed insurgents. As violence increased and the insurgents became more and more militarily organized, the situation qualified as armed conflict under Common article 3 and APII would seem to have been applicable in early March 2011 when the insurgents managed to assume control over major parts of Libyan territory after a rapid retreat by government forces.[36] The Protocol may also be applicable in relation to at least some of the hostilities that, at the time of writing, rage in the civil war in Yemen[37] and in relation to the armed conflict in Ukraine where pro-Russian militants appear to be in effective control of parts of Eastern Ukraine.[38] In practice, though, Russia may be so involved in the armed conflict in Ukraine that it should not be considered 'non-international' but rather 'international' (see Section 14.3.5).

In *Tadić*, the ICTY stated that the laws of armed conflict continue to apply in a non-international armed conflict until 'a peaceful settlement is achieved'.[39] In practice,

---

[31] Pictet (n 30) 37. See also art. 8(2)(b) of the Rome Statute of the International Criminal Court.

[32] *Prosecutor v Limaj et al.*, Judgment, IT-03-66-T (30 November 2005), para. 89.

[33] ICRC, *International Humanitarian Law and Terrorism: Questions and Answers* (2004). See also *Limaj* (n 32) para. 90 and *Prosecutor v Harandinaj et al.*, Trial Judgment (3 April 2008), para. 60. See also *Prosecutor v Thomas Lubanga Diyalo*, Judgment, ICC-01/14-01/06-2842, para. 537.

[34] See the discussion in Arimatsu and Choudhury (n 26) 15.   [35] APII art 1.

[36] Arimatsu and Choudhury (n 26) 34–38.   [37] Ibid, 29–30.

[38] Robert Heinsch, 'Conflict Classification in Ukraine: The Return of the "Proxy War"?' (2015) 91 *International Law Studies* 356.

[39] *Tadić* (n 15) para. 70.

though, violence may cease to qualify as a non-international armed conflict if it falls below the minimum threshold or if it no longer involves two parties that can be said to be sufficiently militarily organized. In addition, a non-international armed conflict may also be considered to have been brought to an end if the conflict evolves into an international armed conflict (see Section 14.3.5).[40]

14.3.4 'Transnational' armed conflict

It is not clear how one should classify an armed conflict that involves hostilities between a state and a private actor that is located on the territory of another state. The issue is relevant, for example, in relation to classification of the use of force by a number of states against the so-called Islamic State (ISIL) in Syria and Iraq and it is also of interest for the US programme for targeted killings—often with the use of unmanned aerial vehicles—of suspected terrorists in places such as Pakistan, Yemen and Somalia. As is well known, the US government adopts the position that the United States is engaged in an armed conflict with members of al Qaida and associated forces.[41] In the wake of the 9/11 attacks, the United States argued that the conflict should be considered as a new and entirely different form of armed conflict from the traditionally recognised types of armed conflict and that the 'war on terror' was therefore not governed by international humanitarian law.[42] That position has been discarded and attention is instead aimed at determining whether a transnational armed conflict should be classified as one of an international or non-international character.

One option is for the classification of the armed conflict to depend on the existence of consent to the use of force by the state in whose territory the private actor is located.[43] Thus, if the territorial state has consented to the use of force against the private actor by the foreign state, it will be a non-international armed conflict; and if it has not, the use of force by the foreign state should then be considered to be aimed *against* the territorial state and the conflict should therefore be found to be an international armed conflict The ICJ's judgment in *Armed Activities* appears to lend support to this position.[44] An alternative view—endorsed by the present author—holds that a transnational armed conflict is a non-international armed conflict as long as the foreign state only uses force against the non-state actor.[45] If the acts of the private actor cannot be attributed to a state, the conflict (remains) non-international in character.

---

[40] Yoram Dinstein, *Non-International Armed Conflicts in International Law* (Cambridge University Press, 2014) 47–50.

[41] Harold H. Koh, 'The Obama Administration and International Law', Remarks at the Annual Meeting of the American Society of International Law, Washington DC, 25 March 2010.

[42] *Memorandum From Alberto R. Gonzales, Counsel to the President, to President Bush*, 25 January 2002. See also *Salim Ahmed Hamdan, Petitioner v Donald H. Rumsfeld et al., Brief for Respondents*, pp. 38 and 48.

[43] Dapo Akande, 'Classification of Armed Conflicts: Relevant Legal Concepts' in Wilmshurst (n 3) 73–79.

[44] *Armed Activities on the Territory of the Congo (Democratic Republic of the Congo v Uganda)*, Judgment [2005] ICJ Rep 168, paras 163–165.

[45] See also Noam Lubell, *Extraterritorial Use of Force Against Non-State Actors* (Oxford University Press, 2010) 100–104.

This position was endorsed by the International Criminal Court (ICC) in the *Lubanga* case[46] and by the US Supreme Court.[47]

Much debate has surrounded the US claim that it is involved in an armed conflict with al Qaida and its associated forces. Conceptually, nothing precludes a state from engaging in armed conflict with a terrorist organization provided the *Tadić* conditions are fulfilled.[48]

14.3.5 **Changes to conflict status**

It is not infrequent that armed conflict develops and thus requires a new classification. First of all, a non-international armed conflict can be 'internationalized' and develop an international character if another state becomes so involved that it becomes a party to the conflict. This may occur in two instances. First, when the foreign state introduces its own forces into the hostilities on the side of the non-state actor. Secondly, case law from the ICTY indicates that 'internationalization' also occurs when the foreign state exercises 'overall control' over the militarily organized private actor. According to the ICTY, the traditional 'effective control' test for state attribution for acts of private individuals should be replaced with an 'overall control' test whereby attribution is in effect as soon as a state 'has a role in organizing, coordination or planning the military actions' of a militarily organized group in addition to financing, training and equipping or providing operational support.[49] While the ICJ has rejected the 'overall control' test for the purposes of state attribution under general international law, it has left open the possibility that it could be 'suitable' for determining whether or not an armed conflict is international.[50] A non-international armed conflict may also evolve into one or more international armed conflicts if the state in which the conflict occurs disintegrates and is replaced by new sovereign states. In *Tadić*, the ICTY concluded that the Federal Republic of Yugoslavia's continued participation in the armed conflict in Bosnia after the latter acquired status as an independent state in 1992, ignited an international armed conflict between those two states.[51]

An international armed conflict may be 'internalized' if a state ceases to exercise 'overall control' over a private actor involved in an armed conflict with a state or if the private actor in question succeeds in replacing the former government and subsequently gives its consent to the continued foreign intervention. The latter occurred in 2001 in Afghanistan when the international armed conflict between Afghanistan and a number of states in an international US-led coalition evolved into a non-international armed conflict when the Taleban were ousted and replaced with a new Afghan government led by Hamid Karzai.[52]

---

[46] *Lubanga* (n 33) para. 539.
[47] *Hamdan v Rumsfeld*, 548 US 557 (2006), see pp. 65–69 of the judgment.
[48] Noam Lubell, 'The War (?) against Al-Qaeda' in Wilmshurst (n 3) 434–437.
[49] ICTY, *Tadić* (n 15) Appeals Chamber, Judgment, para. 137.
[50] *Application of the Convention on the Prevention and Punishment of the Crime of Genocide (Bosnia and Herzegovina v Serbia and Montenegro)*, Judgment [2007] ICJ Rep 43, para. 404.
[51] ICTY, *Tadić* (n 49) para. 162.
[52] For a discussion, see Françoise J. Hampson, 'Afghanistan 2001–2010' in Wilmshurst (n 3) 242–258.

The 2011 armed conflict in Libya is a particularly interesting case study of conflict classification. As we saw earlier, the armed conflict between pro- and anti-government forces constituted a non-international armed conflict governed by Common article 3 and—after the rebels' successful seizure of substantial parts of Libyan territory— seemingly also APII to the Geneva Conventions. Following the initiation in March 2011 of an aerial bombing campaign by an international coalition against the Libyan regime, the existing non-international armed conflict was supplemented by an international armed conflict. It also bears noting that a number of states rendered extensive support to the rebels and that the support would have had the effect of 'internationalizing' the non-international armed conflict between the rebels and the government forces if it equated to exercising 'overall control' of the rebels.[53] The Libyan case is complicated even further because France decided to recognize the rebels as the legitimate representatives of the Libyan people *before* the launch of the air campaign and the physical ousting of Gaddafi and the government forces. This raises the question of whether the recognition transformed the international armed conflict between France and the pro-Gaddafi forces to one of a non-international character.[54] The relationship between classification of armed conflict and the role of recognition—an issue also of relevance to the ongoing armed conflict in Syria—is complicated and the law may be far from settled.

14.4 Battlefield status in international armed conflict

14.4.1 Introduction

The protection offered to individuals in times of armed conflict depends in part on the classification of armed conflict in question and on the specific status of the individuals. International humanitarian law offers a much more detailed regime of protection in times of international armed conflict than in non-international armed conflict and the overview in this section is limited to regulation in international armed conflict. Non-international armed conflict is dealt with in Section 14.6. In international armed conflict, everyone has a status and an accompanying level of legal protection.[55] The most relevant categories are those of 'combatants' and 'civilians'.

14.4.2 Combatants

Combatants consist of members of the armed forces of the parties to the armed conflict and other individuals who take a direct part in the hostilities. All other individuals are considered to be civilians.[56] Since they take part in the armed conflict, combatants can lawfully be the object of lethal force at 'all times and in all circumstances'[57] or detention until the end of hostilities. Importantly, detention of enemy combatants

---

[53] For a discussion, see Arimatsu and Choudhury (n 26) 39–40.   [54] Ibid, 40.
[55] For an overview, see Solis (n 4) 186–238.   [56] APII art. 50(1).   [57] Dinstein (n 16) 34.

is not meant as a punishment but simply as a means of disabling the combatant from participating in the combat. In a sense, the combatant trades his liberty for the safety of his life. Unlike in times of peace, detention is therefore not conditioned on prosecution for wrongful conduct.

Conceptually, it is possible to distinguish between lawful/privileged and unlawful/unprivileged combatants.[58] A combatant may be considered to be lawful if the individual is entitled to take part in the hostilities and unlawful if they are not so entitled. The determination of the entitlement to participate in the hostilities is crucial because lawful and unlawful combatants are treated very differently. A lawful combatant possesses so-called 'combatant's privilege' which means that the individual is offered immunity by international law from prosecution for merely participating in the armed conflict.[59] In addition, if a lawful combatant is captured by the enemy, the individual is entitled to protection as a prisoner of war under the Third Geneva Convention on Prisoners of War.[60] An unlawful combatant, on the other hand, does not benefit from 'combatant's privilege' and may therefore be criminally prosecuted under the national laws of the detaining state for acts perpetrated in the course of the hostilities. Unlike a lawful combatant, then, an unlawful combatant may be prosecuted for murder if the individual has used deadly force against a member of the enemy's armed forces. Furthermore, an unlawful combatant does not benefit from protection as a prisoner of war under the Third Geneva Convention. An unlawful combatant is not devoid of protection, however. Despite occasional claims to the contrary,[61] it is now well established that unlawful combatants are protected under the Fourth Geneva Convention on Civilians[62] and, if applicable to the conflict, under API.[63] In addition, article 75 of the Protocol lists a number of fundamental guarantees that protect individuals 'who do not benefit from a more favourable protection' that are generally considered to reflect customary international law.

The requirements for being a lawful combatant have undergone a number of historical changes. For those states that are (still) not parties to API, the laws of armed conflict operate with three main types of lawful combatants, reflected in the Third Geneva Convention on Prisoners of War. The first category is that of 'members of the armed forces of a state as well as members of militias or volunteer corps forming part of such forces'.[64] The second type is 'members of other militias and members of other volunteer corps, including those of organized resistance movements' that fulfil four cumulative conditions. They must be 'commanded by a person responsible for his subordinates', have 'a fixed distinctive sign recognizable at a distance', carry 'their

---

[58] Ibid, 33–35. Some presentations of battlefield status use a different terminology and desist from relying on two categories of combatant (lawful/unlawful) in order to operate with two categories of civilians (privileged/unprivileged), see e.g. *Public Committee Against Torture* (n 9) remarks by Vice President E. Rivlin, para. 2. In practical terms, the differences in approach lead to the same results.

[59] APII art. 43(2).   [60] APII art. 44(1).

[61] See, inter alia, Inter-AmCtHR, *Response of the United States to Request for Precautionary Measures—Detainees in Guantanamo Bay, Cuba* (2002), pp. 22f. See also *Public Committee Against Torture* (n 9) para. 27.

[62] Pictet (n 30) 51. See also *Prosecutor v Delalić et al*, Judgment, IT-96-21-T (16 November 1998), para. 271. *Public Committee Against Torture* (n 9) para. 28.

[63] See, inter alia, arts 44(4) and 45(3).   [64] GC III art. 4(1).

arms openly' and conduct their 'operations in accordance with the laws and customs of war'.[65] The third and final category of lawful combatants contained in the Third Geneva Convention is the rare case of *levée en masse* where the inhabitants of a non-occupied territory 'spontaneously take up arms' to resist an invading force 'without having had time to form themselves into regular armed units, provided they carry arms openly and respect the laws and customs of war'.[66]

API erases the formal distinction between regular and irregular forces in the Third Geneva Convention and introduces a less strict standard for being considered a lawful combatant. First, the Protocol's article 43(1) stipulates that the armed forces 'consist of all organized armed forces, groups and units which are under a command responsible to that Party for the conduct of its subordinates'. Secondly, although article 44(3) states that combatants must distinguish themselves from the civilian population when engaged in an attack or in a military operation preparatory to an attack, it also notes that 'the nature of the hostilities' may make that requirement hard to comply with. Thus, according to API, an individual will remain a lawful combatant as long as he, 'in such situations', carries his arms openly: (1) 'during each military engagement' and (2) 'during such time as he is visible to the adversary while he is engaged in a military deployment preceding the launching of an attack in which he is to participate'. The more relaxed standards in article 44(3) have been criticized by powerful states and scholars for reducing '*ad absurdum* the conditions for lawful combatancy' to the detriment of the protection of the civilian population who will suffer from any blurring of the boundaries between combatants and civilians.[67] For that reason, the content of article 44(3) cannot be said to reflect customary international law.

The laws of armed conflict contain a number of provisions that are meant to ensure that an individual is not deprived of the rightful status as a lawful combatant. For parties who are not bound by API, the relevant provision is article 5 of the Third Geneva Convention according to which a person who has 'committed a belligerent act' and 'has fallen into the hands of enemy' shall be protected by the Convention 'until such time as their status has been determined by a competent tribunal'. In API, the protection against 'mistaken' status is contained in article 45(1) which stipulates that anyone who has taken part in hostilities and fallen into the 'power of an adverse Party shall be presumed to be a prisoner of war … if he claims the status of prisoner of war, or if he appears to be entitled to such status'.

14.4.3 Civilians

The concept of a 'civilian' is delimited negatively, in the sense that all individuals who are not considered to be combatants are therefore deemed to be civilians. All civilians

---

[65] GC III art 4(2)(a)–(d). See also art. 1 of Annex to the 1907 Hague Convention IV Concerning the Laws and Customs of War on Land.

[66] GC III art. 4(6). See also art. 2 of the 1907 Hague Convention IV Concerning the Laws and Customs of War on Land.

[67] See e.g. the critique in Dinstein (n 16) 54.

must enjoy general protection from the dangers of military operations and civilians shall not be the object of attack unless they take a direct part in hostilities (conceptually, when a civilian participates in the fighting he or she ceases to be considered as a 'civilian').[68] Thus, while the laws of armed conflict do not prohibit a civilian from taking part in the hostilities, they do specify that it is not without practical consequences. If a civilian falls into the hands of the enemy in an international armed conflict, they will enjoy protection under the Fourth Geneva Convention and—if applicable—the protection offered to civilians in API.[69] According to article 50(1) of that Protocol, in case of doubt, a person 'shall be considered to be a civilian'.

Since civilians lose protection from direct attack when they take a direct part in hostilities, it is not surprising that much effort has been put into defining when, more exactly, the line that separates acts that constitute 'direct/active participation' and those that do not is crossed. In an interpretive guidance on the concept of direct participation the ICRC lists three cumulative conditions that must be met for acts to constitute 'direct participation'.[70] First, the act must be 'likely to adversely affect the military operations or military capacity of a party to an armed conflict or, alternatively, to inflict death, injury, or destruction on persons or objects protected against direct attack'. There is, in other words, a threshold regarding the damage or harm that is likely to result from the act in question and some acts are simply deemed not to be of sufficient character to qualify. Secondly, there must be a 'direct causal link between the act and the harm likely to result either from that act, or from a coordinated military operation of which that act constitutes an integral part'. Thirdly, the act must be linked to the armed conflict in the sense that it is 'specifically designed to directly cause the required threshold of harm in support of a party to the conflict and to the detriment of another'.[71] In most cases, of course, in their practical application, the three elements may be interlinked. A particular cause of contention among states relates to the issue of when a civilian loses their right to protection.[72] According to article 51(3) of API, civilian protection is only lost 'for such time' as an individual takes a direct part in the hostilities. Thus, as the ICRC notes in its interpretive guidance, 'suspension of protection lasts exactly as long as the corresponding civilian engagement in direct participation in hostilities'. In effect, civilians lose and regain protection against direct attack in parallel with the intervals of their engagement.[73] The law of armed conflict thereby seemingly acknowledges the existence of a so-called 'revolving door' in international armed conflict where a civilian can cross in and out between protection and non-protection from direct attack.[74] As we shall see later, the temporal aspect of direct participation thereby differs from international to non-international armed conflict.

---

[68] APII art. 51(2) and (3).   [69] See in particular Part IV.

[70] See, inter alia, *Interpretive Guidance on the Notion of Direct Participation in Hostilities under International Humanitarian Law* (ICRC, 2009).

[71] Ibid, 46.   [72] *Public Committee Against Torture* (n 9) paras 38–40.

[73] *Interpretive Guidance* (n 70) 70.   [74] For a critique, see, inter alia, Dinstein (n 16) 147–149.

14.5 The basic principles of the conduct of hostilities

In a 1996 advisory opinion on the legality of nuclear weapons, the ICJ referred to two 'cardinal' principles of international humanitarian law: the principle of distinction and the prohibition against causing unnecessary suffering to combatants.[75] In fact, both principles are derived from the even more basic premise in international law that the 'right of belligerents to adopt means of injuring the enemy is not unlimited'.[76]

The principle of distinction dictates that when launching an attack belligerents are obliged to distinguish between, on the one hand, combatants and military objectives and, on the other, civilians and civilian objects. The principle is reflected in articles 48 and 52(1) and (2) of API and is a well-established principle in customary international law.[77] We saw earlier that combatants in an international armed conflict consist of members of the armed forces of a party to the conflict as well as other individuals who take a direct part in the hostilities. Article 52(2) of the Protocol defines a military objective as 'objects which by their nature, location, purpose or use make an effective contribution to military action and whose total or partial destruction, capture or neutralization, in the circumstances ruling at the time, offers a definite military advantage'. Thus, whereas some objectives are deemed to be military objectives by nature, others will only qualify if they are used in a manner in which they make an effective contribution to military action. If there is doubt about the military character of an objective, it will be presumed to be a civilian object.[78] Article 51 prohibits attacks that are designed to spread terror among the civilian population as well as 'indiscriminate attacks'. The latter refer to attacks that are not 'directed at a specific military objective', attacks 'which employ a method or means of combat which cannot be directed at a specific military objective' or attacks that 'employ a method or means of combat the effects of which cannot be limited'.[79]

It is important to realize, however, that while the laws of armed conflict do not allow *direct* attacks against civilians or civilian targets, they are not categorically opposed to civilian casualties and civilian destruction that is the result of attacks on military targets. As mentioned in the introduction to this chapter, international humanitarian law is an inherently pragmatic discipline that seeks to find a sensible balance between military necessity and humanitarian considerations.[80] The doctrine of so-called 'collateral damage' stipulates that even though states must seek to spare civilians and civilian objects, it allows attacks on a military objective as long as the expected 'incidental loss of civilian life, injury to civilians, damage to civilian objects, or a combination thereof' is not 'excessive in relation to the concrete and direct military advantage

---

[75] *Nuclear Weapons* (n 5) para. 78.

[76] See 1899 Convention (II) with Respect to the Laws and Customs of War on Land and its annex: Regulations concerning the Laws and Customs of War on Land, art. 22 and 1907 Convention (IV) respecting the Laws and Customs of War on Land and its annex: Regulations concerning the Laws and Customs of War on Land, art. 22. See also Dinstein (n 16) 8–10.

[77] Henckaerts and Doswald-Beck (n 8) rule I.   [78] APII art. 52(3).   [79] APII art. 51(4).

[80] Dinstein (n 16) 5–8.

anticipated'.[81] Like all tests of proportionality, the assessment of acceptable 'collateral damage' is always context-specific and must take account of the operational realities of the battlefield. Thus, there is no fixed formula for determining when civilian casualties are acceptable and when they are not. It is important to note, however, that the assessment must be based on the information that was available to the decision-maker *at the time of the decision* to launch an attack and not afterwards when the results of the attack become evident. Israel is often criticized for causing excessive civilian casualties in the course of its military operations[82] but one should always be apprehensive about jumping to the conclusion that attacks against military targets that may have resulted in what seems to be excessive civilian casualties constitute a violation of the laws of armed conflict. According to Israel, it does its utmost to avoid excessive civilian casualties and the Israeli military seem to have adopted a number of novel measures intended to minimize the effects of its military operations on innocent civilians.[83]

The *prohibition against causing unnecessary suffering* to combatants is primarily reflected in treaties that outlaw the use of certain weapons[84] and is well established in customary international law.[85] In practice, of course, suffering is an inherent feature of armed conflict and the prohibition only extents to suffering that is deemed to be 'unnecessary' or 'superfluous'.[86] What is prohibited are weapons the effects of which go beyond those required to put a combatant out of action—generally referred to as *hors de combat*. We are concerned here with weapons that increase suffering without increasing military advantage or, as the ICJ has formulated it, cause 'a harm greater than the unavoidable'.[87] The decisive factor is the nature and not the intention of the weapon and the prohibition against causing unnecessary suffering has played a role in banning the use of certain projectiles, poison, poisonous gases, non-detectable fragments, booby-traps, incendiary weapons, blinding laser weapons, cluster munitions as well as chemical and biological weapons.[88]

The compatibility of *nuclear weapons* with international humanitarian law has been debated since the invention of the atomic bomb in the 1940s.[89] In its 1996 advisory opinion, the ICJ concluded that neither the treaties that specifically deal with nuclear weapons nor customary international law as such prohibit the use of nuclear weapons.[90] The Court did find, however, that the established rules and principles of the laws of armed conflict, including the principle of distinction and the prohibition on inflicting unnecessary suffering to combatants, is applicable to nuclear weapons and that 'the unique characteristics of nuclear weapons' seem to make 'the use of

---

[81] APII arts 51(5)(b) and 57(2).

[82] See e.g. the now infamous 'Goldstone Report' concerning Israel's 2008 *Operation Cast Lead* in Gaza, Human Rights Council, Report of the United Nations Fact-Finding Mission on the Gaza Conflict' (25 September 2009), UN Doc. A/HRC/12/48.

[83] 'How is the IDF Minimizing Harm to Civilians in Gaza?', IDF blog, 16 July 2014.

[84] See also the 1868 St Petersburg Declaration. For a thorough overview, see William H. Boothby, *Weapons and the Law of Armed Conflict* (Oxford University Press, 2009) 55–68.

[85] Henckaerts and Doswald-Beck (n 8) rule 70.

[86] APII art. 35(2). For a debate, see Dinstein (n 16) 63–67.   [87] *Nuclear Weapons* (n 5) para. 78.

[88] For a full overview and discussion, see Boothby (n 84).   [89] Ibid, 215–223.

[90] *Nuclear Weapons* (n 5) paras 62–63 and 67.

such weapons ... scarcely reconcilable with respect for such requirements'.[91] Since the legality of nuclear weapons turns on the risk of excessive collateral damage, it would appear that the deployment of such weapons can only comply with the laws of armed conflict if they are used as a tactical weapon against a military target located far from a civilian population (such as in a desert or on the high seas).[92]

There has recently been much discussion about the legality of a number of *emerging technologies* that increasingly find their way into the military arsenal of states. For example, the use of *armed unmanned aerial vehicles* ('combat drones') has garnered a lot of attention and in 2009 a former judge of the UK House of Lords suggested that drones could potentially be outlawed as a particularly cruel weapon.[93] It is, however, hard to follow the logic of such a statement. The combat drones currently in use fire conventional missiles and as such they are no different from other conventional weapon systems, such as manned fighter jets, battleships, submarines, helicopter gunships etc.[94] While the introduction of remotely operated vehicles may raise both strategic and ethical issues,[95] they should raise few of an international legal character. What should be of interest to international lawyers is not that a drone is operated from the ground but, rather, how (where and against whom) it is used.[96]

Another issue of modern technology that has drawn substantial attention is the emergence of cyber-related means of warfare and the compatibility with the laws of armed conflict of *computer network operations*. While there is certainly room for debate about the likelihood of so-called 'cyberwar',[97] it seems fairly straightforward to conclude that the ordinary principles contained in the laws of armed conflict apply to attacks conducted through computer networks.[98] This, of course, should not distract from the challenges associated with applying the existing legal framework to the use of cyber means in times of armed conflict. More profound challenges may be posed by the invention and subsequent introduction of *autonomous weapons systems* that, once activated, will be able to select and strike targets without human intervention.[99] Like the technology, the legal debate is in its infancy and while some adopt a pragmatic

---

[91] Ibid, para. 95.   [92] See also Boothby (n 84) 222–223 and Dinstein (n 16) 86.

[93] British Institute of International and Comparative Law, 'Joshua Rozenberg's interview with Lord Bingham on the rule of law' (2009), <http://www.biicl.org/files/4415_bingham_interview_transcript.pdf> (accessed 9 October 2013).

[94] See also Philip Alston, 'Report of the Special Rapporteur on extrajudicial, summary or arbitrary executions, Addendum: Study on targeted killings' (28 May 2010), UN Doc. A/HRC/14/24/Add.6, para. 79.

[95] Paul W. Kahn, 'The Paradox of Riskless Warfare' (2002) 22(3) *Philosophy & Public Policy Quarterly* 2; Christopher Coker, *Waging War Without Warriors? The Changing Culture of Military Conflict* (Lynne Rienner, 2002).

[96] See also Philip Alston, 'The CIA and Targeted Killings Beyond Borders' (2011) 2 *Harvard National Security Journal* 282, 325.

[97] See, inter alia, Thomas Rid, *Cyber War Will Take Place* (Oxford University Press, 2013).

[98] For an overview, see Michael N. Schmitt (ed.), *Tallinn Manual on the International Law applicable to Cyber Warfare* (Cambridge University Press, 2013).

[99] For a debate, see Nehal Bhuta, Susanne Beck, Robin Geiss, Hin-Yan Liu and Claus Kress (eds), *Autonomous Weapons Systems: Law, Ethics, Policy* (Cambridge University Press, 2016). See also Hin-Yan Liu, 'Categorization and Legality of Autonomous and Remote Weapons Systems' (2012) 94 *International Review of the Red Cross* 627–652.

view and argue that there need not be anything particularly disconcerting about the introduction of automated weapons,[100] others are more critical.[101] The question has even been raised whether the laws of armed conflict are the proper lens through which autonomous weapons should be viewed.[102]

14.6 Non-international armed conflict

On the face of it, the vast majority of legal instruments in international humanitarian law are limited in their application to international armed conflict.[103] This, of course, stands in stark contrast to the undeniable reality that the world has witnessed an increase in non-international armed conflict since the end of the Second World War and that civil wars may be just as bloody as those of an interstate character. Currently, treaty-based regulation of non-international armed conflict is limited to Common article 3 of the 1949 Geneva Conventions, the 1977 Additional Protocol II, the 1954 Hague Convention for the Protection of Cultural Property in the Event of Armed Conflict, the 1992 Chemical Weapons Convention, the 1996 Protocol II on Prohibitions or Restrictions on the Use of Mines, Booby-Traps and Other Devices and the 1997 Ottawa Landmine Convention.

In the light of the limited applicability of treaty law, it is therefore of paramount importance that there has been a gradual movement in the direction of *greater application of customary international law* in times of non-international armed conflict.[104] Thus, as a rule of thumb at least, the limits imposed by customary international law on the conduct of international armed conflict are equally applicable to non-international armed conflict.[105] As the ICTY stated in *Tadić*, 'the distinction between interstate wars and civil wars is losing its value as far as human beings are concerned'.[106] Surely, what 'is inhumane, and consequently proscribed, in international wars, cannot but be inhumane and inadmissible in civil strife'.[107] Within the areas of protection of civilians from hostilities, 'in particular from indiscriminate attacks, protection of civilian objects, in particular cultural property, protection of all those who do not (or no longer) take active part in hostilities, as well as prohibition of means of warfare proscribed in international armed conflicts and ban of certain methods of conducting hostilities,' customary rules govern non-international armed conflict.[108] The expansion of customary legal principles into the domain of non-international armed

---

[100] See Kenneth Anderson, Daniel Reisner and Matthew Waxman, 'Adapting the Law of Armed Conflict to Autonomous Weapon Systems' (2014) 90 *International Law Studies* 386–411.

[101] Human Rights Watch, 'Losing Humanity: The Case Against Killer Robots', Human Rights Watch and International Human Rights Clinic, 2012.

[102] See, Hin-Yan Liu, 'Refining Responsibility: Differentiating Two Types of Responsibility Issues Raised by Autonomous Weapons Systems' in Bhuta et al. (n 99).

[103] For a thorough analysis, see Sandesh Sivakumaran, *The Law of Non-International Armed Conflict* (Oxford University Press, 2012).

[104] See the debate in Dinstein (n 40) 205–223.   [105] Henckaerts and Doswald-Beck (n 8) xxix.

[106] *Tadić* (n 15) para. 97.   [107] Ibid, para. 119.

[108] Ibid, para. 127. See also *Prosecutor v Blaškić*, Appeals Chamber (2004), para. 157.

conflict has led to a discussion of what some have termed a 'unification' of the regulation of armed conflict.[109]

In a number of ways, however, notable differences remain in the regulation of international and non-international armed conflicts. First, although the conceptual distinction between 'combatants' and 'civilians' is also applicable to non-international armed conflict in the sense that some individuals will participate in the fighting (and therefore be liable to being targeted and/or detained) and some will not, captured 'combatants' cannot benefit from protection as prisoners of war. Insurgents do not benefit from 'combatants' privilege' and upon apprehension by government forces are liable to criminal prosecution before national courts for simply participating in hostilities.

A second significant difference relates to the temporal aspect of the concept of 'direct participation in hostilities'. As we saw earlier, in an international armed conflict a civilian only loses protection from direct attack 'for such time' as they participate in the hostilities thus enabling a 'civilian' to disengage from the fighting on an on/off basis. In a non-international armed conflict, on the other hand, members of an organized armed group that belong to a non-state party to the conflict are not considered 'civilians' as long as they remain members of the organized group by virtue of their 'continuous combat function'. Thus, when members of a private actor 'go beyond spontaneous, sporadic, or unorganized direct participation' and become members as an organized armed group, they are deprived of protection from direct attack 'as long as they remain members of that group'.[110] Unlike a civilian in an international armed conflict, then, a member of an organized armed group in a non-international armed conflict can be targeted at all times, including in situations where the individual is not actively engaged in acts that are harmful to the enemy.

A third difference between the regulation of international and non-international armed conflicts concerns the interaction between the laws of armed conflict and international human rights law.

14.7 The relationship between international humanitarian law and human rights law

We saw in Chapter 9 that it is now well established that human rights law—with due regard to its territorial limitations—applies alongside international humanitarian law in times of armed conflict.[111] In relation to the practical application of the two regimes, the ICJ has stated that some rights may be governed exclusively by either

[109] Lindsay Moir, 'Towards the Unification of International Humanitarian Law' in Richard Burchill and Nigel D. White, *International Conflict and Security Law* (Cambridge University Press, 2005) 108–127. But see also Rogier Bartels, 'Timelines, Borderlines and Conflicts' (2009 91 *International Review of the Red Cross* 35–67.

[110] *Interpretive Guidance* (n 70) 71–72.

[111] See, inter alia, *Nuclear Weapons* (n 5) para. 25; *The Wall* (n 9) para. 105; *Armed Activities* (n 44) para. 216.

international humanitarian law or human rights law, whereas other rights 'may be matters of both these branches of international law'.[112] In most situations, the simultaneous application of the two branches of law is unproblematic. After all, as the ICTY has noted, both human rights law and the laws of armed conflict seek to protect the human dignity of every person and the 'general principle of respect for human dignity is the basic underpinning and indeed the very *raison d'être*' of the two legal regimes.[113] Thus, where possible, the relationship between the law of armed conflict and human rights law is one of coexistence.[114] One of the ways in which the application of human rights law in times of armed conflict may have practical significance is in relation to the interpretation of terms and standards contained in the law of armed conflict. Thus, when interpreting a provision in the law of armed conflict reference may often be made to the interpretation of similar provisions in human rights law. In *Delalić et al.*, for example, the ICTY found that the definition of torture in the Convention against Torture could be relied on in order to define torture for the purposes of the law of armed conflict.[115]

When it comes to the application of human rights law in times of armed conflict, two things must be stressed, though. First, the application of human rights norms into the law of armed conflict must take account of the 'specificities of the latter body of law'.[116] Secondly, in certain circumstances, the norms contained in human rights law and the law of armed conflict differ fundamentally. Most pertinently, international humanitarian law allows substantial room for military necessity and thus tolerates not only the killing of innocent civilians as a result of justifiable collateral damage assessment but also deprivations of liberty for security purposes without criminal prosecution.[117] When the norms of human rights law and international humanitarian law cannot be reconciled, one must be given priority over the other.

The interaction between human rights law and the laws of armed conflict is most interesting in relation to the use of deadly force and detention for security purposes where the norms differ substantially. It is generally established that the standards contained in international humanitarian law fulfil the role as the *lex specialis* and thus inform the content of the human right to, respectively, life and liberty in times of *international armed conflict*. Thus, in *Nuclear Weapons*, the ICJ referred to international humanitarian law in relation to the prohibition against arbitrary deprivation of life in human rights law. According to the Court, although 'the right not arbitrarily to be deprived of one's life applies also in hostilities', the 'test of what is an arbitrary deprivation of life ... falls to be determined by the applicable *lex specialis*, namely, the law applicable in armed conflict which is designed to regulate the conduct of hostilities'. To the Court, then, 'whether a particular loss of life, through the use of a certain weapon

---

[112] *The Wall* (n 9) para. 106. See also *Armed Activities* (n 44) para. 216.

[113] *Prosecutor v Furundžija*, Judgment, IT-95-17/1-T (10 December 1998), para. 183. See also *Prosecutor v Kunarac et al.*, Trial Chamber (2001), para. 467.

[114] For a debate, see Sivakumaran (n 103) 87–99.   [115] *Delalić* (n 62) para. 459

[116] *Kunarac* (n 113) para. 471.

[117] See also Kenneth Watkin, 'Controlling the Use of Force: A Role for Human Rights Norms in Contemporary Armed Conflict' (2004) 98 *American Journal of International Law* 10.

in warfare, is to be considered an arbitrary deprivation of life ... can only be decided by reference to the law applicable in armed conflict' and the human rights convention in question.[118] The practical effect of this approach is that the rule in human rights law is applied by reference to the relevant standard contained in the laws of armed conflict.

In *non-international armed conflict*, however, the relationship between human rights law and international humanitarian law is less clear when it comes to the protection of the right to life and the right to liberty. The problem is the limited treaty-based regulation of non-international armed conflict and the absence of any explicit authority for the use of deadly force and/or preventive detention of insurgents in both Common article 3 and APII. A number of approaches have been advanced. Some argue that the gap in the treaty-based regulation of non-international armed conflict in international humanitarian law must be filled by human rights law.[119] The argument is particular visible in relation to the issue of security detention. In *Hassan v UK*, for example, the European Court of Human Rights stated that 'the taking of prisoners of war and the detention of civilians who pose a threat to security' are 'only accepted features of international humanitarian law' in international armed conflict and that it is therefore only in such armed conflict that the right to liberty in article 5 of the European Convention on Human Rights could be 'interpreted as permitting the exercise of such broad powers'.[120] A recent decision by a UK High Court reached a similar decision in relation to detention by British forces of a suspected member of the Taleban in Afghanistan.[121]

Other sources—including (seemingly) the ICRC[122] and the US Supreme Court[123]—adopt the view that the gap in the treaty-based regulation of non-international armed conflict in international humanitarian law is filled by customary international law and principles derived from international armed conflict.[124] According to that view, the identification of the legal norms that govern non-international armed conflict is by and large an exercise in 'analogical or deductive reasoning' according to which states are generally deemed to have the authority to undertake the same practices in non-international conflict as they are in international armed conflict.[125] Since the law of armed conflict permits a state to use deadly force against combatants and detain civilians in international armed conflict, the law also permits a state to do the same in a non-international armed conflict.

---

[118] See also *Nuclear Weapons* (n 5) para. 25 and ECtHR, *Hassan v UK*, App. no. 29750/09, Judgment, 16 September 2014, paras 102–104.

[119] See the overview and positions reflected in Sivakumaran (n 103) 93–99.

[120] *Hassan* (n 118) para. 102.

[121] *Serdar Mohammed v Ministry of Defence* [2014] EWHC 1369 (QB), [239]–[268].

[122] On the use of deadly force, see ICRC, *Interpretive Guidance* (n 70) 27–36. On security detention, see ICRC, *Strengthening Legal Protection for Persons deprived of their Liberty in relation to Non-International Armed Conflict*, Background Paper, Regional Consultations 2012–13, see 3 and 10.

[123] On security detention, see US Supreme Court, *Hamdan* (n 47) 12–15.

[124] See, inter alia, Dinstein (n 16) 226–230 and Sivakumaran (n 103) 98–99. See also Jelena Pejic, 'Procedural Principles and Safeguards of Violence' (2005) 87 *International Review of the Red Cross* 377.

[125] Ryan Goodman, 'The Detention of Civilians in Armed Conflict' (2009) 103 *American Journal of International Law* 50.

As a point of departure, at least, the present author is inclined to side with the latter approach and the proposition—seemingly advanced by the UK High Court—that the authority to detain for security purposes can somehow be disentangled from an authority to use deadly force appears misguided. The two authorities must go together in the sense that it can only be demanded of soldiers that they must accept surrender by the enemy if they can be certain that the latter can be kept in detention and thus removed from the battlefield until the fighting is over. In the practical application of force, however, a state must be under an obligation to take account of the overall circumstances that surround the armed conflict, including the ability of government forces to exercise physical control over an area. As stressed by both the ICRC and the Israeli Supreme Court, government forces should generally not resort to the use of lethal force if capture is possible without undue risk to government officials.[126]

Summary

The law of armed conflict regulates *how military operations must be conducted*. It is an inherently pragmatic discipline that offers balanced solutions that take account of both military necessity and humanitarian sentiments. The law of armed conflict applies in times of armed conflict and the law differentiates between 'international armed conflict' involving the armed forces of two or more states and 'non-international armed conflict' that involves fighting between either a state and a private organized armed group or between two or more such groups. Regulation differs to a certain extent. All individuals have a status in times of armed conflict and the two most notable categories are those of civilians and combatants. While civilians must be protected from the effects of the conflict, combatants may generally be targeted and detained until the end of hostilities. The conduct of hostilities is based on a number of basic principles, the most important being the principle of distinction and the prohibition against causing unnecessary suffering to combatants. While human rights law also applies in times of armed conflict, its practical application will sometimes be informed by the content of the law of armed conflict.

Recommended reading

There is an extensive literature on the laws of armed conflict. Solid comprehensive works include the contributions by Yoram Dinstein, including his *The Conduct of Hostilities under the Law of International Armed Conflict* (2nd edn, Cambridge University Press, 2010), *The International Law of Belligerent Occupation* (Cambridge University Press, 2009) and *Non-International Armed Conflicts in International Law* (Cambridge University Press, 2014). See also Dieter Fleck, *The Handbook of International Humanitarian Law* (2nd edn, Oxford University Press, 2008) and Gary Solis, *The Law of Armed Conflict* (Cambridge University Press, 2010).

---

[126] See also *Public Committee Against Torture* (n 9) para. 40. See also *Interpretive Guidance* (n 70) 81–82.

On non-international armed conflict, see Sandesh Sivakumaran, *The Law of Non-International Armed Conflict* (Oxford University Press, 2012).

For treatment of relevant customary international law, see Jean-Marie Henckaerts and Louise Doswald-Beck, *Customary International Humanitarian Law*, Vol. I (Cambridge University Press, 2005).

On weaponry, see William H. Boothby, *Weapons and the Law of Armed Conflict* (Oxford University Press, 2009).

On the interplay between human rights and the laws of armed conflict, see Kenneth Watkin, 'Controlling the Use of Force: A Role for Human Rights Norms in Contemporary Armed Conflict' (2004) 98 *American Journal of International Law* 1.

Questions for discussion

1. Why may one reasonably consider the law of armed conflict as a pragmatic discipline?

2. Has the international armed conflict between North and South Korea been brought to an end?

3. Are Ukraine and Russia engaged in an international armed conflict?

4. In 2011, US Special Forces killed the leader of al Qaida, Osama bin Laden, in Pakistan. Did the killing of bin Laden violate international humanitarian law?

5. In November 2015, individuals with alleged ties to the Islamic State perpetrated a series of terrorist attacks in Paris, France. Could the attacks be considered as part of an armed conflict?

6. When it comes to the use of deadly force against individuals who are not members of the armed forces of a state, why does it matter if the armed conflict is classified as an international and not a non-international armed conflict?

7. How is the right to liberty regulated in a non-international armed conflict?

15

International criminal law

CENTRAL ISSUES

1. This chapter presents and discusses the purposes and principles of international criminal law.

2. It discusses the concept of an 'international crime' and the basic principles of international criminal liability as well as some of the relevant grounds for excluding criminal responsibility.

3. The chapter examines the prosecution of international crimes before international criminal courts, including the conditions for prosecuting suspected international criminals before the International Criminal Court.

4. The chapter also discusses the national prosecution of international crimes and the obligation found in a number of conventions to criminalize and prosecute certain conduct.

15.1 Introduction

International criminal law seeks to ensure that perpetrators of certain heinous acts are criminally liable for their acts either before national or international criminal courts or tribunals.[1] It is a fairly recent addition to international law and it was not until after the end of the Second World War that it became accepted that international law authorizes the criminal prosecution of individual perpetrators of serious offences. The Nuremberg trials famously established that international law imposes obligations *directly* on individuals without the need for the interposition of national law. After the successful establishment and operation of two ad hoc criminal tribunals—the International Criminal Tribunal for the former Yugoslavia (ICTY) and the International Criminal Tribunal for Rwanda (ICTR)—in the 1990s, international criminal law has developed at an impressive pace and is now well on the way to becoming a legal regime in its own right. A noteworthy accomplishment was the adoption in 1998 of a statute for a permanent international criminal court. At the current stage

---

[1] In the following, the term 'international court' will cover both international tribunals and international courts.

of its development, international law limits criminal responsibility to individuals. An attempt by the International Law Commission to introduce 'state crimes' did not find support among states and corporate criminal responsibility has yet to be developed.

International law does not authoritatively define an 'international crime' and there are numerous ways of approaching the field. One approach is to limit the concept of an international crime to four 'core' offences directly criminalized under international law: genocide, crimes against humanity, certain war crimes and aggression.[2] This book adopts a more expansive view and includes in the definition of an international crime a range of offences that international law obliges states to criminalize and in most cases also prosecute before their national courts, such as piracy, torture and a number of terrorism-related offences.[3] While the legal basis for prosecuting the 'core' international crimes is international law directly, prosecution for other international crimes is based on the national laws of the states.

International criminal law is heavily influenced and informed by other branches of international law. For example, due to its original focus on prosecuting war crimes, it draws extensively on the law of armed conflict and the definitions and distinctions contained therein. It is also influenced by international human rights law that is instrumental in defining some international crimes, such as crimes against humanity and torture. Human rights law also provides the procedural guarantees afforded to those individuals prosecuted for international crimes. Other relevant branches of international law include the principles of state responsibility and those relating to immunity from national jurisdiction.

We begin the chapter in Section 15.2 with the most important sources of international criminal law. Section 15.3 discusses prosecution of international crimes before *international* criminal courts before Section 15.4 examines prosecutions before *national* courts.

Before proceeding, it is important to clarify the distinction between 'international' and 'national' courts. Despite frequent references to so-called 'hybrid' or 'internationalized' criminal courts, this chapter is based on the premise that only two types of criminal court exist. A criminal court is either 'international' or 'national' depending on *the legal nature of the founding document*. So if a court derives its existence and legal authority from an instrument of international law, it is an international court and it is a national court if its existence is derived from an instrument of national law.[4] For present purposes, then, it is immaterial whether the court is composed of

---

[2] See, inter alia, A. Cassese et al., *Cassese's International Criminal Law* (3rd edn, Oxford University Press, 2013) 18–21 and Robert Cryer, 'International Criminal Law' in Malcolm D. Evans (ed.), *International Law* (4th edn, Oxford University Press, 2010) 752, 754.

[3] For this approach, see Roger O'Keefe, *International Criminal Law* (Oxford University Press, 2015) 56– 57. See also *Questions relating to the Obligation to Prosecute or Extradite (Belgium v Senegal)*, Judgment [2012] ICJ Rep 422, para. 75. International criminal law would thus include what some scholars (for lack of a better term) call 'transnational criminal law', see Neil Boister, 'Transnational Criminal Law?' (2003) 14 *European Journal of International Law* 953.

[4] For a persuasive analysis, see Astrid Kjeldgaard-Pedersen, 'What Defines an International Criminal Court? A Critical Assessment of "the Involvement of the International Community" as a Deciding Factor' (2015) 28 *Leiden Journal of International Law* 113. See also O'Keefe (n 3) 85–114.

a mix of national and international judges or if it has jurisdiction to deal with violations of both international and national law. Since the International Military Tribunal (IMT) at Nuremberg was created pursuant to a treaty between the UK, the United States, France and the Soviet Union, it was an international court. The same goes for the International Criminal Court (ICC) set up by the 1998 Rome Statute (a treaty). The ICTY and the ICTR, the International Residual Mechanism for the International Criminal Tribunals (MICT) and the Special Tribunal for Lebanon (STL) were created by the Security Council under its treaty-based powers in Chapter VII of the Charter and they are therefore also international courts. Similarly, the Special Court for Sierra Leone (SCSL) and the Residual Court for Sierra Leone (RCSL) created under a treaty between Sierra Leone and the UN. In contrast, the Extraordinary Chambers of the Courts of Cambodia for the Prosecution of Crimes Committed during the Period of Democratic Kampuchea (ECCC) derive their existence and authority from the national laws of Cambodia and are therefore 'national courts'. The many military criminal courts set up by the occupying powers in Germany after the end of the Second World War were also national criminal courts.

15.2 Sources of international criminal law

The primary sources of international criminal law are the treaties that establish the international courts, such as the 1945 London Agreement that created the IMT at Nuremberg and the 1998 Statute of the ICC. The statutes only apply to the tribunal or court they establish and not to other courts. This, of course, does not rule out that the statutes—or at least parts of them—may reflect customary international law or may assist in the creation of a customary norm. Other important treaties include the 1949 Geneva Conventions and the 1977 Additional Protocols I and II, the universal human rights conventions and the 1948 Genocide Convention. Mention should also be made of the numerous treaties that authorize and/or oblige states to prosecute certain offences, such as the 1984 Convention against Torture and the numerous 'counter-terrorism' conventions, including the 1971 Montreal Convention for the Suppression of Unlawful Acts against the Safety of Civil Aviation, the 1979 Convention against the Taking of Hostages and the 1999 Convention for the Suppression of the Financing of Terrorism.

Customary international law is an important source of international criminal law and, as we shall see later, prosecution of international crimes before international criminal courts is based on the premise that the crimes are prescribed under customary international law. Customary international law is also frequently relied on by international and national criminal courts when determining how to define an international crime.[5]

---

[5] *Prosecutor v Anto Furundžija*, Judgment, ICTY-95-17/1-T (10 December 1998), paras 137–138, 168–169. See also the lengthy discussion of how to define the crime of persecution as a crime against humanity in *Prosecutor v Kupreškić et al.*, Judgment, ICTY-95-16-T (14 January 2000), paras 567–626.

International courts have also relied on 'general principles of international law' typically derived from domestic legal systems and over time recognized as principles of the international legal system. Noteworthy examples include the principle of legality and the disallowance of the application of *ex post facto* law whereby an individual is punished for an act that was not criminalized when the act was performed (*nullum crimen sine lege*).[6] Another general principle is the presumption of innocence according to which the burden of proof rests upon the prosecution. As a supplement to general principles of international criminal law, courts have also referred to legal principles that are 'borrowed' from the national criminal systems of states.[7] Both international and national courts often make extensive references to relevant case law and seminal trials and there is little doubt that judicial decisions play an important interpretative role in the development of international criminal law. Seminal cases include the judgment in the trial of the major German war criminals at the IMT at Nuremberg,[8] the *Tadić* case from the ICTY,[9] the *Akayesu* case from the ICTR[10] and the *Lubanga* case from the ICC.[11]

15.3 Prosecution of international crimes before international courts

15.3.1 Introduction

This section provides an overview of prosecution of international crimes before international courts. We begin with a brief introduction to the international courts so far established, including the ICC (Section 15.3.2). Attention then turns to individual crimes that have been included in the jurisdiction of the international courts (Section 15.3.3) and a select number of issues concerning criminal liability (Section 15.3.4) and possible defences (Section 15.3.5). We conclude with a brief overview of relevant due process guarantees (Section 15.3.6) and a discussion of the extent to which immunity serves as a bar to criminal prosecution before international courts (Section 15.3.7).

15.3.2 International criminal courts

15.3.2.1 Ad hoc international criminal courts

The modern history of international criminal prosecution starts with the adoption in August 1945 of the London Charter that established the *IMT in Nuremberg* that

---

[6] For an overview, see Cassese et al. (n 2) 22–36.

[7] *Prosecutor v Anto Furundžija* (n 5) paras 177–178.

[8] *Judgment of the Nuremberg International Military Tribunal 1946* (1947) 41 *American Journal of International Law* 172.

[9] See in particular *Prosecutor v Tadić*, Decision on the Defence Motion for Interlocutory Appeal on Jurisdiction, ICTY-91-1 (2 October 1995).

[10] *Prosecutor v Akayesu*, Judgment, ICTR-95-4 (2 September 1998).

[11] *Prosecutor v Thomas Lubanga Dyilo*, Judgment, ICC-01/04-01/06 (14 March 2012).

criminally prosecuted some of the major war criminals of the Axis powers.[12] The Tribunal had jurisdiction over crimes against peace, crimes against humanity and war crimes and it made a number of important contributions to the development of international criminal law. As already noted, the IMT famously articulated the principle that individuals may be held criminally responsible directly under international law. The IMT has also been criticized, however, for violating the prohibition against applying *ex post facto* law in relation to (at least) crimes against peace.[13] The 1946 *Tokyo International Military Tribunal* was created to prosecute those with the greatest responsibility for the Japanese atrocities in the Eastern theatre of the Second World War.[14] Like the IMT in Nuremberg, the Tokyo Tribunal had jurisdiction over crimes against peace, crimes against humanity and war crimes. On most of the legal issues, the Tokyo Tribunal reached conclusions that were similar to those of the Nuremberg Tribunal and it also concluded that aggressive war constituted a crime under international law at the time. The Tokyo Tribunal has been criticized as a particularly clear example of 'victor's justice'.[15]

After the Nuremberg and Tokyo trials, no international courts were created until after the end of the Cold War. In 1993, the UN Security Council reacted to the atrocities committed in the war in Yugoslavia by establishing the ICTY in The Hague, the Netherlands.[16] The ICTY was given jurisdiction over a range of war crimes, the crime of genocide and crimes against humanity and afforded primacy over national courts in the sense that it could oblige states to defer criminal proceedings to the ICTY.[17] The Court got off to a slow start but things began to improve when Serbia began to cooperate with the Court, and the ICTY actually ended up indicting all the main culprits of the worst atrocities in the Balkan war. The high-water mark was the indictment and subsequent surrender to the Court of the former Yugoslavian President Slobodan Milošević[18] and former President of the Bosnian Serbs Radovan Karadžić.[19] Although Milošević died in his prison cell before the Tribunal could render its judgment in the case against him, in 2016 Karadžić was found guilty of genocide, crimes against humanity and war crimes and sentenced to 40 years' imprisonment.[20] In general, the

---

[12] Agreement for the Prosecution and Punishment of the Major War Criminals of the European Axis, and Charter of the International Military Tribunal, London, 8 August 1945.

[13] For an overview and debate about Nuremberg, see Kevin Jon Heller, *The Nuremberg Military Tribunals and the Origins of International Criminal Law* (Oxford University Press, 2011).

[14] Special Proclamation, Establishment of an International Military Tribunal for the Far East, 19 January 1946. For a thorough overview, see Neil Boister and Robert Cryer, *The Tokyo International Military Tribunal: A Reappraisal* (Oxford University Press, 2008).

[15] See, inter alia, Richard Minear, *Victor's Justice: The Tokyo War Crimes Trial* (Princeton University Press, 1971). See also Philip R. Piccigallo, *The Japanese On Trial: Allied War Crimes Operations in the East, 1945–1951* (University of Texas Press, 1979).

[16] SC Res. 827 (25 May 1993), UN Doc. S/RES/827.   [17] Ibid, art. 9(2).

[18] For the initial indictment (concerning Kosovo), see *Prosecutor v Slobodan Milošević et al.*, Initial Indictment, ICTY-99-37 (22 May 1999).

[19] For the initial indictment (concerning Bosnia and Herzegovina), see *Prosecutor v Radovan Karadžić*, Initial Indictment, ICTY-95-5/18 (22 July 1995).

[20] *Prosecutor v Radovan Karadžić*, Judgment, ICTY-95-5/18 (24 March 2016). By July 2016, the last high-profile case, the proceedings against the former general in the Bosnian Serb Army, Ratko Mladić, are still

ICTY has been highly successful and some of its decisions and judgments have already had a noticeable impact on the development of international criminal law.[21]

The Security Council also set up the International Criminal Tribunal for Rwanda (ICTR)—in Arusha, Tanzania, for prosecuting the horrendous crimes committed in 1994 in Rwanda.[22] The Court was given jurisdiction over genocide, crimes against humanity and certain war crimes, namely violations of Common article 3 of the Geneva Conventions and of Additional Protocol II. Like the ICTY, the ICTR was given primacy over national courts. Lack of cooperation on the part of Rwanda was an obstacle from the beginning and the ICTR has overall been less successful than its sister court in The Hague. The ICTR and the ICTY shared an appeals chamber in order to ensure consistency in their interpretation and application of the law.

In 2010, the Security Council established the International Residual Mechanism for Criminal Tribunals (IRMCT) (also known as the Mechanism for International Criminal Tribunals—MICT)—that will take over and finish the remaining tasks of the ICTY and the ICTR.[23] While the MICT cannot issue new indictments, it can prosecute already indicted individuals arrested after the completion of the mandate of the 'old' courts. It will also supervise the enforcement of the sentences rendered and make decisions on pardons.[24] The ICTY and the ICTR had been requested to complete 'all their remaining work' by 31 December 2014,[25] but both tribunals are likely to remain in operation for the foreseeable future.

The *Special Court for Sierra Leone* (SCSL) was set up in 2002 to prosecute crimes committed in Sierra Leone from 1996.[26] The Court had jurisdiction over crimes against humanity and certain war crimes, namely violations of Common article 3 of the Geneva Conventions and of Additional Protocol II as well as certain other serious violations of international humanitarian law.[27] It operated from July 2002 until December 2013 when its essential functions were taken over by a Residual Special

---

ongoing. For the initial indictment, see *Prosecutor v Ratko Mladić*, Initial Indictment, ICTY-95-5-I (24 July 1995).

[21] For a debate see, inter alia, Muhammed Shahabuddeen, *International Criminal Justice at the Yugoslav Tribunal: A Judge's Recollection* (Oxford University Press, 2012).

[22] SC Res. 935 (1 July 1994), UN Doc. S/RES/935.

[23] SC Res. 1966 (22 December 2010), UN Doc. S/RES/1966. See also Statute of the International Residual Mechanism for Criminal Courts in Annex I of the aforementioned resolution. For an overview, see Wayde T. Pittman, 'The Road to the Establishment of the International Residual Mechanism for Criminal Tribunals: From Completion to Continuation' (2011) 9 *Journal of International Criminal Justice* 797.

[24] Following the arrest and subsequent surrender to the ICTY in 2011 of Goran Hadžić (former president of the self-proclaimed Republic of Serbian Krajina) and Ratko Mladić (former general in the Bosnia Serb Army), none of the 161 individuals indicted by the ICTY remain at large. The ICTR indicted a total of 98 individuals of whom nine remain at large.

[25] See SC Res. 935 (1 July 1994), UN Doc. S/RES/953, para. 3.

[26] Agreement between the United Nations and the Government of Sierra Leone on the Establishment of a Special Court for Sierra Leone, 16 January 2002 www.rscsl.org/Documents/scsl-agreement.pdf (accessed 22 August 2016). For a general discussion of the SCSL, see Jalloh C. Chernor (ed.), *The Sierra Leone Special Court and its Legacy: The Impact for Africa and International Criminal Law* (Cambridge University Press, 2014).

[27] The SCSL also had jurisdiction over certain crimes under Sierra Leonean law but never relied on that jurisdiction.

Court for Sierra Leone (RSCSL).[28] Apart from successfully prosecuting the former president of Liberia, Charles Taylor,[29] the Court contributed to the development of international criminal law by concluding that the enlistment of child soldiers is a war crime under customary international law.[30]

The *Special Tribunal for Lebanon* (STL) was set up in Leidschendam, the Netherlands, by the UN Security Council to prosecute those responsible for the February 2005 assassination of former prime minister of Lebanon, Rafiq Hariri, and a number of other individuals.[31] As an international court, the STL is noteworthy because its jurisdiction covers crimes under Lebanese criminal law, most notably certain acts of terrorism.[32]

15.3.2.2 The International Criminal Court

The international courts listed in Section 15.3.2.1 were established with the purpose of prosecuting crimes committed within a certain predefined context. The ICC, on the other hand, is a permanent international court for criminally prosecuting the 'most serious crimes of international concern'.[33] The Statute of the Court was adopted in Rome in 1998 and it entered into force on 1 July 2002. By July 2016, it had 124 state parties. The Court is based in The Hague, the Netherlands, and its primary legal instruments are the Statute, the Elements of Crime and the Rules of Procedure and Evidence. The Statute of the ICC explicitly lists the sources available to the Court.[34] The primary organs of the ICC are the three divisions (the Pre-Trial Division, the Trial Division and the Appeals Division), the Office of the Prosecutor and the Registry. The Court has jurisdiction over genocide, crimes against humanity, war crimes and—at some point in the not too distant future—aggression, but the jurisdiction of the Court is limited to crimes committed after the entry into force of the Statute (1 July 2002).[35] With regard to states that have subsequently become parties to the Statute, the Court can only exercise jurisdiction for crimes committed *after* the Statute entered into force for that state unless the latter has declared its acceptance of the Court's exercise of jurisdiction in relation to a particular crime.[36]

From the outset, the ICC has been embroiled in high politics. The attitude of the United States has been particularly delicate and it has been critical of the Court from

---

[28] See Agreement between the United Nations and the Government of Sierra Leone on the Establishment of a Residual Special Court for Sierra Leone (n 26).

[29] *Prosecutor v Charles Taylor*, Judgment, SCSL-03-01-T (18 May 2012). For the sentencing, see *Prosecutor v Charles Taylor*, Sentencing Judgment, SCSL-03-01-T (30 May 2012).

[30] *Prosecutor v Norman (Fofana intervening)*, Decision on Preliminary Motion Based on Lack of Jurisdiction, SCSL-2003-04-14 AR72 (E) (31 May 2004), para. 25. See also Matthew Happold, 'International Humanitarian Law, War Criminality and Child Recruitment: The Special Court for Sierra Leone's Decision in *Prosecutor v. Samuel Hinga Norman*' (2005) 18 *Leiden Journal of International Law* 283.

[31] SC Res. 1757 (30 May 2007), UN Doc. S/RES/1757.

[32] See art. 2 of the Statute of the Special Tribunal for Lebanon annexed to SC Res. 1757 (n 31). By July 2016, the court had indicted a total of nine individuals, five of whom remain at large. Two of the defendants have been acquitted and the court has yet to issue a conviction.

[33] Rome Statute of the International Criminal Court (adopted 17 July 1998, entered into force 1 July 2002), 2187 UNTS 90, art. 1. See generally William Schabas, *An Introduction to the International Criminal Court* (4th edn, Cambridge University Press, 2011).

[34] Art. 21.   [35] Art. 11(1).   [36] See arts 11(2) and 12(3).

the beginning.[37] Along with only seven other states, the United States voted against the Rome Statute in 1998. The US is concerned that the Court will conduct politically motivated investigation and prosecution of members of the US armed forces and other public officials. Although then-US President Bill Clinton signed the Rome Statute on 31 December 2000, it was accompanied by a recommendation that his successor should not move forward with the ratification process until US 'fundamental concerns' were satisfied.[38] On 6 May 2002, the administration of President George W. Bush famously 'withdrew' the US signature to the Statute and informed the UN Secretary-General that the United States did not intend to become a party to the treaty.[39] US–ICC relations improved to some degree during the Obama administration[40] but, at the time of writing, it does not appear likely that the United States will become a party to the ICC in the foreseeable future.

More recently, criticism of the Court and the Prosecutor has emerged from African states which have protested against what they perceive to be an unjustified and allegedly politicized focus on prosecuting crimes committed in Africa, including the prosecution of acting heads of state. In response to the ICC's indictment of the sitting president of Kenya, in 2013 members of the African Union (AU) issued strong protests and even threatened to withdraw from the ICC.[41] Tension flared again in reaction to the commencement of the trial against former president of the Ivory Coast, Laurent Gbagbo. In early 2016, Kenya tabled a proposal before the AU to initiate a withdrawal from the Court[42] and, in October 2016, South Africa, Burundi and Gambia declared their intention to withdraw.[43]

Only a few points about the ICC will be noted here. For one thing, in contrast to the ICTY and the ICTR, the ICC has not been given primacy over national courts and the Court cannot therefore oblige states to defer criminal proceedings to it. According to

---

[37] For an overview of the US position on the Court, see John P. Cerone, 'Dynamic Equilibrium: The Evolution of US Attitudes toward International Criminal Courts and Tribunals' (2007) 18 *European Journal of International Law* 277.

[38] 'Statement by US President Bill Clinton, authorizing the US signing of the Rome Statute of the International Criminal Court', Camp David, Maryland (31 December 2000) www.iccnow.org/documents/USClintonSigning31Dec00.pdf (accessed 22 August 2016).

[39] John R. Bolton, Under Secretary of State for Arms Control and International Security, 'International Criminal Court: Letter to UN Secretary General Kofi Annan', Washington DC (6 May 2002) http://2001-2009.state.gov/r/pa/prs/ps/2002/9968.htm (accessed 22 August 2016).

[40] Harold Hongju Koh, 'U.S. Engagement With the ICC and the Outcome of the Recently Concluded Review Conference', Special Briefing (15 June 2010).

[41] See, inter alia, African Union, Extraordinary Session of the Assembly of the African Union: Decisions and Declarations (12 October 2013), Ext/Assembly/AU/Dec.1–2, Ext/Assembly/AU/Decl.a-1, Addis Ababa, Ethiopia.

[42] Agence France-Presse, 'African Union members back Kenyan plan to leave ICC', *The Guardian*, London (1 February 2016) www.theguardian.com/world/2016/feb/01/african-union-kenyan-plan-leave-international-criminal-court (accessed 21 August 2016).

[43] Sewell Chan and Marlise Simons, 'South Africa to Withdraw from International Criminal Court', *New York Times* (21 October 2016) http://www.nytimes.com/2016/10/22/world/africa/south-africa-international-criminal-court.html?_r=1 (accessed 8 November 2016). See also 'Gambia Says It Is Leaving International Criminal Court', *Wall Street Journal* (26 October 2016) http://www.wsj.com/articles/gambia-says-it-is-leaving-international-criminal-court-1477483387 (accessed 8 November 2016).

article 17 of the Statute, a case is inadmissible if it is being investigated or prosecuted by a state that has jurisdiction over it 'unless the State is unwilling or unable genuinely to carry out the investigation or prosecution'.[44] This principle of so-called 'complementarity' in practice means that national criminal jurisdiction takes precedence over the jurisdiction of the ICC.[45] Insufficient willingness may be found to exist if national proceedings do not seem consistent with a genuine intention to bring the person concerned to justice.[46]

Another interesting feature of the ICC is the competence of the Prosecutor to initiate an investigation of potential crimes under the Court's jurisdiction. According to article 13 of the Statute, the Prosecutor may initiate an investigation in three situations.[47] First, a state party may refer a 'situation' to the Prosecutor and request the latter to investigate (art. 13(a)). Secondly, the UN Security Council may rely on its powers under Chapter VII of the UN Charter and refer a situation to the Prosecutor (art. 13(b)). Thirdly, the Prosecutor may initiate an investigation on his or her own initiative (*proprio motu*) provided they obtain authorization from a pre-trial chamber (art. 13(c)).[48] By July 2016, nine situations had been referred to the Prosecutor of which six had been referred by a state party[49] and two by the Security Council.[50] The Prosecutor has opened three own-initiative investigations, the most recent concerning the situation in Georgia in relation to the international armed conflict between 1 July and 10 October 2008. Three trials have so far been completed. On 14 March 2012, Thomas Lubanga was the first individual convicted by the ICC.[51] Since then, two more individuals have been convicted[52] while one individual has been acquitted.[53]

In practice, the jurisdiction of the Court depends on the manner in which a situation has been referred to it. Thus, when a case has been referred by a state party or if the Prosecutor has initiated an investigation on his or her own initiative, article 12(2) states that the Court may exercise its jurisdiction over conduct:

---

[44] Art. 17(1)(a). Art. 17(1)(b) stipulates that a case is inadmissible if it 'has been investigated by a State which has jurisdiction over it and the State has decided not to prosecute the person concerned, unless the decision resulted from the unwillingness or inability of the State genuinely to prosecute'.

[45] See also *Prosecutor v Katanga and Ngudjolo*, Judgment on the Appeal of Mr Germain Katanga against the Oral Decision of Trial Chamber II of 12 June 2009 on the Admissibility of the Case, ICC-01/04-01/07-1497 (25 September 2009), para. 85. On the principle of complementarity, see Jann K. Kleffner, *Complementarity in the Rome Statute and National Criminal Jurisdictions* (Oxford University Press, 2008).

[46] Art. 17(2). See also O'Keefe (n 3) 556–562 and *Prosecutor v Saif Al-Islam Gaddafi and Abdullah Al-Senussi*, Judgment on the appeal of Mr Abdullah Al-Senussi against the decision of Pre-Trial Chamber I of 11 October 2013 entitled 'Decision on the admissibility of the case against Abdullah Al-Senussi', ICC-01/11-01/11-565 (24 July 2014), para. 2.

[47] Art. 13.   [48] Art. 15(4).

[49] These investigations relate to post-election violence in Kenya in 2007–2008 and the situation in the Ivory Coast from 19 September 2002.

[50] See, respectively, SC Res. 1593 on the situation in Darfur, Sudan (31 March 2005), UN Doc. S/RES/1593 and SC Res. 1970 regarding Libya (26 February 2011), UN Doc. S/RES/1970.

[51] *Prosecutor v Thomas Lubanga Dyilo* (n 11).

[52] See *Prosecutor v Germain Katanga*, Judgment, ICC-01/04-01/07 (7 March 2014); *Prosecutor v Jean-Pierre Bemba Gombo*, Judgment, ICC-01/05-01/08 (21 March 2016).

[53] *Prosecutor v Mathieu Ngudjolo Chui*, Judgment, ICC-01/04-02/12 (18 December 2012).

(a) that has occurred on the territory of, or on board, a vessel or aircraft registered in a state that is a party to the Statute or that has accepted the jurisdiction of the Court with respect to the crime; or

(b) when the accused individual is a national of a state party or a state that has accepted the jurisdiction of the Court.[54]

If, however, the case is referred to the Prosecutor by the Security Council, the Court may exercise its jurisdiction *regardless* of where the alleged crime was committed and the nationality of the suspected offender. The rationale for the absence of the limitations in these cases stems from the Security Council's powers under Chapter VII of the UN Charter to uphold international peace and security.

15.3.3 **Crimes in international criminal law**

15.3.3.1 Introduction

The legal basis for criminal prosecutions before international courts is that the prosecuted crimes are directly applicable to individuals in customary international law without the need for the interposition of national law and domestic criminal laws. In fact, it is of no relevance if the offence in question is prescribed under national criminal law.[55] Four crimes are generally considered to be directly binding on individuals under customary international law: genocide, crimes against humanity, certain war crimes and aggression.[56] In the following, we will discuss each in turn. Before proceeding, it is important to note that a crime always consists of both a physical and a mental element. The physical element—known by its Latin term *actus reus*—is the conduct itself, such as the physical act of killing another human being. The metal element—in Latin, *mens rea*—is the psychological state of mind of the offender required for the conduct to be subject to punishment (the 'guilty mind').

Brief mention must also be made of the unusual case of the crime of piracy. Despite occasional indications to the contrary,[57] piracy is not a crime under customary international law.[58] As noted in Chapters 5 and 8, there is, however, both a treaty-based rule

---

[54] With regard to aggression, see, however, art. 15*bis*(5).

[55] See also ILC, Draft Code of Crimes against the Peace and Security of Mankind, art. 1 and the commentaries to the article in *Yearbook of the International Law Commission*, 1996, vol. II, Part Two, 17, paras 6–10.

[56] Some include the crimes of torture and terrorism, see Cassese et al. (n 2) 131–135, 146–158. See also Claus Kress, 'International Criminal Law' in Rüdiger Wolfrum (ed.), *Max Planck Encyclopedia of Public International Law* (Oxford University Press, 2009) para. 10. The ILC Draft Code of Crimes (n 55) includes crimes against UN and associated personal, see art. 19. The Appeals Chamber for the Special Tribunal for Lebanon concluded that terrorism is a crime under customary international law, see *Prosecutor v Ayyash et al.*, Interlocutory Decision on the Applicable Law: Terrorism, Conspiracy, Homicide, Perpetration, Cumulative Charging, STL-11-01/I/AC/R176bis (16 February 2011), paras 83–113. However, since states have still not been able to agree on a definition of terrorism, this judgment is considered to be controversial.

[57] See *Arrest Warrant of 11 April 2000 (Democratic Republic of the Congo v Belgium)*, Joint Separate Opinion of Judges Higgins, Kooijmans and Buergenthal [2002] ICJ Rep 3, paras 39 and 61.

[58] For a definition of piracy, see the discussion in Chapter 8.

in the 1982 UN Law of the Sea Convention and a principle in customary international law whereby all states may assert universal prescriptive jurisdiction over the crime of piracy.[59]

15.3.3.2 Genocide

As an international crime, genocide is part of customary international law and the prohibition against genocide is recognized as *jus cogens*.[60] Although it was not included in the jurisdiction of the IMT at Nuremberg, it was prosecuted as a form of persecution contained in the wider notion of crimes against humanity.[61] Genocide is included in the jurisdiction of the ICTY, the ICTR and the ICC. The definition of genocide is authoritatively put forward in article II of the 1948 Genocide Convention according to which:

> genocide means any of the following acts committed with intent to destroy, in whole or in part, a national, ethnical, racial or religious group, as such:
>
> (a) Killing members of the group;
> (b) Causing serious bodily or mental harm to members of the group;
> (c) Deliberately inflicting on the group conditions of life calculated to bring about its physical destruction in whole or in part;
> (d) Imposing measures intended to prevent births within the group;
> (e) Forcibly transferring children of the group to another group.

With the regard to the element of conduct (*actus reus*), the intentional killing of other human being is the most straightforward way to perpetrate the crime of genocide. It may, however, be committed by other means, such as causing serious bodily harm or deliberately inflicting conditions that may bring about the destruction of life.[62] It is unclear whether forcefully expelling civilians of a particular group from a given area or town—ethnic cleansing—can fulfil the conduct element; nevertheless, the ICTY concluded that the customary definition of genocide is limited to acts that seek the 'physical or biological destruction of all or part of the group'.[63] It is always a requirement that the conduct in question forms part of a 'manifest pattern of similar conduct'

---

[59] United Nations Convention on the Law of the Sea (LOSC, also known as UNCLOS) (adopted 10 December 1982, entered into force 16 November 1994) 1833 UNTS 2, art. 105. For an overview, see also O'Keefe (n 3) 17–21.

[60] *Reservations to the Convention on Genocide*, Advisory Opinion [1951] ICJ Rep 15, 23. See also *Application of the Convention on the Prevention and Punishment of the Crime of Genocide (Bosnia and Herzegovina v Serbia and Montenegro)*, Judgment [2007] ICJ Rep 43, para. 161. See also *Prosecutor v Goran Jelisić*, Judgment, ICTY-95-10-T (14 December 1999) and ICTR, *Prosecutor v Akayesu* (n 10) para. 495. For early affirmation of the crime of genocide, see GA Res. 96(I) (11 December 1946), UN Doc. A/RES/96(I).

[61] See also commentary to art. 17 of the ILC Draft Code of Crimes (n 55) 44, paras 1–2.

[62] See also the discussion in *Prosecutor v Akayesu* (n 10) para. 731. See also the Elements of Crimes for the International Criminal Court (adopted 9 September 2002), UN Doc. PCNICC/2000/1/Add.2, art. 6(c).

[63] *Prosecutor v Radislav Krstić*, Judgment, ICTY-98-33-T (2 August 2001), para. 580. See also the commentary to art. 17 of the ILC Draft Code of Crimes (n 55) 46, para. 12. See, however, *Prosecutor v Nikola Jorgić*, Federal Constitutional Court, 4th Chamber, 2nd Senate, ruling of 12 December 2000, 2 BvR 1290/99, para. 9. See also GA Res. 47/121 on the situation in Bosnia and Herzegovina (18 December 1992), UN Doc. A/RES/47/121.

directed at the group in question or that the conduct in itself is able to bring about the destruction of the group.[64]

The subjective or mental element of the crime of genocide (*mens rea*) is what sets it apart from other crimes. The distinguishing feature is the 'genocidal intent' and the intention to 'destroy, in whole or in part,' one of the groups listed in the definition 'as such'.[65] The intention to destroy the group need not be realized—the intention suffices. Also, the intention need only be to destroy the group 'in part,' such as within a limited geographical area. Both the International Court of Justice (ICJ) and the ICTY concluded that the massacre of around 7,000 Muslim men at Srebrenica constituted genocide.[66] The victims must be chosen due to their membership of the group whose destruction is sought. In most cases, intent must be inferred from the factual circumstances surrounding the case.[67] In addition, what is important is not whether an individual actually belongs to the groups in question, but whether the perpetrator believes that that is the case.[68]

15.3.3.3 Crimes against humanity

One of the novelties of the Nuremberg trials was the inclusion in the Statute of the IMT of 'crimes against humanity'.[69] At the time, the crime sought to make up for the fact that the laws of war only covered acts perpetrated against enemy forces or enemy populations and not Germany's atrocities against its own population. It is questionable if crimes against humanity existed as an international crime at the time.[70] But that is no longer the case and crimes against humanity can be committed both in times of armed conflict and in peacetime. The ICTY, the ICTR, the ICC and the SCSL all have jurisdiction over crimes against humanity, but the definition of the crime is not identical.[71]

The physical element (*actus reus*) of 'crimes against humanity' are acts of serious violence committed during a large-scale or systematic attack against a civilian population. Under the Rome Statute, the physical element consists of any of the following acts: murder, extermination, enslavement, deportation or forcible transfer of populations, imprisonment or other severe deprivation of physical liberty in violation of fundamental rules of international law, torture, rape, sexual slavery, enforced

---

[64] See also ICC Elements of Crimes (n 62) art. 6.

[65] See also *Prosecutor v Jean Kambanda*, Judgment, ICTR 97-23-S (4 September 1998), para. 16. See also GA Res. 96(I) (n 60).

[66] *Application of the Convention on the Prevention and Punishment of the Crime of Genocide* (n 60) para. 297. *Prosecutor v Radislav Krstić* (n 63) para. 598. See also *Prosecutor v Vidoje Blagojević and Dragan Jokić*, Judgment, ICTY-02-60-T (17 January 2005), paras 670–677.

[67] See also *Prosecutor v Akayesu* (n 10) para. 523. See also *Prosecutor v Radovan Karadžić* (n 20) para. 550.

[68] *Prosecutor v Radislav Krstić* (n 63) paras 556– 557.

[69] See art. 6(c) of the Statute of the Tribunal (n 12). For an overview, see O'Keefe (n 3) 137–145.

[70] For a discussion, see Cassese et al. (n 2) 86–88. It is worth noting that the crime had to be committed in connection with one of the other crimes within the jurisdiction of the IMT.

[71] The ICTY Statute limited crimes of humanity to acts committed in times of armed conflict. Updated Statute of the International Criminal Tribunal for the Former Yugoslavia (September 2009) www.icty.org/x/file/Legal%20Library/Statute/statute_sept09_en.pdf (accessed 22 August 2016).

prostitution, forced pregnancy, enforced sterilization, or any other form of sexual violence of comparable gravity, persecution, enforced disappearance of persons, the crime of apartheid or other inhumane acts of a similar character intentionally causing great suffering, or serious injury to body or to mental or physical health.[72] It is a requirement that the physical act forms part of a more widespread or systematic pattern of violent acts against a civilian population. It is, in other words, the *context* in which the acts occur that elevates the acts to crimes against humanity under international law.[73]

The term 'civilian population' refers to *any* civilian population and neither the nationality not the geographic location of the population is decisive. The term 'civilian' is defined in accordance with the law of armed conflict and it thus excludes members of the armed forces of a state and members of certain organized resistance movements.[74] The requirement that the act of violence forms part of a wider pattern of violence means that the perpetrator of the act must be aware of the existence of the widespread or systematic practice of violence against a civilian population and that his or her acts constitute a part thereof.[75] In practice, therefore, there are two relevant mental elements (*mens rea*) that must be fulfilled. The first is the mental element required for the underlying offence (murder, torture, rape etc.) and the second is an awareness of the context of which the offence is part. It is not a requirement that the perpetrator agrees with a policy that may or may not provide the rationale for the overall attack on the civilian population and a crime against humanity may therefore be committed for purely personal ends.[76]

15.3.3.4 War crimes

A war crime is the 'classic' international crime and has been included in the jurisdiction of all the international criminal courts with the exception of the Special Tribunal for Lebanon. As a legal concept, the term is linked to the relevant provisions in the law of armed conflict, but it is not all violations of the many provisions in international humanitarian law that constitute war crimes covered by individual criminal responsibility under customary international law. As the ICTY Appeals Chamber noted in *Tadić*, a war crime 'must constitute a breach of a rule protecting important values'.[77] There is no authoritative list of which acts constitute war crimes and the content of the jurisdictional clauses of the international courts are not identical. It is, however, well settled that the term covers the so-called 'grave

---

[72] Rome Statute art. 7(1)(a)–(k). For an overview of the various acts, see Cassese et al. (n 2) 91–98. For a discussion of the status of art. 7 under customary international law, see Cassese et al. (n 2) 105–108.

[73] See also *Prosecutor v Kunarac et al.*, Judgment, ICTY-96-23 and IT-96-23/1-A (12 June 2002), paras 93–94, 98, and *Prosecutor v Tihomir Blaškić*, Judgment, ICTY-95-14-A (29 July 2004), para. 120. See also the commentary to art. 18 of the ILC Draft Code of Crimes (n 55) 47, paras 3–4.

[74] See also *Prosecutor v Tihomir Blaškić* (n 73) paras 110–114. For the distinction in the laws of armed conflict, see Chapter 14.

[75] *Prosecutor v Kunarac et al.* (n 73) para. 102; *Prosecutor v Tihomir Blaškić* (n 73) para. 124.

[76] *Prosecutor v Kunarac et al.* (n 73) para. 103.

[77] *Prosecutor v Tadić* (n 9) 94. See also art. 20 of the ILC Draft Code of Crimes (n 55) and the requirement that a crime is 'committed in a systematic manner or on a large scale'.

breaches' of the four 1949 Geneva Conventions and the 1977 Additional Protocol I[78] and other serious violations of the regulation of means and methods of warfare in international armed conflict, such as the 1899 and 1907 Hague Regulations as well as the 1977 Additional Protocol I.[79]

Certain acts committed in non-international armed conflicts may also constitute war crimes giving rise to individual criminal responsibility under customary international law.[80] In *Tadić*, the Appeals Chamber of the ICTY concluded that customary international law imposes criminal liability for 'serious violations of common Article 3, as supplemented by other general principles and rules on the protection of victims of internal armed conflict, and for breaching certain fundamental principles and rules regarding means and methods of combat in civil strife'.[81] The recognition that acts committed in times of non-international armed conflict may also constitute war crimes for the purposes of international criminal law has made the proper classification of an armed conflict as one of an 'international' or 'non-international' character less important.[82]

15.3.3.5 Aggression

The crime of aggression was prosecuted as a 'crime against the peace' at the Nuremberg and Tokyo IMTs. Like crimes against humanity, however, it was doubtful if aggression constituted a crime under customary international law at the time. As an international crime, aggression has always been controversial and it was not included in the Statutes of the ICTY, the ICTR or the SCSL.[83] It was inserted in the Rome Statute, however, but agreement on a definition and the Court's jurisdiction over the crime was not reached until 2010 when a new article was inserted into the Rome Statute.[84] The new article defines aggression in accordance with the General Assembly's 1974 Definition of Aggression but includes a higher threshold for criminal conduct.[85] Thus, the *crime* of aggression is defined as the 'planning, preparation, initiation or execution' 'of an act of aggression which, by its character, gravity and scale, constitutes a manifest violation of the Charter of the United Nations.'[86] A violation of the 1974 General Assembly Definition must therefore be 'manifest' in order to be prosecuted.[87] The crime is limited to the absolute leadership of a state. Special provisions and procedures were

---

[78] See, inter alia, the Rome Statute art. 8(2)(a) and (b). See also ILC Draft Code of Crimes (n 55) art. 20(a)–(c).

[79] See ILC Draft Code of Crimes (n 55) arts 8(2)(c) and 20(e).   [80] See also ibid, art. 20(f).

[81] *Prosecutor v Tadić* (n 9) para. 134. See also ILC Draft Code of Crimes (n 55) art. 8(2)(c)–(e).

[82] The classification of armed conflict is still important in a number of respects, though, and as we saw in the previous chapter substantial differences remain between international and non-international armed conflicts in relation to, e.g., the point in time when the laws of armed conflict begin to apply and the temporal dimensions of the concept of direct participation in hostilities.

[83] But see ILC Draft Code of Crimes (n 55) art. 16.

[84] See art. 8*bis*. See also Claus Kress and Leonie von Holtzendorff, 'The Kampala Compromise on the Crime of Aggression' (2011) 8 *Journal of International Criminal Justice* 1179.

[85] The GA Res. 3314 (XXIX) (14 December 1974), UN Doc. A/RES/3314(XXIX).

[86] Rome Statute art. 8*bis*(2).

[87] See also commentary to art. 16 of the ILC Draft Code of Crimes (n 55) 43, para. 5.

inserted in relation to the Court's exercise of jurisdiction over aggression, including with regard to Security Council referrals.[88] Among other things, the Court can only exercise jurisdiction over alleged acts of aggression that are committed one year after the ratification or acceptance of the aggression amendments by 30 state parties. In July 2016, 28 states had ratified the amendments.

15.3.4 **Criminal liability**

The majority of the principles of criminal liability in international criminal law are familiar to the national lawyer. According to article 2 of the 1996 Draft Code of Crimes against the Peace and Security of Mankind, for example, an individual shall be held responsible for an international crime when he or she:

(a) intentionally commits such a crime;

(b) orders the commission of the crime;

(c) under certain circumstances fails to prevent or repress the crime;

(d) knowingly aids, abets or otherwise assists in the commission of the crime;

(e) directly participates in the planning or conspiring to commit the crime;

(f) directly and publicly incites another individual to commit the crime which then in fact occurs; or

(g) attempts to commit such a crime.[89]

One of the more interesting forms of international criminal liability is the concept of *joint criminal enterprise* (JCE) applied in cases where more than one person is involved in the commission of an offence.[90] The rationale of JCE is that anyone who takes part in a common criminal act with an awareness of its purpose and who shares its requisite criminal intent must share the criminal liability. The core elements of JCE were discussed and articulated by the ICTY Appeals Chamber in *Tadić*.[91] Conceptually, conviction for a JCE requires:

(a) the existence of more than one individual involved in the commission of the crime;

(b) a common plan; and

(c) that the accused made a significant contribution to the crime.

In practice, three forms of JCE have been created. The first, JCE I, is where all the accused individuals act under a common design possessing the same criminal intention, such as an intention to kill.[92] The second form is JCE II—also referred to as the 'concentration camp' cases—where JCE is applied to offences committed by members

---

[88] See Rome Statute arts 15*bis* and 15*ter*.   [89] ILC Draft Code of Crimes (n 55) art. 2(3)(a)–(g).
[90] For an overview, see the discussion in Cassese et al. (n 2) 163–178.
[91] *Prosecutor v Tadić*, Judgment, IT-94-1-A (15 July 1999), paras 195–220.
[92] Ibid, paras 196–201.

of military or administrative units, such as those who run concentration camps and in that regard can be considered to be acting according to a concerted plan.[93] JCE II is a variant of JCE I. The third and last category of JCE is the controversial JCE III. Here, an individual is found criminally liable for participation in a 'common design to pursue one course of conduct where one of the perpetrators commits an act which, while outside the common design, was nevertheless a natural and foreseeable consequence of the effecting of that common purpose'.[94] When JCE III is applied, all participants in 'the common design' are held responsible for the crime regardless of the role they have played.[95] JCE III is controversial because it paves the way for prosecution for offences that did not form an explicit part of the common design but was merely a 'foreseeable' result thereof. Most cases against high-ranking political and military officials have relied on JCE III.[96]

Liability may arise not only due to the commission of a positive act but also due to a failure to take action—an omission. Under *the principle of superior responsibility*, for example, international law imposes criminal liability on a superior if he or she has failed to prevent or punish the criminal acts of a subordinate. In *Yamashita*, the US Supreme Court famously convicted a Japanese general for the large-scale atrocities perpetrated by his subordinates in the Philippines during the Second World War even though the prosecution had not shown that the general had any knowledge of the atrocities.[97] The doctrine of superior responsibility was subsequently extended to civilian leaders and supplemented with a requirement that the superior knew or had reason to know about the criminal acts of the subordinates.[98] In *Delalić et al.*, the Trial Chamber of the ICTY listed three essential elements to command responsibility for failure to act:

(i)   the existence of a superior-subordinate relationship
(ii) the superior knew or had reason to know that the criminal act was about to be or had been committed, and
(iii) the superior failed to take the necessary and reasonable measures to prevent the criminal act or punish the perpetrator thereof.[99]

---

[93] Ibid, paras 202–203.   [94] Ibid, paras 204–219.

[95] For a critique see, inter alia, Jens David Ohlin, 'Joint Intentions to Commit International Crimes' (2011) 11 *Chicago Journal of International Law* 693, 706–709 and the decision in the Extraordinary Chambers in the Courts of Cambodia, Public Decision on the Appeals Against the Co-Investigative Judges Order on Joint Criminal Enterprise, 002-D97/17/6 (20 May 2010), paras 75–89. See also the debate in Antonio Cassese, 'The Proper Limits of Individual Responsibility under the Doctrine of Joint Criminal Enterprise' (2007) 5 *Journal of International Criminal Justice* 109.

[96] See, inter alia, *Prosecutor v Radovan Karadžić* (n 20) para. 3524. See also *Prosecutor v Radovan Karadžić*, Second Amended Indictment, ICTY-02-54-T (23 October 2002), para. 8.

[97] US Supreme Court, *Yamashita v Styer*, 327 US 1 (1946). The principle of superior responsibility is reflected in Additional Protocol to the Geneva Conventions of 12 August 1949, Relating to the Protection of Victims of International Armed Conflicts (API) (adopted 8 June 1977, entered into force 7 December 1978) 1125 UNTS 3, art. 86.

[98] See, inter alia, *United States v Soemu Toyoda* cited in *Prosecutor v Zejnil Delalić et al.*, Judgment, ICTY-94-1-A (15 July 1999), para. 339. See also the ILC Draft Code of Crimes (n 55) art. 6 and the Rome Statute art. 28.

[99] *Prosecutor v Zejnil Delalić et al.* (n 98) para. 346.

The superior–subordinate relationship can be either an official (*de jure*) relationship or one based on effective (*de facto*) subordination.[100] Regardless of the relationship, however, the control of the superior must be effective.[101] International law thereby recognizes that a situation may arise in which a superior is aware that unlawful conduct occurs but is incapable of preventing or repressing the conduct. Conviction of a superior is conditioned on the existence of information available which would have put him or her 'on notice of offences committed by subordinates'.[102]

15.3.5 **Defences**

As with national criminal law, international criminal law recognizes that the existence of certain grounds may exclude criminal responsibility. Under the Rome Statute, for example, a person shall not be criminally responsible if, at the time of the conduct, the person is mentally incapacitated and did not know that what they were doing was wrong.[103] Other grounds for excluding criminal responsibility include intoxication, self-defence, the defence of others and the defence of certain property.[104] Mention should also be made of 'duress' that refers to those situations where a person defends their conduct by claiming that it followed from 'a threat of imminent death or of continuing or imminent serious bodily harm against that person or another'.[105] Duress was recognized as a possible defence in some of the trials after the Second World War.[106] In the *Erdemović* case, the Trial Chamber of the ICTY accepted that fear for an accused's own life and that of his wife and child could constitute a valid defence, but it also found that the general duty to disobey manifestly illegal orders only receded in 'the face of the most extreme duress'.[107]

It is controversial whether an individual can defend their unlawful conduct by pleading that the acts or omissions were mandated by an order from a superior.[108] Although a plea of superior orders was generally accepted historically, things changed after the end of the Second World War and it is now generally accepted that an individual who receives an unlawful order is under a duty to disobey rather than obey.[109] The Statute of the IMT explicitly states that the 'fact that the defendant acted pursuant

---

[100] Ibid, paras 377–378. See also the decision from the Appeals Chamber in the same case, *Prosecutor v Zejnil Delalić et al.*, Judgment, ICTY-96-21-A (20 February 2001), paras 197–198.

[101] *Prosecutor v Zejnil Delalić et al.* (n 98) para. 192. See also *Fofana and Kondewa*, Judgment, SCSL-04-14-A (28 May 2008), para. 175.

[102] *Prosecutor v Radovan Karadžić et al.* (n 96) para. 393 and *Prosecutor v Zejnil Delalić et al.* (n 98) para. 214.

[103] Rome Statute art. 31(1)(a). See also *Prosecutor v Zejnil Delalić et al.* (n 98) para. 582.

[104] Rome Statute art. 31(1)(b) and (c).   [105] Ibid, art. 31(1)(d).

[106] See the overview in the commentary to art. 14 of the ILC Draft Code of Crimes (n 55) 40, para. 10.

[107] *Prosecutor v Erdemović*, Sentencing Judgment No. 1, ICTY-96-22-T (29 November 1996), para. 18. It must be noted, however, that some of the Chamber's statements could be read to the effect that a plea of duress cannot be advanced in relation to crimes against humanity, see para. 19. For a debate, see Cassese et al. (n 2) 218–219.

[108] See Cassese et al. (n 2) 228–240.

[109] See, inter alia, *Trial of Wilhelm List and Others*, US Military Tribunal, Nuremberg, 8 July 1947–19 February 1948, LRTWC, Case No. 47, Vol. VIII, pp. 50–52.

to the order of his Government or of a superior shall not free him from responsibility, but may be considered in mitigation of punishment'.[110] Similar provisions have since been concluded in the Statutes of the ICTY, the ICTR and the SCSL. In contrast, the Statute of the ICC seems to leave a small window open to a plea of superior orders. Thus, under article 33(1) an individual may be relieved of criminal responsibility if the individual was legally obliged to obey 'orders of the Government or the superior in question', if he or she 'did not know that the order was unlawful' and the order 'was not manifestly unlawful'. The article also stipulates, however, that an order to commit genocide or crimes against humanity is always considered 'manifestly unlawful'.[111] In practice, pleas of superior orders are rarely successful.[112]

15.3.6 **Due process guarantees**

It is well established that criminal proceedings must comply with the overall fair trial guarantees and principles of due process contained in human rights law.[113] The right to a fair trial was recognized in article 14 of the Statute of the IMT, and both the Statutes of the ICTY and the ICTR contain a number of fair trial provisions. Procedural protection is particularly strong in the Rome Statute where article 21(3) provides that the ICC's application and interpretation of law 'must be consistent with internationally recognized human rights'.[114] The protection offered in the Statute is modelled on article 14 of the UN Covenant on Civil and Political Rights and the rights contained therein. Thus, international criminal law protects the well-established rights of an accused, including protection from self-incrimination,[115] the presumption of innocence,[116] the right to be informed of the charges and the opportunity to challenge them,[117] the right to trial without delay,[118] a public hearing[119] and the right to be present at trial.[120]

15.3.7 **The question of immunity as a procedural bar to prosecution before international criminal courts**

The Statutes of international criminal courts generally specify that the official capacity of an accused individual is no bar to criminal prosecution and that the court may also prosecute heads of state or heads of government.[121] The immunities for criminal prosecution for state representatives before *national* courts were discussed in Chapter 6 and we saw there that personal immunity/immunity *ratione personae* offers extensive

---

[110] See Nuremberg Charter (n 12) art. 8. See also ILC Draft Code of Crimes (n 55) art. 5.

[111] See also *Prosecutor v Erdemović* (n 107) para. 15.

[112] For a brief overview of relevant case law, see Cassese et al. (n 2) 232–237.

[113] See also art. 11 of the ILC Draft Code of Crimes (n 55). For an overview and discussion of the protections offered, see Cassese et al. (n 2) 347–362.

[114] See also art. 64(2): 'The Trial Chamber shall ensure that a trial is fair and expeditious and is conducted with full respect for the rights of the accused.' See also art. 64(8).

[115] Art. 55(1)(a).   [116] Art. 66.   [117] Art. 67(1)(a) and (d).   [118] Art. 67(1)(c).

[119] Art. 67.   [120] Art. 63.   [121] See, inter alia, art. 27.

protection from criminal jurisdiction to certain high-ranking state representatives. It was also noted, however, that the ICJ in the *Arrest Warrant* case stated that a high-ranking state representative can be prosecuted before international criminal courts, where they have jurisdiction.[122] In 2004, in a decision concerning the immunity of Charles Taylor, who was indicted while he was the head of state of Liberia, the Appeals Chamber of the SCSL relied on the ICJ *Arrest Warrant* case in holding that 'the principle seems now established that the sovereign equality of states does not prevent a Head of State from being prosecuted before an international criminal tribunal or court'.[123] And in the *Bashir* case concerning the criminal prosecution of the incumbent head of state of Sudan, the Pre-Trial Chamber of the ICC in 2011 concluded that neither sitting nor former heads of state can invoke immunity in opposition to prosecution by an international criminal court.[124]

If the decisions to deny immunity were based solely on the *international* rather than national character of the courts in question, they were misguided.[125] The reason why a state may not be entitled to invoke immunity before an international criminal court in relation to criminal prosecution of one of its officials or ex-officials is not due the international character of the court. Rather, it is because the state has given its consent to the court's jurisdiction.[126] So when determining if Charles Taylor was entitled to personal immunity from prosecution before the SCSL, the Court needed to ascertain whether Liberia had consented to the Court's jurisdiction.[127] In a similar vein, in the case against Bashir, the ICC needed to examine the extent to which Sudan had consented to the Court's jurisdiction. Two states cannot adopt a treaty that alters the legal rights of a third state unless the third state gives its consent. The ICC also seems to have corrected its practice.[128]

Consent to an international criminal court's jurisdiction may be both explicit and implicit. First, a state will be found to have explicitly given its consent if it has chosen to become a party to a treaty that establishes an international criminal court. Since the Rome Statute is a treaty, state parties to the Statute have consented to the Court's exercise of jurisdiction and cannot therefore invoke immunity. Secondly, consent will also—implicitly—exist if an international criminal court has been established

[122] *Arrest Warrant of 11 April 2000* (n 56) 3, para. 61.

[123] *Prosecutor v Charles Ghankay Taylor*, Decision on Immunity from Jurisdiction, SCSL-2003-01-I (31 May 2004), paras 50–52.

[124] *Prosecutor v Omar Hassan Ahmad al-Bashir*, Corrigendum to the Decision Pursuant to Article 87(7) of the Rome Statute on the Failure by the Republic of Malawi to Comply with the Cooperation Requests Issued by the Court with Respect to the Arrest and Surrender of Omar Hassan Ahmad al-Bashir, ICC-02/05-01/09 (13 December 2011), paras 18, 34–36.

[125] The claim does, however, find support in the literature, see, inter alia, Cassese et al. (n 2) 320–322.

[126] See also the overview in O'Keefe (n 3) 106–110.

[127] Since the Security Council did not adopt the Statute of the SCSL it would appear that the Court's indictment of Taylor constituted a violation of his personal immunity, see also O'Keefe (n 3) 523–524. It is worth noting, however, that Liberia gave its consent to the arrest and subsequent prosecution of Taylor when he left office.

[128] See also *Prosecutor v Omar Hassan Ahmad al-Bashir*, Decision on the Cooperation of the Democratic Republic of the Congo Regarding Omar al-Bashir's Arrest and Surrender to the Court, ICC-02/05-01/09 (9 April 2014), para. 26.

by the UN Security Council in accordance with its powers under Chapter VII of the UN Charter. Article 25 of the Charter stipulates that the members of the UN accept the decisions of the Security Council. The ICTY and the ICTR are examples of international courts set up by the Council. It is the implied consent of all member states to accept the decisions of the Security Council that is the basis for the ICC being able to exercise jurisdiction over a situation involving a state that is not a party to the Statute (e.g. Sudan) if it has been referred by the Security Council.[129]

15.4 National prosecution of international crimes

Despite the widespread attention garnered by the establishment of international courts, including the ICC, it remains an undeniable fact that international crimes are primarily supposed to be prosecuted at the national level by the states themselves. In fact, the inherently subsidiary role of international prosecution is reflected in the principle of 'complementarity' mentioned in Section 15.3.2.2. For reasons of legitimacy, speed and overall logistics, and proximity to the place of the crime, domestic prosecutions are in most cases to be preferred over trials before international courts. In addition, unlike international prosecutions, national prosecution of international crimes is not limited to those core offences that derive their criminalization directly from customary international law.

There is a rich history of national prosecutions of individuals suspected of having committed international crimes, including one or more of the 'core crimes'. The majority of cases are connected to atrocities committed during the Second World War. More recently, many national cases have been brought against individuals for crimes committed in the former Yugoslavia and Rwanda in the 1990s, including in Denmark where in 1998 a criminal court convicted a Bosnian national of war crimes committed in a Croatian detention camp.[130] In 2001, a Belgian court successfully prosecuted a number of Rwandan nationals for crimes, including war crimes, committed in Rwanda in 1994,[131] and Sweden has twice prosecuted former Rwandan citizens for genocide. In the last such case, in May 2016 a Swedish court convicted a (now) Swedish national of participating in widespread massacres of Tutsis.[132] Domestic prosecutions of international crimes have also been conducted before a number of national courts with 'special jurisdiction' set up with international assistance, such as the criminal prosecution of former high-ranking members of the Khmer Rouge before the Extraordinary Chambers of the Courts of Cambodia (ECCC).[133] Other

---

[129] See Rome Statute art. 13(b). See also *Prosecutor v Omar Hassan Ahmad al-Bashir* (n 124) paras 29–30.

[130] UfR1995.838H.

[131] *Public Prosecutor v the 'Butare Four'*, Assize Court of Brussels, verdict of 8 June 2001. For an overview, see Luc Reydams, 'Belgium's First Application of Universal Jurisdiction: the *Butare Four* Case' (2003) 1 *Journal of International Criminal Justice* 428.

[132] B 12882-14, 16 May 2016.

[133] Law on the Establishment of Extraordinary Chambers in the Courts of Cambodia (as amended on 27 October 2004), art. 2 www.eccc.gov.kh/sites/default/files/legal-documents/KR_Law_as_amended_27_Oct_2004_Eng.pdf (accessed 22 August 2016). See also Agreement between the United Nations

examples include the special courts set up under the District Court of Dili in East Timor by the UN Transitional Administration in East Timor (UNTAET),[134] the introduction of specialized sections for war crimes in Bosnia and Herzegovina,[135] an International Crimes Tribunal in Kosovo,[136] an International Crimes Division in the High Court of Uganda[137] and the Extraordinary African Chambers in Senegal which in May 2016 convicted the former president of Chad, Hissène Habré for crimes against humanity.[138]

The primary basis for prosecuting international crimes nationally is the many conventions that oblige states to criminalize and/or prosecute certain international crimes before their national courts. The purpose of these conventions is, of course, to prevent individuals suspected of the conduct in question from going unpunished.[139] While the precise content of the treaties differ, they generally oblige states to enact legislation that will enable them to assert prescriptive jurisdiction over certain offences on the basis of the principles of universal jurisdiction we visited in Chapter 5.[140] At times, national prosecution of international crimes is complicated by the existence of legal impediments particular to the state in question. Most states operate with *statutes of limitation* according to which prosecution for certain crimes may not be initiated after a specified period of time (e.g. 10 or 20 years) has elapsed. Restrictions on limiting the period during which international crimes can be prosecuted are found in treaty law.[141] Another domestic legal impediment is a *grant of amnesty* where national decision-makers have decided that conduct which was once criminal is no longer considered unlawful, with the consequence that the authorities are then barred from initiating criminal proceedings.[142] An amnesty for genocide would appear to be incompatible with article 1 of the 1948 Genocide Convention, according to which the state parties undertake to 'prevent and to punish' the crime of genocide. Amnesties may also violate a treaty-based obligation to prosecute or extradite (*aut dedere aut*

---

and the Royal Government of Cambodia concerning the prosecution under Cambodian law of crimes committed during the period of Democratic Kampuchea, Phnom Penh, 6 June 2003 (ECCC Agreement), art. 1.

[134] See SC Res. 1272 (25 October 1999), UN Doc. S/RES/1271.   [135] See O'Keefe (n 3) 389–390.
[136] Ibid, 401–402.   [137] Ibid, 395.
[138] BBC News, 'Hissene Habre: Chad's ex-ruler convicted of crimes against humanity' (30 May 2016) www.bbc.com/news/world-africa-36411466 (accessed 22 August 2016). For an overview and discussion, see Sarah Williams, 'The Extraordinary African Chambers in the Senegalese Courts: An African Solution to an African Problem?' (2013) 11 *Journal of International Criminal Justice* 1139.
[139] See also *Questions relating to the Obligation to Prosecute or Extradite* (n 3) para. 120.
[140] See also ILC Draft Code of Crimes (n 55) art. 8.
[141] See the Convention on the Non-Applicability of Statutory Limitations to War Crimes and Crimes Against Humanity (adopted 26 November 1968, entered into force 11 November 1970), 754 UNTS 73; International Convention for the Protection of All Persons from Enforced Disappearance (adopted 20 December 2006, entered into force 23 December 2010), 2716 UNTS 48088, art. 8(1) and the OECD Convention on Combating Bribery of Foreign Public Officials in International Business Transactions (adopted 17 December 1997, entered into force 15 February 1999), DAFFE/IME/BR(97)20. See also *Prosecutor v Anto Furundžija* (n 5) para. 157 and from the Inter-American Court of Human Rights, *Barrios Alto v Peru*, 14 March 2001, para. 41. See Cassese et al. (n 2) 315.
[142] For a debate and overview, see John Duggard, 'Dealing with the Crimes of the Past Regime: Is Amnesty Still an Option?' (1999) 12 *Leiden Journal of International Law* 1001.

judicare), especially if the grant of amnesty is not a result of a genuine wish to promote reconciliation in society.[143]

Summary

International criminal law is a fairly recent addition to international law. It seeks to ensure that perpetrators of certain heinous acts are criminally liable for their acts either before national or international criminal courts or tribunals. Prosecution of international crimes occurs either before international courts or before national courts. International courts consist of both ad hoc and permanent criminal courts—the ICC. International courts generally have jurisdiction over a number of core international crimes that are directly prescribed under customary international law: genocide, crimes against humanity, war crimes and aggression. The principles of liability and possible defences are well known to national lawyers. National prosecution of international crimes may relate to both the core international crimes as well as the offences listed in a number of conventions that generally oblige states to either prosecute or extradite individuals suspected of committing the listed offences if located on their territory.

Recommended reading

The literature on international criminal law is growing rapidly. Major general works include Roger O'Keefe, *International Criminal Law* (Oxford University Press, 2015); Antonio Cassese et al., *Cassese's International Criminal Law* (3rd edn, Oxford University Press, 2013); William A. Schabas (ed.), *The Cambridge Companion to International Criminal Law* (Cambridge University Press, 2016); and Robert Cryer et al., *An Introduction to International Criminal Law and Procedure* (3rd edn, Cambridge University Press, 2014).

On the distinction between international and national criminal courts, see Astrid Kjeldgaard-Pedersen, 'What Defines an International Criminal Court? A Critical Assessment of "the Involvement of the International Community" as a Deciding Factor' (2015) 28 *Leiden Journal of International Law* 113.

For the ICC, see William Schabas, *An Introduction to the International Criminal Court* (4th edn, Cambridge University Press, 2011). On the principle of complementarity, see Jann K. Kleffner, *Complementarity in the Rome Statute and National Criminal Jurisdictions* (Oxford University Press, 2008). For an overview of the process that led to the agreement on the crime of aggression in the ICC, see Claus Kress and Leonie von Holtzendorff, 'The Kampala Compromise on the Crime of Aggression' (2010) 8 *Journal of International Criminal Justice* 1179. A debate about JCE is available in Jens David Ohlin, 'Joint Intentions to Commit International Crimes' (2011) 11 *Chicago Journal of International Law* 693, 706–709.

---

[143] See also ECtHR, *Ould Dah v France*, App. no. 13113/03, 17 March 2009, 17; Human Rights Committee, 'General Comment 20: Article 7: Compilation of General Comments and General Recommendations Adopted by Human Rights Treaty Bodies' (1994), UN Doc. HRI/GEN/1/Rev.1, para. 15; O'Keefe (n 3) 474–475.

On immunity and the ICC, see Dapo Akande, 'International Law Immunities and the International Criminal Court' (2004) 98 *American Journal of International Law* 407.

Questions for discussion

1. Conceptually, what is the difference between an 'international' and a 'national' criminal court?

2. Why are some international crimes referred to as 'core' crimes?

3. What does the principle of 'complementarity' in the Rome Statute mean?

4. The United States is not a party to the Rome Statute. What would it require for US servicemen to be prosecuted before the ICC?

5. What are the differences between the three forms of Joint Criminal Enterprise (JCE)? Why is the third form deemed to be controversial?

6. The power of the Security Council to refer a situation to the ICC Prosecutor includes a situation that involves nationals of a state that is not a party to the Rome Statute. Why does a Council referral not violate the consensual nature of the jurisdiction of the ICC?

Glossary

AD HOC Formed for a particular purpose.

AUT DEDERE AUT JUDICARE The principle that requires a state to either prosecute or extradite an individual to another state.

DE JURE As of right or law.

DELICTA JURIS GENTIUM Crimes against public international law.

DEROGATION The non-application of a rule.

ERGA OMNES OBLIGATIONS Obligations not merely owed to another state but to the international community as a whole.

EX AEQUO ET BONO A decision or judgment based on such general principles as a court find appropriate.

EX INJURIA JUS NON ORITUR A principle that legal rights cannot arise from wrongful conduct.

FORCE MAJEURE The occurrence of an irresistible or unforeseen force.

FORUM PROROGATUM A court's jurisdiction on the basis of consent after a case has been submitted.

GOOD FAITH A principle that stipulates that states must act honestly in the fulfilment of their international obligations.

IN ABSENTIA Trials conducted without the presence of the accused.

INTER ALIA Among other things.

INTER SE Between the parties.

JURE GESTIONIS State acts of a commercial character.

JURE IMPERII State acts of a sovereign or governmental nature.

JUS AD BELLUM The international legal regulation of the use of force.

JUS COGENS OBLIGATIONS Norms accepted and recognized by the international community of states as a whole as obligations from which no derogation is permitted.

JUS GENTIUM A law of people or nations, in the Middle Ages considered inferior to *jus naturale* (see below).

JUS IN BELLO The international regulation of the conduct of hostilities.

JUS NATURALE Natural law meaning an all-embracing range of ideas about natural and social life in the universe.

LEX POSTERIOR A principle that stipulates that law which is later in time prevails.

LEX SPECIALIS A principle that stipulates that in a case of conflict between a norm of general and specific character, the latter prevails.

MALA CAPTUS, BENE DETENTUS A principle whereby a state can prosecute an individual even if he or she was brought before the court by irregular means.

NE BIS IN IDEM A principle that specifies that an individual should not be punished twice for the same offence. Also referred to as 'double jeopardy'.

NULLUM CRIMEN SINE LEGE The principle that no crime can be committed unless it was considered a crime at the time of its commission. Also referred to as the principle of legality.

OPINIO JURIS The belief that a practice is obligatory and a requirement in the formation of customary international law.

PACTA SUNT SERVANDA The fundamental rule that a treaty is binding on the parties.

PERSONA NON GRATA An unwelcome individual. Used in diplomatic relations to refer to an individual that is considered unwanted on the territory of the receiving state.

RATIONE MATERIAE By reason of the subject matter in question.

RATIONE PERSONAE By reason of the person.

REBUS SIC STANTIBUS A claim that an obligation has terminated due to a fundamental change in circumstances.

RES COMMUNIS Territory not open to acquisition by any states but instead available for the enjoyment of any member of the international community.

RES JUDICATA The principle that a decision is final and a matter already dealt with should not be reopened.

RESERVATION A caveat or an exception to acceptance of a treaty.

SUI GENERIS Falling outside the normal categories.

TERRA NULLIUS Territory that does not belong to any state or people. Also known as 'no man's land'. Unlike *res communis, terra nullius* is open to occupation and acquisition.

TRAVAUX PRÉPARATOIRES Material preparatory to a treaty, often derived from a conference.

ULTRA VIRES Not authorized by a legal power.

UTI POSSIDETIS A principle that stipulates that borders and frontiers of emerging states conform to those of the 'old' state or territory.

Index